TRANSBOUNDARY WATER DISPUTES

One of the most challenging aspects of climate change has been the increased pressure on water resources limited by droughts and new rain patterns, exacerbated by rapid modernization. Due to these realities, disputes across national borders over use and access to water have now become more commonplace. This study analyzes the history and adjudication of North American transboundary water disputes in five international courts and tribunals, three US Supreme Court cases, and boundary water disputes between the United States and Canada and the United States and Mexico. Explaining the circumstances and outcomes of these cases, Kornfeld asks how effective courts and tribunals have been in adjudicating them. What kind of remedies have they fashioned and how have they dealt with polycentric and sovereignty issues? This timely work examines the doctrine of equitable allocation of transboundary water resources and how this norm can be incorporated into international law.

Itzchak E. Kornfeld, Ph.D. (Hebrew University) is General Counsel and Vice President of MEJ Development Group, Ltd. (a non-profit development concern) and teaches international and transboundary water law and consults to governments and indigenous peoples on transboundary water issues. He has earned several degrees in both law and geology, and he has worked for the US EPA as a Senior Geohydrologist, working on surface and ground water issues, and for Texaco/Chevron as an environmental geologist, where he dealt with migration of contaminants in water.

Transboundary Water Disputes

STATE CONFLICT AND THE ASSESSMENT OF THEIR ADJUDICATION

ITZCHAK E. KORNFELD, Ph.D.

General Counsel and Vice President,
MEJ Development Group, Ltd., formerly,
Faculty of Law
The Hebrew University of Jerusalem

CAMBRIDGE
UNIVERSITY PRESS

CAMBRIDGE
UNIVERSITY PRESS

University Printing House, Cambridge CB2 8BS, United Kingdom

One Liberty Plaza, 20th Floor, New York, NY 10006, USA

477 Williamstown Road, Port Melbourne, VIC 3207, Australia

314–321, 3rd Floor, Plot 3, Splendor Forum, Jasola District Centre,
New Delhi - 110025, India

79 Anson Road, #06-04/06, Singapore 079906

Cambridge University Press is part of the University of Cambridge.

It furthers the University's mission by disseminating knowledge in the pursuit of
education, learning, and research at the highest international levels of excellence.

www.cambridge.org
Information on this title: www.cambridge.org/9781107186606
DOI: 10.1017/9781316890776

© Itzchak E. Kornfeld 2019

First published 2019

Printed and bound in Great Britain by Clays Ltd, Elcograf S.p.A.

A catalogue record for this publication is available from the British Library

Library of Congress Cataloging-in-Publication data
Names: Kornfeld, Itzchak E., author.
Title: Transboundary water disputes : state conflict and the assessment of their
adjudication / Itzchak E. Kornfeld, Hebrew University of Jerusalem.
Description: Cambridge : Cambridge University Press, [2017] | Includes
bibliographical references.
Identifiers: LCCN 2017026492 | ISBN 9781107186606
Subjects: LCSH: Water – Law and legislation. | Water rights. | Riparian rights. | Water
rights (International law) | Rivers – Law and legislation.| Interstate controversies – United
States | United States – Boundaries – Canada. | Canada – Boundaries – United States. |
United States – Boundaries – Mexico. | Mexico – Boundaries – United States.
Classification: LCC K3496.K67   2017 | DDC 341.4/4097 – dc23
LC record available at https://lccn.loc.gov/2017026492

ISBN 978-1-107-18660-6 Hardback

Contents

The Adjudication of Transboundary Disputes

This work makes the following findings and contributions to international water law and to international dispute resolution:

(1) This is the very first study of its kind in any geographic venue/location.

(2) Transboundary water disputes are resolved by courts and tribunals' use of equity, or equitable remedies, such as *equitable apportionment* and the *equitable and reasonable utilization* of international watercourses. The present research finds that this is the first study of its kind that definitively demonstrates this fact.

(3) State sovereignty is a hallmark of transboundary water disputes.

(4) The apportionment of water is best done by treaty or compact between states in the United States.

(5) In one respect, *ad hoc* international tribunals are more effective than international courts in adjudicating transboundary disputes because they are more adept at addressing polycentric issues.

(6) The results yielded in this volume demonstrate that within the universe of disputes *ad hoc* tribunals adjudicate disputes quicker – than do courts.

(7) I also compare the length of time from the execution of the *compromis* until the issuance of the arbitral awards for the three arbitrations analyzed herein: the *Chamizal Dispute* the *Gut Dam Arbitration*; and the *Bayview Irrigation District Case*, with the *Bering Sea Arbitration (Fur Seals)*, the *Trail Smelter Case*, The *San Juan River Case* and the *Lac Lanoux Arbitration*, and found that the average time for resolution of these disputes is between 1.9 years and 2.2 years, while most court cases, particularly those of the United States Supreme Court whose cases are analysed herein take much longer – for two SCOTUS disputes analyzed here it took 86 years and 102 years respectively to resolve. Thus, I

argue that arbitral tribunals are more effective, in resolving these types of case.

(8) The use of precedents and the development of norms is one major thread that runs through the cases that are analyzed herein, particularly to fill lacunae. The use of precedents, which I term "cross-pollination," leads to greater coherence in international law, and helps the development of new norms; regardless of whether an adjudicative body employs its own case law or imports it from another jurisdiction. Thus, if we think of the use of precedents as pieces of a puzzle that fit together to provide a fully integrated archetype, we can comprehend and envisage the building of a system of international law.

Table of Authorities

CONSTITUTIONS

STATUTES

RULES

Rules of Procedure of the International Joint Commission
Rules of the United Nations Commission on International Trade Law
U.S. Supreme Court Rule 17

TREATIES

Boundary Convention of March 1, 1889, 26 Stat. 1512
Canadian United States Boundary Waters Treaty of 1909
Chamizal Tract Arbitration, Jan.15, 1911,U.N. Rpts. of Int'l Arb., vol. XI
    pp. 309–347
Chamizal Convention of August 29, 1963; and the November 1970 Treaty
Convention for the Arbitration of the Chamizal Case, June 24, 1910,
    U.S.–Mex., 36 Stat. 2481. 11 R.I.A.A
Convention Between the United States of America and the Mexico States
    Touching the International Boundary Line Where it Follows the Bed of
    the Rio Grande and the Rio Colorado, U.S.–Mex., Nov. 12, 1884, 24
    Stat.1011
Convention for the Rectification of the Rio Grande (Rio Bravo) in the El
    Paso-Juarez Valley of February 1, 48 Stat. 1621
Convention of July 29, 1882
Convention of May 21, 1906
Convention of November 12, 1884, 24 Stat. 1011
Convention on Protection and Use of Transboundary Watercourses and
    Lakes, (Helsinki, 17 March 1992), 3 I.L.M. 1312 (entered into force Oct. 6,
    1996)
Convention for the Solution of the Problem of the Chamizal, U.S.-Mex.,
    Aug. 29, 1963, 15 U.S.T. 21
Convention of 21 May 1997 on the Law of the Non-Navigational Uses of
    International Watercourses by the United Nations General Assembly
Convention and Supplemental Protocol between the United States and
    Mexico; Award and Dissenting Opinion – Gadsden Treaty, Dec. 30, 1853,
    U.S.–Mex., 10 Stat. 1031
Hague Convention for the Pacific Settlement of International Disputes, 29
    July 1899, Art. 1, 32 Stat. 1779, 1 Bevans 230, 26 Martens Nouveau Recueil
    (ser. 2) 720, 187 Consol. T.S. 410, entered into force Sept. 4, 1900
Hague Convention for the Pacific Settlement of International Disputes, Oct.
    18, 1907, Art. 38, 36 Stat. 2199, TS No. 536
North American Agreement on Environmental Cooperation (NAAEC)
    NAAEC
North American Agreement on Environmental Cooperation,
    U.S.–Can.–Mex., Sept. 14, 1993, T.I.A.S. No. 12,516, 32 I.L.M. 1480

United Nations Convention on International Bills of Exchange and
International Promissory Notes (New York, 1988) (UNCITRAL)

COMPACTS

Arkansas River Compact
Colorado River compact

Other Authorities

BOOKS

Robin A. Abell, *et al.*, Freshwater Ecoregions of North America: A Conservation Assessment (2000)

Jack L. August, Jr., Dividing Western Waters: Mark Wilmer and Arizona v. California xvi (2007)

Robert Beckman and Dagmar Butte, *Introduction to International Law* (undated)

Ian Brownlie, Principles of Public International Law (5th ed. 1998)

Antonio Cassese, *International Law* (2nd ed. 2005)

Joseph Dellapenna, Building International Water Management Institutions: The Role of Treaties and Other Legal Arrangements, in *Water in the Middle East: Legal, Political, and Commercial Implications*, in, Water in the Middle East: Legal, political, and commercial implications (J.A. Allan and Chibli Mallat, with Shai Wade and Jonathan Wild, ed. 1995) 55

Joseph W. Dellapenna & Joyeeta Gupta (eds.), The Evolution of Law and Politics of Water (2008)

William Cullen Dennis, International Boundary & Water Commission United States & Mexico, *Chamizal Arbitration: The Countercase of the United States of America, with Appendix and Portfolio Maps* (1911) 562

George Finch & Harold G. Moulton, Forward, to Manley O. Hudson, International Tribunals v. (1944)

Jerome Frank, *Courts on Trial: Myth and Reality in American Justice* (1949) 3 (Reissued 1973)

Hugo Grotius (Huig de Groot), De Jure Belli ac Pacis Libris Tres (1625)

Ellen Hanak, *et al. Managing California's Water: From Conflict to Reconciliation* (2011)

Louis Henkin, General Course on Public International Law, in IV Recueil des Cours (1989)

Oliver Wendell Holmes, The Common Law (Mark DeWolf Howe ed., 1963) 103

Manley O. Hudson, International Tribunals (1944)

Norris Hundley Jr., Water and the West: The Colorado River Compact and the Politics of Water in the American West (2009)

Institutes of Justinian 2. 1.1 (S. Scott trans. reprinted ed. 1973)

Katharine L. Jacobs & Bonnie G. Colby (eds.), Arizona Water Policy: Management Innovations in an Urbanizing, Arid Region (2006)

Philip C. Jessup, Transnational Law (Extracts), in Philip C. Jessup's Transnational Law Revisited – On the Occasion of the 50th Anniversary of its Publication, (Christian Tietje, *et al.* eds. 2006)

Hans Kelsen, General Theory of Law and State (1945)

Alexandre Kiss, Dinah Shelton & Kanami Ishibashi (eds.), Economic Globalization and Compliance with International Environmental Agreements (2003)

H. G. Koeningsberger, Republicanism, Monarchism and Liberty, in Robert Oresko *et al.*, Royal and Republican Sovereignty in Early Europe, Essays in Memory of Ragnhild Hatton (2006)

Martti Koskenniemi, Report of the Study Group of the International Law Commission, Fragmentation of International Law: Difficulties Arising from the Diversification and Expansion of International Law, UN GA, Doc. A/CN.4/L.682 (2006)

Luna B. Leopold and Thomas Maddock, Jr., The Hydraulic Geometry of Stream Channels and Some Physiographic Implications, United States Geological Survey (1953)

Francesco Maiolo, Medieval Sovereignty: Marsilius of Padua and Bartolus of Saoferrato (2007)

Ed Marston (ed.), Quenching the Big Thirst, in Char Miller, *Rivers of the American West* (2009)

Stephen C. McCaffrey, *The Law of International Watercourses: Non-Navigational Uses* (2001)

Owen McIntyre & Alistair Rieu-Clarke, UN Watercourses Convention, Online Users Guide, Article 5, 5.1.1 Theories of Allocation

NASA, NASA Finds Drought in Eastern Mediterranean Worst of Past 900 Years (Mar. 1, 2016)

National Assessment Synthesis Team (Eds.), Climate Change Impacts on the United States – Foundation Report: The Potential Consequences of Climate Variability and Change (2001) 113. (Cambridge, New York, NY)

Roger K. Newman, Hugo Black: A Biography 531–32 (1994)

Abigail Ofri Amoah, Water Wars and International Conflict (2008)

L. Oppenheim, Oppenheim's International Law, (9th ed). Robert Jennings and Arthur Watts eds. (1992)

Roland Paris, The Devils Lake Dispute between Canada and the United States (Feb. 2008), University of Ottawa, Centre for International Policy Studies

Kenneth Pennington, Sovereignty and Rights in Medieval and Early Modern Jurisprudence: Law and Norms Without State, in Joanna Sondel *et al.*, Roman Law as Formative of Modern Legal Systems: Studies in Honour of Wiesław Litewski (2003)

Joseph Raz, *Ethics in the Public Domain* (1995)

Joseph Raz, The Authority of Law (1979)

Edward Re, Chairperson, U.S. Foreign Claims Settlement Commission, Gut Dam Arbitration, Report of by 4 May 1965, *reproduced in* International Environmental Law Reports, vol. I: Early Decisions (Cairo A. R. Robb ed.) (1999) 386

W. Michael Reisman, Nullity and Revision (1971)

Alistair Rieu-Clarke, *et al.*, UN Watercourses Convention – User's Guide (2012)

Cairo A. R. Robb (ed.), International Environmental Law Reports, Volume 1, Early Decisions (1990)

Alfred P. Rubin, Pollution by Analogy: The Trail Smelter Arbitration (1971)

Hal Shelton, *Geology Illustrated* (1966)

Igor Shiklomanov, World Fresh Water Resources, in Peter H. Glick, Water in Crisis: *A Guide to the World's Fresh Water Resources* (1993) 13

Milan Sahovi & William Bishop, The Authority of the State: Its Range with Respect to Persons and Places, in *Manual of Public International Law* 311, 314 (Max Serensen ed., 1968)

The International Bank for Reconstruction and Development's Inspection Panel

Barton Thompson, Jr. John Leshy, & Robert Abrams's Legal Control of Water Resources, Cases and Materials, (6th ed. 2016)

Elsie G Turnbull, Trail Between Two Wars: The Story of a Smelter City (1980)

Robert M. Utley *Changing Course* (1996)

Joseph Vining, *From Newton's Sleep* (1995)

John D. Wirth, Smelter Smoke in North America: The Politics of Transborder Pollution (1999)

World Bank Group, ICSID, International Centre for Settlement of
Investment Disputes of the World Bank (2015)

Kenneth Duane Yielding, The Chamizal Dispute: An Exercise in
Arbitration, 1845–1945, Ph.D. Dissertation, Texas Tech University (May
1973)

ARTICLES

Henk Aarts *et al.*, Automatic Normative Behavior in Environments: The
Moderating Role of Conformity in Activating Situational Norms, 21 Social
Cognition (2003) 447

Leisy Abrego, Legitimacy, Social Identity, and the Mobilization of Law: The
Effects of Assembly Bill 540 on Undocumented Students in California, 33
Law & Social Inquiry (2008) 709

Melissa Albert, Meuse River, Europe, Encyclopedia Britannica (Sept. 10,
2010)

Australian Government Department of Agriculture, Drought and Rural
Assistance

Jeffrey D. Azarva, Note, Conflict on the Nile: International Watercourse Law
and Elusive Effort to Create a Transboundary Water Regime in the Nile
Basin, 25 Temp Int'l & Comp. L J (2011) 457

Banyan Asia, Xayaburi and Vientaine, The Mekong River: Lies, Dams and
Statistics, *The Economist* (July 26, 2012)

C. Richard Bath, Alternative Cooperative Arrangements for Managing
Transboundary Air Resources along the Border, 18 Nat Res J (1978) 181

Eyal Benvenisti, Asian Traditions and Management of Water Resources:
Ancient Practices Informing Regional Cooperation, (Asian Law Inst.)
Proceedings of the Role of Law in a Developing Asia (2004) 617

Rinaldo Bianchi, The Role of Adjudication in International River Disputes:
The Lake Lanoux Case, 53 Am J Int'l L (1959) 30

L. J. Bouchez, The Fixing of Boundaries in International Boundary Rivers, 12
Int'l & Comp L Q (1963) 789, 793

BBC News, South Africa Grapples with Worst Drought in 30 Years (2015)

Dante A. Caponera, Patterns of Cooperation in International Water Law:
Principles and Institutions, 25 Nat. Res. J. (1985) 563

Paulo Canelas de Castro, Trends of Development of International Water
Law, 6 Beijing Law Review 285 (2015)

Joseph W. Dellapenna, The Customary International Law of Transboundary
Waters, 1 Int'l J. Global Envtl Issues (2001) 264

John W. Donaldson, Paradox of the Moving Boundary: Legal Heredity of River Accretion and Avulsion, Water Alternatives (2011) 155

Lesley Downer, Pyrenees: Criss-Crossing the Spanish-French Border, *The Telegraph (UK)*, May 9, 1998

Dr. Lambertus Erades, The Gut Dam Arbitration, 16 Netherlands Int'l L. Rev. 161 (1969)

Par Engstrom, Effectiveness of International and Regional Human Rights Regimes, The Int'l Studies Encyclopedia (Robert A. Denemark ed., 2010)

Jay Famiglietti, Can We End the Global Water Crisis? *National Geographic*, June 10, 2013

John Fellas, A Fair and Efficient International Arbitration Process, 59 Dispute Res. J (2004) 78

Andreas Follesdal, The Legitimacy Deficits of the Human Rights Judiciary: Elements and Implications of a Normative Theory, 14 Theoretical Inquiries L (2013) 339

Joe Gelt, Sharing Colorado River Water: History, Public Policy and the Colorado River Compact, 10 *Arroyo*, Aug. 1997, No. 1

Tom Ginsburg and Richard H. McAdams, Adjudicating in Anarchy: An Expressive Theory of International Dispute Resolution, 45 Wm & Mary L R (2004) 1229, 1304, 1308

Peter Gleick, *et al.*, Water, War & Peace in the Middle East, 36 Environment (Apr. 1994) 6

Andrew T. Guzman, International Tribunals: A Rational Choice Analysis, 157 U Pa L R (2008) 171

Peter M. Haas, Banning Chlorofluorocarbons: Epistemic Community Efforts to Protect Stratospheric Ozone, 46 Int'l Org (1992) 187

Peter M. Haas, Introduction: Epistemic Communities and International Policy Coordination, 46 *Int'l Org* (1992)

Peter M. Haas, Do Regimes Matter? Epistemic Communities and Mediterranean Pollution Control, 43 *Int'l Org* (1989) 377

Noah Hall, Bilateral Breakdown: U.S.-Canada Pollution Disputes, 21 Nat. Resources & Envt (2006) 18

Günther Handl, State Liability for Accidental Transnational Environmental Damage by Private Persons, 74 Am J Int'l L. (1980) 525

Laurence R. Helfer & Anne-Marie Slaughter, Toward a Theory of Effective Supranational Adjudication, 107 Yale L J (1997) 273, 282

Laurence R. Helfer & Anne-Marie Slaughter, Why States Create International Tribunals: A Response to Professors Posner and Yoo, 93 *Calif L R* (2005) 899, 901

James Landes & Richard Posner, The Independent Judiciary in an Interest Group Perspective, 18 *J L & Econ* (1975) 875

Maximo Langer, The Rise of Managerial Judging in International Criminal Law, 53 *Am J Comp L* (2005) 835

Malcolm Langford, Another Rip in the Arbitration Veil? Transparency in the Wake of Forresti and Giovanna 1, *available at* http://ssrn.com/abstract=2238495

Matthew Lister, The Legitimating Role of Consent in International Law, 11 *Chi J Int'l L* (2011) 663

Ryke Longest, Opinion Analysis: Bargaining in the Shadow of Equitable Apportionment, *SCOTUSblog*, Mar. 3, 2015

Yonatan Lupu, International Judicial Legitimacy: Lessons from National Courts, 14 *Theoretical Inquiries L* 2103 (437)

Brunson MacChesney, Judicial Decisions: Lake Lanoux Case, 53 Am J Int'l L (1959) 156

James G. Mandik, The Modification of Decrees in the Original Jurisdiction of the Supreme Court, 125 Yale L J (2016) 1880

Jenny S. Martinez, Towards an International Judicial System, 56 *Stan L R* (2003) 429

Leah H. Martinez, Post Industrial Revolution Human activity and Climate Change: Why the United States Must Implement Mandatory Limits Industrial Greenhouse Gas Emissions, 20 *J Land Use* (2005) 407

Paul Mason, Catalonia, Lombardy, Scotland . . . why the fight for self-determination now? The Guardian (UK) 23 Oct. 2017

Stephen C. McCaffrey, The Harmon Doctrine One Hundred Years Later: Buried, Not Praised, 36 Nat. Resources J (1996) 549

John O. McGinnis, *The President, the Senate, the Constitution, and the Confirmation Process: A Reply to Professors Strauss and Sunstein*, 71 Tex L R (1993) 633

Augusto P Miceli, Forum Juridicum: Bartolus of Sassoferrato, 37 La. L.R. (1977) 1027

Charles Meyers, The Colorado River, 19 Stan. L. Rev. (1967) 1

Dan Morrison, Can Uganda and Ethiopia Act as Egypt's "Water Bankers"? *National Geographic Voices*, Aug. 3, 2010

Monica Moyo, Egypt, Sudan, and Ethiopia Sign Nile Dam Agreement (March 23, 2015), American Society of International law, International Law Brief (Mar. 27, 2015)

P. Godfrey Okoth, The Nile River Question and the Riparian States: Contextualising Uganda's Foreign Policy Interests, 11 *African Soc R* (2007) 81

Andreas Osiander, International Relations, and the Westphalian Myth, 55 Int'l Organizations (2001), 251

Fred Pearce, Mideast Water Wars: In Iraq, A Battle for Control of Water, Environment 360 (Aug. 25, 2014)

Eric A. Posner & John C. Yoo, Judicial Independence in International Tribunals, 93 Calif L R (2005) 1

Muhammad Mizanur Rahaman, Principles of International Water Law: Creating Effective Transboundary Water Resources Management, 3 Int'l J Sustainable Soc (2009) 207

Kal Raustiala, Compliance & Effectiveness in International Regulatory Cooperation, 32 Case W Res J Int'l L (2000) 387

W. Michael Reisman, Control Mechanisms in International Dispute Resolution, 2 US–Mex LJ (1994) 129

Cesare P. R. Romano, The Shift from Consensual to the Compulsory Paradigm in International Adjudication: Elements for a Theory of Consent, 39 NYU J Int'l L & Pol (2007) 791

Cesare P. R. Romano, The Proliferation of International Judicial Bodies: The Pieces of the Puzzle, 31 NYU J. Int'l L & Pol. 709, 712 (1999)

John Gerard Ruggie, International Responses to Technology: Concepts and Trends, 29 *Int'l Org* (1975) 557

Salman M. A. Salman, The Helsinki Rules, the UN Watercourses Convention and the Berlin Rules: Perspectives on International Water Law, 23 Water Res Develop (2007) 625

Yuval Shany, Assessing the Effectiveness of International Courts – A Goal-Based Approach, 106 AJIL (2012)

Marat Seidakhemtov, *et al.*, Mechanism of Trans Boundary Water Resources Management for Central Asia Countries, 143 Procedia – Social and Behavioral Sciences 600 (2014)

Bruno Simma, Universality of International Law from the Perspective of a Practitioner, 20 Eur J Int'l L (2009) 265

Peter S. Smedresman, The International Joint Commission (United States-Canada) and the International Boundary and Water Commission (United States-Mexico): Potential for Environmental Control Along the Boundaries, 6 NYU J Int'l L & Pol (1973) 499

Caroline Spiegel, International Water Law: The Contributions of Western United States Water Law to the United Nations Convention on the Law of Non-Navigable Uses of International Watercourses, 15 Duke J Comparative & Int'l L (2005) 333

David M. Solzman, Des Plaines River, Encyclopedia of Chicago (2005)

Joyce R. Starr, Water Wars, Foreign Pol'y (Spring 1991) 17, 19

David A. Strauss & Cass R. Sunstein, The Senate, the Constitution, and the Confirmation Process, 101 Yale L J (1992) 1491

Mark C. Suchman, Managing Legitimacy: Strategic and Institutional Approaches, 20 Acad Manag J (1995), 571

Ishaan Thaoor, The Middle East Just Suffered its Worst Drought in 900 Years, Wash. Post, Mar. 4, 2016

Jonathan Thompson, Drought, Glen Canyon Dam, Climate Change and God: Stopping by the dam during a days-long experimental flood, it's clear that even this massive feat of engineering can't fix the arid West, High Country News, (Nov. 18, 2013)

Alezah Trigueros, The Human Right to Water: Will Its Fulfillment Contribute to Environmental Degradation? 19 Indiana J of Global Legal Stud (2012) 599

United States National Park Service, Chamizal National Memorial, Flood and the Chamizal Issue, The Rio Grande Floods: The Beginning of the Chamizal Dispute (undated)

US Department of the Interior, Bureau of Reclamation, *The Bureau of Reclamation: A Very Brief History* (Last Updated July 5, 2011)

William Van Alstyne, International Law and Interstate River Disputes, 48 Calif L R (1960) 596

Pieter van der Zaag, Southern Africa: Evolving Regional Water Law and Politics, in in Joseph W. Dellapenna & Joyeeta Gupta (eds.), *The Evolution of Law and Politics of Water* (2008) 245

John Vidal, How Water Raises the Political Temperature Between Counties, The Guardian (UK) Jun 25, 2010

John D. Walsh, *et al.*, Our Changing Climate. Climate Change Impacts in the United States: The Third National Climate Assessment, in Jerry M. Melillo *et al.* (eds.) U.S. Global Change Research Program (2014)

Rodrick E. Walston, The Public Trust Doctrine in the Water Rights Context 29 Nat R J (1989) 585

Percy Don Williams, Jr., Fifty Years of the Chamizal Controversy – A Note on International Arbitral Appeals, 25 Tex L R (1947) 455

John Wright, Planning Arizona's Future Begins with Education, *Arizona Daily Star*, Mar. 4, 2008

1

Adjudication and the Scope of Transboundary
Water Disputes

Transboundary water disputes have been a constant in the universe of international conflicts since time immemorial. The first recorded dispute occurred in Mesopotamia around 450 BCE between Lagash and Umma over the king of Umma's diversion of water from the Shatt al-Gharraf, an ancient Iraqi canal connecting the Euphrates and Tigris Rivers.[1] Others include those adjudicated by the United States Supreme Court, including *Kansas v. Colorado*,[2] which resulted in the espousal of the doctrine of equitable allocation, *New Jersey v. New York*[3] and *Texas v. New Mexico*,[4] conflicts between Mexico and the United States over the Rio Grande and Colorado Rivers, the *Lac Lanoux Arbitration* (Spain and France),[5] and the recently decided *Indus Waters Kishenganga Arbitration* (India and Pakistan).[6] Today, the issues that led to these disputes are much more prevalent than they were in the past,[7]

---

[1] *See*, e.g., Oxford Cuniform Digital Library Initiative, The Umma–Lagash Border Conflict (Last updated September 5, 2013), http://cdli.ox.ac.uk/wiki/doku.php?id=umma_lagash_border_conflict; Les Belles English, Classical Wisdom Weekly, A War for Water – The Tale of Two City-States (April 30, 2013), http://classicalwisdom.com/a-war-for-water-the-tale-of-two-city-states.

[2] 206 US 46 (1907).

[3] 283 US 336 (1931). (New Jersey sued both New York State and New York City to enjoin them from diverting water from nonnavigable tributaries of the Delaware River.)

[4] 462 US 554 (1983). (Allocation of waters from the Pecos River between the two states as per their compact (treaty).).

[5] 12 RIAA 281 (1957). (Diversion of water from a stream that flows from Lake Lanoux to the Carol River in Spain.)

[6] PCA Case No. 2011–01.

[7] *See generally*, Itzchak E. Kornfeld, Mesopotamia: A History of Water and Law, in Joseph W. Dellapenna and Joyeeta Gupta (eds.), *The Evolution of Law and Politics of Water* (2008) 21; Robbie Sabel, The Jordan Basin: Evolution of the Rules, Dellapenna and Gupta, *The Evolution of Law and Politics of Water* 263; Pieter van der Zaag, Southern Africa: Evolving Regional Water Law and Politics, Dellapenna and Gupta, *The Evolution of Law and Politics of Water*

as a consequence of the persistent growth in population[8] and the expansion of worldwide agriculture,[9] industrialization and climate change[10] – the latter resulting in droughts in Australia,[11] South Africa,[12] sub-Saharan Africa,[13] the Middle East,[14] the Glen Canyon and Lake Mead in Arizona and southern California.[15] Economic expansion also accounts for an increased use of water as a consequence of higher standards of living for the world's poor.[16]

245; Eyal Benvenisti, Asian Traditions and Management of Water Resources: Ancient Practices Informing Regional Cooperation, (Asian Law Inst.) *Proceedings of the Role of Law in a Developing Asia* (2004) 617; Eyal Benvenisti, *Sharing Transboundary Resources: International Law and Optimal Resource Use* (2002).

[8] Per the United States Census, International Programs, World Population (last revised July 9, 2015), www.census.gov/population/international/data/worldpop/table_population.php. In 1950 the world's population was 2,557,628,654. By 1980 it had climbed to 4,451,362,735, and by 2000 it grew to 6,088,571,383. As of 2017, the population is expected to reach 7,412,778,971, and by 2050 the world's population is expected to rise to 9,408,141,302. That is a 3.7-fold increase over a century. Compare that growth to that from 1800 (approx. 950 million) to that in 1900 (1.65 billion), a 1.7-fold increase. Figures available at Carl Haub, How Many People Have Ever Lived on Earth, Population Reference Bureau (October 2011), www.prb.org/Publications/Articles/2002/HowManyPeopleHaveEverLivedonEarth.Aspx.

[9] *See e.g.*, Natasha Gilbert, African Agriculture: Dirt Poor, 498 *Nature* (2012) 525, *available at* www.nature.com/news/african-agriculture-dirt-poor-1.10311; Food and Agricultural Organization of the United Nations, Livestock Environment and Development (LEAD), South & Central America (Undated), www.fao.org/agriculture/lead/lead/networks/americao/en.

[10] *See*, Leah H. Martinez, Post Industrial Revolution Human Activity and Climate Change: Why the United States Must Implement Mandatory Limits Industrial Greenhouse Gas Emissions, 20 *J Land Use* (2005) 407.

[11] *See generally*, Australian Government Department of Agriculture, Drought and Rural Assistance (last reviewed July 1, 2014) www.daff.gov.au/agriculture-food/drought.

[12] BBC News, South Africa Grapples with Worst Drought in 30 Years (November 30, 2015), www.bbc.com/news/world-africa-34884135.

[13] IRIN, Drought in Africa 2017: Farmers, traders and consumers across East and Southern Africa are feeling the impact of consecutive seasons of drought that have scorched harvests and ruined livelihoods, (Mar. 17, 2017), https://www.irinnews.org/feature/2017/03/17/drought-africa-2017.

[14] NASA, NASA Finds Drought in Eastern Mediterranean Worst of Past 900 Years (March 1, 2016), www.nasa.gov/feature/goddard/2016/nasa-finds-drought-in-eastern-mediterranean-worst-of-past-900-years. ("New NASA study finds that the recent drought that began in 1998 in the eastern Mediterranean Levant region, which comprises Cyprus, Israel, Jordan, Lebanon, Palestine, Syria, and Turkey, is likely the worst drought of the past nine centuries.")

[15] Jonathan Thompson, Drought, Glen Canyon Dam, Climate Change and God: Stopping by the dam during a days-long experimental flood, it's clear that even this massive feat of engineering can't fix the arid West, *High Country News*, (November 18, 2013), www.hcn.org/articles/drought-glen-canyon-dam-climate-change-and-god. ("We're now 14 years into the current drought, the driest 14 years of the past century."); Eric Holthaus, The California Drought Isn't Going Anywhere, *Slate* (October 16, 2014), www.slate.com/blogs/future_tense/2014/10/16/noaa_forecast_suggests_california_drought_isn_t_going_anywhere.html. ("For a state racked by drought, there couldn't be much worse news. 'California's record-setting drought will likely persist or intensify in large parts of the state . . . '.")

[16] E.g., Organization for Economic Cooperation and Development, Dept. For International Development, Growth Building Jobs and Prosperity in Developing Countries (undated),

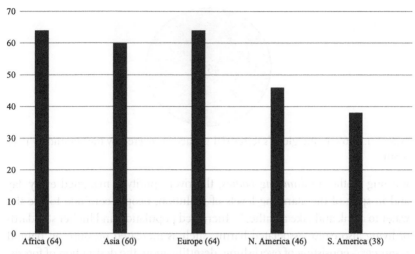

FIGURE 1.1 Transboundry river basins by Continent

However, this growth has been accompanied by a concomitant need for greater access to potable water.[17] In some regions of the world neither potable water[18] nor proper sanitation are available.[19] These two factors have had numerous negative effects on transboundary waters, including overuse and pollution.[20] For example, the Ganges River is one of the five most polluted rivers in the world:[21] "In certain areas in Ganga River *the bacteria levels are more than 100 times higher than the limits set by the government.* From

www.oecd.org/derec/unitedkingdom/40700982.pdf. ("Asian countries are increasingly tackling [poverty via an] agenda of 'inclusive growth'. India's most recent development plan has two main objectives: raising economic growth and making growth more inclusive, policy mirrored elsewhere in South Asia and Africa.")

[17] World Health Organization. Making Water a Part of Economic Development: The Economic Benefits of Improved Water Management and Services 4 (2005), www.who.int/water_sanitation_health/waterandmacroecon.pdf. ("Improved water supply and sanitation and water resources management boosts countries' economic growth and contributes greatly to poverty eradication.")

[18] United Nations, International Decade for Action "Water for Life" 2005–2015, UN Water, Water Scarcity (2015), www.un.org/waterforlifedecade/scarcity.shtml. ("Water scarcity already affects every continent. Around 1.2 billion people, or almost one-fifth of the world's population, live in areas of physical scarcity, and 500 million people are approaching this situation. Another 1.6 billion people, or almost one quarter of the world's population, face economic water shortage . . .")

[19] 2.5 billion people worldwide lack access to proper sanitation. World Health Organization, *Water Sanitation Health: Water Supply, Sanitation and Hygiene Development* (2016), www.who.int/water_sanitation_health/hygiene/en.

[20] Ganapati Information Technology Services, Ganga [Ganges] India's National River (2006), www.gits4u.com/water/ganga.htm# Introduction and map of Ganga.

[21] *Ibid.*

FIGURE 1.2 46% of the globe's terrestrial surface is covered by transboundary river basins

washing clothes to *dumping bodies*, the river's purity is maligned every day and in spite of the alarming levels of pollution, people continue to use the water to drink and take a bathe."[22] Increased population and higher standards of living also cause associated harms, such as increased pressure on natural resources – consisting of overfishing, desertification, the destruction of forests, and increased waste from mining – and, at the same time, a dramatic increase in the allocation of water.[23]

Transboundary water resources are also scarcer.[24] Water use has been increasing at more than twice the rate of population growth over the last century, and, while there is no *per se* global water shortage, a mounting number of the world's regions are persistently water starved.[25] Indeed, the United Nations estimates that some "1.2 billion people, or almost one-fifth of the world's population, live in areas of physical scarcity, and 500 million people are approaching this situation."[26] Moreover, a further 1.6 billion

---

[22] *Ibid.* (emphasis added).

[23] Papua New Guinea Department of National Planning and Monitoring & the United Nations Development Programme in Papua New Guinea, Papua New Guinea – Millennium Development Goals Second National Progress Comprehensive Report for Papua New Guinea (2010) 10, 201, www.pg.undp.org/content/dam/papua_new_guinea/docs/MDG/UNDP_PG_MDG%20Comprehensive%20Report%202010.pdf (emphasis added).

[24] *See*, e.g., Marat Seidakhemtov *et al.*, Mechanism of Trans Boundary Water Resources Management for Central Asia Countries, 143 *Procedia – Social and Behavioral Sciences* 600 (2014). (The Republic of Kazakhstan, a water-scarce country in Central Asia, is confronting an urgent problem of managing the waters of its transboundary rivers, such as the Horergusi and Sumubai Rivers.)

[25] The United Nations, International Decade for Action "Water for Life" 2005–2015, Water Scarcity (last updated November 24, 2014), www.un.org/waterforlifedecade/scarcity.shtml.

[26] "Water scarcity is defined as the point at which the aggregate impact of all users impinges on the supply or quality of water under prevailing institutional arrangements to the extent that the demand by all sectors, including the environment, cannot be satisfied fully." *Ibid.* *See also* United Nations World Water Development Report 4. Volume 1: Managing Water under Uncertainty and Risk (2012), www.unesco.org/new/en/natural-sciences/environment/water/wwap/wwdr/wwdr4-2012.

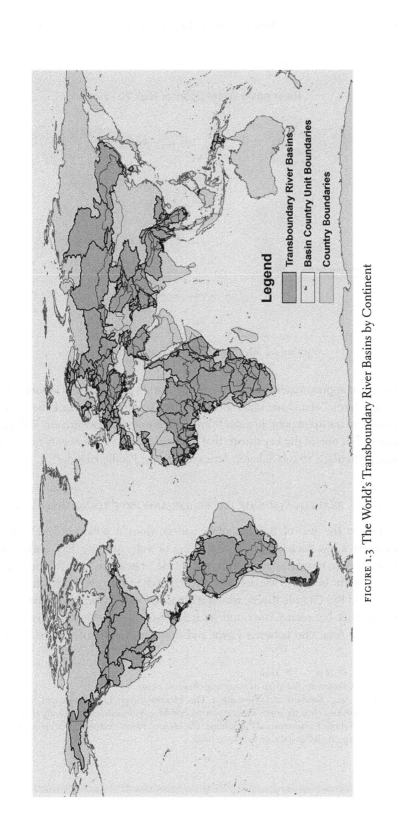

Legend

☐ Transboundary River Basins
☐ Basin Country Unit Boundaries
☐ Country Boundaries

FIGURE 1.3 The World's Transboundary River Basins by Continent

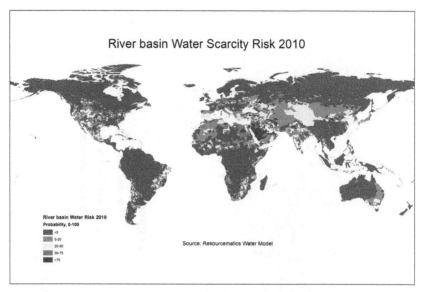

River basin Water Scarcity Risk 2010

Source: Resourcematics Water Model

River basin Water Risk 2010
Probability, 0-100

FIGURE 1.4 River basin Water Scarcity Risk 2010

people, or approximately one quarter of the world's population, confront what the UN terms "economic water shortage," that is, where states lack the infrastructure to transport potable water from aquifers and adjacent streams.[27] Water scarcity[28] is one of the key threats that the world faces in the twenty-first century, particularly in sub-Saharan Africa and in the Pacific Islands.[29]

I THE REALLOCATION OF WATER USE AND IMPENDING DISPUTES

A shift in the use of transboundary waters, from a policy of unchecked water use a few decades ago, to today's era of water scarcity, has resulted in disputes over transboundary rivers worldwide. These include the decades-long dispute between Mexico and the United States, over both the Colorado and Rio Grande Rivers, which is discussed in the *Chamizal Dispute*;[30] the conflict between China and its neighbors on the Mekong River[31] in Southeast Asia; one between Egypt and upstream riparians over the White

---

[27] *Ibid.*   [28] *Ibid.*   [29] *Ibid.*
[30] These two rivers are discussed in upcoming chapters, *infra.*
[31] Banyan Asia, Xayaburi and Vientiane ; The Mekong River: Lies, Dams and Statistics, *The Economist* (July 26, 2012), www.economist.com/blogs/banyan/2012/07/mekong-river; The United Nations Environmental Programme, *The Mekong River – Survival for Millions* (2008), www.unep.org/dewa/vitalwater/article120.html.

and Blue Nile Rivers in Africa;[32] the decades-long clash between Iraq and
Syria over the Euphrates and Tigris Rivers, in Asia Minor;[33] and recent
"[t]ensions ... between Uzbekistan, Kazakhstan, Kyrgyzstan and Tajikistan
over the Amu Daria and Syr Daria rivers, as well as the severely depleted Aral
Sea."[34]

Each of these disputes will require resolution within the next few decades,
either by diplomatic means or by adjudication – before an international court
or tribunal – or, there is, of course, the possibility that hostilities will break out.
Moreover, as populations upstream and downstream modernize, their need
for additional water resources will become more acute. These peoples will
need to fight against agricultural interests, who are inefficient, and use 80 percent of the world's water – a figure that has not changed in millennia.[35] The
main problem, however, is that the quantity of water will shift geographically,
due to climate change,[36] and become scarcer in some locales where today it
may be abundant.[37] And, as noted above, this scarcity may cause disputes that

---

[32] Jeffrey D. Azarva, Note, Conflict on the Nile: International Watercourse Law and Elusive
Effort to Create a Transboundary Water Regime in the Nile Basin, 25 *Temp Int'l & Comp. L
J*(2011) 457. In 1979, following the execution of the Camp David Accords, Egyptian president
Anwar Sadat declared that "[t]he only matter that could take Egypt to war again is water."
Joyce R. Starr, Water Wars, *Foreign Pol'y*, (Spring 1991) 17, 19.

[33] Fred Pearce, Mideast Water Wars: In Iraq, A Battle for Control of Water, *Environment*
360 (August 25, 2014), http://e360.yale.edu/feature/mideast_water_wars_in_iraq_a_battle_for_
control_of_water/2796. ("There is a water war going on in the Middle East this summer.
Behind the headline stories of brutal slaughter as Sunni militants carve out a religious state
covering Iraq and Syria, there lies a battle for the water supplies that sustain these desert
nations.") Itzchak E. Kornfeld, Trouble in Mesopotamia: Can America Deter a Water War
Between Iraq, Syria and Turkey? 34 *Envtl L Reporter* (2004) 10632.

[34] John Vidal, *How Water Raises the Political Temperature Between Countries*, The Guardian
(UK) Jun 25, 2010, www.theguardian.com/environment/2010/jun/25/river-water-disputes-
tension-shortages.

[35] United States Department of Agriculture, Economic Research Service, Irrigation & Water
Use (last updated, July 19, 2012). "Agriculture is a major user of ground and surface water in
the United States, accounting for approximately 80 percent of the Nation's consumptive water
use and over 90 percent in many Western States."

[36] United States Environmental Protection Agency (EPA), Water Resources: Climate Impacts
on Water Resources (last updated February 23, 2016), www3.epa.gov/climatechange/impacts/
water.html. "[S]tresses that are likely to be exacerbated by climate change. In many areas,
climate change is likely to increase water demand while shrinking water supplies. This shifting balance would challenge water managers to simultaneously meet the needs of growing
communities, sensitive ecosystems, farmers, ranchers, energy producers, and manufacturers."

[37] See e.g., Global Policy Forum, Water in Conflict (2016), www.globalpolicy.org/
the-dark-side-of-natural-resources-st/water-in-conflict.html. ("As demand for water hits the
limits of finite supply, potential conflicts are brewing between nations that share transboundary freshwater reserves. More than 50 countries on five continents might soon be caught up
in water disputes unless they move quickly to establish agreements on how to share reservoirs,

may lead to wars.[38] Indeed, what we see in the cases assessed herein and elsewhere, is that attempts at diplomacy have failed and thus international courts and tribunals are utilized to resolve these disputes.

Due to their impact on human health and the environment, these international conundrums and conflicts are critical today, and will likely grow more so in the future.[39] These issues are finally being taken seriously, and are being addressed within the legal academy, the political branches of many governments, and society in general. They are also being adjudicated in international courts, e.g., the ICJ's *Case Concerning Pulp Mills on the River Uruguay* (Argentina v. Uruguay).[40] Moreover, clearly, such conflicts do not stop at the artificially drawn borders of individual states, which, of course, do not coincide with natural systems, such as rivers. Rather, they are transboundary phenomena. Indeed, one expert recently observed that

> [i]t is now recognized that the planet faces a diverse and growing range of environmental challenges which can only be addressed through international co-operation. Acid rain, ozone depletion, climate change, loss of biodiversity, toxic and hazardous products and wastes, *pollution of rivers and depletion of fresh water resources*, are some of the issues which international law is being called upon to address.[41]

A *The Hydrological Cycle*

The volume of freshwater available for human use and consumption, including groundwater (1.65 percent), lakes (0.013 percent), and rivers (.0002 percent), amounts to just 1.66 percent of the available fresh water on the planet.

---

rivers, and underground water aquifers."); Abigail Ofri Amoah, Water Wars and International Conflict (2008), http://academic.evergreen.edu/g/grossmaz/oforiaa. ("For centuries war and conflict has been tied to the protection of water resources. With the risk of water shortages around the world becoming more of an issue, water has become fuel of certain conflicts in many regions of the world.")

38 One example is the past and current conflict between Sudan and South Sudan. One study that has examined that conflict noted that "[e]ach plausible scenario ... holds great uncertainty and risk regarding the potential impacts on oil, land, and water. The effects of each scenario could drastically change if the political and economic situations on the ground become more fragile." Paul Sullivan and Natalie Nasrallah, Improving Natural Resource Management in Sudan: A Strategy for Effective State Building and Conflict Resolution, US Institute for Peace, Special Report 242 (June 2010) 1, *available at* www.usip.org/sites/default/files/SR242SullivanNasrallah.pdf.

39 Vidal, *ibid.* ("Water wars haven't started yet, but shortages certainly cause tensions between states to rise.")

40 Judgment, ICJ Reports 2010, 14.

41 Philippe Sands, *Principles of International Environmental Law* (2nd ed. 2003) 3 (emphasis added).

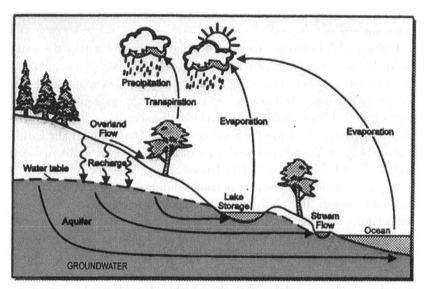

FIGURE 1.5 The Water/Hydrological Cycle

Moreover, 96.5 percent of the global water is contained in the oceans, seas and bays and the ice caps contain 1.74 percent of the total, adding up to 99.9 percent of earth's total water budget, while the remaining 0.1 percent is either bound up in the soil as soil vapor, constitutes saline water in aquifers, is in swamps, or is in the atmosphere.[42] Indeed, the amount of water that exists on earth is unchanged and constant – and has not changed since primordial times.

Moreover, hydrologists and geologists refer to the earth's water system on as a "closed system." That is, nothing either leaves or enters the system – it is fixed. Water is controlled by a model called the water/hydrological cycle[43] that describes the existence and movement of water "on, in and above the earth"[44] (Figure 1.5). The cycle also depicts the always changing phases/types of water, whether liquid, gas (in the atmosphere), or solid (bound up as ice), at any given time. Indeed, the phases or types of the water cycle are mutable. They may occur for seconds, e.g., the vaporization of water or melting of ice or as in the situation of water traveling through an aquifer, take millions of

[42] Igor Shiklomanov, World Fresh Water Resources, in Peter H. Glick, Water in Crisis: A Guide to the World's Fresh Water Resources (1993) 13.
[43] United States Geological Survey (USGS) The Water Cycle (last modified September 13, 2012), http://ga.water.usgs.gov/edu/watercycle.html.
[44] United States Geological Survey (USGS) Summary of the Water Cycle. What is the Water Cycle? (Last Modified May 2, 2016), http://water.usgs.gov/edu/watercyclesummary.html.

years to move a few meters.[45] Indeed, the hydrological cycle has no starting or end-point.

The impacts of climate change will likely profoundly impact the water cycle. Warmer temperatures will increase the degree of water evaporation into the atmosphere, thereby expanding its capacity to "hold" more moisture, i.e., water.[46] Indeed, "[w]hile it sounds counterintuitive, a warmer world produces both wetter and drier conditions."[47] Accordingly, increasing evaporation may dry out some areas,[48] such as the Southwest United States, the Middle East,[49] and sub-Saharan Africa,[50] and flood other areas, including the southern states, and the Great Lakes Region,[51] of the United States and northern Europe.

Disparities in the accumulation of rainfall during storms offer confirmation that the hydrological cycle is currently experiencing changes.[52] Since 1895 temperatures have increased by 1.3°F to 1.9°F (0.72° to 1.05°C), with most of this increase occurring since 1970,[53] causing increased precipitation. Warming winter temperatures result in more rain than snowfall.[54] Moreover, these increasing temperatures trigger earlier snow melts, which modify the timetables of streamflow in watercourses whose highlands are located in mountainous regions.[55]

Another problem caused by rising temperatures is that both people and animals require greater amounts of water, in order to sustain their health and to flourish.[56] Numerous human activities, including raising food and non-food

[45] USGS, The Water Cycle (Last Modified Dec. 15, 2016).

[46] Thomas R. Karl *et al.* (eds.), *Global Climate Change Impacts in the United States* (2009) 15. (Cambridge and New York). ("[S]ince a warmer climate increases evaporation and allows the atmosphere to hold more moisture. This creates an amplifying 'feedback loop,' leading to more warming.")

[47] *Ibid.* at 44.   [48] *Ibid.*

[49] Ishaan Thaoor, The Middle East Just Suffered its Worst Drought in 900 Years, WASH. POST, March 4, 2016, https://www.washingtonpost.com/news/worldviews/wp/2016/03/04/the-middle-east-suffered-its-worst-drought-in-900-years; John Vidal, Middle East Faces Water Shortages for the Next 25 Years, Study Says, The Guardian (UK) August 27, 2015, https://www.theguardian.com/environment/2015/aug/27/middle-east-faces-water-shortages-for-the-next-25-years-study-says.

[50] BBC News, South Africa Grapples with Worst Drought in 30 Years, November 30, 2015, http://www.bbc.com/news/world-africa-34884135.

[51] National Assessment Synthesis Team (eds.), *Climate Change Impacts on the United States – Foundation Report: The Potential Consequences of Climate Variability and Change* (2001) 113 (Cambridge, New York, NY).

[52] Karl, *Global Climate Change Impacts in the United States.*

[53] John D. Walsh, *et al.*, Our Changing Climate. Climate Change Impacts in the United States: The Third National Climate Assessment, in Jerry M. Melillo *et al.* (eds.), *US Global Change Research Program* (2014) 19–20, *available at* http://s3.amazonaws.com/nca2014/low/NCA3_Full_Report_02_Our_Changing_Climate_LowRes.pdf?download=1.

[54] Karl, *Global Climate Change Impacts in the United States* at 44.   [55] *Ibid.*

[56] EPA, Climate Impacts on Water Resources *ibid.*, at note 36.

crops and livestock, maintaining healthy fish populations, as well as maintaining hydroelectric and other energy-producing power plants also require stable water supplies. As the earth warms, these activities may be curtailed due to diminishing amounts of water in certain geographic locales, as well as increasing competition for freshwater resources.[57]

---

[57] Karl, *Global Climate Change Impacts in the United States* at 44. [T]he Rio Grande . . . river is in bad shape this year. It has already dried to a dusty ribbon of sand in some parts . . . "If we use up [the limited amount of water we have] early in the season and don't get any rain further on, the whole [agricultural and irrigation system is] going to crash." . . . But whatever happens this spring and summer, the long-term outlook for the river is clouded by climate change." Henry Fountain, In a Warming West, the Rio Grande Is Drying Up, NY Times, May 26, 2018, at 1, *available* at https://www.nytimes.com/interactive/2018/05/24/climate/dry-rio-grande.html.

2

The Proliferation of Dispute Resolution Fora

People tend to behave in ways that they believe other people approve of, and avoid those behaviors they think others disapprove of. This normative social influence is based on the fundamental human need to be liked and accepted by others. Furthermore, people's behavior can also be shaped by informational social influence.[1]

Transnational law includes "all law which regulates actions or events that transcend national frontiers."[2]

I INTRODUCTION

In 1944, during the depths of World War II, George A. Finch and Harold G. Moulton, of the Carnegie Endowment for International Peace, wrote that "current suggestions are unanimous in their insistence upon the strengthening of international law and upon the maintenance of courts to administering it."[3] Similarly, during that era Judge Manley O. Hudson wrote that "[i]f any attempt is made to forge new directions for international law, attention will doubtless be given to some remodelling and adaptation of

---

[1] Henk Aarts *et al.*, Automatic Normative Behavior in Environments: The Moderating Role of Conformity in Activating Situational Norms, 21 *Social Cognition* (2003) 447, 448.

[2] Philip C. Jessup, Transnational Law (Extracts), in *Philip C. Jessup's Transnational Law Revisited–On the Occasion of the 50th Anniversary of its Publication*, (Christian Tietje, *et al.* eds. 2006), 45–55. Halle-Wittenberg: Martin-Luther-Universitat. www.wirtschaftsrecht .uni-halle.de/sites/default/files/altbestand/Heft50.pdf (accessed April 18, 2011).

[3] George Finch and Harold G. Moulton, Forward, to Manley O. Hudson, *International Tribunals* v. (1944). (George A Finch, was the Assistant Director, Division of International Law, Carnegie Endowment for International Peace; Secretary, American society of International Law; and Managing Editor, *American Journal of International Law*. Harold G. Moulton, PhD, was an economist at the University of Chicago, and the first Director of the Brookings Institution.)

international judicial institutions."[4] These three men could not have been more prescient. Today, we are in the midst of a twenty-year-long revolution in international law.[5] That transformation encompasses the proliferation of international courts and tribunals, many of which have discrete *ratione materia* jurisdiction.[6] It also incorporates the development of new fields of international law, including those of environmental and natural resources law, or international environmental law ("IEL").[7]

A *The Proliferation of Dispute Resolution Fora*

Over the past twenty-six years, the legal world has been witness to an expansive proliferation in the number of pacific dispute settlement bodies. The growth of these fora offers scholars the opportunity for comparing their effectiveness. Indeed, recently numerous scholars have turned their attention to the question of international court and tribunal effectiveness.[8] For instance in 2005, Eric Posner and John Yoo asserted that international courts "are likely to be ineffective when they neglect the interests of state parties and, instead, make decisions based on moral ideals, the interests of groups or individuals within a state, or the interests of states that are not parties to the dispute."[9] However, others have questioned that thesis.[10] This author also disagrees with Posner and Yoo's hypothesis.

Indeed, the judgments and awards of international courts and tribunals established post-1992, which address a host *rationae materia*, e.g., international war crimes, law of the sea/maritime and investor–state disputes – each of which has compulsory jurisdiction – demonstrate that Posner and

---

4　Manley O. Hudson, *International Tribunals* vii. (1944). (Manley Ottmer Hudson was a professor of international law at Harvard University from 1923–1954; He was a member of the International Law Commission, and became the editor of the *American Journal of International Law* in 1924. A member of the Permanent Court of Arbitration, beginning in 1933; he was appointed to the position of judge at the Permanent Court of International Justice in 1936 and served in that position until January 31, 1946, when the judges of the Permanent Court of International Justice resigned and the court was dissolved.)

5　Of course, the world in the twenty-first century has also devolved into many zones of conflict, e.g., Sudan v. South Sudan, ISIS/DA'ASH, the Taliban, the conflicts in Iraq and Syria, and the like.

6　These include investment dispute under Chapter 11 of the North American Free Trade Agreement, war crime disputes at the International Criminal Tribunal for Yugoslavia, and at the International Criminal Tribunal for Rwanda ("ICTR"), and the International Criminal Court.

7　The Trump Administration's efforts to undermine international law notwithstanding.

8　Eric A. Posner and John C. Yoo, *Judicial Independence in International Tribunals*, 93 *Calif L R* (2005) 1, 7. (Hereinafter Posner and Yoo.)

9　*Ibid.*

10　See e.g., Yuval Shany, *Assessing the Effectiveness of International Courts* (2014) (Oxford Univ. Press, Oxford).

Yoo's hypothesis is facile at best. Nevertheless, to date there have been no international adjudicative bodies that have been solely invested with the subject matter of transboundary water or environmental disputes. Accordingly, each adjudicative body assessed herein has general jurisdiction. Furthermore, considering the growth in the number of international courts and tribunals, international lawyers and scholars are presented with the perfect opportunity to assess various questions regarding the contributions of international courts and tribunals to the dispute resolution process of transboundary water disputes.

As for post-1992 adjudicative bodies created in North America, only one was established: The North American Free Trade Agreement ("NAFTA" or "Agreement"). NAFTA governs disputes involving Canada, the United States of Mexico and the United States of America. The Agreement's Chapter 11, the investor–state dispute resolution section, requires investors, who feel aggrieved by the actions of one of the state-parties, to bring that dispute before the International Centre for Settlement of Investment Disputes of the World Bank ("ICSID").[11] Moreover, NAFTA's jurisdiction is compulsory.

In addition, one of the issues created by the multiplication of international dispute resolution fora is the fragmentation of international law.[12] "The fragmentation of the international social world has attained legal significance especially as it has been accompanied by the emergence of specialized and (relatively) autonomous rules or rule-complexes, legal institutions and spheres of legal practice."[13] Indeed, the work of each of these "legal institutions" is regulated by a specific set of laws, rules, and procedures which, in many cases, result from *ad hoc* negotiations, and bear little likeness to one another. Nevertheless, many of the international judicial bodies evaluated herein, often, also have common aspects and approaches.

B *The Development of North American Pacific Dispute Settlement Bodies*

The development of pre- and post-1992 dispute settlement bodies in North America has been robust and primarily a creature of treaty negotiations. By

---

[11] ICSID panels have been adjudicating private party disputes for some fifty years, that is, since ICSID was created in 1966, for mediating disputes between countries and investor/foreign nationals. For a thorough explanation of what ICSID does, *see generally*, World Bank Group, ICSID, *International Centre for Settlement of Investment Disputes of the World Bank* (2015), https://icsid.worldbank.org/apps/ICSIDWEB/Pages/default.aspx.

[12] *See* e.g., Report of the Study Group of the International Law Commission, Fragmentation of International Law: Difficulties Arising from the Diversification and Expansion of International Law, Finalized by the Chair, Prof. Martti Koskenniemi, UNGA Doc. A/CN.4/L.682 (April 13, 2006), available at http://legal.un.org/ilc/documentation/english/a_cn4_l682.pdf.

[13] *Ibid.* at 11, ¶ 8.

1993 most were firmly established within the universe of adjudicative bodies. North American international courts and tribunals differ from those established by the United Nations, e.g., the International Tribunal for the Law of the Sea, and the International Criminal Court. As discussed above, only one, the North American Free Trade Agreement (NAFTA), was founded to address disputes in North America, and to resolve specific types of disputes. However, several of the pseudo-adjudicative North American bodies were similarly created post-1993. These include the North American Agreement on Environmental Cooperation's Commission on Environmental Cooperation:[14] a forum that was also created by a 1994 treaty between the three states.

For the most part Canada, Mexico, and the United States have a history of cooperation, particularly with regards to transboundary rivers and lakes. That history dates back to the 1848 US–Mexico Guadalupe–Hidalgo Treaty. Additionally, the cultural affinity between Canada and the United States – both arising from English patrimony – may also have enhanced these two states joint cooperation.[15] Furthermore, the United States and Canada were among the earliest states to enact their own municipal environmental laws.[16] They also have a robust history of resolving environmental disputes, since 1909, when they executed their joint Boundary Waters Treaty.[17]

C The Unique Challenge of Transboundary Water Disputes

The adjudication of transboundary water and natural resources disputes is, in many ways, distinct from other legal claims. A critical difference between these conflicts and other disputes is the answer to the following question: how does one measure the effectiveness of the remedy or the resolution of the dispute, in allocating water and restoring the environment? For example, in a contract dispute a party that has suffered a breach is made whole by being compensated so that the pre-contract *status quo ante* is achieved. However, in water allocation or natural resources disputes, the first question that generally comes before a court or tribunal – that is attempting to resolve a disagreement – is: how can the resource be apportioned? And second, in an environmental dispute, how can the environment be returned to the *status*

---

[14] North American Agreement on Environmental Cooperation, September 14, 1993, 32 ILM 1480, reprinted in the NAFTA Supplemental Agreements (United States Government Printing Office ed., 1993).

[15] By cultural affinity I mean that both Canadians and Americans spoke English, and were of white European stock, and also many of them were former British subjects. In contrast, Mexicans were browner and spoke another language.

[16] For example, one of the United States' oldest laws is the National Environmental Policy Act of 1969, 42 USC §4321 et seq. (1969).

[17] US–Gr. Brit., Jan. 11, 1909, 36 Stat. 2448.

quo ante? The April 2010 BP Deepwater Horizon oil spill is a good example of both questions in search of an answer.[18]

How then is the outcome of such a dispute to be measured? The legal response to this question will require the development of several qualitative as opposed to quantifiable variables and determinants, including: (1) the scientific validity and gravity of the transboundary injury; (2) the existing conservation and protective measures; (3) the degree of compliance with the court's or tribunal's order, whether total or partial; (4) in the event of noncompliance, how – if at all – are sanctions[19] applied to sovereign states? (In a system that is essentially consensual, coercive measures are difficult to apply); (5) whether interim relief is granted,[20] e.g., ensuring that certain evidence is not destroyed ("spoliation of evidence"); and (6) the success of the resolution and/or remedy in resolving the dispute, but also in protecting the environment or the natural resource. By resolving the dispute I mean that the controversy has finality, as opposed to the resolution of individual or separate phases of the dispute.[21]

D *The Normative Impacts of Transboundary Water Dispute Resolution*

Another key measurement of the success of a resolved dispute is the normative impact that its decision or award has on international law. This metric is used to describe the development or growth of legal doctrine. For example, the United States Supreme Court, over the course of its two-century-long adjudication of interstate disputes, has developed legal principles that have been employed in subsequent disputes and in completely different fora, e.g., the principle of equitable allocation, which the Court developed in 1907. That principle is now a fundamental canon in international water law. Similarly, the *Trail Smelter Arbitration* established the principle that an upstream state may not cause any harm to a downwind or downgradient state, which is now part of customary international law.

[18] *See e.g.,* Itzchak E. Kornfeld, Of Dead Pelicans, Turtles, and Marshes: Natural Resources Damages in the Wake of the BP Deepwater Horizon Spill, 38 *B.C. Envtl. Aff. L. Rev.* (2011) 317. (Addressing the valuation of species.)

[19] Sanctions as defined herein denote a tribunal's ability to enforce its award or decision against parties who fail to comply with its judgment.

[20] An example of a procedure where interim measures are provided for is the United Nations Commission on International Trade Law's (UNICTRAL) Model Law Article 17, which provides that, "unless otherwise agreed by the parties, the arbitral tribunal may, at the request of a party, order any party to take such interim measure of protection as the arbitral tribunal may consider necessary in respect of the subject matter of the dispute."

[21] Two instances, in cases that are analyzed *infra* – *California v. Arizona* and *Kansas v. Colorado* – the Court resolved different phases of the dispute at different times. In both cases the parties had to return to the Court multiple times; sometimes to relitigate similar issues, and sometimes other issues. These two cases are discussed in Chapter 8, *infra*.

1 Measuring the Effectiveness of International Courts and Tribunals

Alternatively, with regards to the first criterion, i.e., the scientific validity and gravity of the transboundary injury, the key is fact-finding. During the discovery phase, one must assess the role assigned to the tribunal in this stage of the dispute. Some judges argue that the principal undertaking of a tribunal is "the specific application, in particular law suits, of [legal rules] to the particular facts of those suits. A court's task [they assert] thus divides into two parts: First, it finds the facts of a case... Second, it determines what legal rules cover those facts. The court's decision then results."[22] Fact-finding, according to some jurists, is therefore such a critical function of courts and tribunals that former United States Second Circuit Judge Jerome Frank asserted that "it is the toughest part of the judicial function... [Moreover, i]t is there that most of the very considerable amount of judicial injustice occurs."[23]

Indeed, a tribunal's fact-finding task, if properly carried out, may "effectively dispose"[24] of certain claims or of the entire dispute. Additionally, a tribunal's fact-finding ability has been identified as a measure of the effectiveness of the adjudicative body. For example, one commentator has observed that the International Court of Justice (ICJ) "may not be the best forum to resolve a treaty dispute... [because] the Court has not lived up to its potential and few states consistently look to it to solve their disputes. The problems involve perceived structural deficiencies such as... *inadequate fact finding abilities*... "[25] Finally, international lawyers and "[t]he public ha[ve] a compelling interest in the effective functioning of [international] courts as fact-finding tribunals."[26] In this regard, the theoretical literature on international justice, concerns the transparency of the process and invites an assessment of the quality of the court's reasoning.[27]

From the limited population of courts and tribunals assessed here, it appears that *ad hoc* international tribunals are more effective than are international courts in solving and/or adjudicating transboundary disputes. One reason may be the phenomenon of judicial or adjudicative functions. That is, the

---

[22] Jerome Frank, *Courts on Trial: Myth and Reality in American Justice* (1949) 3 (reissued 1973).

[23] *Ibid.* at 4.

[24] Judge James A. Dennis, Judicial Power and the Administrative State, 62 *La. L R* (2001) 59, 76.

[25] Edwin J. Nazario, Note & Comment, The Potential Role of Arbitration in Nuclear Non-Proliferation Treaty Regime, 10 *Am Rev Int'l Arb* (1999) 139, 145. (Emphasis added.)

[26] Edward J. Imwinkelried, The Alienability of Evidentiary Privileges: Of Property and Evidence, Burden and Benefits, Hearsay and Privilege, 80 *St John's L R* 497 (2006) 511–512.

[27] *See e.g.*, Martin A. Gramatikov *et al.*, Measuring the Costs and Quality of Paths to Justice: Contours of a Methodology, 3 *Hague J Rule L* (2011) 349, 360, http://papers.ssrn.com/sol3/papers.cfm?abstract_id=1269328.

mechanisms of adjudicative decision-making have an impact on the outcome of a particular case, as well as upon the effectiveness of the adjudicative process itself. One example is the issue of the polycentricity of the dispute – which is discussed *infra* – and whether such issues have a significant bearing on the judicial function, i.e., fact-finding and legal conclusions drawn (as described previously).

Furthermore, another issue raised by the adjudication of a dispute is, what is the influence of a judge or arbitrator on the adjudicative process? Is it rooted in whether or not the adjudicator has specialized knowledge regarding the operation of specific substantive regulations of a case. In response to these two questions, I posit that generalist judges and arbitrators who have both experience and knowledge in international law are just as effective as those who have specific knowledge of the issue being adjudicated.

One other factor that is considered herein, is the power of adjudicators in policymaking. The latter is contingent upon the strategic importance of the institutions and substantive areas in which they are active, e.g., in NAFTA arbitrations the tribunals arguably seek only to resolve disputes, and not to establish or formulate policy, whereas courts are known as policy creators. Thus, it may be the institutional structure of a specific court or tribunal and the rules it places upon those hearing the dispute, that is, the "primary institutional sphere" of the judges or arbitrators (as well as of the legal profession in general), that governs policy outcomes.

II SELECTION OF THE CASES AND SELECTION BIAS

In initially surveying the international fora and the environmental cases available in North America, I sought to determine whether there could be a problem with selection bias. Accordingly, in order to mitigate this issue, I examined the number of available cases, from the adjudicative bodies whose effectiveness I would measure – the International Joint Commission (USA/Canada), the International Boundary and Water Commission, the North American Free Trade Agreement's Chapter 11 (investor–state dispute chapter) – and discovered that there was a relative paucity of cases. Thus, any problem with selection bias quickly became moot.

The final series of disputes is from the suite of cases adjudicated by the Supreme Court of the United States. Here, I selected three of the most complex and famous disputes, two of which were also coincidentally the court's most time-consuming. Nevertheless, within that universe of cases, I utilized three criteria in selecting the cases: (1) the dispute had to be a transboundary one; (2) the dispute had to involve water allocation; and (3) the dispute had to have been resolved. International disputes were defined as those either occurring between state-parties or between a state and a non-state party.

A *North America as a Microcosm for International Disputes*

One other issue in the selection process was geographic locality. Following a review of the available suite of transboundary water allocation disputes, North America was chosen because the continent is rich in territorial jurisdictions, including: Canada, the United States, and Mexico; the fifty states within the United States; Canada's ten provinces and three territories, as well as Mexico's thirty-one states, many of whom have executed agreements between themselves for governing water and other natural resources.

Moreover, North America has numerous courts and tribunals that have addressed, and continue to adjudicate with, interstate disputes. Indeed, there is no other continent where there are as many independent dispute resolution fora that adjudicate disputes that do not involve human rights. North America is also an ideal geographic region to study and evaluate transboundary disputes, as it has many of the same climates and terrains as other parts of the world. Consequently, it is a geographic microcosm of the world. For example, in the southwestern United States and northern Mexico deserts, droughts and water allocation problems are key issues. Similarly, on the Canadian–United States border water disputes occur across a spectrum of climatic conditions and over a host of issues.

One example of the latter issue is the Devils Lake Outlet controversy between Canada and the United States, a case which is not assessed here. This controversy developed due to the diversion northward of water that is heavily contaminated with heavy metals and other pollutants, from Devils' Lake, located in the US state of North Dakota, into the Red River, and then into Lake Winnipeg, located in Manitoba, Canada.[28]

Additionally, there are regular ongoing conflicts over water allocation between the three North American nation-states, as well as internally between their constitutive federal units. These include a host of water rights disputes adjudicated by the United States Supreme Court.[29] They also involve water rights and allocation disputes litigated before other fora, which includes a

[28] Roland Paris, *The Devils Lake Dispute between Canada and the United States* (Feb. 2008), University of Ottawa, Centre for International Policy Studies, http://aix1.uottawa.ca/~rparis/CIPS_Devils_Lake_Feb2008.pdf.

[29] *See e.g. Florida v. Georgia*, US Supreme Court Docket No. 22O142 ORG, Original 142, October 4, 2013. (The issue is, whether Florida is entitled to equitable apportionment of the waters of the Apalachicola–Chattahoochee–Flint River Basin and appropriate injunctive relief against Georgia to sustain an adequate flow of fresh water into the Apalachicola Region.)

dispute litigated under NAFTA between parties in Texas and the Mexican government.

Other reasons why North America is a paradigm for issues that are examined here include: (1) the fact that the three North American states have entered into, and ratified, numerous transboundary water conventions; and (2) a history that can be surveyed to assess the impacts that these decisions and awards have had within the realm of dispute resolution and the development of norms.

Finally, the North American continent has a long-standing history of legal initiatives and dispute avoidance agreements vis-à-vis transnational water distribution (as well as long-standing effects of pollution, e.g., The Great Lakes Water Quality Agreement, a commitment between the United States and Canada to restore and protect the waters of the Great Lakes).[30]

These include, in part, (1) the Treaty of Guadalupe-Hidalgo of 1848[31] entered into between the United Mexican States and the United States of America, as noted above; (2) the Water Treaty of February 3, 1944, between Mexico and the USA, which formed the International Boundary and Water Commission (IBWC), a dispute resolution forum; and (3) the Boundary Waters Treaty of 1909, entered into between Canada and the United States, which created the International Joint Commission (IJC). The IJC has either adjudicated cases on its own or referred them to arbitration, as occurred, e.g., in the *Trail Smelter Arbitration*. Indeed, as early as 1972 the IJC also fashioned a plan to remedy and inhibit the pollution in the Great Lakes.

In light of the foregoing, the following section addresses the selected international courts and tribunals, as well as the respective cases that are analyzed herein. It also discusses why certain other fora were not selected.

B *The Selected Suite of International Courts and Tribunals and Their Cases That Are Analyzed Herein*

The fora and their respective cases that are to be assessed here are as follows:

(1) the Supreme Court of the United States' *Kansas v. Colorado, Nebraska v. Wyoming* and *Arizona v. California*;

(2) the Canadian–American International Joint Commission's (IJC's) *Gut Dam Arbitration*;

---

[30] International Joint Commission (IJC), The Great Lakes Water Quality Protocol of 2012 (2017), http://www.ijc.org/en_/great_lakes_water_quality.

[31] Ratifications Exchanged at Queretaro, May 20, 1848. Proclaimed, July 4, 1848.

(3) the Mexican–American International Boundary Waters Commission's (IBWC's) *Chamizal Dispute*; and

(4) the North American Free Trade Agreement's (NAFTA's) *Bayview Irrigation District v. Mexico*.

One other noteworthy characteristic of these fora, is that they have the jurisdiction to bring a dispute to finality. That is, there exists no other body, including appellate courts, which can change, modify, or overturn the selected court's and tribunal's judgment or award. One might argue, of course, that the Supreme Court of the United States is a domestic court rather than an international one, and in one respect that assertion is correct. However, that court, via its constitutionally granted original jurisdiction, is empowered to adjudicate disputes between the fifty states, as a trial court, or court of first instance. In this context, the Court's justices have characterized it as a *quasi-international court*. Consequently, it is treated as an international court for purposes of this work.

Of the six cases assessed here: The first three disputes, *Kansas v. Colorado*, *Nebraska v. Wyoming*, and *Arizona v. California*, were adjudicated by the US Supreme Court. These conflicts involved interstate water allocation between two sovereigns. Two of the three cases considered here, *Kansas v. Colorado* and *Arizona v. California*, were selected over numerous others because each of them was at the time the longest in Supreme Court history, 86 years for the first and 102 for the second, respectively. They are also, in this author's opinion, among the most complex of the Court's water allocation cases.

The next three disputes were *ad hoc* arbitrations. The first of these, the *Gut Dam Arbitration*, was adjudicated by a panel appointed by the International Joint Commission. The next dispute selected is the Mexican–American International Boundary Commission's *Chamizal Dispute*. The final adjudication is the *Bayview Irrigation District v. Mexico Arbitration*, which arose under the North American Free Trade Agreement's ("NAFTA") Chapter 11, the investor dispute section. *Bayview* was adjudicated by an ICSID panel.

Disputes involving either the Mexican federal government or its states, or between the individual states, were not found. Similarly, there are no such similar disputes between Canada's provincial governments, or between a provincial government and the federal government, because of the special features of the Canadian legal regime.[32] Moreover, with the exception of disputes between individual states in the United States, I identified no other international water disputes, in North America. Finally, the *Trail Smelter Arbitration*

---

[32] Interview with Professor Joel Bakan, Faculty of Law, the University of British Columbia.

was not considered because (1) it is not a water dispute; and (2) it has been the subject of so much attention in recent years,[33] and I felt that I could not add anything substantial to the previous scholarship.

Finally, each adjudicative institution's judgments and awards are examined, in order to learn how they resolved their respective cases, and to tease out or extract from these judgments or awards what their impact is upon: (1) norm development; (2) the adjudicative process; (3) the fairness of the procedures; and finally; (4) to determine the contribution the court or tribunal under review made to the development of transboundary water disputes.

C *The International Bodies That Were Excluded*

Two North American institutions were not selected because they do not issue binding decisions and are neither a court nor a tribunal. They are: (1) the North American Agreement on Environmental Cooperation's Commission for Environmental Cooperation, a fact-finding body that makes findings on whether the three NAFTA parties are abiding by their *own* environmental laws.[34] It has no binding adjudicative role; and (2) the World Bank's Inspection Panel. The Panel is an investigative body, whose jurisdiction is limited solely to reviewing whether the Bank ensured compliance with its policies, in carrying out its loan obligations.[35] Moreover, the Inspection Panel assesses whether deviations from these policies caused the harm or injury complained of by project-affected individuals, i.e., it may only evaluate whether the Bank's performance measured up to the standards set forth within the Bank's operational policies and procedures.[36] The Inspection Panel is also precluded from

[33] *See, e.g.,* Rebecca M. Bratspies and Russell A. Miller (eds.), *Transboundary Harm in International Law: Lessons from the Trail Smelter Arbitration* (2006); John D. Wirth, *Smelter Smoke in North America: The Politics of Transborder Pollution* (1999); Elsie G. Turnbull, *Trail Between Two Wars: The Story of a Smelter City* (1980); Alfred P. Rubin, *Pollution by Analogy: The Trail Smelter Arbitration* (1971); Allen L. Springer, From Trail Smelter to Devils Lake: the Need for Effective Federal Involvement in Canadian-American Environmental Disputes, 37 Am. R Canadian Stud (2007) 77.

[34] *See generally,* North American Agreement on Environmental Cooperation, US–Can.–Mex., September 14, 1993, TIAS No. 12,516, 32 ILM 1480, at Arts. 10–15, *available at* http://www.cec.org/Page.asp?PageID=1226&SiteNodeID=567 (last visited September 4, 2012). For the procedure of how the Commission establishes a factual record, *see* Art. 15.

[35] The International Bank for Reconstruction and Development's Inspection Panel, The World Bank Group, The Inspection Panel, About Us (2008), http://web.worldbank.org/WBSITE/EXTERNAL/EXTINSPECTIONPANEL. For a general discussion of how the Panel operates, *see* Dana L. Clark, A Citizen's Guide to the World Bank Inspection Panel (CIEL 2nd ed. 1999), *available at* www.ciel.org/Publications/citizensguide.pdf.

[36] David Hunter, Using the World Bank Inspection Panel to Defend the Interests of Projected-Affected People, 4 Chi J Int'l L (2003) 201.

determining whether Bank officials have acted inappropriately within the framework of its policies and procedures. Nor is the Panel charged with overruling Bank policies or procedures. Finally, it too is not an adjudicative tribunal.

D *The Scope of the Problem that the Book Addresses*

This volume seeks to evaluate the effectiveness of international courts and tribunals in their adjudication of disputes involving the allocation of fresh water. However, direct measurement of the effectiveness of the courts and the *ad hoc* tribunals assessed herein is difficult, due to the fact that direct measurement is simply not possible at this juncture, as no methodology has been developed to do so. Therefore, the determination of the effectiveness of an adjudicative body must be done via proxies.

Prior to discussing and selecting proxies, one must confront a more fundamental issue: "When can adjudication be said to be 'effective'?"[37] The effectiveness of an individual court or *ad hoc* tribunal rapidly becomes enmeshed with bigger jurisprudential questions that include "the nature of law and the sources of compliance."[38] Moreover, in seeking to define a tribunal's effectiveness one is required to ask, "effective for what purpose?"[39]

Indeed, such an inquiry is contingent upon the perception of what the specific role or purpose of a particular court or tribunal is within specific legal systems.[40] For example, such tasks may incorporate "dispute resolution, 'social control'...lawmaking...articulating social and political ideals...and securing social change."[41] However, each of these tasks may conflict with one or more of the others, and may produce different measures of "effectiveness."[42] For instance, many transboundary water disputes, as well as the delimitation and natural resource cases brought before the International Court of Justice, are resolved by recourse to equitable principles.[43] Alternatively, a case-by-case adjudication, attempting to assess their overall normative impact or measuring a court's effectiveness may prove to be vexing or may provide inconclusive results. How then can we characterize effectiveness within the universe of the adjudicatory process?

---

[37] Laurence R. Helfer and Anne-Marie Slaughter, Toward a Theory of Effective Supranational Adjudication, 107 *Yale L J* (1997) 273, 282.

[38] *Ibid.*   [39] *Ibid.*   [40] *Ibid.*   [41] *Ibid.*   [42] *Ibid.*

[43] *See e.g., Delimitation of Maritime Boundary in Gulf of Maine Area (Can/US)*, 1984 ICJ 246, 278. ("The Chamber is, furthermore, convinced for the purposes of such a delimitation operation as is here required, *international law, as will be shown below, does no more than lay down in general that equitable criteria are to be applied...*") (Emphasis added.)

E *Measuring the Effectiveness of International Courts and Tribunals*

Laurence Helfer and Anne-Marie Slaughter propose a very stripped-down or basic definition of effective adjudication. For them, "the effectiveness of a particular court [or tribunal] rests on its power to compel a party to a dispute to defend against a plaintiff's complaint and to comply with the resulting judgment. This power [they stress] is the characteristic that typically distinguishes courts from other dispute resolvers such as go-betweens, mediators, and arbitrators."[44] Indeed, under Helfer and Slaughter's rubric every adjudicative body analyzed here is "effective" since the respondent in each case defended the claim against it.

Alternatively, Yuval Shany argues that effectiveness for the majority of international courts and tribunals is measured by evaluating whether these adjudicative bodies satisfy four goals established for them by their mandate providers. These objectives are: (1) promoting compliance with the prevailing international norms; (2) resolving disputes; (3) supporting applicable international regimes; and (4) legitimizing the legal regime and its norms.[45] Pursuant to this agenda, legitimacy may correspondingly serve to reinforce other goals and assist an international court or tribunal in fulfilling them. These proxies suggest that courts have to pursue or assume tradeoffs between diverse goals.[46]

I adopt Shany's criteria and add one more. These five proxies, as I reformat them, are utilized herein to measure a court's or ad hoc tribunal's effectiveness. They are: (1) Compliance: did this court promote compliance with the governing international norms (primary norm compliance), and was there an impact on state conduct, finally, was there improved compliance by states and other relevant actors? (2) Resolution and Satisfaction: did the court or tribunal resolve this particular dispute and the specific problem it was asked to solve? (3) Normative Impact: did the court resolve this international dispute while providing new remedies (lawmaking) and, did the court contribute to the operation of related institutional and normative regimes? (4) Fairness and Legitimation: was this court perceived as being fair, just and independent forum, and did the judgment or award add to the legitimization of the regime and its norms? and (5) Efficiency: was the court or tribunal efficient in issuing its judgment?

Each of these proxies has both positive and negative aspects. Both figure into the interpretation of the correlation between the proxy and a prospective

---

[44] Helfer and Slaughter, Toward a Theory of Effective Supranational Adjudication at 283.
[45] Yuval Shany, Assessing the Effectiveness of International Courts – A Goal-Based Approach, 106 *AJIL* (2012) 225, 244–247.
[46] Ibid. at 246.

direct measurement. For example, we might consider the fourth proxy: "Was this court perceived as a being fair, just and independent forum?" This would lead to the following question: How can this proxy be measured? Unless we have direct evidence, e.g., a statement from, or acknowledgment of, a party's satisfaction, we are required to read between the lines.

Similarly, the third proxy, "Was there an overall impact that the resolution of the dispute had on international legal norms?" This surrogate may also be difficult to measure because in some cases it can take years for a norm to have an impact on international law. For example, although today we accept equitable allocation as a principle of international law, that was not always the case,[47] it took many years for the doctrine to take hold. Likewise, assessing whether a particular judgment or award, or even a settlement, has any effects on international legal norms may be problematic, since the "[r]ecognition of international law itself as a valid corpus of rules has been a gradual process."[48]

F *The Problem of Evaluating Transboundary Water Issues and Disputes*

Transboundary water conflicts pose unique difficulties both for international law and for international courts and tribunals. Among these dilemmas are: (1) the technical and/or scientific complexity of pollution, water scarcity and allocation; (2) a lack of information regarding how natural systems work; and (3) the impact on future generations. Furthermore, the transnational environmental problematique incorporates the involvement and overtones of various and dissimilar domestic laws, political regimes, cultural features, and diverse priorities.

Due to their impact on human health and the environment today's international conundrums and conflicts over water are more critical than in the past. These issues, including a paucity of fresh water and climate change,[49] are

---

[47] See e.g., Dante A. Caponera, Patterns of Cooperation in International Water Law: Principles and Institutions, 25 *Nat. Res. J.* 563 (1985); Joseph Dellapenna, Building International Water Management Institutions: The Role of Treaties and Other Legal Arrangements, in *Water in the Middle East: Legal, Political, and Commercial Implications* (1995) 55.

[48] See generally, L. Oppenheim, *Oppenheim's International Law*, (9th ed. Robert Jennings and Arthur Watts eds. 1992), Vol. 1, p. 3 *et seq*. In contrast, in domestic systems, the presence and therefore validity of the law is quite well-defined. Moreover, law is fashioned and enforced as a consequence of the State's power, which is upon its citizenry. Indeed, as has been observed, "[i]n systems of municipal law the concept of formal source [of law] refers to the constitutional machinery of law-making and the status of the rule is established by constitutional law." Ian Brownlie, *Principles of Public International Law* (5th ed. 1998), at 1.

[49] See generally, Blanca E. Jiménez Cisneros, *et al.*, Freshwater Resources. In: Ch. 3, of Climate Change 2014: Impacts, Adaptation, and Vulnerability. Part A: Global and Sectoral Aspects. Contribution of Working Group II to the Fifth Assessment Report of the Intergovernmental

currently being addressed within the legal academy, the political branches of many governments, and society in general. They are also being adjudicated in international courts, e.g., the ICJ's *Case Concerning Pulp Mills on the River Uruguay* (Argentina v. Uruguay).[50]

Moreover, today, nation-states, non-state actors, including nongovernmental organizations, and aboriginal populations, among others, face numerous critical issues within the universe of transboundary water and international environmental law. These issues raise numerous questions for international courts and tribunals. For example, can each adjudicative body, within the confines of its dispute resolution system, address questions concerning scientific issues related to frequent droughts,[51] overpopulation[52] – which causes human waste to pollute rivers and groundwater[53] – and a lack of access to potable water? Furthermore, which, if any, international adjudicative forum has been able to provide meaningful resolution to transboundary disputes?

Panel on Climate Change. Field, C.B., *et al.*, (eds.). (Cambridge Univ. Press, Cambridge, U.K. and N.Y., NY, USA, pp. 229–269.

[50] Judgment, ICJ Reports 2010, 14.

[51] *See, e.g.,* Global Development, Africa drought pushes Kenya and Somalia into pre-famine conditions, *The Guardian* (UK), June 28, 2011, *available at* www.guardian.co.uk/environment/ 2011/jun/28/africa-drought-kenya-somalia-famine; Vikas Bajaj, Drought in India Devastates Crops and Farmers, *NY Times*, September 3, 2012, *available at* www.nytimes.com/2012/09/ 04/business/global/drought-in-india-devastates-crops-and-farmers.html?hpw; UN Newscenter, With Drought Intensifying Worldwide, UN Calls for Integrated Climate Policies, August 21, 2012, www.un.org/apps/news/story.asp?NewsID=42716&Cr=climate&Cr1=drought ("Climate change is projected to increase the frequency, intensity, and duration of droughts, with impacts on many sectors, in particular food, water, and energy," said World Meteorological Organization (WMO) Secretary-General Michel Jarraud in a press release. "We need to move away from a piecemeal, crisis-driven approach and develop integrated risk-based national drought policies," he added.)

[52] *See e.g.,* Science Daily, *Worst Environmental Problem? Overpopulation, Experts Say,* April 20, 2009, www.sciencedaily.com/releases/2009/04/090418075752.htm. ("Overpopulation is the world's top environmental issue, followed closely by climate change and the need to develop renewable energy resources to replace fossil fuels . . .")

[53] *See generally,* Pacific Institute, *World Water Quality Facts and Statistics,* March 22, 2010, www.pacinst.org/reports/water_quality/water_quality_facts_and_stats.pdf.

Every day, 2 million tons of sewage and industrial and agricultural waste are discharged into the world's water . . . the equivalent of the weight of the entire human population of 6.8 billion people. The UN estimates that the amount of wastewater produced annually is about 1,500 km³ six times more water than exists in all the rivers of the world . . . Lack of adequate sanitation contaminates water courses worldwide and is one of the most significant forms of water pollution. Worldwide, 2.5 billion people live without improved sanitation.

Finally, although inter-state cooperation is the ideal that state and non-state actors strive for in resolving transboundary environmental problems, conflicts between states do periodically occur. When these situations do arise, pacific dispute settlement methods are preferable to non-pacific ones, e.g., war. Consequently, over the past two decades[54] international lawyers and diplomats alike have developed a better understanding of the transboundary environmental problematique and the potential for disputes over these issues. This awareness has caused numerous states within the international community to establish – generally via bi- and multilateral agreements and other mechanisms – a mélange of pacific dispute settlement fora, which are prepared to adjudicate transboundary water issues.

G *The Outline of the Ensuing Chapters*

The present book is divided into ten chapters. Chapter 3 is chiefly dedicated to the scope of environmental problems, and polycentricity and a discussion of whether international *ad hoc* arbitral tribunals are more effective than international courts. This chapter also elaborates upon a bedrock principle of environmental and natural resource disputes. That is, they are more complex than other disputes. Why is this the case? Because these disputes possess multifaceted or polycentric issues that inexorably change or fluctuate for every slight variation in a court's judgment or resolution of a given matter. This is particularly true of the United States Supreme Court's *Arizona* v. *California* dispute.

In Chapter 4, I address the scope of the process of pacific dispute resolution and the limitations on adjudication. Within that framework one examines the proliferation of international courts and tribunals, as well as the founding of international courts, particularly those created post-1992. In that context, I address the creation of transboundary water and environmental norms and how courts and tribunals function as an important element in fashioning legal regimes and bolstering their regimes.

In Chapter 5, the impacts of sovereignty are addressed, as are theories of sovereignty and sovereignty and transboundary water allocation. Chapter 6 reviews the courts and *ad hoc* tribunals that are assessed in this book. It

---

[54] *See e.g.*, Bruno Simma, Universality of International Law From the Perspective of a Practitioner, 20 *Eur J Int'l L* (2009) 265; Cesare P. R. Romano, The Shift from Consensual to the Compulsory Paradigm in International Adjudication: Elements for a Theory of Consent, 39 *NYU J Int'l L & Pol* (2007) 791; Benvenisti, *Sharing Transboundary Resources*.

examines the histories and procedures of the following adjudicative bodies: (1) the United States Supreme Court; (2) the International Boundary Waters Commission (Mexico/USA); (3) the International Joint Commission (Canada/USA); and (4) the North American Free Trade Agreement's Chapter 11 dispute resolution system. Chapter 7 outlines the factors employed in analyzing the effectiveness of the court and *ad hoc* tribunals, discussed above, and assesses the goal-based approach to court effectiveness. As noted earlier, since direct measurement of court effectiveness is not possible, I utilize five proxies to measure effectiveness.

In Chapter 8, I summarize and analyze the transboundary water disputes adjudicated by the United States Supreme Court, while in Chapter 9 I assess the three ad hoc transboundary water arbitrations included herein: the *Chamizal Arbitration*, the *Gut Dam Arbitration*, and the *Bayview Irrigation District v. Mexico Arbitration*. Finally, in Chapter 10, I offer some conclusory remarks.

3

The Scope of Transboundary Water Issues and Polycentricity

I THE UNIQUE CHALLENGES OF ADJUDICATING TRANSBOUNDARY WATER DISPUTES

Transboundary water issues pose unique challenges for international law and for international courts and tribunals. Among these difficulties are: (1) the technical and/or scientific complexity of pollution, water scarcity and allocation; (2) the lack of information regarding the workings of natural systems; and (3) the impact on future generations.[1] They also include disputes over natural resources such as groundwater, e.g., the Soconusco–Suchiate/Coatán Aquifer (Guatemala/Mexico), the Karoo-Carbonate Aquifer (Central African Republic/Congo/South Sudan), and the Lower Fars Aquifer (Syria/Iraq); as well as the Jordan and the Amazon Rivers, and the Amazonian rainforests, none of which respect manmade artificial boundaries such as borders.

These issues pose three significant complications for international adjudicative bodies, but more so, for international courts, because (1) future generations do not have standing. For

> Our growing [environmental crisis] demands that our laws take seriously the legal rights of children and future example, with regards to inter-generational issues, commentators have observed that generations to inherit a clean, healthy and sustainable environment... In turn, the present generation must take legal responsibility for the ecological legacy we leave behind. It is a rank injustice to our heirs if our behavior does not change.[2]

---

[1] *See generally*, Edith Weiss Brown, *In Fairness to Future Generations* (1989).

[2] University of Iowa News Release, Law Professor Leads Initiative to Protect Environment for Future Generations (Apr. 17, 2009) (*citing* Burns Weston, Professor Emeritus at the University of Iowa, College of Law) *available at* www.news-releases.uiowa.edu/2009/april/041709climate_legacy_initiative.html.

Legal philosophers[3] similarly assert that the moral questions of the law's responsibility to future generations – who have no voice whatsoever in any current decision that impacts the environment – include: What is the extent of our duty to posterity? And, whether humanity and the law possess sufficient motivation to provide for future generations? They also point to other issues related to future generations, which include: what is the scope of our efforts to protect the rights of future generations? And how these policies relate to environmental protection, and water allocation, among others? These questions, legal philosophers, further emphasize, (1) that our obligation to develop the historical consciousness and moral judgment to ensure future generations the necessities of life; (2) the complexity of scientific concepts that are polycentric and which, courts have difficulty in dealing with – as is further discussed below, and as will become clear from the succeeding chapters; and (3) issues of water allocation may take courts years and sometimes decades to resolve – meanwhile, the dispute lingers and the parties may suffer. Furthermore, transnational water and environmental issues incorporate various diverse national priorities, dissimilar domestic laws, e.g., civil versus common law, national political regimes, or, cultural attributes. Such questions, as well as those related to whether there are coherent norms within international law and whether adjudicative bodies can add to these norms, are discussed *infra*. However, we now turn to an examination of the concept of polycentricity.

A *Complexity and Polycentricity in Transboundary Water Disputes*

Transboundary water and environmental or natural resource disputes are atypical in the universe of international law. That is, because of a bedrock principle of transboundary water, environmental, and natural resource disputes: They tend to be more complex than other types of dispute.[4] This is because these disputes may possess multifaceted scientific issues and unpredictable societal ramifications that inexorably change or fluctuate for every slight variation in a court's judgment or the resolution of a particular issue. Within the sphere of transboundary water and environmental law, these complex effects are the result of a host of difficulties which include science's

---

3   *See e.g.*, Matthew D. Adler, Future Generations: A Prioritarian View, 77 *Geo Wash L R* (2009) 1478; David Dyzenhaus, Are Legislatures Good at Morality? Or Better at it Than the Courts? 7 *Int'l J Const L* (2009) 50.

4   [Judge] Patricia M. Wald, Negotiation of Environmental Disputes: A New Role for the Courts, 10 *Colum. J Envtl L* (1985) 1; [Judge] Harold Leventhal, Environmental Decisionmaking and the Role of Courts, 122 *U Penn L R* (1974) 509.

incomplete knowledge of how hydrological ecosystems function; or how courts and tribunals can determine the associations between biological or chemical variables, as well as the allocation formulae that incorporate the universe of water users.

Transboundary water and environmental disputes also involve multifaceted and scientific issues, such as the impacts of climate change. This phenomenon is said to have caused droughts, and lowered groundwater tables.[5] As former United States Supreme Court Associate Justice William O. Douglas observed in 1972, such thorny issues grow out of the destructive pressures of modern technology and modern life. And their impact is not only felt by

> valleys, alpine meadows, rivers, lakes, estuaries, beaches, ridges, groves of trees, swampland...[but] even [by the very] air [we breathe]...The river, for example, is the living symbol of all the life it sustains or nourishes – fish, aquatic insects, water ouzels [a stocky dark grey bird that bobs its body up and down into the bottom of fast-running rivers as it feeds], otter, fisher, deer, elk, bear, and all other animals, including man, who are dependent on it or who enjoy it for its sight, its sound, or its life.[6]

These complexities lead to polycentric problems, and to impediments that have proven difficult for courts to address.

During the 1970s Lon Fuller coined the term "polycentricity," in an effort to describe issues "that have *many complex and unpredictable social and economic repercussions,* which inevitably vary for every subtle difference in a court's decision."[7] In most cases, polycentric and similar issues, whose resolution requires significant expertise, are regarded as "unsuitable for judicial resolution."[8] Hence, some scholars suggest that "[a]djudication is best suited to bilateral disputes over *private claims of rights;* it is least well-suited to

---

5 *See generally,* Institute for Water Resources, Drought in Texas December 2011, NASA Research Reveals Low Aquifer Levels and Conservation Districts Continue Local Work (Last updated 2014), http://twri.tamu.edu/publications/drought/2011/december/nasa-research-reveals-low-aquifer-levels; Amy Hardberger, What Lies Beneath: Determining the Necessity of International Groundwater Policy Along the United States–Mexico Border and a Roadmap to an Agreement, 35 *Tex Tech L R* (2004) 1211.

6 *Sierra Club* v. *Morton,* 405 US 727, 743 (1972) (Douglas, J. Dissenting).

7 Lon L. Fuller, The Forms and Limits of Adjudication, 92 *Harv L R* (1978) 353, 394–404. (Emphasis added.) ("coining the term 'polycentric' and providing examples of polycentric decision-making to demonstrate what types of tasks are inherently unsuited for resolution via adjudication").

8 Jeff A. King, Institutional Approaches to Judicial Restraint, 28 *Oxford J Legal Stud* (2008) 409, 420.

disputes that implicate polycentric issues requiring a weighing of interests and the capacity to seek out and evaluate complex data."[9]

B *Polycentricity and its Discontents*[10]

There are two definitional views of the term "polycentricity." The first of these, described above, is the one coined by Professor Lon Fuller. Another view, expressed by Professor William A. Fletcher, holds that polycentricity

> is the property of a complex problem with a number of subsidiary problem "centers," each of which is related to the others, such that the solution to each depends on the solution to all of the others. A classic metaphor for a polycentric problem is a spider web, in which the tension of the various strands is determined by the relationship among all the parts of the web, so that if one pulls on a single strand, the tension of the entire web is redistributed in a new and complex pattern.[11]

Whichever definition one subscribes to, there is no question that polycentric issues present two principal impediments to adjudication by courts. First, the difficulty in a polycentric situation lies in the inability of a court to hear from all the parties that will be affected by a judgment, i.e., the entire suite of stakeholders, only the parties before it. A second problem with judicial review in polycentric situations lies in the nature of adjudication. Decision-making in polycentric cases involves a back-and-forth interaction among the centers of interest. Thus, any proposal is subject to adjustment to accommodate the responses of others.[12]

Indeed, United States Supreme Court Associate Justice Oliver Wendell Holmes addressed the issue of polycentricity when he asserted that "[t]he trouble with many cases of negligence is... that the elements are so complex that courts are glad to leave the whole matter in a lump for the jury's determination."[13] Consequently, in most disputes involving polycentric issues, resolution requires significant expertise, which, as noted above, is frequently

---

[9] Hoi Kong, The Spending Power, Constitutional Interpretation and Legal Pragmatism, 34 *Queen's L J* (2008) 305, 357 (emphasis added).

[10] Parts of the discussion here on the topic of polycentricity are reproduced from Itzchak E. Kornfeld, Polycentricity and the International Joint Commission 54 *Wayne L R* (2008) 1695.

[11] William A. Fletcher, The Discretionary Constitution: Institutional Remedies and Judicial Legitimacy, 91 *Yale L J* (1982) 635, 645. ("The concept of polycentricity may help to clarify the problems involved in trial court remedial discretion...")

[12] James Leonard, Judicial Deference to Academic Standards under Section 504 of the Rehabilitation Act and Titles II and III of the Americans with Disabilities Act, 75 *Neb L R* (1996) 27, 76–77.

[13] Oliver W. Holmes, *The Common Law* (Mark DeWolf Howe ed., 1963) 103.

regarded as "unsuitable for judicial resolution."[14] Nevertheless, one commentator has observed that "judges are not neutral arbiters of single conflicts, but instead are actively engaged in ongoing intervention with polycentric problems."[15]

Nonetheless, courts have had to address polycentric issues. Why do they do so when the subject matter is so complex? One simple reason is because they must. As one court has observed "to say that a problem is polycentric is not to say that it is insoluble."[16] The complexity of transboundary water and environmental disputes is addressed next.

Indeed, transboundary water and natural resource disputes are polycentric, since they contain numerous variables or inputs. For example, when allocating a river's water there are prospective gaps in information between water demand and water supply in the future. Some of the variables include the various forecasts of water use, population estimates, anticipated per capita growth, industrial and agricultural uses. These forecasts must then be compared to the existing or measured available water resources.

Similarly, consider the BP Deepwater Horizon oil spill which began on April 20, 2010.[17] A suite of different ecosystems, e.g. shorelines, marshes, deep water, were polluted or destroyed, including oil-laden shallow brackish water where shrimp and oysters spawned. The oil also caused the eradication of marshland grasses and the death of birds and dolphins that perished because they were soaked in oil and could not breath.[18]

Years after the spill, scientists – whether biologists, ecologists or geologists – still do not have a full understanding of how the various ecosystems were impacted. Nor do they fully comprehend how these ecosystems operate; or, how one life form, e.g., birds or fish, interact with one another, within their individual niches. Thus, science is unable to describe the entire ecological

[14] Jeff A. King, *ibid.* at Institutional Approaches to Judicial Restraint, 28 *Oxford J L Stud* (2008) 409, 420.

[15] Chrysanthi S. Leon, Should Courts Solve Problems? Connecting Theory and Practice, 43 *Crim L Bull Art* (Winter 2007) 2.

[16] *Plata v. Schwarzenegger*, 2005 WL 2932253 (ND Cal.), *at * 26.

[17] "Beginning on April 20, 2010, and continuing for nearly ninety days thereafter, millions of barrels of oil gushed into the Gulf of Mexico, producing one of the most devastating eco-disasters since the Exxon Valdez's grounding in Prince William Sound, Alaska." Itzchak E. Kornfeld, Of Dead Pelicans, Turtles, and Marshes: Natural Resources Damages in the Wake of the BP Deepwater Horizon Spill, 38 *BC Envtl Aff L R* (2011) 317, 318.

[18] *See generally,* Lori H. Schwacke *et al.*, Health of Common Bottlenose Dolphins (*Tursiops truncatus*) in Barataria Bay, Louisiana, Following the *Deepwater Horizon* Oil Spill, 48 *Environ Sci Technol*, 93 (2013); National Wildlife Federation, Oil Spill Impacts on Mammals (2014), www.nwf.org/What-We-Do/Protect-Habitat/Gulf-Restoration/Oil-Spill/Effects-on-Wildlife/Mammals.aspx.

system with any degree of precision. Consequently, any answer that scientists provide, regarding the Deepwater Horizon's injury, is to a great extent, based on hypotheses or conjecture, because it is based on an incomplete data-set of how these systems work. Accordingly, because science is unable to either decipher or describe what has been lost, lawyers, for any party, cannot present a full evidentiary depiction to a court or tribunal of the harm or damage that occurred or, is occurring.

Similarly, assume a hazardous substance spill, such as that caused by the United States Environmental Protection Agency into the transboundary Animas River (Colorado/New Mexico), from the Gold King mine, near Durango, Colorado in August 2015.[19] That spill of hundreds of gallons a minute of acidic metals laced sludge killed thousands of fish, beavers, and other aquatic creatures. The lost use value of the beavers would be measured by the market value of their pelts (which would be approximately $9.14–$15.46 each).[20] But what of the value of freshwater fish, birds, etc., and the groundwater polluted, as well as any adjacent land,[21] and the cost of litigation?[22] Of course, the issues of negligence and corporate malfeasance are simple and have been resolved.

However, a court that was confronted with assessing the valuation of similar natural resources held that

> [w]hile *it is not irrational* to look to market price as *one* factor in determining the use value of a resource, it is unreasonable to view market price as the *exclusive* factor, or even the predominant one. From the bald eagle to the blue whale and snail darter, natural resources have values that are not fully captured by the market system.[23]

In conclusion, these two phenomena fully describe the classic polycentric problem in environmental and natural resource disputes.

---

[19] Jesse Paul and Bruce Finley, Animas River Fouled by 1 Million Gallons of Contaminated Mine Water, Denver Post, August 6, 2015, www.denverpost.com/2015/08/06/animas-river-fouled-by-1-million-gallons-of-contaminated-mine-water; Mariano Castillo, Pollution Flowing Faster than Facts in EPA Spill, CNN August 10, 2015, www.cnn.com/2015/08/10/us/colorado-epa-mine-river-spill. ("The mustard hue of the Animas River in Colorado – the most visible effect of a mistake by the Environmental Protection Agency that dumped millions of gallons of pollutants into the water – is striking.")

[20] Trapping Today, April 11, 2015, http://trappingtoday.com/category/fur-prices.

[21] Kornfeld, Of Dead Pelicans at 329. (*Citing Ohio v. Dep't of Interior*, 880 F.2d 432, 442 (D.C. Cir. 1989).)

[22] Michael Bastach, New Mexico Will Sue EPA For Polluting A River With Mine Waste, *The Daily Caller*, Jan. 14, 2016, http://dailycaller.com/2016/01/14/new-mexico-will-sue-epa-for-polluting-a-river-with-mine-waste/#ixzz4FMgdGhVD. ("New Mexico will sue the EPA for accidentally unleashing three million gallons of mine wastewater into state waters and contaminating drinking water for thousands of people.")

[23] *Ohio v. Dep't of Interior ibid.* at 462–463 (first emphasis added).

C *The Limitations of Dispute Resolution*

Dispute resolution bodies have very limited means of reflecting the interests of all stakeholders. For instance, NAFTA's ICSID arbitration panels *only hear* the case presented by the individual disputants – the investor and state-party, unless both the claimant and the responding state consent to have third parties intervene or attend.[24] Consequently, an investment dispute that has spillover effects onto a larger community,[25] does not address such issues. Moreover, potential intervenors may have to seek another forum in which to litigate their issues. This may lead to a waste of limited domestic judicial resources, and a host of legal questions.

Similarly, NAFTA's ICSID arbitration panels, pursuant to ICSID's Article 44,[26] generally do not accept *amicus curiae* briefs. There is one exception to this general rule, *amicus curiae* briefs are permitted upon agreement by the panel members when a third party petitions to do so.[27] However, this does not mean that the tribunal will consider the brief. Alternatively, in *Bayview Irrigation District* v. *Mexico*, a dispute that is analyzed herein, the arbitrators *sua sponte* requested the input of the three state-parties.

Alternatively, municipal courts allow third parties to intervene, once they demonstrate a real interest in the proceedings or the outcome, even when the petitioner and respondent objects. For example, *Arizona v. California*, venued in the United States Supreme Court, is a good example of the

---

[24] World Bank, ICSID Arbitration Rule 32(2), states that: "The tribunal shall decide, *with the consent of the parties*, which other persons besides the parties, their agents, counsel and advocates, witnesses and experts during their testimony, and officers of the Tribunal may attend the hearings." (Emphasis supplied.)

[25] *Metalclad v. United Mexican States*, ICSID Additional Facility, Case No. ARB (AF)/97/1 (Award, Aug. 30, 2000) (Professor Sir Elihu Lauterpacht, QC, CBE, President). The dispute arose out of the activities of the Claimant, Metalclad Corporation ... in the Mexican Municipality of Guadalcazar ... located in the Mexican State of San Luis Potosi ... Metalclad alleges that Respondent, the United Mexican States ... through its local governments of SLP and Guadalcazar, interfered with its development and operation of a hazardous waste landfill. Metalclad claims that this interference is a violation of the Chapter 11 investment provisions of the North American Free Trade Agreement ...
Ibid. at 4.

[26] International Centre for Settlement of Investment Disputes, ICSID Convention, Regulations and Rules (Apr. 2006), 24, https://icsid.worldbank.org/ICSID/StaticFiles/basicdoc/CRR_English-final.pdf.

[27] *See e.g., In the Proceedings Between Aguas Argentinas, S.A., Suez, Sociedad General de Aguas de Barcelona, S.A. and Vivendi Universal, S.A. (Claimants) and The Argentine Republic (Respondent)* ICSID Case No. ARB/03/19 (Order in Response to a Petition for Transparency and Participation as Amicus Curiae) (May 19, 2005) ¶ 16 ("The Tribunal unanimously concludes that Article 44 of the ICSID Convention grants it the power to admit amicus curiae submissions from suitable nonparties in appropriate cases.").

concerns raised by a court regarding intervention – there by Indian tribes. That case is discussed *infra*.

The foregoing raises the following question: which dispute resolution bodies – courts of general subject matter jurisdiction or tribunals with specific jurisdiction – are more effective or better able to address the issues in a given case, where polycentric and thorny transboundary water allocation or, environmental problems are present?

D *Arbitral Tribunals' Superior Facility for Integrating Scientific Data?*

At the outset of this study, I posited that non-court adjudicative fora, such as *ad hoc* arbitral tribunals, and the non-confrontational Canadian–US International Joint Commission ("IJC") and Mexican–US International Boundary Waters Commission ("IBWC"), are much more effective in resolving polycentric transboundary natural resource and environmental disputes. That hypothesis is based upon the fact that arbitral tribunals have the capacity to adapt to evolving scientific developments and polycentric issues. This adaptation, I believe, is a result of the parties' ability to select different arbitrators on an *ad hoc* basis, depending on the dispute. For example, two investment disputes currently before the Permanent Court of Arbitration are: *Louis Dreyfus Armateurs SAS* (France) v. *Republic of India*, Case No. 2014–26 and *Mytilineos Holding S.A.* (Greece) v. *The Republic of Serbia*, Case No. 2014–30, have different arbitrators, as selected by the parties.

Thus, adjudicators with diverse skills and knowledge may be selected because they may be better suited to the subject of a dispute. They may also be selected for different disputes; as opposed to judges in courts of general jurisdiction, e.g., the ICJ, who are selected for a fixed term, and are required to hear cases with manifold *ratione materiae*. Furthermore, *ad hoc* tribunals'flexibility, and their resultant ability to assimilate data and scientific concepts, even in treaty interpretation disputes, may provide litigants with an opportunity to more quickly present their case, and to add to international norms.[28] The latter, may lead to greater impact on state behavior. This proposition has however, been questioned.[29] Finally one failing of the arbitral process is that it is not open to the public, as are international courts.

---

[28] *See, e.g.,* Mia Swart, Judicial Lawmaking at the ad hoc Tribunals: The Creative Use of the Sources of International Law and "Adventurous Interpretation," 70 *Heidelberg J Intl L* 459, 460 (2010), http://www.zaoerv.de/70_2010/70_2010_3_a_459_486.pdf. ("The ad hoc International ... Tribunals have been widely praised for playing a pioneering role in the formation and implementation of international ... law.")

[29] Personal communication from Yuval Shany, Nov. 4, 2015.

There is little argument that the ICJ's case law in disputes where water is the *casus decidendi and rationale*, has had an impact on state behavior and normative development.[30] *See e.g. Case Concerning the Gabcikovo Nagymaros Project*[31] and the *Pulp Mills on the River Uruguay Case*.[32] However, I am unable to accept the viewpoint that tribunal awards have a lesser impact on state behavior and normative development than court judgments, in disputes involving transboundary water and harm to the environment. *See e.g., Indus Waters Kishenganga Arbitration;*[33] the *Lac Lanoux Arbitration*,[34] or the *Trail Smelter Arbitration*.[35]

For purposes of this volume, the argument presented above for arbitral tribunals also applies to the US–Canada IJC and US–Mexico IBWC. Additionally, unlike international courts which have their own fixed rules of procedure, *ad hoc* tribunals generally do not. The latter may offer greater flexibility to the disputing Parties since they negotiate the procedural rules in their *compromis*. This topic is more fully addressed in succeeding chapters.

For all their differences, however, one characteristic that international courts and tribunals share is the fact that they do not have "juries as triers of fact, [consequently] no criteria exist for the exclusion of any evidence which may be offered on the ground of irrelevance."[36] Moreover, both adjudicative bodies have conducted site visits to assess issues related to the dispute *sub judice*. For example, the tribunals in the 1902 *Lake Meerauge Boundary Arbitration;*[37] and the 1909 *Grisbardånra Case*[38] visited the sites in the respective disputes. Similarly, the ICJ conducted a site visit during its hearing of the *Case Concerning the Gabcikovo Nagymaros Project*.[39]

---

[30] *See e.g.*, Paulo Canelas de Castro, Trends of Development of International Water Law, 6 Beijing Law Review 285 (2015), *available at* http://file.scirp.org/Html/5-3300377_61741.htm# p294.

[31] (Hungary v Slovakia) [1997] Judgment ICJ Rep. p. 7.

[32] (Argentina v. Uruguay), Judgment, [2010] ICJ Rep.o, p. 14. Other disputes before the ICJ include *Kasikili/Sedudu Island* (Botswana v. Namibia), Judgment, [1999] IC J Rep. p. 1045; *Land and Maritime Boundary between Cameroon and Nigeria* (Cameroon v. Nigeria: Equatorial Guinea intervening), Preliminary Objections, Judgment [1998] IC J Rep., p. 275; and the *Frontier Dispute* (Benin/Niger), Judgment, [2005] ICJ Rep., p. 90.

[33] (Pakistan/India), PCA Case No. 2011–01.

[34] 12 RIAA 281 (1957).   [35] (USA v. Canada), 3 RIAA 1965 (1941).

[36] Manley O. Hudson, *International Tribunals, Past and Future* (1944) 93.

[37] (Austria /Hungary) (1908 RDILC 38), (Formally known as the Decision of the Arbitral Tribunal Established to Settle the Dispute Concerning the Course of the Boundary between Austria and Hungary Near the Lake Called the "Meerauge", Decision of 13 September 1902.)

[38] (Norway/Sweden), Award, PCA 1908.

[39] (Hungary v. Slovakia) [1997] ICJ Rep. 7. In that case the International Court of Justice conducted its first ever visit to the Nagymaros or Pilismarót waterworks, on Danube River, as part of its adjudication.

The foregoing should not be taken to mean that courts are not confronted with applications to resolve extremely complex, multi-issue scientific transboundary disputes. They certainly are.[40] But, both international and municipal courts are limited in their ability to deal with these types of issues. An ideal instance of a court that was confronted with a complex scientific issue is demonstrated by the *Massachusetts* v. *EPA* case.[41] There the Supreme Court of the United States was asked to decide whether carbon dioxide was a pollutant that could be regulated under the Clean Air Act.[42] At the oral argument, Associate Justice Antonin Scalia had the following colloquy with counsel for the State of Massachusetts:

JUSTICE SCALIA: Mr. Milkey, I always thought an air pollutant was something different from a stratospheric pollutant, and your claim here is not that the pollution of what we normally call "air" is endangering health. That isn't, that isn't – your assertion is that after the pollutant leaves the air and goes up into the stratosphere it is contributing to global warming.

MR. MILKEY: Respectfully, *Your Honor, it is not the stratosphere. It's the troposphere.*

JUSTICE SCALIA: *Troposphere, whatever.* I told you before I'm not a scientist.

JUSTICE SCALIA: That's why I don't want to have to deal with global warming, to tell you the truth.[43]

Similarly, in the *Gabcikovo* Danube River Dam Case[44] a number of the judges on the International Court of Justice expressed difficulty with the scientific issues that confronted that Court. The inflexibility or disinterest, as demonstrated by Justice Scalia and the ICJ's Justices inability to deal with scientific issues, cannot provide comfort to litigants. Indeed, Justice Scalia's dismissal of critical facts raises a number of questions, regarding his Court's effectiveness – despite his dissent in this case. For example, how much did the Justice's unwillingness or his inability to understand the science influence his decision – indeed, how could it not? Moreover, how could Justice Scalia rule on the central legal issue if he did not grasp the facts and the technical data that underpinned the case? Did he decide the case "unencumbered" by the facts? How frequently do such situations occur among judges?

---

[40] *See, e.g., In re Agent Orange Prod. Liab. Litig.,* 304 F. Supp. 2d 404 (EDNY 2004) (Weinstein, J.), *aff'd,* 517 F.3d 76 (2d Cir. 2008); *Sterling* v. *Velsicol Chem. Corp.,* 647 F. Supp. 303 (W.D. Tenn. 1986), *aff'd* in part and *rev'd* in part, 855 F.2d 1188 (6th Cir. 1988); *United States* v. *Hooker Chem. & Plastics Corp.,* 607 F. Supp. 1052 (WDNY 1985).

[41] 549 US 497 (2007).   [42] *Ibid.* at 532 (discussing 42 USC § 7521(a) (1) (1977)).

[43] Transcript of Oral Argument at 22–23, *Massachusetts* v. *EPA,* 549 US 497 (Nov. 29, 2006). (Emphasis added.)

[44] *Gabcikovo-Nagymaros Project, ibid.*

Finally, when judges like Justice Scalia mentally shy away, or worse, do not consult experts who can assist them in understanding the scientific concepts that arise in many transboundary water disputes or, those presented in the *Massachusetts* v. *EPA* case, what will they do when truly demanding or persistent issues or cases come before them? One possibility is that they will ignore the science and instead employ hyper-legal reasoning in arriving at their decision.

E *The Problem of Polycentrism*

The difficulty that Justice Scalia may have been grappling with, is what has been referred to as the "polycentric problem." It becomes a significant factor for courts when complex factual issues, balancing complex policies or too many litigants confront the judiciary in a particular dispute. Numerous courts and commentators have observed that "the nature of adjudication is not such as to be amenable to competent evaluation of polycentric problems."[45] Nevertheless, this issue has been dealt with tangentially by a handful of United States courts. Only one reported case explicitly, however, addresses the issue of polycentricism in the environmental context.[46]

Those courts that have been confronted by the issue of polycentrism have observed that, but for the fortuity of the situation, the court may or may not be faced with an unanticipated independent effect. "Partly this is due to the basic complication of assessing any multi-factor decision, [such as the] limits of adjudication in the face of 'polycentric' problems, especially a decision that will not yet have been made and may in any event never be backed by any formal explanation."[47] For example, in a case of assisted suicide by a doctor, the Ninth Circuit Court of Appeals, sitting *en banc*, observed:

> Even more appropriate for a controversial polycentric issue involving the active taking by a state licensed medical doctor of the life of a gravely ill yet somehow competent person are the words of Justice William O. Douglas:
>
> The changes suggested implicate so many policies and raise so many problems of a political, economic, and social nature that it is fit that the Judiciary recuse itself. At times judges must legislate "interstitially" to resolve ambiguities in laws. But [certain] problem[s are] not "interstitial" or as Mr. Justice

---

[45] *Owens* v. *Allis-Chalmers Corp.*, 326 N.W.2d 372, 377 (Mich. 1982).

[46] *United States* v. *Conservation Chem. Co.*, 106 F.R.D. 210, 221 (W. D. Mo. 1985).

[47] *United States* v. *Smith*, 27 F. 3d 649, 655 (D.C. Cir. 1994).

Holmes once put it [they are] "molecular." It is a massive or "molar" action for which the judiciary is ill-equipped.[48]

In another case, *Williams* v. *City of New Orleans*,[49] the court cited Lon Fuller's classic work on polycentrism,[50] stating that:

> [i]t is a classic "polycentric" dispute that sorely taxes the judicial role: [S]uppose in a socialist regime it was decided to have all wages and prices set by courts which would proceed after the usual forms of adjudication. It is, I assume, obvious that here is a task that could not successfully be undertaken by the adjudicative method. The point that comes first to mind is that courts move too slowly to keep up with a rapidly changing economic scene. The more fundamental point is that the forms of adjudication cannot encompass and take into account the complex repercussions that may result from any change in prices or wages... Each of these separate effects may have its own complex repercussions in the economy. In such a case [*sic*] it is simply impossible to afford each affected party a meaningful participation through proofs and arguments.[51]

Finally, in an environmental case, *United States* v. *Conservation Chemical Co.*,[52] the trial court issued an injunction against the defendants ordering them to cleanup a chemical waste disposal site, which was to be overseen by a court ordered Special Master.[53] When the defendants moved to revoke the reference to the Special Master, the court noted that because the issue bore the hallmarks of a polycentric problem the master was best equipped to oversee the cleanup.[54] The Court also observed that "the public interest in a prompt resolution of the issues constitute [d an] exceptional circumstance"[55] and justified the reference to the Special Master. Moreover, it carefully defined the Special Master's authority and the delegation of his powers, and observed that the delegation did not deprive the court of essential attributes of its judicial power.[56]

---

[48] *Compassion in Dying* v. *Wash.*, 85 F.3d 1440, 1450 (9th Cir. 1996). (*Citing Saxbe* v. *Bustos*, 419 US 65, 79–80 (1974).) (Emphasis added.)

[49] 729 F.2d 1554, 1567 (5th Cir. 1984).

[50] Fuller, The Forms and Limits of Adjudication, *ibid.*

[51] *Williams ibid.* 729 F.2d at 1567 n. 2. (*Citing* Fuller n. 3 at 394–395.)

[52] 106 FRD 210 (W. D. Mo. 1985).

[53] *Ibid.* at 219. ("A trial court may appoint a Master to achieve the resolution of a complicated case where promptness is required by the public Interest.")

[54] *Ibid.* at 221.   [55] *Ibid.* at 224.   [56] *Ibid.* at 233.

F Polycentricity and Transboundary Disputes

Transboundary disputes involve panoply of issues that adjudicative bodies are asked to resolve. These may include complex hydrological phenomena that can have an interactive role with one another.[57] In addition, there may be questions regarding the interaction of groundwater and surface water, or the impact that a given resolution of an allocation of a stream will have on an entire basin. Addressing these issues requires numerous scientific experts, each of whom will need to provide expert reports, and may also be required to testify.[58] International courts and tribunals are then required to analyze and assess these reports and witness testimony.

In addition, since transboundary water disputes may often involve at least one governmental party and numerous scientific issues, polycentric problems will routinely arise. That is, because in water allocation disputes, for example, most government choices involve "polycentric problems" in which it is impossible to affect just one variable in a complicated web of interconnecting relationships. Because the government cannot restrict its effects to one area, analysis of these side effects is extremely difficult especially when second, third or nth order consequences are involved.[59]

[57] For an example, a court's allocation of water may not foresee the impact of future uses, users or climatic changes. Similarly, a court's order to reduce one pollutant may impact a water body in ways that the court may not have anticipated.

[58] Of course, arbitral tribunals are not the only adjudicative bodies that can call and hear testimony form expert witnesses. However, appellate courts such as Supreme Courts of the United States only have paper records to rely on. *But see* Article 62 and 63 of the ICJ's Rules of Court. International Court of Justice, Basic Documents, Rules of Court (1978) Adopted on April 14 and Entered into Force on 1 July 1978, *available at* http://www.icj-cij.org/documents/index .php?p1=4&p2=3&p3=0.

Art. 62

1. The Court may at Any Time call upon the Parties to Produce such evidence or to give Explanations Such as the Court may be Necessary to Consider for the elucidation of Any appearance of the matters in issue, or may seek other information Itself for this purpose.

2. The Court may, if Necessary, arrange for the attendance of a witness or expert to give evidence in the proceedings.

Article 63

1. The parts may call Any Witnesses or experts appearing on the list Communicated to the Court Pursuant to Article 57 of These Rules. If At Any Time falling on the hearing a party wishes to call a witness or expert whose name was not included in that list, it shall so inform the Court and the other party, and shall supply the information required by Article 57. The witness or expert may be called either if the other party makes no objection or if the Court is satisfied that his evidence seems likely to prove relevant.

[59] James V. DeLong, *Informal Rulemaking and the Integration of Law and Policy*, 65 Va. L. Rev. 257, 329 & n. 342 (1970). (*Citing* Fuller, *ibid.* at 394–404.)

4

Pacific Dispute Resolution & the Limitations on Adjudication

I INTRODUCTION

The proliferation of international courts[1] and tribunals over the past century, has led to numerous studies aimed at gaining an understanding of the pacific dispute resolution process and its "effectiveness."[2] Both international courts and *ad* hoc tribunals expand the universe of pacific settlement venues for transboundary water disputes. They do so, via international arbitration or court adjudication, which has developed since the execution of the 1899 Hague Convention for the Pacific Settlement of International Disputes[3] and, in response to the failure of dispute resolution by diplomatic means. With

---

[1] As used herein international courts and tribunals are independent judicial bodies, founded by bilateral or multilateral treaties or conventions that are endowed with the jurisdiction to utilize international law in order to resolve specific disputes which are brought before them. Cesare P. R. Romano, The Proliferation of International Judicial Bodies: The Pieces of the Puzzle, 31 *N.Y.U. J. Int'l L & Pol.* 709, 712 (1999). Defining international judicial bodies as those possessing five specific features: (1) permanence, (2) established by an international instrument, (3) use of international law to decide cases, (4) reliance upon preexisting rules of procedure in deciding cases, and (5) result of process is a binding decision. Note however, that the Supreme Court of the United States, as discussed *infra* is also considered to be an international or *quasi*-international court.

[2] *See generally*, Jenny S. Martinez, Towards an International Judicial System, 56 *Stan L R* (2003) 429; Andrew Guzman, International Tribunals: A Rational Choice Analysis; 157 *U Pa L R* (2008) 171; Anna Spain, Using International Dispute Resolution to Address the Compliance Question in International Law, 40 *Geo J Int'l L* (2009) 807.

[3] *See e.g.*, Hague Convention for the Pacific Settlement of International Disputes, 29 July 1899, Art. 1, 32 Stat. 1779, 1 Bevans 230, 26 Martens Nouveau Recueil (ser. 2) 720, 187 Consol. T.S. 410, entered into force Sept. 4, 1900. ("With a view to obviating, as far as possible, recourse to force in the relations between States, the Signatory Powers agree to use their best efforts to insure the pacific settlement of international differences.") *See also*, Hague Convention for the Pacific Settlement of International Disputes, Oct. 18, 1907, Art. 38, 36 Stat. 2199, TS No. 536. ("In questions of a legal nature, and especially in the interpretation or application of international conventions, arbitration is recognized by the contracting Powers as the most

regards to the resolution of international disputes by means of diplomacy, Yuval Shany has observed that these "processes [are] subject to the parties' full control – to resolve sensitive and volatile international disputes."[4]

Moreover, the founding of independent international courts and *ad hoc* tribunals functions as an important element in fashioning legal regimes and bolstering their own individual powers.[5] Accepting autonomous judicial review also eliminates – from the predominant authority of State jurisdiction – the need for the construction and application of international legal norms, since these are now established by judges and arbitrators. Moreover, it also provides two other functions: (1) the development of international law; and (2) a pragmatic means by which States acknowledge their obligation to adhere to existing and newly developed norms.

Indeed, each of these adjudicative bodies has the capacity, within its jurisdiction, to (1) interpret treaties; (2) settle disputes; and where possible (3) to enforce international commitments. These three traits have provided for a growth in the number of international legal norms and rules fostering greater transboundary water cooperation, *e.g.*, the 1997 United Nations Convention on the Law of the Non-Navigational Uses of International Watercourses.

In evaluating the impact of international courts and *ad hoc* tribunals on international legal norms, three major criteria have been employed in measuring their effectiveness. They are: (1) judgment compliance; (2) usage rates; and (3) the impact on state behavior. Each of these criteria is flawed and its usage has been criticized.[6] A number of these criticisms are discussed below. However, at this juncture I seek only to point out that these factors also do not consider international adjudicative bodies' institutional needs, such as their need to be aware of their audience, a subject which is similarly elaborated upon below. But can these criteria be utilized for measuring the "effectiveness" of the courts and tribunals that have had to deal with transboundary

effective, and, at the same time, the most equitable means of settling disputes which diplomacy has failed to settle.")

[4] Yuval Shany, Assessing the Effectiveness of International Courts: A Goal Based Approach, 106 *AJIL* (2012) 225, 259.

[5] *Ibid.*

[6] *See e.g.*, Shany Assessing Effectiveness *ibid.* at 227, providing.

Yet, complicated links exist between the effectiveness of international courts, on the one hand, and each of the three aforementioned factors: judgment compliance, usage rates, and impact on state conduct. For instance, judgment-compliance rates may depend as much on the nature of the remedies issued by a court as on the actual or perceived quality of the court's structures or procedures. [Footnote omitted.] Thus, a low-aiming court, issuing minimalist remedies, may generate a high level of compliance but have little impact on the state of the world.

water? The answer is no: Indeed, these three criteria are not employed here for measuring effectiveness. Rather, other measurements of/for effectiveness are utilized.

A *The Effectiveness of Remedies*

One issue that routinely comes up in any discussion of the effectiveness of international courts or tribunals is, whether a given adjudicative body provided the parties to the litigation with an effective remedy, *i.e.*, where a breach has occurred, did the applicable remedy restore the injured party to the *status quo ante*? In the PCIJ's *Factory at Chorzów* case,[7] the Court held that "[i]t is a principle of international law that the breach of an engagement involves an obligation to make reparation in an adequate form. Reparation therefore is the indispensable complement of a failure to apply a convention . . . "[8]

Occasionally, the remedial norms laid down by the PCIJ in its *Factory at Chorzów* judgment, as well as other remedies, are not appropriate in transboundary water and environmental disputes. Accordingly, one needs to consider the effectiveness of a court's or tribunal's remedies. Indeed, within the realm of transboundary water disputes, it is well known that effective remedies[9] and enforcement – whether by public pressure, shaming, or by a court's or tribunal's "long shadow"[10] – are critical to building the confidence of the Parties involved. These remedies however, are diplomatic in nature, and therefore, cannot be ascribed to courts or tribunals. For example, if the tribunal is viewed as fair, just and equitable, then it will likely enhance the legitimacy[11] and reputation of its umbrella body, *e.g.*, the Permanent Court of Arbitration, and provide future litigants with the confidence to employ the forum.

Another factor that will build confidence in a dispute resolution, is access for aggrieved parties who were heretofore precluded from appearing before

---

7   *Chorzów Factory* (Ger. v. Pol.), 1928 PCIJ (ser. A) No. 17, (Sept. 13), at 47. ("It is a principle of international law that the breach of an engagement involves an obligation to make reparation in an adequate form. Reparation therefore is the indispensable complement of a failure to apply a convention . . . ") *Ibid.* at 21.

8   *Ibid.* at 21.

9   The term *effective remedy* is used herein is defined as follows: *effective* is defined as a legal process that is successful in producing a desired or intended result; and the term *remedy* is defined as "the manner in which a right is enforced or satisfied by a court when some harm, injury or wrongful act is inflicted upon an individual or a state."

10   On the "long shadow" *see e.g*, Michael S. Kang & Joanna M. Shepherd, The Long Shadow of Bush v. Gore, 68 *Stan L R* 1411 (2016) 1141.

11   On legitimacy *see* Thomas Franck, *ibid.*

international adjudicative bodies, where previously only states could litigate disputes. Post-1993 fora, for example, have provided *in personam* jurisdiction. These parties may include individual citizens, community groups and non-governmental organizations.

In fact, over the past few decades, treaty bodies have developed new rights, which often provide transparency, particularly within the realm of transboundary water and international environmental law and management. These include the human right to water[12] and the 1997 United Nations Convention on the Law of the Non-Navigational Uses of International Watercourses, *see e.g.* Art. 9 ¶ 2.[13] Similarly, within the adjudicative realm, the environmental impact assessment, a by-product of government transparency efforts, is demonstrated by the ICJ's recent *Pulp Mills* case.[14]

There, the ICJ's judgment addressed issues related to an environmental assessment; which in turn, provided more information for the relevant non-governmental organizations ("NGOs") and other stakeholders. Indeed, recent judgments, awards and multilateral environmental agreements ("MEAs") all provide information to the wider-public, and "shine a light" on both governmental action, as well as on the judicial and arbitral process – including how judges and arbitrators arrive at their decisions, and their logic and rationale in doing so. As has been noted elsewhere, "[i]n debates over the democratic deficit of international institutions, transparency is usually the legitimacy criteria most easily satisfied."[15]

We now move to the topic of measuring the effectiveness of international adjudicative bodies.

B *Measuring the Effectiveness of International Courts and Tribunals: Compliance and Usage Rates*

The rate of compliance with a judgment or award,[16] as was noted previously, is one of the metrics that is generally utilized in measuring an international

---

[12] *See e.g.*, UNGAA/RES/64/292, The Human Right to Water and Sanitation28 July 2010, http://www.un.org/es/comun/docs/?symbol=A/RES/64/292&lang=E.

[13] "If a watercourse State is requested by another watercourse State *to provide data or information that is not readily available,* it shall employ its best efforts to comply with the request but may condition its compliance upon payment by the requesting State of the reasonable costs of collecting and, where appropriate, processing such data or information."

[14] *Case Concerning Pulp Mills on the River Uruguay* (Argentina vs. Uruguay). Judgment [2010], ICJ Rep., p. 14.

[15] *See e.g.*, Malcolm Langford, Another Rip in the Arbitration Veil? Transparency in the Wake of Forresti and Giovanna 1, *available at* http://ssrn.com/abstract=2238495.

[16] *See e.g.*, Posner & Yoo, *ibid* at 1, 7.

court or tribunal's effectiveness. This section addresses why I reject that measure. As utilized herein compliance "generally refers to a state of conformity or identity between an actor's behavior and specified rule . . . In the international context, compliance is often specified as 'an actor's behavior that conforms to a treaty's explicit rules.'"[17]

One of the difficulties in using compliance as a measure for effectiveness is that it is out of the court or tribunal's control. Thus, when a state refuses to abide by a judgment or award, it is not necessarily due to the adjudicative body's decision. There may be political or other considerations that states make. Indeed, Kal Raustiala has observed that although compliance "is typically an important aspect of the production of institutional effectiveness . . . [it is] not the only aspect."[18] He finds that there "exists a complex relationship between compliance . . . and effectiveness."[19] Moreover, he contends that "high levels of compliance may signal low effectiveness."[20]

Additionally, Yuval Shany argues that "judgment-compliance rates fail to capture either out-of-court settlements conducted under the court's shadow [Footnote omitted] or the court's more general compliance-inducing effect."[21] Alternatively, Posner and Yoo focus on the usage rates of courts and tribunals as a *sine qua non* for effectiveness. For instance, they cite data demonstrating low usage rates for the ICJ.[22] From these data, Posner & Yoo posit that a "low usage rate no doubt stems in part from the reluctance of countries to agree to compulsory jurisdiction."[23]

I find the latter's logic faulty. Compulsory jurisdiction is the hallmark of international courts, particularly, in post-1992 courts and tribunals, *e.g.*, the World Trade Organization, NAFTA's Chapter 11 Investor-State disputes, and the Yugoslavia and Rwanda Criminal Tribunals. These examples appear to belie Posner & Yoo's hypothesis. Furthermore, there are numerous factors that states examine prior to selecting a forum for their dispute. These may include forum shopping, political considerations, and nationalistic ones, *e.g.*, how a negative result will play out at home. Accordingly, compliance is not utilized here as a measure of/for court and tribunal effectiveness.

C *The Role of Judicial Independence in International Adjudication*

Court and tribunal independence is another poor proxy for measuring effectiveness. Several authors[24] take the position that dependent tribunals are more

---

[17] Kal Raustiala, Compliance & Effectiveness in International Regulatory Cooperation, 32 *Case W Res J Int'l L* (2000) 387, 391.
[18] Raustiala *ibid.* at 388.   [19] *Ibid.*   [20] *Ibid.*
[21] Shany Assessing Effectiveness *ibid.* at 227.   [22] Posner & Yoo, *ibid.* at 37.
[23] *Ibid.*   [24] Posner & Yoo *ibid.* at 72.

effective than independent ones. They define "dependent" tribunals as those where arbitrators or judges are "party appointed." In contrast, independent tribunals are characterized as those peopled by fixed-term judges, *e.g.*, the ICJ or the ITLOS, as opposed to tribunals where the adjudicators are *ad hoc* arbitrators.

These authors also assert that dependent adjudicators are more successful than those who populate independent tribunals.[25] That claim is based on the following reasoning: the success of dependent tribunals is grounded in the fact that if these arbitrators/judges fail to please the State-party that engaged them, they won't be employed again. In contrast, Richard Epstein finds that "judicial independence [or dependence] offers no guarantee that judicial decisions will serve the public interest, even if we could all agree as to how it should be defined."[26] Although I agree with Epstein's view, the implications for any differences regarding the assessment between independent and dependent tribunals is immaterial for my analysis. As one will recall the criteria for effectiveness that are utilized herein do not make any distinction between whether a judge or arbitrator is either dependent or independent of a party.

D *The Use of Equity in Transboundary Water Disputes*

The principle of equity is an essential doctrine that is routinely utilized by international adjudicative bodies, particularly in transboundary water disputes. In fact, equity is the hallmark of transboundary water disputes. For example, in adjudicating these conflicts, unless a treaty governs the allocation of the resource, the default mechanism is the equitable doctrine of equitable allocation, e.g., The Bellagio Draft Treaty.[27]

Equity, as employed herein refers to a "sense of considerations of fairness, reasonableness, and policy often necessary for the sensible application of the more settled rule of law."[28] Indeed, equity, by its nature, requires a balancing of interests. However, the question should be, is the use of equity fair and reasonable to both parties? And is the court or tribunal effective when it employs equity in resolving a dispute? Courts have, of course, demonstrated that they can be fair, reasonable and sensible.[29]

---

[25] *Ibid.*

[26] Richard Epstein, The Independence of Judges: The Uses and Limitation of Public Choice Theory, 1990 *BYULR* (1990) 827, 827.

[27] Robert D. Hayden and Albert E. Utton, Transboundary Groundwaters: The Bellagio Draft Treaty, 29 Nat. Res. J. (1989) 668, 676. ("Governments apply the general principles of international law applicable to the water resources which include *inter alia* the right of each basin State to an *equitable utilization*."). (Emphasis added.)

[28] Ian Brownlie, *Principles of Public International Law* (5th ed. 1998) 25.

[29] *Ibid.* at 314.

Recently introduced instruments, including the 1997 United Nations Convention on the Law of Non-Navigational Uses of International Watercourses, also include equity and equitable principles, such as equitable and reasonable utilization.[30] These principles have also been incorporated into case law,[31] and will be addressed below.

[30] 36 ILM 700 (1997); GA Res. 51/229, UN GAOR, 51st Sess., 99th mtg., UN Doc A/RES/51/229 (1997) (Entered into force on 17 August 2014. GA Res. 51/229, annex, Official Records of the General Assembly, Fifty-first Session, Supplement No. 49 (A/51/49)), *available at* http://legal .un.org/ilc/texts/instruments/english/conventions/8_3_1997.pdf, at Art. 5, Equitable and Reasonable Utilization and Participation. *See also*, Convention on the Protection and Use of Transboundary Watercourses and International Lakes, 1936 UNTS 269; 31 ILM 1312 (1992), at Art. 2, "1 (c) To ensure that transboundary waters are used in a reasonable and equitable way...."

[31] Krishna Water Tribunal II, Report and Decision: *In the Matter of Water Disputes Regarding the Inter-State River Krishna and the River Valley Thereof, Between 1. The State of Maharashtra; 2. The State of Karnataka; and 3. The State of Andhra Pradesh* (2010), *available at* http://www.indiawaterportal.org/sites/indiawaterportal.org/files/Krishna%20Water %20Disputes%20Tribunal_II_Report_2010.pdf (at p. 40 "(2) In equitable allocation, future uses requiring diversion of water outside the basin are relevant...").

5

The Impacts of Sovereignty

I THEORIES OF SOVEREIGNTY

In its purest form sovereignty is defined as the supreme, absolute, and untrammeled power by which an independent State is governed.[1] The modern conception of sovereignty began with the Treaty of Westphalia of 1648, which marked both the end of the Thirty Years' War and the development of the contemporary state. It was executed in Munster and Osnabrug in Westphalia in 1643. The Treaty is also regarded as the foundation of the international system of sovereignty.

A *The Classic View*

According to the classical view, the Thirty Years War was a battle between two main opponents. One side was populated by the emperor and the Spanish King, the members of the Habsburg Dynasty, all faithful to Pope Alexander VII, and the Church of Rome. They were seen as the "universalists,"[2] who affirmed their right, and the right of the Pope, to exclusively control Christendom. Their adversaries, Denmark, the Dutch Republic, France, the German Princes and Sweden, were referred to as "particularists."[3] They rejected the Pope's authority as well as the prevailing imperial overlords, preferring instead the sovereignty or independence of states.

---

[1] *Black's Law Dictionary* (1985) 1936. *See also*, Milan Sahovi & William Bishop, The Authority of the State: Its Range with Respect to Persons and Places, in *Manual of Public International Law* 311, 314 (Max Serensen ed., 1968). ("The jurisdiction of the state over its territory is called territorial sovereignty." Indeed, "the jurisdiction of a state over its territory is the basis of its activity." *Ibid.* at 313.)

[2] Andreas Osiander, International Relations, and the Westphalian Myth, 55 *Int'l* Organizations (2001), 251, 252.

[3] *Ibid.*

The Treaty was founded on Christian principles, whose first paragraph included the following:

> In the name of the *most holy and individual Trinity*: Be it known to all, and everyone whom it may concern, or to whom in any manner it may belong, That for many Years past, Discords and Civil Divisions being stir'd up in the Roman Empire, which increas'd to such a degree, that not only all Germany...and the most Serene, and the most Puissant Prince, Lewis the Thirteenth, most *Christian* King of France and Navarre...from whence ensu'd great Effusion of *Christian* Blood...[4]

The Treaty's principle provision is article I, which provides the following in pertinent part:

> That there shall *be a Christian and Universal Peace*, and a perpetual, true, and sincere Amity...That this Peace and Amity be observ'd and cultivated with such a Sincerity and Zeal, that each Party shall endeavour to procure the Benefit, Honour and Advantage of the other; that thus on all sides they may see this Peace and Friendship in the Roman Empire, and the Kingdom of France flourish, by entertaining a good and faithful Neighbourhood.[5]

Some have interpreted Article I as meaning that with peace, and continual friendship, the now sovereign parties will seek to work to aid not only their interests, but also the interests of their neighbors, so that a "family of nations"[6] is formed. Moreover, this line of thought, in its unalloyed form provides the overarching tenet of Westphalian sovereignty: that sovereignty rises and sets with the state.[7] Consequently, no external actor or establishment can undermine national institutions.[8] Under this doctrine, Westphalian sovereignty also imputes "legal equality between states" and prohibits states from interfering in the domestic affairs of other states.[9]

---

[4] Yale Law School, The Avalon Project, Treaty of Westphalia, Peace Treaty between the Holy Roman Emperor and the King of France and their Respective Allies (1648), *available at* http://avalon.law.yale.edu/17th_century/westphal.asp.

> While, originally, the peacemakers entertained visions of a settlement ending all conflict in Christendom, four years of negotiations brought "only" the Peace of Münster between Spain and the Dutch Republic and the Peace of Westphalia for the empire; the war between Spain and France continued until 1659. It is to the empire, not to the European system at large, that the Peace of Westphalia is devoted.

[5] *Ibid.*

[6] Francis G. Castles, *Families of Nations: Patterns of Public Policy in Western Democracies* (1993).

[7] Ankit Panda, China's Westphalian Attachment, *The Diplomat*, May 22, 2014, http://thediplomat.com/2014/05/chinas-westphalian-attachment. ("The world may be moving on from the Westphalian international system, but China isn't playing along.")

[8] *Ibid.*   [9] *Ibid.*

Yet, other scholars assert that the Peace of Westphalia, in fact did not inaugurate "a system" that is rooted in the sovereign state.[10] Rather, it established and perfected something completely different: "a system of mutual relations among autonomous political units that *was precisely not based on* the concept of sovereignty."[11]

Of course, regardless of how one views the Westphalian system, sovereignty did not form in a vacuum. It had its origins in the *Ius Commune*,[12] which was one of the key contributions of Catholic jurisprudence during the medieval era.[13] Since Latin was the language of the Church and that of academia in medieval times, the *Ius Commune* was a universal European legal canon that was taught in every law school across the continent. It was also the foundation of law practice among the European states.[14]

The conception of territorial sovereignty had its roots in the Roman law, "which regarded as *ius commune* applicable to cities and *signori* whether they obeyed the Emperor or not."[15] Indeed, the Italian jurist and law professor Bartolus of Saoferrato[16] opined that the basis of self-government was obtained by custom and the consent of the governed and the governor, *i.e.*, both the people and the Emperor, and was taken as fact, as opposed to law.[17] Bartolus further suggested that the *ius commune* was the basis for the laws that municipalities and states drew from.[18]

As the Renaissance spread to northern and western Europe so did the concept of city-states. However, in this part of Europe they were called Republics, or at minimum political entities which, exhibited several important attributes of the conventional republic,[19] sovereignty among them. This then was the basis for the current view of Westphalian sovereignty.

---

[10] Osiander *ibid.* at 270.   [11] *Ibid.* (emphasis added).

[12] *ius commune* is the Latin term for "common law." It is the body of Roman Cannon law that jurists studied, which became the universal law of Europe, from the early twelfth to the seventeenth century. *See generally*, D. David J. Ibbetson, *Common Law and Ius Commune* (2001).

[13] Kenneth Pennington, Sovereignty and Rights in Medieval and Early Modern Jurisprudence: Law and Norms Without State, in Joanna Sondel *et al.*, *Roman Law as Formative of Modern Legal Systems: Studies in Honour of Wiesław Litewski* (2003) 26.

[14] *Ibid.* at 35.   [15] *Ibid.*

[16] (1313/14–1357). Bartolus developed many novel legal concepts, which became part of the civil law tradition. Augusto P. Miceli, Forum Juridicum: Bartolus of Sassoferrato, 37 *La. L.* (1977) 1027, 1028.

[17] Francesco Maiolo, *Medieval Sovereignty: Marsilius of Padua and Bartolus of Saoferrato* (2007) 234.

[18] *Ibid.* at n. 21.

[19] H. G. Koeningsberger, Republicanism, Monarchism and Liberty, in Robert Oresko *et al.*, *Royal and Republican Sovereignty in Early Europe, Essays in Memory of Ragnhild Hatton* (2006) 43, 58.

B *The Contemporary View*

In the modern era, former Secretary General of the North Atlantic Treaty Organization ("NATO"), Javier Solana, observed on the 350th anniversary of the signing of the Treaty of Westphalia,

> the Westphalian system had its limits. For one, the principle of sovereignty it relied on also produced the basis for rivalry, not a community of states; exclusion, not integration. Further, the idea of a strong, sovereign state was later draped with nationalistic fervour that degenerated into a destructive political force. The stability of this system could only be maintained by constantly shifting alliances, cordial and not-so-cordial ententes, and secret agreements.[20]

The foregoing is of course, contrary to the central themes of the United Nations Charter, which fosters a "community of nations", as set forth in its Articles I and II, which provide in pertinent part:

Article 1

The Purposes of the United Nations are:

1. To maintain international peace and security, and to that end: to take effective collective measures for the prevention and removal of threats to the peace, and for the suppression of acts of aggression or other breaches of the peace, and to bring about by peaceful means, and in conformity with the principles of justice and international law, adjustment or settlement of international disputes or situations which might lead to a breach of the peace;
2. To develop friendly relations among nations based on respect for the principle of equal rights and self-determination of peoples, and to take other appropriate measures to strengthen universal peace;
3. To achieve international cooperation in solving international problems of an economic, social, cultural, or humanitarian character, and in promoting and encouraging respect for human rights and for fundamental freedoms for all without distinction as to race, sex, language, or religion...

Article 2

The Organization and its Members, in pursuit of the Purposes stated in Article 1, shall act in accordance with the following Principles.

1. The Organization is based on the principle of the *sovereign equality of all its Members* ...

That rule of sovereign statehood is also embodied in the Statute of the International Court of Justice ("ICJ"), which only has jurisdiction over

---

[20] Dr. Javier Solana, Secretary General of NATO, Securing Peace in Europe, Speech at the Symposium on the Political Relevance of the 1648 Peace of Westphalia, Mnster, 12 Nov. 1998, http://www.nato.int/docu/speech/1998/s981112a.htm.

member-states.[21] The Statute at Article 34, Competence of the Court, declares in pertinent part

1. Only [sovereign] states may be parties in cases before the Court . . .[22]

The foregoing produces three theories of sovereignty. The first is that a State has the authority to regulate its internal affairs, without interference from other states. Second, there is a sovereign equality between states, *i.e.*, internal state action is limited externally by the lawful equality of other states. Third, public international law and international relations are characterized by an absence of a superior entity or power, and state consent.

Indeed, international lawyers have argued that based on their sovereignty, "State consent is the foundation of international law. The principle that law is binding on a State only by its consent remains an axiom of the political system, an implication of State autonomy."[23] Moreover, the majority of international lawyers maintain that the sources of international law listed in Article 38 of the Court's Statute – treaties, custom, and recognized general principles – are rules constituting law by referring to the concept that "the general consent of [sovereign] states creates rules of general application."[24] How then, does the foregoing figure into the adjudication of transboundary disputes?

II ADJUDICATION OF TRANSBOUNDARY WATER DISPUTES

The majority of transboundary water disputes that have been adjudicated by international courts and tribunals were solely between sovereign states. However, consent has not always been the *sine qua non* for jurisdiction. For example, the Supreme Court of the United States has observed that when it adjudicates water disputes "between States [it] is concerned with disputes so serious that they would be grounds for war if the [fifty] States were truly sovereign."[25] Likewise, in *Kansas v. Colorado*, the Court made clear that "[o] ne cardinal rule, underlying all the relations of the States to each other, is that of equality of right. Each State stands on the same level with all the rest."[26]

---

[21] Dr. Javier Solana, Secretary General of NATO, Securing Peace in Europe, Speech at the Symposium on the Political Relevance of the 1648 Peace of Westphalia, Mnster 12 Nov. 1998, http://www.nato.int/docu/speech/1998/s981112a.htm.

[22] The Statute is *available at* http://www.icj-cij.org/documents/?p1=4&p2=2.

[23] Louis Henkin, *General Course on Public International Law*, in IV Recueil des Cours (1989) 46. *On state consent see generally*, Duncan Hollis, Why State Consent Still Matters – Non-State Actors, Treaties, and the Changing Sources of International Law, 23 *Berkeley J Int'l L* (2005) 137.

[24] Hollis *ibid* at 141.   [25] *South Carolina v. North Carolina*, 558 US 256 (2010).

[26] 206 US 46, 97–98 (1907).

Moreover, in *Kansas* v. *Colorado*,[27] Chief Justice Fuller writing for the Court declared: "[s]itting, as it were, *as an international* as well as a domestic *tribunal* we apply . . . *international law*, as the exigencies of the particular case may demand . . . ."[28] In that case the Court also observed that

> Comity demanded that navigable rivers should be free, and therefore the freedom of the Mississippi, the Rhine, the Scheldt, the Danube, the St. Lawrence, the Amazon, and other rivers has been at different times secured by treaty; but if a state of this union deprives another state of its rights in a navigable stream, and Congress has not regulated the subject, as no treaty can be made between them, how is the matter to be adjusted?[29]

Likewise, in *New Jersey* v. *Delaware*[30] the Court proclaimed: "[i]nternational law today divides the river boundaries between states by the middle of the main channel, when there is one, and not by the geographical center, halfway between the banks."[31] Following are two examples of transboundary water disputes, where sovereignty was involved.

A *The Lake Lanoux Arbitration*

The Lacke Lanoux Arbitration[32] is another example where the sovereignty of the two parties, France and Spain is cited. There the Treaties of Bayonne included the following provision in an Additional Act of May 26, 1866:[33]

> Control and Enjoyment of Waters of Common User between the Two Countries
> Article 8: All standing and flowing waters, whether they are in the private or public domain, are *subject to the sovereignty of the State* in which they are located . . . [34]

Similarly, in their Memorial the French side summed up the principles of international law experts as follows:

> As far as this litigation is concerned, the following topics may be particularly borne in mind: *the sovereignty in its own territory of a State* desirous of carrying out hydro-electric developments; the correlative duty not to injure the

---

[27] 185 US 125 (1902).   [28] *Ibid.* at 146–147.
[29] *Kansas* v. *Colorado*, 185 US at 144.   [30] 291 U.S. 361 (1934).
[31] *Ibid.* 291 US at 379. (*Citing* numerous cases and international law texts.)
[32] Lake Lanoux Arbitration (Spain/France), 12 RIAA 281 (Nov. 16, 1957); 24 ILR 101 (Petrén, President; Bolla, De Luna, Reuter, De Visscher). The panel's report is more fully discussed below.
[33] The Additional Act was executed on the same day as the Treaty of Bayonne.
[34] *Ibid.* at 2.

interests of a neighbouring State; the convenience of informing a neighbouring State of contemplated projects, of discussing them with it, If need be;
the opportunity of seeking an agreement, including, if appropriate, guaran-
tees of execution; but, if the interests of the latter State do not suffer serious
prejudice, no duty to obtain its consent before undertaking the work.[35]

Additionally, in the ICJ's *Case Concerning the Gabĉikovo-Nagymaros
Project*[36] the Court observed that with regards to a construction permit, the
parties, Hungary and Slovakia agreed as follows with regards to sovereignty.

However, the positions of the parties [Hungary and Slovakia] were by [1992]
comprehensively defined, and would scarcely develop any further. Hungary
considered, as it indicated in a Note Verbale of 14 February 1992, that Vari-
ant C was in contravention of the Treaty of 1971 ... and the convention ratified in 1976 regarding the water management of boundary waters ... with
*the principles of sovereignty, territorial integrity, with the inviolability of
State borders, as well as with the general customary norms on international
rivers* ... [37]

III SOVEREIGNTY AS APPLIED TO TRANSBOUNDARY WATER LAW

There are four accepted sovereignty doctrines related to transboundary waters.
They are: (1) the Harmon Doctrine, or the doctrine of absolute territorial
sovereignty; (2) the theory of absolute territorial integrity; and (3) the theory of
limited territorial sovereignty. These are elaborated upon below.

A *The Harmon Doctrine*

The Harmon Doctrine or the doctrine of absolute territorial sovereignty provides that an upstream state may utilize the water from a transboundary
river that flows within its domain, as it sees fit, without any concern about
any resulting harm to its downstream neighbors. Thus, under this principle
the upstream state has no duty to cooperate or to consult with its downstream neighbors, even if it diverts the entirety of the flow from such a shared
watercourse.[38] The doctrine has its roots in an 1895 opinion by the then Attorney General of the United States, Judson Harmon.

---

[35] *Ibid.* at 9.
[36] (Hungary/Slovakia), Judgment, 1. C. J. Reports 1997, p. 7.   [37] *Ibid.* at ¶ 46.
[38] Stephen C. McCaffrey, The Harmon Doctrine One Hundred Years Later: Buried, not Praised,
36 *Nat Res J* (1996) 549.

That opinion was issued following ever-increasing diversions of the Rio Grande River by upstream US farmers. The loss of downstream water resulted in the Mexican government's complaints to the United States Department State about these diversions.[39] The history of this episode is complex and detailed – involving several federal agencies, the United States Congress, and President Grover Cleveland[40] – and is therefore, beyond the scope of this book. Nevertheless, for our purposes, the then Secretary of State, Richard Olney, eventually requested the Attorney General, Judson Harmon, to opine upon the respective rights of the USA and Mexico under international law. In establishing the doctrine bearing his name, Harmon responded as follows:

> The fundamental principle of international law *is the absolute sovereignty of every nation, as against all others, within its own territory*. Of the nature and scope of sovereignty with respect to judicial jurisdiction, which is one of its elements, Chief Justice Marshall said (*The Schooner Exchange* v. *McFadden*, 7 Cranch [US Supreme Court Reports] p. [116, at) 136 [(1812)1):
>
> *The jurisdiction of the nation within its own territory is necessarily exclusive and absolute. It is susceptible of no limitation not imposed by itself.* Any restriction upon it, deriving validly from an external source, *would imply a diminution of its sovereignty* to the extent of the restriction, and an investment of that sovereignty to the same extent in that power which could impose such, restriction.[41]
>
> *All exceptions, therefore, to the full and complete power of a nation within its own territories must be traced up to the consent of the nation itself.* They can flow from no other legitimate source.[42]

Harmon continued his legal analysis with the following assertion:

> [t] he fact that the Rio Grande lacks sufficient water to permit its use by the inhabitants of both countries *does not entitle Mexico to impose restrictions on the USA which would hamper the development of the latter's territory or deprive its inhabitants of an advantage with which nature had endowed it and which is situated entirely within its territory*. To admit such a principle would be completely contrary to the principle that USA exercises full sovereignty over its national territory.[43]

---

[39] *Ibid.* at 553.
[40] *Ibid.* at 553–57. *See also*, Stephen C. McCaffrey, *The Law of International Watercourses: Non-Navigational Uses* (2001) 76–83.
[41] *Ibid.* at 82–83.
[42] 21 Op. Atty Gen. 274, 281–82 (1895). (*Cited at* McCaffrey (2001) at 90 (emphasis supplied).
[43] *Ibid.* at 283 (emphasis supplied).

Finally, Harmon went on to erroneously conclude that whether the Government of the United States ought to "take any action from considerations of comity... should be decided as one of policy only, because, in my opinion, the rules, principles and precedents of international law impose no liability or obligation upon the United States."[44]

The foregoing is the essence of the Harmon Doctrine: a declaration of the absolute entitlement of the United States to divert the waters from the Rio Grande River without any interference from Mexico, the downstream riparian. However, as Stephen McCaffrey details,[45] nearly a month prior to Harmon's delivery of his opinion, Secretary of State Olney consulted with others at the State Department and with Minister Romero to resolve the dispute. Indeed, Mexico and the United States referred the problem with the Rio Grande diversion to their joint Boundary Waters Commission, which was established in 1889, for fact-finding and to report on "[t]he best and most feasible mode... of so regulating the use of said [Rio Grande] river as to secure to each country concerned and to its inhabitants their *legal and equitable rights and interests* in said water."[46] Harmon's opinion was therefore never employed.

The Doctrine has similarly been rejected by most states and has found little support in state practice.[47] Indeed, the United States repudiated the doctrine a few years following Harmon's opinion, in both a Supreme Court case involving the issue[48] and in two treaties. The first of these was executed in 1906, and is called the Convention between the United States of America and the Republic of Mexico Concerning the Equitable Distribution of the Waters of the Rio Grande, for irrigation,[49] which, in its articles 8 and 9, acknowledged the "common interest" and the protection of the parties' existing uses. The second, the Boundary Waters Treaty,[50] was executed in 1909 between Great Britain, on behalf of Canada and the United States. As is more fully discussed *infra* both of these treaties appear to be consonant with the doctrine of limited territorial sovereignty.[51] Although, some scholars have argued

---

[44] *Ibid.*   [45] McCaffrey (2001) at 93.

[46] 21 Op. Atty Gen. at 226.   [47] McCaffrey (2001) at 116–128.

[48] *United States v. Rio Grande Irrigation*, 174 US 690 (1899).

[49] Convention between the United States and Mexico Equitable Distribution of the Waters of the Rio Grande, Signed at Washington, U.S.-Mex., May 21, 1906, 34 Stat. 2953.

[50] Treaty Between the United States and Great Britain Relating to Boundary Waters Between the United States and Canada, U.S.-U.K., Jan. 11, 1909, 36 Stat. 2448 (1909).

[51] McCaffrey (2001) at 137 *et seq.* William Van Alstyne, International Law and Interstate River Disputes, 48 *Calif L R* (1960) 596, 605.

that these treaties allocation of water are more in keeping with equitable utilization.[52]

Moreover, in adjudicating transboundary water disputes international courts and tribunals have rejected the Harmon Doctrine of absolute territorial sovereignty, as they must balance the competing equitable interests of state sovereignty,[53] as well as the various communities of interest in the watercourses being allocated.

B *The Doctrine of Sovereign Equality and Absolute Integrity*

The doctrine of sovereign equality or absolute territorial integrity provides that a lower riparian state is entitled to the continual flow of water from its upper riparian, regardless of priority,[54] *i.e.*, the doctrine "embodies the idea that an upstream state may do nothing that might affect the natural flow (quantity and quality) of the water into the downstream state."[55] It is grounded in the principle that all states along a shared transboundary river are free to utilize the flow within their borders, so long as such consumption does not work to injure the interests of its co-riparians. Accordingly, the incidence of sovereignty over the Transboundary River is not absolute; rather, it is qualified, and the co-riparian states have mutual and equitable entitlements as well as obligations in the utilization of their shared watercourse.

Obviously, this principle finds support by downstream riparians. In contrast, upstream states that develop their river water sources slower than downstream states find themselves in a ruinous situation, since their water sources will be limited as they were initially exploited by the downstream state. Nevertheless, it has found little support within the international law community.

The United States incongruously, however, utilized this theory, as the downwind state in the *Trail Smelter Arbitration*.[56] The Trail Smelter case, of course, was not a transboundary water case; rather, it was a transboundary air pollution dispute. There, a zinc and lead mine located in Trail, southern British Columbia, Canada, spewed lead and zinc polluted smoke downwind

---

[52] Owen McIntyre, *Environmental Protection of International Watercourses Under International Law* (2007) 14.

[53] *See e.g.*, Itzchak E. Kornfeld, Is News of "Sovereignty's Death" Exaggerated? 18 *ILSA J International & Comparative L* (2012) 315; Noah Hall, Bilateral Breakdown: U.S.-Canada Pollution Disputes, 21 *Nat. Res. & Envt* (2006) 18, 68.

[54] Van Alstyne, *ibid.* at 605–16.

[55] Caroline Spiegel, International Water Law: The Contributions of Western United States Water Law to the United Nations Convention on the Law of Non-Navigable Uses of International Watercourses, 15 *Duke J Comparative & Int'l L* (2005) 333, 335.

[56] (United States/Canada), 1941, 2 UNRIAA 1905 (1949).

across the border into the US state of Washington, damaging forests and crops, and engendered vehement complaints from residents. Following these complaints, the smelter's owners accepted responsibility for the injuries. Nevertheless, the dispute became an international one. The Trail Smelter arbitrator's award was the first pronouncement which established international liability for damages caused by an up gradient state to a lower one, where no treaty existed between them. The award gave birth to the notion that states are obligated to prevent such damage.

Recall, that Attorney General Harmon cited the case of *The Schooner Exchange* v. *McFadden*, in the development of the absolute territorial sovereignty doctrine as pertained to Mexico. In the *Trail Smelter Arbitration*, the United States again raised that case, when the US Legal Advisor asserted that an international harm was committed by Canada's Trail smelter. These injuries, he argued, involved "acts which deprive us of free and untrammelled use of our territory in a manner which we as a sovereign state have an inherent and incontestable right to use it."[57] Indeed, in *The Exchange*, Chief Justice Marshall declared that

> The jurisdiction of the nation within its own territory is necessarily exclusive and absolute. It is susceptible of no limitation not imposed by itself. Any restriction upon it deriving validity from an external source would imply a diminution of its sovereignty to the extent of the restriction and an investment of that sovereignty to the same extent in that power which could impose such restriction.
>
> All exceptions, therefore, to the full and complete power of a nation within its own territories must be traced up to the consent of the nation itself. They can flow from no other legitimate source.[58]

Consequently, given Canada's "diminution of [American] sovereignty" and the United States' "lack of consent [in allowing the pollution to cross its border]", the United States Legal Advisor contended that it is irrelevant whether an injury is caused by a neighboring sovereign spewing pollution *into* another sovereign's territory or, *withholding* water from a stream that *leaves* a sovereign jurisdiction and courses into another's territory.[59] This approach, however, is problematic. It alters the accepted *status quo* because it restricts a state's right to utilize its territory as it sees fit. Indeed, under this theory diversions of rivers in transboundary water course states would be prohibited: an untenable circumstance.

---

[57] 11 US (7 Cranch) 116, 136 (1812).   [58] *Ibid.* at 136.
[59] *See* McCaffrey (2001) at 129. (Reasoning that "[i]f and to the extent that the former is prohibited, it would seem to follow that the latter should be as well.") *Ibid.*

Similarly, assume a situation where a downstream or lower riparian state could dictate to upstream states how to utilize their portion of a water course. The Nile River Basin offers such a scenario. Egypt and Sudan, the lower riparians, are acutely sensitive to development by the upper riparians, who include Burundi, Uganda, Ethiopia, Kenya, and Rwanda. Indeed, Egypt, as the most downstream riparian along the Nile, does not contribute a drop of water to the basin, but demands a large share of the water. Until recently, a dispute has fulminated over a treaty for the utilization of the Nile River executed in 1959 by Egypt and the Sudan. That treaty divides the entirety of the Nile's flow between these two states,[60] but not the upper riparian states.[61]

Egypt has counted on the Nile River, as a steady source of water, for some 5,000 years.[62] This reliance has led it to assert that it has "natural and historical rights," or "acquired rights" in the Nile's waters.[63] For instance, when in 1978, Ethiopia commenced a study of the feasibility of utilizing the Blue Nile for irrigating crops, the late Egyptian President Anwar Sadat declared that "[a]ny action that would endanger the waters of the Blue Nile will be faced with a firm reaction . . . even if that action should lead to war."[64] Indeed, as late as 1981 Egypt asserted in a public forum that "Each riparian country has the full right to maintain the *status quo* of rivers flowing on its territory"; "it results from this principle that no country has the right to undertake any positive or negative measure that could have an impact on the river's flow in other countries."[65] This logic appears to be the Harmon Doctrine in reverse.

[60] United Arab Republic and Sudan Agreement for the Full Utilization of the Nile Waters, Signed at Cairo, on 8 November 1959; in force 12 December 1959, Registered by the United Arab Republic on 7 February 1963, 6519 UNTS 63. *See also*, Dan Morrison, Can Uganda and Ethiopia Act as Egypt's "Water Bankers"? *National Geographic Voices*, Aug. 3, 2010, http://voices.nationalgeographic.com/2010/08/03/can_uganda_and_ethiopia_be_water_bankers_for_egypt. ("In May, a group of upstream states in eastern and central Africa signed an agreement that seeks to break Egypt's (and, to a much lesser degree, Sudan's) monopoly on the Nile waters–a legacy of colonial-era treaties imposed by Britain on its possessions and clients in the Nile valley. The 1929 and 1959 treaties gave Egypt a veto over its neighbors' irrigation projects and guaranteed it the vast majority of the Nile's flow.")
[61] On March 23, 2105, the leaders of Egypt, Sudan and Ethiopia executed a Declaration of Principles in an effort to resolve their long-standing dispute over sharing the Nile's waters. Monica Moyo, Egypt, Sudan, and Ethiopia Sign Nile Dam Agreement (March 23, 2015), American Society of International law, International Law Brief (Mar. 27, 2015), https://www.asil.org/blogs/egypt-sudan-and-ethiopia-sign-nile-dam-agreement-march-23-2015. The Declaration is available at http://english.ahram.org.eg/NewsContent/1/64/125941/Egypt/Politics-/Full-text-of-Declaration-of-Principles-signed-by-E.aspx.
[62] Peter Gleick, *et al.*, Water, War & Peace in the Middle East, 36 *Environment* (Apr. 1994) 6, 14. ("The Nile valley has sustained civilization for more than 5 millennia.")
[63] McCaffrey (2001) at 130.   [64] Morrison, *ibid.*   [65] McCaffrey (2001) at 130.

Under the principles of international law, no State has the right to use or permit the use of its territory in such a manner as to cause injury by fumes in or to the territory of another or the properties or persons therein, when the case is of serious consequence and the injury is established by clear and convincing evidence.[66]

Indeed, in the transboundary water context, under the *sic utere ut alienum non laedas* doctrine, the injury could be caused by either downstream riparian or the upstream one.[67] For example, if an upstream riparian causes the course of a river to change, or diminishes the river's flow, by constructing a dam and a large reservoir, this could impact the downstream riparian. Alternatively, query if a downstream riparian, such as Egypt, on the Nile River, was guaranteed a specific volume of water and an upstream riparian sought to utilize water from that portion of the Nile that flows through its territory. Such an action, would curtail the volume that Egypt would receive. Would the latter be allowed to veto such a development?

C *The Principle of Limited Territorial Sovereignty or No Significant Harm Rule*

The previously discussed doctrines, absolute territorial sovereignty and absolute territorial integrity, have been utilized solely as bargaining chips, in a negotiating technique known as the "zero-sum game," which is routinely utilized prior to reaching a settlement agreement that is agreeable to all parties.[68] Accordingly, they have not received unanimous backing. The reason should be evident: neither upstream nor downstream riparians along a transboundary river can easily divide the watercourse as it flows through their artificially constructed national borders. Some of these riparians may be in the middle reaches of the watercourse, *e.g.*, Bolivia or Venezuela, along the Amazon, others may lie at its headwaters, *e.g.*, Switzerland upstream on the Rhine, or they may be a downstream riparian, *e.g.*, Vietnam, the lower riparian on the Mekong River.

---

[66] Antonio Cassese, *International Law* (2nd ed. 2005), 484. *See also, Island of Palmas case* (Netherlands/USA), Hague Court Reports 2d 83 (1932) (Perm. Ct. Arb. 1928), 2 UN Rep. Intl. Arb. Awards 829, *available at* http://legal.un.org/riaa/cases/vol_II/829–871.pdf. ("Territorial sovereignty involves the exclusive right to display the activities of a State. This right has as corollary a duty: the obligation to protect within the territory the rights of other States.")

[67] McCaffrey (2001) at 135.

[68] Owen McIntyre & Alistair Rieu-Clarke, UN Watercourses Convention, Online Users Guide, Article 5, 5.1.1 Theories of Allocation, http://www.unwatercoursesconvention .org/the-convention/part-ii-general-principles/article-5-equitable-and-reasonable-utilisation-and-participation/5-1-1-theories-of-allocation.

The preferred water allocation theory is that of Limited Territorial Sovereignty, because it characterizes a middle ground between the former two poles. It also balances the rights and responsibilities[69] between riparians along a transboundary watercourse. That is, under the doctrine co-riparian sovereigns are required to "equitably and reasonably" use/exploit their joint transboundary river. The principle is grounded in the notion that each co-riparian state should have unrestricted access in its utilization of that portion of the river that courses through its territory, so long as that use does not interfere with the uses of its co-riparians. Moreover, under Limited Territorial Sovereignty, the co-riparians obligate themselves not to injure their neighbor in the utilization of the water body.[70] This doctrine, is the only one that has received wide-scale acceptance within transboundary water law community.[71] Furthermore, it is now part of customary international law.[72]

In its most basic form, this is the kindergarten rule: everyone must share, *i.e.*, the doctrine stands for the proposition that a sovereign has limited use of its territory. Stated differently, no state may use its territory to cause significant injury to other states and must respect the rights of all states along a transboundary watercourse. Under the principle of equality of rights in the previous example involving the Nile River, Egypt would not be able to stake out most of the volume of water from the Nile. Rather, it would be obliged to share the river's water with its nine upper riparians.[73] Moreover, equality of rights motivates the theory behind the doctrine of *sic utere tuo ut alienum non laeda* (one state may not cause damage or harm to its transboundary neighbor), that was discussed above. Finally, the theory of equality of rights gave rise to the United States Supreme Court's doctrine of equitable allocation,[74] and

---

[69] McCaffrey (2001) at 137.

[70] Muhammad Mizanur Rahaman, Principles of International Water Law: Creating Effective Transboundary Water Resources Management, 3 *Int'l J Sustainable Soc* (2009) 207, 210.

[71] Salman M. A. Salman, The Helsinki Rules, the UN Watercourses Convention and the Berlin Rules: Perspectives on International Water Law, 23 *Water Res Develop*, (2007) 625, 628.

[72] Joseph W. Dellapenna, The Customary International Law of Transboundary Waters, 1 *Int'l J. Global Envtl Issues* (2001) 264.

[73] The other nine states include Burundi, the Democratic Republic of the Congo, Eritrea, Ethiopia, Kenya, Rwanda, Sudan, Tanzania, and Uganda.

[74] *Kansas v. Colorado*, 206 US 46, 118 (1907). ("It shall appear that, through a material increase in the depletion of the waters of the Arkansas by Colorado, its corporations or citizens, the substantial interests of Kansas are being injured to the extent of destroying the *equitable apportionment* of benefits between the two states resulting from the flow of the river.") (Emphasis supplied.)

to the recently adopted doctrine of equitable apportionment and utilization ("equitable utilization"), adopted in the 1997 United Nations Non-Navigable Watercourse agreement.[75]

The principle of equitable allocation was expanded to include "equitable division"[76] (or utilization) in the US Supreme Court case of *New Jersey* v. *New York*.[77] There, in a dispute between the two states over the diversion of the Delaware River[78] by the State of New York, in order, to increase the drinking water supply of New York City. New Jersey sued both the State of New York and New York City to enjoin them from diverting water from the Delaware and its non-navigable tributaries.[79] Justice Oliver Wendell Holmes, writing for the Court, noted the following:

> A river is more than an amenity, it is a treasure. It offers a necessity of life that must be rationed among those who have power over it. New York has the physical power to cut off all the water within its jurisdiction. But clearly the exercise of such a power to the destruction of the interest of lower states could not be tolerated. And, on the other hand, equally little could New Jersey be permitted to require New York to give up its power altogether in order that the river might come down to it undiminished. Both states have real and substantial interests in the river that must be reconciled as best they may. The different traditions and practices in different parts of the country

---

75 United Nations Convention on the Law of Non-Navigable Uses of International Watercourses, annexed to UN GA Res. 51/229, 21 May 1997, *available at* http://legal.un.org/ilc/texts/instruments/english/conventions/8_3_1997.pdf.

76 283 US 336, 343 (1931). (Holmes, J.)

> [T]he principle of equitable division which clearly results from the decisions of the last quarter of a century. Where that principle is established, there is not much left to discuss. The removal of water to a different watershed obviously must be allowed at times unless states are to be deprived of the most beneficial use on formal grounds. In fact, it has been alowed (*sic*) repeatedly, and has been practiced by the states concerned...

77 283 US 336 (1931). Equitable Allocation has also been applied to anadromous fish. *See Idaho* v. *Evans*, 462 US 1017, 1024 (1983).

78 The Delaware River is a major river that flows for approximately 350 miles from New York through Pennsylvania, New Jersey and Delaware on its way to the Atlantic Ocean. Its headwaters lie in New York State's Catskill Mountains, and it discharges into Delaware Bay, in both Cape May, New Jersey and Cape Henlopen, Delaware. The River forms the border between southwestern New York and northeastern Pennsylvania, flows through the entire state of New Jersey, forms the Border between New Jersey and Pennsylvania, and finally, between New Jersey and Delaware.

79 283 US at 343. New Jersey alleged that among other injuries "the proposed diversion will transgress its rights in many respects. That it will interfere with the navigability of the Delaware... That it will deprive the state and its citizens who are riparian owners of the undiminished flow of the stream to which they are entitled..."

may lead to varying results, but the effort always is to secure an equitable apportionment without quibbling over formulas.[80]

One other Supreme Court dispute bears upon this subject: *Nebraska v. Wyoming*,[81] lists the factors to be considered by a Court when it equitably apportions a transboundary river's waters. There the Court held that

> Apportionment calls for the exercise of an informed judgment on a consid-
> eration of many factors . . . *[P]hysical and climatic conditions, the consump-*
> *tive use of water in the several sections of the river, the character and rate of*
> *return flows, the extent of established uses, the availability of storage water,*
> *the practical effect of wasteful uses on downstream areas, the damage to*
> *upstream areas as compared to the benefits to downstream areas if a limita-*
> *tion is imposed on the former – these are all relevant factors.* They are merely
> an illustrative, not an exhaustive, catalogue. They indicate the nature of the
> problem of apportionment and the delicate adjustment of interests which
> must be made.[82]

These factors must be weighed for both riparians, since the Court points to damages caused by both downstream and upstream uses. Thus, when states share the waters of a transboundary river, their allocations must be shared in a manner that is appropriate for each sovereign's uses. Under this formula the court or tribunal, is duty-bound to employ an approach that is even-handed, so that neither side is injured. Alternatively, the state that is injured most should be compensated for its injury.[83]

1 The Doctrine of Equitable Allocation as Applied to Polluted Water

The doctrine of equitable allocation or of limited territorial sovereignty gen-
erally applies to fresh and unpolluted waters. However, cases do arise where a tribunal or court must adjudicate cross-border pollution. That, of course, was the case in the *Trail Smelter Arbitration*, an air pollution dispute, which yielded the doctrine of no significant harm. In the water pollution case of

---

[80] 283 US at 343–34. The Court cited the following cases in support of its view that "different traditions and practices in different parts of the country." *See also, Missouri v. Illinois*, 200 US 496, 200 US 520; *Kansas v. Colorado*, 206 US 46, 206 US 98, 206 US 117; *Georgia v. Tennessee Copper Co.*, 206 US 230, 206 US 237; *Wyoming v. Colorado*, 259 US 419, 259 US 465, 259 US 470; *Connecticut v. Massachusetts*, 282 US 660, 282 US 670.

[81] 325 US 589 (1945). (Douglas, J.) Order Modifying and Supplementing Decree of October 8, 1945, 345 US 98 (1953).

[82] *Ibid.* 325 US at 618.

[83] The compensation can be in money damages or a re-allocation of water.

Missouri v. Illinois,[84] the Supreme Court of the United States was asked by Missouri to restrain a discharge of sewage which the City of Chicago released through an artificial channel into the Desplaines River,[85] in the State of Illinois. That river, along with the Kankakee River, merges to produce the Illinois River, a significant tributary of the Mississippi River, above the City of St. Louis.[86] Missouri's complaint alleged that a threatened discharge of some "1,500 tons of poisonous filth daily into the Mississippi,"[87] would imperil the sediments of a portion of the bed of that river which flows within petitioner's borders.[88]

Justice Holmes, writing for the Court, noted that the plaintiff state must prove that its water body was injured/polluted by the offending state. Here, "the defendant's evidence shows a reduction in the chemical and bacterial accompaniments of pollution in a given quantity of water . . . It affirms that the Illinois is better or no worse at its mouth than it was before,"[89] and therefore the Court could not determine if the pollution was caused by discharges of sewage from the City of Chicago or, whether it should be attributed to sources downstream.[90]

2 Application of the Doctrine in Resolving Disputes

One of the first international courts to address the Doctrine of Equitable Allocation was the Permanent Court of International Justice ("PCIJ"), in its judgment in the case of the *Diversion of Water from the Meuse River*.[91] There, the Court was asked to both interpret and to apply a Treaty executed on May 12, 1863, between Belgium and the Netherlands.[92] The purpose of the Treaty was "to settle permanently and definitively the regime governing diversions

---

[84] 200 US 496 (1906). The case was a precursor to both *Kansas v. Colorado* and *New Jersey v. New York*, and demonstrates the development of the equitable allocation doctrine.

[85] The Des Plaines' headwaters rise near Union Grove, Wisconsin, and flows 150 miles (105 miles in Illinois) through the City of Chicago. David M. Solzman, Des Plaines River, Encyclopedia of Chicago (2005), http://www.encyclopedia.chicagohistory.org/pages/375.html

[86] 200 US at 517.   [87] *Ibid.*   [88] *Ibid.*   [89] 200 US at 525.   [90] *Ibid.*

[91] (Neth. v. Belg.), 1937 P.C.I.J. (ser. A/B) No. 70 (June 28), Judgment, reproduced in Cairo A. R. Robb (ed.), International Environmental Law Reports, Volume 1, Early Decisions (1990) 169. The Meuse's headwaters rise in northeastern France, and flows in a northerly direction for approximately 950 km (590 miles) across Belgium and the Netherlands, emptying into the North Sea. Melissa Albert, Meuse River, Europe, Encyclopedia Britannica (Sept. 10, 2010), *available at* https://www.britannica.com/place/Meuse-River.

[92] More formally known as Treaty of May 12, 1863, Between Belgium and the Netherlands, which was annexed to the Treaty of July 20, 1863, executed by the United States and Belgium. Reproduced by the Yale Law School, The Avalon Project, Documents in Law, History and Diplomacy, *available at* http://avalon.law.yale.edu/19th_century/bel005.asp.

of water from the Meuse for the feeding of navigation canals and irrigation channels."[93]

The 1863 Treaty grew out of an 1856 dispute between the Netherlands and Belgium, wherein, Belgium diverted water from the Meuse into the Campine Canal, situated in the Province of Antwerp.[94] Further differences between the two States caused them to enter into a new agreement intended to reconcile their disagreements, arising from their respective building plans. However, the Netherlands repudiated the agreement, and began the construction of a new canal, lock, and a barrage. Similarly, on its end, Belgium commenced the construction of comparable structures. Ultimately, the parties were unable to settle their differences, and therefore the Netherlands unilaterally applied to the Court for relief. Both states accepted the Court's jurisdiction.

Several of the PCIJ's judges argued that equitable allocation of the Meuse River's waters was either contemplated by the Treaty or was required pursuant to equity. For example, Judge Jonkheer Van Easing, in his dissent and separate opinion, found that

> [56] The essential feature of the Treaty was that a considerable portion of the discharge of the international river was assigned [57] to Belgium, even at periods of the year when the Meuse is very low. The Treaty, therefore, derogated from the normal state of affairs, according to which the discharge of an international river belongs to the river. *The quantity of water to be withdrawn for Belgium... is fixed... The Netherlands have also to receive a certain quantity of water, which however, is far less than that allotted to Belgium; on the other hand, it is liable to be increased, within certain limits* and subject to certain conditions.[95]

Judge Manley Hudson concurred in the Court's opinion but appended his separate observations, in which he declared that these two co-riparian sovereigns are to equitably and reasonably utilize the transboundary Meuse River. His view is that equity and equitable principles should govern, and he stresses that the Court should not grant relief to either party if it would upset the fairness that is equity. A portion of Hudson's exact statement follows:

> [77] It would seem to be an important principle of equity that where two parties have assumed an identical or a reciprocal obligation; *one party which is engaged in a continuing nonperformance of that obligation should not be permitted to take advantage of a similar non-performance of that obligation by the other party.* The Principle finds expression in the so-called maxims

---

[93] Judgment at ¶ 1.   [94] *Ibid.* at Facts.   [95] Judgment at ¶¶ 56–57 (emphasis added).

of equity ... Some of these maxims are, "Equality is equity." "He who seeks equity must do equity." It is in line with such maxims that "a court of equity refuses relief to a plaintiff whose conduct in regard to the subject-matter of the litigation has been improper."

* * *

[78] In equity, the Netherlands cannot ask Belgium to discontinue the operation of the Neerhaeren Lock when the Netherlands remain free to continue the operation of the Bosscheveld Lock ... *Neither of these two requests should be granted where the circumstances are such that the judgment would disturb that equality which is equity.*[96]

Another case where the doctrine of equitable allocation or of Limited Territorial Sovereignty was a key feature was the *Lake Lanoux Arbitration*. There, a forty-year dispute (1917–57), between France and Spain, took place, over France's planned diversion for the production of hydroelectric power from Lake Lanoux, which lies solely in France.[97] The lake is the source of the River Carol's headwaters. Following a course of 25 kilometers totally through French territory, the river passes into Spain, thereafter joining the Serge River.[98] Prior to entering Spanish territory, the Carol's waters feed the Puig Cerda Canal, which is situated on private property in the Catalonian[99] town of Puig Cerda.[100] The canal is the source of irrigation water for Spanish farmers.

The Franco-Spanish border was established by the Treaty of Bayonne of 1866. The portion pertinent in the arbitration was denominated "Control and Enjoyment of Waters of Common User between the Two Countries." The panel cited articles 8–19 as applicable to the resolution of the

---

[96] *Ibid.* at ¶¶ 77–78. (Emphasis added.)

[97] The Lake is situated in the southern Pyrenees Mountains. "It is fed by streams which have their source in French territory [footnote omitted] and which run entirely through French territory only." *Lake Lanoux* Arbitration, 12 RIAA 281 (1957), *available at* http://www2.ecolex.org/server2.php/libcat/docs/COU/Full/En/COU-143747E.pdf *See also*, Brunson MacChesney, Judicial Decisions: Lake Lanoux Case, 53 Am J Int'l L (1959) 156; John Laylin and Rinaldo Bianchi, The Role of Adjudication in International River Disputes: The Lake Lanoux Case, 53 Am J Int'l L (1959) 30.

[98] 12 RIAA 281 *ibid.*

[99] For centuries, the Catalonian "people have been pawns in the struggle between Paris and Madrid. In 1659 the once-proud kingdom of Catalonia was partitioned. France took a small but strategically vital strip, Spain took the rest. Ever since, the Catalans in Spain have fought for self-determination and the use of their own language." Pyrenees: Criss-Crossing the Spanish-French Border, *The Telegraph (UK)*, May 9, 1998, *available at* http://www.telegraph.co.uk/travel/destinations/europe/spain/catalonia/721037/Pyrenees-Criss-crossing-the-Spanish-French-border.html.

[100] 12 RIAA 281 *ibid.* All further factual information regarding this arbitration are from the Tribunal's award.

dispute. Only a few of these will be reproduced here. Beginning in 1917 France began contemplating the diversion of Lake Lanoux. France and Spain exchanged views over the project over a series of years. In 1918, Spain concerned that its interests in the River Carol could be harmed, advised France that the latter should maintain the *status quo* until firm plans for the diversion were in hand. In a communication dated January 15, 1920, the Spanish Government reminded the French Ministry of Foreign Affairs of its desire to be consulted about the proposed project and requested that the two parties take steps to appoint an international commission which, in accordance with the provisions of the Bayonne Treaty, would examine the question in the name of the two Governments, and would agree on the works to be undertaken so as to safeguard both the French and the Spanish interests involved.

Some weeks later, the Ministry advised Spain's Ambassador in Paris of the fact that the French Government agreed with the Spanish Government that any issue related to the diversion of the waters of Lake Lanoux would only be resolved with Spain's concurrence. Concomitantly, the Ministry specified that the diversion studies were incomplete, and, thus, the Government of France, could not at that juncture provide Spain with any concrete proposals. The two governments continued their exchanges and established committees of engineers, among other efforts, to have a meeting of the minds regarding the diversion.

Then, on September 21, 1950, the French Utility Electricité de France ("EDF") sought a concession from the French Government to produce electricity, from power generated by the diversion of Lake Lanoux waters into the River Adige, wholly located in France. According to EDF's plan, the diverted water was to be completely returned to the Carol River via a tunnel, which was situated above the outlet to the Puigcerda Canal. Nevertheless, the French Government, while acceding to the notion that waters should be restored, considered itself not obliged to return the entirety of the diverted water; only an amount equivalent to the Spanish users' genuine requirements. The foregoing suggests that France, at that juncture, was subscribing to the Doctrine of Absolute Sovereignty.[101]

---

[101] *See* the Harmon Doctrine as expressed at 21 Op. Atty Gen. 274, 281–82 (1895).

> *The jurisdiction of the nation within its own territory is necessarily exclusive and absolute. It is susceptible of no limitation not imposed by itself.* Any restriction upon it, deriving validly from an external source, *would imply a diminution of its sovereignty* to the extent of the restriction, and an investment of that sovereignty to the same extent in that power which could impose such, restriction.

The parties agreed to establish a mixed commission of engineers. However, side-stepping the commission, on May 26, 1953, the French Government, advised Spanish authorities that France would likely begin to develop Lake Lanoux by diverting its waters towards the Ariège. Nonetheless, a certain restricted amount of water "corresponding to the actual needs of the Spanish [riparians] would be assured at the level of the outlet to the Puigcerda Canal." France also invited the Government of Spain to prepare a monetary amount of compensation which EDF would owe pursuant to the terms of an Additional Act to the Bayonne Treaty.

In response, on June 18, 1953, the Government of Spain requested that France halt its work on Lake Lanoux, until such time that the Mixed Commission of Engineers could meet. In a rejoinder dated, June 27, 1953, the French Government advised that although the Additional Act does not provide for a suspension of water projects that are likely to affect the parties' joint water system; if requested, it would freely provide Spain with assurances that nothing, in connection with Lake Lanoux, had yet been commenced or was about to be undertaken. Moreover, the French agreed to a meeting of the Mixed Commission of Engineers. In the interim, France initiated a review of its stance regarding the capacity of water which was to be returned to the River Carol. It also elected to accept EDF's proposal contained in its application for the concession, of what that company called, "integral restitution."[102]

The following year (1954), the French Prefect of the Department of Pyrénées Orientales provided the technical papers relating to this proposal to the Governor of Gerona, Spain. In the accompanying letter, the Perfect intimated that the entirety of the water diverted towards the Ariège would be restored to the Carol. During the next two years, the parties went back and forth on a series of respective proposals. Moreover, several meetings, aimed at resolving the disagreement, took place over the next few years, including two meetings of the Mixed Commission of Engineers, during 1955. At each of these meetings France provided a variety of proposals. However, Spain rejected them all, because France was determined to pursue the diversion. Indeed, the Government of France, by a Note dated March 21, 1956, advised the Government of Spain of its resolve "to assume freedom of action within the limits of their rights." In taking that extreme position Spain asserted

All exceptions, therefore, to the full and complete power of a nation within its own territories must be traced up to the consent of the nation itself. They can flow from no other legitimate source.(Emphasis supplied)

[102] This term is not defined in the Tribunal's report.

the Doctrine of Absolute Territorial Integrity. The parties then executed a *compromis* for arbitration. In their respective applications and counterstatements, the two states asked the Tribunal for the following relief:

(1) Spain requested a declaration that France be prohibited from diverting the waters of Lake Lanoux, as set forth by the EDF project, since the erstwhile lack of agreement between the two Governments regarding the diversion, would mean that France would be a breach of the relevant provisions of the Treaty of Bayonne of 1866, and its Additional Act.

(2) The French Government requested the Tribunal to declare that it was not in breach of the Treaty of Bayonne and its Additional Act, because it sought to divert and utilize the waters of Lake Lanoux under the terms of the parties' *compromis* of November 19, 1956.

The panel unanimously found that the French Government's proposed diversion would not be in breach of the Bayonne Treaty or its Additional Act. Nor, did the French proposal and actions in support thereof "contravene any rule of international law." Moreover, *the Treaty and the Additional Act, by their agreed terms, encroached upon "the principle of territorial sovereignty, which must yield to such and other limitations of international law."* Indeed, the panel also maintained that the "conflicting interests aroused by the industrial use of international rivers must be reconciled by mutual concessions embodied in comprehensive agreements" – which include the two instruments at issue in this dispute.

> States have a duty to seek to enter into such agreements. The "interests" safeguarded in the Treaties between France and Spain included interests beyond specific legal rights. A *State wishing to do that which will affect an international watercourse cannot decide whether another State's interests will be affected; the other State is the sole judge of that and has the right to information on the proposals.* [Furthermore, any c]onsultations and negotiations between the two States must be genuine, must comply with the rules of good faith and must not be mere formalities. The rules of reason and good faith are applicable to procedural rights and duties relative to the sharing of the use of international rivers; and the subjecting by one State of such rivers to a form of development which causes the withdrawal of some supplies from its basin, are not irreconcilable with the interests of another State.[103]

---

[103] Lake Lanoux Arbitration (Spain/France), 12 RIAA 281 (Nov. 16, 1957); 24 ILR 101. (Petrén, President; Bolla, De Luna, Reuter, De Visscher.) The panel's report is more fully discussed below.

Moreover, the Tribunal declared the following:

"I. The public works envisaged in the French scheme are wholly situate in France; *the most important part if not the whole of the effects of such works will be felt in French territory; they would concern waters which Article 8 of the Additional Act submits to French territorial sovereignty:* "Article 8. All standing and flowing waters, whether they are in the private or public domain, are subject to the sovereignty of the State in which they are located, and therefore to that State's legislation, except for the modifications agreed upon between the two Governments. "Flowing waters change jurisdiction at the moment when they pass from one country to the other, and when the watercourses constitute a boundary, each State exercises its jurisdiction up to the middle of the flow." "This text itself imposes a reservation on the principle of territorial sovereignty ('except for the modifications agreed upon between the two Governments')."[104]

This Article, the panel observed, is located under the heading "Control and enjoyment of waters of common user between the two countries." Consequently, the Tribunal found that Article 8, "itself imposes a reservation on the principle of territorial sovereignty ('except for the modifications agreed upon between the two Governments'); some provisions of the Treaty and of the Additional Act of 1866 contain the most important of these modifications; there may be others."[105]

Spain also argued that these modifications should be strictly construed because they are in derogation of its sovereignty. In rebuffing this argument, the Tribunal declared that it "could not recognize such an absolute rule of construction," since *"territorial sovereignty plays the part of a presumption. It must bend before all international obligations, whatever their origin, but only before such obligations."*[106]

Here, again, a tribunal rejected any doctrine expressing some aspect of absolute sovereignty, and established the rule of equitable allocation. That is, an upstream state *may* undertake actions related to a transboundary river or lake, so long as it does not injure the interests of its downstream neighbor. The Tribunal also held that the parties to a transboundary watercourse must consult in good faith with each other prior to undertaking any alteration in the flow of a fresh water body. Indeed, the panel declared that a *"State wishing to do that which will affect an international watercourse cannot decide whether another State's interests will be affected; the other State is the sole judge of that and has the right to information on the proposals."*[107]

---

[104] *Ibid.*   [105] *Ibid.*   [106] *Ibid.*   [107] *Ibid.* at 115.

D The Theory of Community or Shared Interests

The final concept of the four allocation principles is the doctrine of Community of Interests[108] also termed Shared Interests. This principle has its roots in the Roman law pertaining to water, as expressed in the *Corpus Juris Civilis* or Code of Justinian.[109] In his now-classic work of 1694, Jean Domat, a French Judge, reduced that country's civil law to writing, so far as these were either indistinguishable or founded upon Roman law.[110] He included the following in his civil code: "Rivers, the banks of rivers, and highways are things public, the use of which is common to all persons, And these kinds of things do not appertain to any particular persons, nor do they enter into commerce, but it is the sovereign that regulates them."[111]

If rivers are common property,[112] then they are governed solely by the sovereign[113] for the benefit of all of its citizens, i.e., the public or the greater community. Thus, the notion of a *community of interests* "can be seen as a step beyond the theory of limited territorial sovereignty,"[114] and appears to be the vector in which the law and practice of transboundary water disputes is heading. The theory stems from the view that a community of interests in rivers is shaped by the natural, physical and societal needs of transboundary watercourses, and therefore should be considered a commons, which ought to be shared by these various communities.

[108] *Ibid.* at 27.

[109] Eugene R. Ware, *Roman Water Law: Translated from the Pandects of Justinian* (1905) 16.

[110] Domat (1625–1696) was a renowned French jurist in the reign of Louis XIV. His 1694 book is titled, *Le lois civiles dans leur ordre naturel (The Civil Law in its Natural Order)*.

[111] Ware *ibid.* at 18–19. Roman law is also progenitor to the Public Trust Doctrine. *See* Institutes of the Emperor Justinian, which stated that water, like air, is incapable of private ownership and that the resource belongs to everyone and thus can be owned by no one. *Institutes of Justinian* 2. 1.1 (S. Scott trans. reprinted ed. 1973). "Under the English common law, the King was held to have sovereign power in navigable waters, and his sovereign power was paramount to private proprietary interests." Rodrick E. Walston, The Public Trust Doctrine in the Water Rights Context 29 *Nat R J* (1989) 585, 586.

[112] *See e.g.*, Louisiana Civil Code Art. Art. 482, which provides "Among those [things] which are not susceptible of ownership, there are some which can never become the object of it; as things in common, of which all men have the enjoyment and use." *See also*, Art. 450. "Things, which are common, are those the ownership of which belongs to nobody in particular, and which all men may freely use, conformably with the use for which nature has intended them; such as air, *running water*, the sea and its shores" and Art. 453. "Public things are those, the property of which is vested in a whole nation, and the use of which is allowed to all the members of the nation: of this kind are *navigable rivers*, seaports, roadsteads and harbors, highways and the *beds of rivers*, as long as the same are covered with water." (Emphasis added.)

[113] *See also, Virginia v. Maryland*, 540 US 56, 80 (2003). The State of "Virginia its governmental subdivisions, and its citizens may withdraw water from the Potomac River and construct improvements appurtenant to the Virginia shore of the Potomac River free of regulation by [the State of] Maryland."

[114] Alistair Rieu-Clarke, *et al.*, *UN Watercourses Convention – User's Guide* (2012) 104.

Similarly, Hugo Grotius, incorporating Roman Law, in his treatise, states the following in paragraph 11: "That men possess the right to use things which have become the property of another, for a purpose which involves no detriment to the owner."[115] A second right is that of innocent use. "'Why,' says [the Roman] Cicero, 'when a man can do so without loss to himself, should he not share with another things that are useful to the recipient and can be spared without annoyance to the giver?' . . ."[116] Accordingly Grotius, 1625 Book 2, Chapter 2, "Things Which Belong to Men in Common" provides.

Article XII. *Hence the right to the use of running water*, provides:

> Thus *a river*, viewed as a stream, *is the property of the people through whose territory it flows, or of the ruler under whose sway that people is.* It is permissible for the people or king to run a pier out into it, and to them all things produced in the river belong. *But the same river, viewed as running water, has remained common property, so that any one may drink or draw water from it.*[117]

The foregoing, of course, accords with the current *opinio juris*.[118] A transboundary river may be utilized by the citizens of an upstream state, or its sovereign, so long as they do not impact a downstream state's interests. Nevertheless, that river is also a common or community property, and, therefore, the various riparians along the river, have a community of interests in maintaining and improving the quality and quantity of the watercourse.

In the modern era, the concept of a *community of interests* was revitalized in the 1929 Case involving the River Oder.[119] There, the PCIJ found that

> the fact that a single waterway traverses or separates the territory of more than one State, and the possibility of fulfilling the requirements of justice and the considerations of utility which this fact places in relief, it is at once seen that *a solution of the problem has been sought not in the idea of a right* of passage in favour of upstream States, but *in that of a community of interest of riparian States*. This *community of interest* in a navigable river becomes

[115] Hugo Grotius, The Law of War and Peace, Book 2, Chapter: Of Things Which Belong to Men in Common, XI, (1625), http://lonang.com/library/reference/grotius-law-war-and-peace/gro-202.

[116] *Ibid.*   [117] *Ibid.*

[118] The classic description of *opinion juris* is "Oppenheim's elegant definition . . . as state practice 'under the aegis of the conviction' that the practice is 'according to international law, obligatory or right' or take the standard Restatement of Foreign Relations' definition of *opinio juris* as a 'sense of legal obligation.'" Anthony D'Amato, Customary International Law: A Reformulation, 4 *Int'l L Theory* 1 (1998), *available at* https://law.ubalt.edu/centers/cicl/publications/docs/ILT_04_1_1998.pdf.

[119] *Case Relating to the Territorial Jurisdiction of the International Commission of the River Oder*, PCIJ Series A, Judgment No. 16 (1929) 27, *available at* http://www.icj-cij.org/pcij/serie_A/A_23/74_Commission_internationale_de_l_Oder_Arret.pdf.

the basis of a common legal right, the essential features of which are the perfect equality of all riparian States in the user of the whole course of the river and the exclusion of any preferential privilege of any one riparian State in relation to the others.[120]

This principle was re-enunciated in 1997, in the ICJ's non-navigational Danube River Dam case,[121] where the Court declared that

Modern development of international law has strengthened this principle for non-navigational uses of international watercourses as well, as evidenced by the adoption of the Convention of 21 May 1997 on the Law of the Non-Navigational Uses of International Watercourses by the United Nations General Assembly.

The Court considers that Czechoslovakia, *by unilaterally assuming control of a shared resource, and thereby depriving Hungary of its right to an equitable and reasonable share of the natural resources of the Danube* – with the continuing effects of the diversion of these waters on the ecology of the riparian area ... failed to respect the proportionality which is required by international law.[122]

Indeed, in stressing Czechoslovakia's unilateral actions in diverting the water of the Danube River, the Court "pointed out ... [that] the fact that Hungary had agreed in the context of the original Project to the diversion of the Danube [but later backed out of the agreement] ... cannot be understood as having authorized Czechoslovakia to proceed with a unilateral diversion of this magnitude without Hungary's consent."[123]

Here, the ICJ employed logic similar to that utilized by the Tribunal in the *Lake Lanoux Case*. As was noted above, France did not assume unilateral control of either Lake Lanoux or the River Carol. That was not the case with Czechoslovakia. Moreover, the fact that in both cases one party rejected the entreaties of its co-riparian – Spain rejecting France and Hungary rejecting Slovakia – to divert water may be coincidental. However, both adjudicative bodies did not and would countenance self-help or unilateral acts. Consent is the hallmark of international law.[124]

---

[120] *Ibid.* at 27.
[121] *Case Concerning the Gabčíkovo-Naymaros Project* (Hungary/Slovakia), Judgment, ICJ Rep. 1997, p. 7.
[122] *Ibid.* at ¶ 85 (p. 56) (emphasis added).   [123] *Ibid.*
[124] Matthew Lister, The Legitimating Role of Consent in International Law, 11 *Chi J Int'l L* 663, 664 (2011). ("To a large degree, international law ... depends on the consent of those (states) that are governed by it.")

6

The Courts and Tribunals Assessed Here

This chapter summarizes the attributes of the international courts and tribunals that will be evaluated herein. They are: (1) the United States Supreme Court; (2) the International Boundary Waters Commission (Mexico & the USA); (3) the International Joint Commissions (Canada & the USA); and (4) the North American Free Trade Agreement.

I THE SUPREME COURT OF THE UNITED STATES: A BRIEF HISTORY

A *Introduction*

The Supreme Court of the United States ("SCOTUS" or "Court")[1] was provided with the jurisdiction to hear disputes between the states of the Union, by the Constitution's Article III and the Judiciary Act of 1789.[2] In that role, its jurisdiction and procedures differ from those of private litigants and its appellate jurisdiction. These distinctions grow out of the history of the Court's creation, following the establishment of the original thirteen sovereign states. The SCOTUS' original jurisdiction[3] provides, for our purposes, "the Supreme Court shall have *original and exclusive jurisdiction of all*

---

[1] On the Supreme Court *see generally*, (Justice) Stephen Breyer, *Making Our Democracy Work: A Judge's View* (2011); (Justice) William Rehnquist, *The Supreme Court* (1987).

[2] 1 Stat. 73, Sept. 24, 1789, Ch. XX, § 13, *available at* http://www.constitution.orguslaw/judiciary_1789.htm. ("*And be it further enacted*, That the Supreme Court shall have exclusive jurisdiction of all controversies of a civil nature, where a state is a party...")

[3] The original jurisdiction of the US Supreme Court is governed by Article III, Section 2 of the Constitution, provides the following in pertinent part: "(a) The Supreme Court shall have *original and exclusive jurisdiction of all controversies between two or more States...*" (Emphasis added.) Enacted by 62 Stat. 927, ch. 646 (June 25, 1948). *See generally*, 28 Ch. 81 – Supreme Court (Jan. 2009), *available at* http://uscode.house.gov/download/pls/28C81.txt.

controversies between two or more States..."[4] In exercising this jurisdiction the Court hears interstate disputes for the first time, *i.e.*, it sits as a trial court, as opposed to its typical appellate jurisdiction. Thus, in interstate cases the SCOTUS effectively sits as an international or *quasi*-international court, since the states were/are considered *quasi*-sovereigns.

Accordingly, pursuant to the United States' Constitution's Article III,[5] only the Supreme Court has the plenary jurisdiction to adjudicate disputes between the several states. This jurisdiction was a substitute in the absence of diplomatic settlement of controversies between the sovereign states. These controversies must be disputes "by a state for an injury to it in its capacity as a *quasi*-sovereign. In that capacity, the state has an interest independent of and behind the titles of its citizens, in all the earth and air of its domain."[6]

The Constitution's framers did not, of course, divine the Court's original jurisdiction in a vacuum. Indeed, they realized that "[i]nterstate competition, conflict, and cooperation are products of a confederate or a federal system of governance as semiautonomous states may employ their constitutional powers to promote their respective self-interest at the expense of sister states."[7] Accordingly, the framers included provisions intended to promote cooperative and amicable interstate dealings between the states and also endorsed the efforts of two or more states to enter into interstate compacts with Congressional assent.[8] Compacts are treaties between states that must be approved by Congress.[9]

B *The First Court*

The SCOTUS spent its first session organizing itself and attempting to determine the ambit of its jurisdiction and duties. The new Justices heard and

---

[4] *Ibid. See also*, US CONST. Art. III § 2, states in pertinent part that "[t]he judicial power shall extend to all cases, in law and equity, arising under this Constitution, the laws of the United States, and treaties made, or which shall be made, under their authority... *to controversies between two or more states*...." (Emphasis added.)

[5] US Const. Art. III, § 2, cl. 2, which provides in pertinent part: "The judicial power shall extend to all... to controversies between two or more states... In all cases... in which a state shall be party, the Supreme Court shall have original jurisdiction."

[6] *North Dakota v. Minnesota*, 263 US 365, 373 (1923).

[7] Joseph F. Zimmerman, *Interstate Disputes: The Supreme Court's Original Jurisdiction* (2006) ix.

[8] *Ibid.*

[9] US Const. Art. I, § 10, Cl. 3, reads: "No State shall, without the Consent of Congress... enter into any Agreement or Compact with another State, or with a foreign Power." The Compact Clause applies to agreement between states whose aim is the founding of any entity that enhances the political power of the agreement's member States in relation to that of the Federal Government. *See also, New Hampshire v. Maine*, 426 US 363, 369 (1976).

decided their first case two years later, in 1792. Due to the lack of any specific constitutional direction, the American Judiciary spent its first decade as
the weakest of the three branches of government. Early federal courts failed
to issue strong judgments or even to accept controversial cases. Indeed, the
Court's justices were uncertain whether they had the power to consider the
constitutionality of laws passed by Congress.

1 Disputes Between the States: The Supreme Court's Original Jurisdiction

In *Chisholm* v. *Georgia*,[10] the Supreme Court's fourth case, and its first
"major" one, the Justices were requested to invoke the Court's original jurisdiction, in a suit against a state by an individual. The *Chisolm* Court was asked
to decide whether the state of Georgia was subject to the laws of the federal
government and to the Court's jurisdiction. The dispute arose from events that
occurred during the Revolutionary War, wherein Georgia authorized the purchase of supplies from a South Carolina merchant, Robert Farquhar. Following receipt of the supplies, Georgia breached the contract by refusing to pay
Farquhar, who died without receiving payment. The executor of Farquhar's
estate, Alexander Chisolm, brought a suit for breach of contract to collect the
debt from Georgia. The suit was filed in the SCOTUS by the Attorney General of the United States on behalf of Chisolm, asserting the Court's original
jurisdiction.

The Court's opinion cited

[t]he part of the Constitution concerning the Judicial Power is as follows, *viz*:
Art.3. sect. 2. The Judicial Power shall extend...
(5) To controversies between two or more States; *between a State and citizens of another State*; between citizens of different States; between citizens of
the same State, claiming lands under grants of different States, and between
a State or the citizens thereof and foreign states, citizens or subjects.[11]

Subsequently, addressing the Court's original jurisdiction in one of its foremost water disputes, *Illinois* v. *City of Milwaukee*,[12] Justice Douglas writing
for the Court, observed that

'It has long been this Court's philosophy that 'our original jurisdiction should
be invoked sparingly...' we... honor our original jurisdiction but... make it
obligatory only in appropriate cases. And the question of what is appropriate

---

[10] 2 US (2 Dall.) 419 (1793). The case invoked Article III, § 2's grant of federal jurisdiction to the
Supreme Court over suits "between a State and Citizens of another State" and annulled Georgia's sovereign immunity, which was established at common law, consequently permitting an
individual to sue the State into the federal court system.

[11] *Ibid.* 2 US at 430–431.   [12] 406 US 91 (1972).

concerns, of course, the seriousness and dignity of the claim . . . and whether there is another forum available for litigating the dispute.[13]

Justice Douglas's observation that the Court uses its original jurisdiction sparingly has withstood the test of time. Through the Court's 2015–2016 term ending with *Montana v. Wyoming*[14] – a period of 224 years (1792–2016), since the SCOTUS heard its first case – it has adjudicated some 140 original juris-diction cases for an average of approximately 1.6 cases per annum.

The *Illinois* dispute was a seminal case, as it defined the outlines of which entity a state could sue under the Court's original jurisdiction. There, the State of Illinois, in its role as a *parens patria*, sought to invoke the Court's original jurisdiction in a suit alleging that four cities and other defendants in Wisconsin, including the City of Milwaukee, were polluting Lake Michi-gan by discharging some 200 million gallons per day of "raw or inadequately treated sewage and other waste materials . . . "[15] Lake Michigan is an interstate water body, in the Milwaukee area alone. Illinois claimed that "the defendants are instrumentalities of [the State of] Wisconsin and that this suit was there-fore one against that State that must be brought in this Court under Art. III, 2, cl. 2, of the Constitution . . . "[16] The SCOTUS denied Illinois request to invoke its original jurisdiction against the four municipalities because the Constitu-tion only confers original jurisdiction on the Court "[i]n all cases . . . *in which a State* shall be a party." Accordingly, as the defendant entities sub-divisions of the state of Wisconsin, they could not be subject to the Court's original juris-diction. Finally proceedings under the Court's original jurisdiction are "basi-cally equitable in nature."[17] Accordingly, "the court may regulate and mould the process it uses in such a manner as in its judgment will best promote the purposes of justice."[18]

C *Appointment of the Court's Justices & the Court's Term*

Article II § 2 of the United States Constitution states that the President "shall nominate, and by and with the advice and consent of the Senate, shall appoint . . . judges of the Supreme Court . . . ."[19] The nomination must

---

[13] *Illinois v. City of Milwaukee, ibid.* at 93.
[14] 137 Original, 577 US ___, 136 S. Ct. 1034 (2016).   [15] 406 US 91, 93.   [16] *Ibid* at 91.
[17] *Ohio v. Kentucky*, 410 US 641, 648 (1973). (*Citing Rhode Island v. Massachusetts*, 39 US 210 (1840).)
[18] *Kentucky v. Dennison*, 24 How. 66, 98 (1861).
[19] US Const. Art. II, § 2, Cl. 2. Known as the "Appointments Clause," the Senate's "advice and consent" function can be at best described as dysfunctional and flawed. *See e.g.*, David A. Strauss & Cass R. Sunstein, The Senate, the Constitution, and the Confirmation Process,

be approved by a majority vote of the Senate, and, once confirmed, the Justices have life tenure. Presidents appointing the most Supreme Court Justices include George Washington, with ten appointments, and Franklin D. Roosevelt, who appointed eight Justices. Before settling at nine in 1869, the number of Supreme Court Justices changed six times. In its entire history, the Supreme Court has had only sixteen Chief Justices, and over one hundred Associate Justices.

By law, the Court's Term begins on the first Monday in October and ends the first Monday in October of the next year. Approximately 10,000 petitions are filed with the Court during each Term. In addition, some 1,200 applications of various kinds are filed annually that can be acted upon by a single Justice.

D *The Court's Original Jurisdiction in Water Cases*

"Water disputes between states are a recurring issue arising across the nation. Traditionally, such water disputes were seen only in the arid west. However, as populations have increased and demand for water has grown, these disputes have become more frequent in the eastern part of the nation."[20] Indeed, the Court has recently seen an unparalleled increase in the quantity of original jurisdiction disputes regarding water allocation issues. That trend is likely to continue.[21] Moreover, the SCOTUS has noted that its "original jurisdiction over actions between States is concerned with disputes so serious that they would be grounds for war if the States were truly sovereign."[22]

The case of *Arizona v. California*[23] exemplifies the considerable import of these types of disputes. That case – which is more fully discussed *infra* – is one of the longest and most adjudicated cases in the Supreme Court's history. The dispute concerned the water rights of six different states, as well as twenty-five Native American tribes. It involved the use of the Colorado River, which the Court declared "is a navigable stream of the United States. [And therefore, t]he privilege of the states through which it flows and their inhabitants to

101 *Yale L J* (1992) 1491. (Finding the confirmation of Justices to be deeply flawed.) *Cf.* John O. McGinnis, *The President, the Senate, the Constitution, and the Confirmation Process: A Reply to Professors Strauss and Sunstein*, 71 *Tex L R* (1993) 633 (arguing that the system is not flawed but, for the most part, as expected to work by the Framers).

[20] Courtney T. Kerwin, Note, The US Supreme Court Addresses the Battle for Control Over the Potomac River, 12 *Southeastern Envtl L J* (2004) 183, 183.

[21] Paul Stinson, *Increase in Water Battles among States Seen, Cruden Says*, Bloomberg BNA *Daily Envtl R* (Mar. 31, 2016), http://www.bna.com/increase-water-battles-n57982069272.

[22] *South Carolina v. North Carolina, ibid.* 130 S. Ct. at 876 (2010).

[23] 298 US 558 (1936) (Stone, J.).

appropriate and use the water is subject to the paramount power of the United States to control it for the purpose of improving navigation."[24]

Indeed, Justice Stone, writing for the Court in 1936, observed that "[e]very right which Arizona asserts is so subordinate to and dependent upon the rights and the exercise of an authority asserted by the United States that no final determination of the one can be made without a determination of the extent of the other."[25] Therefore, in cases involving disputes over rivers,[26] where a United States federal government agency has acted to control the flow or some other aspect of a river, the Court will not allow the matter to move forward unless the United States either intervenes or is brought into the case, as an indispensable party, by one of the states to the conflict.[27] One reason for this procedure is likely the finality of the litigation.

In another case, *Nebraska v. Wyoming*,[28] the issue was whether the dependable natural flow of the North Platte River, during the irrigation season, was over-appropriated between three states, Colorado, Nebraska, and Wyoming, and the United States? The Court found that not only were present uses over-appropriated,[29] but that future projections would maintain this over-appropriation.[30] Although the United States was allowed to intervene, on the basis that there was unappropriated water, the SCOTUS found the following: (1) the United States had no vested rights in the water, as Congress appropriated water for the use of the land-owners through the property which the river flows, and not for use by the federal government. Accordingly, the water became the property of the land owners; and (2) the North Platter River water

---

[24] *Ibid.* 298 US at 569. A river's navigability is rooted in Congress' constitutional power to regulate interstate commerce, as set forth in Article I, Section 8, Clause 3, which in pertinent part provides "The Congress shall have Power...To regulate Commerce with foreign Nations, and among the several States, and with the Indian Tribes." In *Gibbons v. Ogden*, 22 US 1 (1824) the Supreme Court Stated that commerce includes navigation.

[25] *Ibid.* 298 US at 571. (Emphasis added.) (*Citing California v. Southern Pacific Co.*, 157 US 229, 251, 257 (1894) and *Minnesota v. Northern Securities Co.*, 184 US 199, 235, 245–247 (1902).)

[26] See e.g., *Colorado v. New Mexico* 459 US 176, 178 (1982), describing the watercourse at issue: "The Vermejo River is a small, nonnavigable river that originates in the snow belt of the Rocky Mountains in southern Colorado and flows southeasterly into New Mexico for a distance of roughly 55 miles before it joins the Canadian River."

[27] *Arizona v. California, ibid.* 298 US at 571–572.

[28] No. 6 Original, 325 US 589 (1945). In which Colorado was impleaded as a defendant and the United States intervened. Nebraska claimed that there existed a shortage and misappropriation of water by Wyoming and Colorado. It also asserted that a future threat of water shortage and diversions would occur. 325 US 599.

[29] 325 US 608.

[30] 325 US 610. ("What we have, then, is a situation where three States assert against a river whose dependable natural flow during the irrigation season has long been over appropriated claims based not only on present uses, but on projected additional uses as well.")

was "wholly distinct from the property right of the [federal] government in the irrigation works."[31]

E The Procedure for Filing Original Actions

In enacting the Judiciary Act of 1789[32] Congress empowered the Court to draft and publicize its own procedural rules,[33] which would allow all United States federal courts to facilitate the systematic running of their affairs.[34] In cases where one state decides to sue a sister state, the movant must file a pleading, petitioning the Supreme Court for its authorization to file a suit, pursuant to the Court's original jurisdiction. Procedurally, the petitioning state must file a motion for leave,[35] with an accompanying brief, requesting the Court's approval or permission to file a complaint against the other state(s).

During the period prior to 1954 the SCOTUS' procedural rules *vis-à-vis* a state's raising the Court's original jurisdiction were extremely general. For instance, former Rule 5 stated that a moving state's motion for leave to file a complaint may be supported by a brief; the filing of supplemental pleadings as requested by the Court; and that rules applicable to the appellate docket were to govern, to the extent relevant. In other words, these rules were not hard and fast. Thus, the Court, at its discretion, could employ rules on a case by case basis, which did not provide litigant states with the certainty that any litigant seeks.

1 The Court's Rule 17: Greater Clarity

Under current US Supreme Court rules, as adopted April 19, 2013, Rule 17, "Procedure in an Original Action," applies expressly "only to an action

---

[31] *Ibid.* at 614.   [32] Judiciary Act *ibid.*

[33] *Ibid.* 1 Stat. 73 at 83. *See generally* the Judiciary Act's § 17, which provides the following in pertinent part: "Sec. 17. *And be it further enacted*, that all the said courts of the United States shall have power... *to make and establish all necessary rules for the orderly conducting business in the said courts*, provided such rules are not repugnant to the laws of the United States." (Emphasis added.)

[34] *See e.g.*, 28 USC §2071, Rule-making power generally

(a) The Supreme Court and all courts established by Act of Congress may from time to time prescribe rules for the conduct of their business. Such rules shall be consistent with Acts of Congress and rules of practice and procedure prescribed under section 2072 of this title.

[35] *South Carolina v. North Carolina*, 585 US 256, 259 (2010). "We granted leave [in 2007] for South Carolina to file its complaint in this matter two years ago." *South Carolina v. North Carolina*, 552 US 804 (2007).

invoking the Court's original jurisdiction under Article III of the Constitution..."[36] The *form* of the pleadings as well as motions is now fixed, and must conform with the Federal Rules of Civil Procedure.[37] The initial filing must be a pleading, which is to be "preceded by a motion for leave to file, and may be accompanied by a brief in support of the motion."[38]

The Court's decision to allow a petitioning state to file the initial request can be quite succinct. For example, in *Oklahoma v. Arkansas*[39] the Court's opinion consisted of one terse sentence, stating that the "Motion for leave to file a bill of complaint [is] granted and [the] defendant [is] allowed sixty days in which to respond."[40] Once the motion for leave to file and its accompanying initial pleading are filed with the Clerk of the Supreme Court the case is placed on the Court's docket.[41] On the occasion that the adverse state party has been served with the moving party's motion for leave to file (and accompanying papers), the responding state has up to 60 days to "file 40 copies of any brief in opposition to the motion, with proof of service as required by Rule 29."[42] The Respondent's brief in opposition is equivalent to a motion to dismiss the complaint.[43] Once the foregoing touchstones are met the Court's Clerk "will distribute the filed documents to the Court for its consideration..."[44]

Where the responding state timely files a brief in opposition, the Clerk is required to circulate this document to the justices for their consideration, "no less than 10 days after the brief in opposition is filed."[45] The Rule further provides that while the petitioning state may file a reply brief, the justices' consideration of the case will not be delayed until it is received.[46] Thereafter, the Court may grant or deny the motion, set it for oral argument, direct that additional documents be filed, or require that other proceedings be conducted.[47]

---

[36] Sup. Ct. R. 17.1 (2009).

[37] *Ibid.* at R. 17.2. ("The form of pleadings and motions prescribed by the Federal Rules of Civil Procedure is followed. In other respects, those Rules and the Federal Rules of Evidence may be taken as guides.")

[38] *Ibid.* at R. 17.3. Moreover, the Rule requires that "Forty copies of each document shall be filed, with proof of service," which is to be made on both the responding state's Attorney General and Governor. *Ibid.*

[39] 439 US 812 (1978).   [40] *Ibid.*

[41] Sup. Ct. R. 17.4. For the matter to be docketed "The Rule 38(a) docket fee shall be paid at that time." *Ibid.* Currently the Rule 38(a) docketing fee is $300.00, as per 28 USC § 1911, wherein Congress declared that "The Supreme Court may fix the fees to be charged by its clerk. The fees of the clerk, cost of serving process, and other necessary disbursements incidental to any case before the court, may be taxed against the litigants as the court directs."

[42] *Ibid.* at R. 17.5. Sup. Ct. R. 29.5 ("5. Proof of service, when required by these Rules").

[43] Zimmerman, *ibid.* at 28.   [44] Sup. Ct. R. 17.5   [45] *Ibid.*   [46] *Ibid.*   [47] *Ibid.*

F Deciding When to Grant or Deny a Motion for Leave

The Court's decision to grant or deny the motion must be by a majority vote of all the justices. This vote contrasts with the consideration of whether to grant or deny an appeal, via a *writ of certiorari*, where only four of the nine Justices must vote to accept a case. However, should the Justices feel that they are required to address a point of law that is unclear to them or, that an issue has not been addressed by the parties, they may set the matter "for oral argument, direct that additional documents be filed, or require that other proceedings be conducted."[48] Where the Court seeks to address the matter via oral argument, it will generally allot a two-hour block of time, double the time that is provided for oral argument in other cases that the justices hear. The SCOTUS has asked for oral argument in a number of original jurisdiction cases. For example, in 1957 and 1958 the Court requested oral argument in *Virginia v. Maryland*[49] and in *California v. Washington*,[50] respectively. After the argument in *Virginia v. Maryland* the Court issued the following *Per Curium* Opinion:

> The Court having heard oral argument by the Attorneys General of the States and having considered the printed briefs of counsel, the Court is of the opinion that the motion for leave to file the bill of complaint should be granted. The State of Maryland is directed to file an answer to the bill of complaint within 60 days and process is ordered to issue accordingly.[51]

In *California v. Washington*[52] the Court ruled that "[t]his case is set for argument on the motion for leave to file a bill of complaint and answer. Two hours allowed for oral argument."[53] In fact, the SCOTUS has made clear that it "interpret[s] 28 USC § 1251(a)[54] with substantial discretion to make case-by-case judgments as to the practical necessity of an original forum in this Court for particular disputes within our constitutional original jurisdiction, [and that the justices] exercise that discretion with an eye to promoting the most effective functioning of this Court within the overall federal system."[55]

Nevertheless, the Court has denied leave in some disputes. For example, in the 1981 case of *California v. West Virginia*,[56] the Court denied California leave when it sought to file a breach of contract claim against West Virginia,

---

[48] *Ibid.*   [49] 355 US 269 (1957).   [50] 365 US 955 (1958).

[51] 355 US 269 (1957).   [52] 356 US 955 (1958).   [53] *Ibid.*

[54] Congressional statute for original jurisdiction. "(a) The Supreme Court shall have original and exclusive jurisdiction of all controversies between two or more States."

[55] *Texas v. New Mexico*, 462 US 554, 570 (1983). *See also, Maryland v. Louisiana*, 451 US 725, 743 (1981).

[56] 454 US 1027 (1981).

subsequent to the refusal of a West Virginia state university football team to play its California opponent. Dissenting from that denial, Justice John Paul Stevens stated that "[t]he fact that two sovereign States have been unable to resolve this matter without adding to our burdens does not speak well for the statesmanship of either party but does not, in my opinion, justify our refusal to exercise our exclusive jurisdiction..."[57]

Alternatively, in a case where a responding state party did not reply to a motion for leave within the required 60-day period, the movant may proceed *ex parte*.[58] That was the case of *New York v. Connecticut*.[59] In that 1799 dispute New York state asked the Court to issue an injunction against Connecticut, seeking to prevent the sale of a parcel of land by Connecticut, known as the "Connecticut Gore." Chief Justice Ellsworth, writing for the Court, held that where the New York Attorney General provided notice to the appropriate parties on behalf of the State of Connecticut and the latter did not attend the hearing on the matter, sufficient notice was provided.[60]

Finally, even in the Rule 17 era states have misfiled their suits. For example, in *Louisiana v. Mississippi*,[61] Louisiana filed her dispute in the Federal District Court (the trial court). Based on the Supreme Court's original jurisdiction, the District Court ruled in favour of defendant Mississippi. However, the Fifth Circuit Court of Appeals reversed that ruling in favour of Louisiana. Mississippi petitioned the SCOTUS for certiorari. Thereafter, the Supreme Court granted Mississippi's petition.[62] Following oral argument before the Court on both the substantive and jurisdictional issues, the case was resolved solely on the latter. The Court held that neither the trial judge nor the Court of Appeals had subject matter jurisdiction over the dispute and therefore they could not grant Louisiana any relief whatsoever. That jurisdiction rests solely with, and is reserved exclusively with the Supreme Court.[63]

G *The Role of the Special Master in Original Jurisdiction Cases*

One of the unique characteristics of the Court's original jurisdiction cases is its routine appointment of a Special Master to hear the case and take

---

[57] *Ibid.* at 1028.
[58] Sup. Ct. R. 17.6. "6. A summons issued out of this Court shall be served on the defendant 60 days before the return day specified therein. If the defendant does not respond by the return day, the plaintiff may proceed *ex parte*."
[59] 4 US (4 Dall.) 1 (1799).
[60] *Ibid.* For subsequent history of the case, *see Lindsey v. Miller* 3 US (3 Dall.) 411 (1799).
[61] *Mississippi v. Louisiana*, 503 US 935 (1992).   [62] *Ibid.*
[63] *See Mississippi v. Louisiana*, 506 US 73, 77–78 (1992). "We remanded the case so the complaint filed by Louisiana could be dismissed in the District Court and for the Court of Appeals to determine what further proceedings were necessary with respect to the claims of the private parties."

evidence.[64] The appointment of a Special Master is based on a simple and practical fact. Although the Constitution grants the Court the jurisdiction to sit as a trial court in interstate or transboundary cases, as established the Court is neither equipped for, nor capable of, performing the functions of a trial court, *e.g.*, to take evidence in the first instance[65] or to rule on motions.

Therefore, the Court generally appoints a Special Master – an experienced lawyer or judge – to compile evidence, rule on motions, and prepare a report that contains a statement of facts and conclusions of law.[66] Indeed, the Special Master's role is akin to that of a federal district court judge or magistrate judge.[67] Moreover, under Supreme Court Rule 17, Special Masters have extremely broad discretion in the handling of the proceedings before them.[68] Supreme Court Rule 17 also governs the procedures and filings of pleadings before the Special Master. Rule 17 has developed into the solitary rule that governs the proceedings before Special Masters, including the use of the Federal Rules of Civil Procedure for the filing of pleadings: "[t]he form of pleadings and motions prescribed by the Federal Rules of Civil Procedure is followed. In other respects, those Rules and the Federal Rules of Evidence may be taken as guides."[69]

---

[64] The master is in some respects akin to European Court of Justice's Advocates-General.

[65] *See e.g.*, Bleich, *ibid.* at 47.

[66] *See e.g.*, *Vermont v. New Hampshire*, 269 US 527, 527 (1925) (naming commissioners "for taking of testimony and documentary evidence"); *New Mexico v. Texas*, 266 US 586, 586–87 (1924) (directing Special Master to "make special findings on all material questions of fact").

[67] US magistrate judges are Article I judges, *i.e.*, their power is granted by Congress. They are judicial officers of the district court, who do not have life tenure. They possess some powers that district court Article III judges have, *e.g.*, they can try civil and criminal cases, handle motions and settlement negotiations, but, they are on a lower tier than federal court judges. Magistrate judges are "appointed by majority vote of the active district judges of the court to exercise jurisdiction over matters assigned by statute as well as those delegated by the district judges…A full-time magistrate judge serves a term of eight years." United States Courts, Frequently Asked Questions, Federal Judges, Q. *What are Federal Magistrate Judges?*, http://www.uscourts.gov/Common/FAQS.aspx.

[68] *See e.g.*, Ryke Longest, Opinion Analysis: Bargaining in the Shadow of Equitable Apportionment, *SCOTUSblog*, Mar. 3, 2015, http://www.scotusblog.com/2015/03/opinion-analysis-bargaining-in-the-shadow-of-equitable-apportionment. ("Clearly, the Court's opinion endorses expansive powers for Court-appointed special masters to resolve disputes.")

[69] *Ibid.* at 2. The rule for pleadings in the Fed.R.Civ.Pro., is Rule 8, which states in part:

A. Rule 8. General Rules of Pleading
   (a) Claims for Relief

A pleading that states a claim for relief must contain:

(1) a short and plain statement of the grounds for the court's jurisdiction, unless the court already has jurisdiction and the claim needs no new jurisdictional support;

(2) a short and plain statement of the claim showing that the pleader is entitled to relief; and

1 The History of the Appointment of Special Masters

The Court's employment of Special Masters appears to be part of its equitable powers and harkens back to the Chancery Courts of England.[70] In
those courts, Special Masters were appointed as fact finders.[71] That practice was carried over to the United States during the colonial period, as
demonstrated by two incidents. The first, a pre-Revolutionary War boundary dispute, between two English royal provinces – Massachusetts and New
Hampshire – which involved what today are the states of Maine and New
Hampshire. New Hampshire's leaders petitioned King George II, who in
1737 appointed twenty commissioners[72] from the adjoining New England
provinces to conduct a boundary survey line dividing the two provinces. In
1740, King George accepted and signed the decree submitted to him by the
commissioners.[73]

The second occurred following the revolutionary war and the independence of the United States. The very first case docketed in the SCOTUS
required a commissioner.[74] The United States Attorney General, Edmund
Randolph, "moved, on behalf of the plaintiffs, that a commission should issue
to examine witnesses in Holland; to which the opposite counsel assented,
although the commissioners were not named. [The Court held that] [w]e
will not award the commission, 'till commissioners are named."[75] Three
years later in *Georgia v. Brailsford*,[76] the Court appointed William Bradford, the Attorney General of the United States, to take testimony[77] concerning whether the state of Georgia's legislature, as a sovereign state, had the
authority to pass a law, which transferred to the state's coffers, the debts it

---

(3) a demand for the relief sought, which may include relief in the alternative or different
    types of relief...
[70] Zimmerman, *ibid.* at 43.   [71] *Ibid.*
[72] *New Hampshire v. Maine*, 426 US 363, 366–367 (1976) (Brennan, J.).

> The legal issues focused on the Merrimack River, but the boundary between New
> Hampshire and the Maine portion of Massachusetts was also involved. When represen-
> tatives of the two provinces were unable in 1731 to reach agreement, the New Hampshire
> representatives presented the matter to King George II. The King referred the dispute
> to the Board of Trade, which, in 1735, recommended that commissioners from the other
> New England Colonies be designated to resolve the question. In 1737 the King accord-
> ingly appointed 20 members of the Provincial Councils of New York, New Jersey, Rhode
> Island, and Nova Scotia to serve as commissioners.

[73] *Ibid.* at 366. The dispute was, in fact, fixed in 1740 by decree of King George II of England.
[74] *Vanstophorst v. Maryland*, 2 US (2 Dall.) 401 (1791).
[75] *Ibid.* 2 US at 401.   [76] 3 Dall. 1 (1794) (Jay, C. J.).
[77] *Ibid.* at note 1. ("Mr. Bradford was appointed in the room of Edmund Randolph, Esq. who
    had accepted the office of Secretary of State.")

owed to two American citizens, who resided in South Carolina and Great Britain, respectively.[78]

The Supreme Court continued to appoint commissioners throughout the nineteenth century. Then in 1908, in *Virginia v. West Virginia*[79] the Court inexplicably replaced commissions when it appointed a Special Master.[80] In that case the Master was selected in order to calculate funds owed for civil war debts by West Virginia to the Commonwealth of Virginia.

a CHANGING OVER: FROM COMMISSIONERS TO MASTERS

The change from commissioners to a Special Master is consistent with the Court's broad delegation of its original jurisdiction to appointees to handle its "trial court" functions. Indeed, a seminal article tracing the development of the Special Masters[81] found that the language in the SCOTUS' memoranda appointing successive Special Masters is quite similar. Additionally, the author points out that in the Court's delegation to the Special Master, it imbues him/her with extensive powers. Nevertheless, the justices generally do not indicate how the Special Master is supposed to carry out the task.[82]

The memoranda also state that the Special Master may, among other things, "summon witnesses, issue subpoenas, and take such evidence as may be introduced and such as [he or she] may deem it necessary to call for."[83] Since 1965, however, the extent of the Special Master's jurisdiction has expanded to the "authority to fix the time and conditions for the filing of additional pleadings and to direct subsequent proceedings."[84] For example, in *Kansas v. Nebraska's* 1999[85] memorandum, the Court declared that the Special Master is provided "with the authority to fix the time and conditions

---

[78] *Ibid.* at 3 Dall. 4. "We are also of opinion that the debts due to Brailsford, a British subject, residing in Great Britain, were by the statute of Georgia subjected not to confiscation, but only to sequestration, and therefore that his right to recover them revived at the peace, both by the law of nations and the treaty of peace."

[79] 209 US 514 (1908), Forms of decree appointing Special Master, submitted April 7, 1908 Form of decree announced May 4, 1908.

[80] 209 US at 536.

> It is further ordered that the Commonwealth of Virginia and the State of West Virginia shall each, when required, produce before the master, upon oath, all such records, books, papers, and public documents as may be in their possession or under their control, and which may, in his judgment, be pertinent to the said inquiries and accounts, or any of them.

[81] Anne-Marie C. Carstens, Lurking in the Shadows of Judicial Process: Special Masters in the Supreme Court's Original Jurisdiction Cases, 86 *Minn L Rev* (2002) 625.

[82] *Ibid.* at 654.   [83] *Ibid.* at 652.   [84] *Ibid.* at note 173.

[85] *Kansas v. Nebraska* & Colorado, 525 U.S. 1101 (1999) (order granting motion for leave to file bill of complaint).

for the filing of additional pleadings and to direct subsequent proceedings, and with authority to summon witnesses, issue subpoenas, and take such evidence as may be introduced and such as he may deem it necessary to call for."[86] Moreover, the Special Master was instructed to tender any reports as he deemed suitable. "The compensation of the Special Master, the allowances to him, the compensation paid to his legal, technical, stenographic and clerical assistants, the cost of printing his report, and all other proper expenses, including travel expenses, shall be charged against and be borne by the parties in such proportion as the Court may hereafter direct. The motion of Nebraska to dismiss the complaint is referred to the Special Master."[87]

However, in some cases the Court curbs the Master's jurisdiction. For example, in *New Mexico* v. *Texas*,[88] the Court specifically limited the Special Master to "make [only] special findings on all material questions of fact."[89]

H *Criticisms of the Use of Special Masters and Suggested Solutions*

Much about the entire Special Masters' appointment process has been criticized[90] – apart from their salaries, which can reach into the millions of dollars. Concern, for example, has been expressed regarding the constitutionality of the use of the Special Master. For example, in *Maryland* v. *Louisiana*, Justice Rehnquist, dissenting, declared that

> [t]he breadth of the constitutional grant of this Court's original jurisdiction dictates that we are able to exercise discretion over the cases we hear under this jurisdictional head, lest our ability to administer our appellate docket be impaired.[91]

* * *

None of these concerns are adequately answered by the expedient of employing a Special Master to conduct hearings, receive evidence, and submit recommendations for our review. It is no reflection on the quality of the work by the Special Master in this case or any other master in any other original

---

[86] *Ibid.*   [87] 120 S. Ct. 519, 519 (1999).

[88] *New Mexico* v. *Texas*, 266 US 586 (1924).   [89] *Ibid.* at 266 US 586–87.

[90] For example, in *Texas* v. *Florida*, 306 US 398, 428 (1939), Justice Frankfurter, in dissenting noted that certain considerations regarding the scope of the Court's original jurisdiction and the appointment of Special Masters

> have from time to time led this Court, or some of its most distinguished members, either to deprecate resort to this Court by states for settlement of their controversies (*see New York* v. *New Jersey*, 256 US 296, 256 US 313) or to oppose assumption of jurisdiction (*see* Mr. Chief Justice Taney in 54 US 579, 54 US 592; *in connection with the Act of August 31, 1852, 10 Stat. 112, and 59 US 605*).

[91] 451 US 762 (1981).

jurisdiction case to find it unsatisfactory to delegate the proper functions of this Court. Of course, this Court cannot sit to receive evidence or conduct trials – but that fact should counsel reluctance to accept cases where the situation might arise, not resolution of the problem by empowering an individual to act in our stead. I, for one, think justice is far better served by trials in the lower courts, with appropriate review, than by trials before a Special Master whose rulings this Court simply cannot consider with the care and attention it should.[92]

One author is also of the opinion that "[m]ost fundamentally, the role of Special Master is one that – with the Court's permission – runs afoul of many of the characteristics of our American federal judicial system: adversarial testing, presentation of witnesses by parties, multilayered review, decision making by constitutionally appointed judicial actors, and adherence to judicially created procedural safeguards."[93] There are also practical limits to the usefulness of the litigation or adjudicative process in the Supreme Court's resolution of interstate water controversies.[94] The shortcomings of litigation, including its episodic nature and repeated need for a Master – for example, Arizona v. California, has come to the Court eleven times between 1931 and 2006, amounting to a period of 74 years, or an average of once every 6.8 years. Similarly, the dispute between Kansas v. Colorado, has been visited upon the Court a half-dozen times over a span of 102 years, from 1902 to 2004, or an average of once every 17 years – and the justices unavoidably constrained capacity for genuine inquiry, limit the SCOTUS' efficacy.

1 A Lack of Openness of the Special Masters' Proceedings

The Special Masters' proceedings are, moreover, closed to non-parties, and are an extremely restricted deliberative or reflective forum for addressing policy issues.[95] In contrast, courts routinely mold policy into their decisions, especially when new social situations arise, e.g., the development of the doctrine of equitable apportionment in the Supreme Court's water decisions;[96] strict

---

[92] Ibid. at 762–763. (Emphasis added). [93] Carstens ibid. at 668.
[94] Texas v. Florida, 306 US 398, 428 (1939) (Frankfurter, J., dissenting).

> (The authority which the Constitution has committed to this Court over 'Controversies between two or more States,' serves important ends in the working of our federalism. But there are practical limits to the efficacy of the adjudicatory process in the adjustment of interstate controversies. The limitations of litigation – its episodic character, its necessarily restricted scope of inquiry ...).

[95] Ibid.
[96] Nebraska v. Wyoming, 325 US 589, 618 (1945). For an excellent, and still timely, summary of the law of interstate water allocation, see A. Dan Tarlock, The Law of Equitable Apportionment Revisited, Updated, and Restated, 56 U Colo L R (1985) 381.

liability for tortuous conduct, involving different types of behavior, or certain factors that impact a court in transboundary law. Additionally, the Master's proceedings are dependent upon the "contingencies of a particular record, and other circumscribing factors [which] often denature and even mutilate the actualities of a problem and thereby render the litigious process unsuited for its solution."[97]

2 The Financial Burden of the Master's Appointment Scheme

Returning to the Court's dissatisfaction with the system of appointing Special Masters, in *Texas* v. *New Mexico*,[98] Justice Blackmun declared in dissent that Special Masters, from what he called "'establishment' law firms, are doing themselves and the public a disservice by asserting fees of this magnitude so persistently over dissents from the Court." Similarly, in an earlier round in *Texas* v. *New Mexico*,[99] Chief Justice Burger, also in dissent – with two other justices joining – found the hourly rates for "junior associates, some of whom were only 'summer law clerks,' were not supported and were unreasonable." Finally, in *Louisiana* v. *Mississippi*,[100] Chief Justice Burger, again in dissent, found that the Special Master's fees were unwarranted and noted that "the public service aspect of the appointment is a factor that is not to be wholly ignored in determining the reasonableness of fees charged in a case like this."

I *Original Jurisdiction Cases: A Body of Transboundary and Common Law*

In *North Dakota* v. *Minnesota*,[101] Chief Justice Taft, writing for the Court, observed that the majority of original jurisdiction cases, and therefore most of the cases in which the Court appointed commissioners or Special Masters, involved boundary disputes.[102] Anne-Marie Carstens similarly observes that "[t]he precedent that guides the Special Master, particularly in boundary dispute cases, *is a fragile body of specialized federal common law, pasted together from international law treatises*, property concepts, contract law,

---

[97] *Texas* v. *Florida ibid.* 306 US at 428. For example, Carstens notes that "[i]n many original jurisdiction cases, which may span many decades and even centuries, the availability of witnesses will be highly curtailed. Accordingly, the interest in the availability of relevant evidence might justify deviation from strict application of hearsay rules. Relaxed hearsay rules – or expanded exceptions – in original jurisdiction cases thus might be necessary." Carstens *ibid.* at 669–700.

[98] 485 US 953, 953–56 (1988).   [99] 475 US 1004, 1004–05 (1986).

[100] 466 US 921, 921–23 (1984).   [101] 263 US 583 (1924).

[102] *Ibid.* at 583. "By far the greater number of suits between states have been brought for the purpose of settling boundaries."

and *sovereignty principles.*"[103] She also notes that, in his 1955 book on the Court's role, Justice Robert Jackson declared, that "the Court has no escape in many cases of this character from the undesirable alternatives of refusing to obey its duty to decide the case or of devising some rule of decision which has no precedent or positive law authority."[104] Jackson provides an example in his book,[105] citing Justice Benjamin Cardozo's opinion in *New Jersey* v. *Delaware*.[106] There, Cardozo cited "ancient law,[107] international law and American and foreign conventional authorities . . . ."[108]

Indeed, the Court's precedents in interstate water disputes are grounded in international law and sovereignty principles. For example, in *Kansas* v. *Colorado*,[109] Chief Justice Fuller writing for the Court declared: "[s]itting, as it were, as an international as well as a domestic tribunal, we apply federal law, state law, and international law, as the exigencies of the particular case may demand . . . ."[110] In that case the Court also observed that

> Comity demanded that navigable rivers should be free, and therefore the freedom of the Mississippi, the Rhine, the Scheldt, the Danube, the St. Lawrence, the Amazon, and other rivers has been at different times secured by treaty; but if a state of this union deprives another state of its rights in a navigable stream, and Congress has not regulated the subject, as no treaty can be made between them, how is the matter to be adjusted?
>
> Applying the principles settled in previous cases, we have no special difficulty with the bare question whether facts might not exist which would justify our interposition, while the manifest importance of the case and the necessity of the ascertainment of all the facts before the propositions of law can be satisfactorily dealt with lead us to the conclusion that the cause should go to issue and proofs before final decision.[111]

In closing, the Supreme Court's original jurisdiction provides the justices with a wide degree of latitude in adjudicating transboundary and interstate disputes. A number of the justices have, however, at various stages of the Court's existence, expressed concern regarding whether the Court is best suited to resolve these types of cases. Moreover, some justices and publicists have articulated their frustrations concerning the system of appointing

---

[103] Carstens *ibid.* at 654, citation omitted (emphasis added).
[104] *Ibid.* (citing Robert H. Jackson, *The Supreme Court in the American System of Government* (1955) 25).
[105] *Ibid.* at 73.   [106] 291 US 361 (1934).   [107] *Ibid.* 291 US 381–382.
[108] Carstens, *ibid.* at 655, *citing* 291 US at 379 ("International law today divides the river boundaries between states by the middle of the main channel, when there is one, and not by the geographical center, halfway between the banks.") (*Citing* numerous cases and international law texts).
[109] 185 US 125 (1902).   [110] *Ibid.* at 146–147.   [111] *Kansas* v. *Colorado*, 185 US at 144.

Masters. In regard to the issue of whether Masters or Special Masters are best equipped to hear disputes, rule on motions and issue reports, for all of the complaints of previous justices and scholars, the Court does not appear to be moving away from the current system.

II THE INTERNATIONAL BOUNDARY AND WATER COMMISSION ("IBWC") (MEXICO/USA)

When the well's dry, we know the worth of water.

Benjamin Franklin (1706–1790)

A Introduction

The history of transboundary water issues between the United States and Mexico is a complex and long-standing one: reaching back into the mid-nineteenth century.[112] Beginning in 1848 the two states executed and ratified a succession of treaties. The first of these was the 1848 Guadalupe–Hidalgo Treaty,[113] which established the international border between the United States and Mexico. That frontier was modified to the one that exists today by the Gadsden Purchase Treaty of December 30, 1853.[114]

These instruments and nine subsequent ones[115] fixed the 3,145 km (1,954 mile) (Figure 6.1) boundary, and delineated the water allocation regime

---

[112] Daene C. McKinney, *CE 397 Transboundary Water Resources US–Mexico Water Issues* (undated), http://www.ce.utexas.edu/prof/mckinney/ce397/Topics/US-Mex/US-Mex%282003%29.htm.

[113] 9 Stat. 92. The treaty is formally known as the Treaty of Peace, Friendship and Limits, Settlement between the United States and the Mexican Republic.

[114] The Gadsden Purchase Treaty (also known as the "Treaty of La Mesilla"), 10 Stat. 1031, was executed in Mexico City on December 30, 1853, by James Gadsden, the United States Minister to Mexico, on the one part and General Antonio López de Santa Anna, president of Mexico, on the other part. The treaty settled the dispute over the precise location of the Mexican border west of El Paso, Texas, and assigned to the United States, for the price of $10 million, an additional 76,800 km² (29,600 square mile) tract of land in what would later become southern New Mexico and Arizona (from approximately Las Cruces, in south central, New Mexico to Yuma, Arizona and encompassing Tucson, Ariz.). The tract that was sold to the USA was called *Venta de La Mesilla* or the "Sale of La Mesilla" by Mexico. *See* Ignacio Ibarra, Land Sale Still Thorn to Mexico: Historians Say United States Imperialism behind Treaty, *Ariz. Daily Star*, Feb. 12, 2004, *available at* http://www.azstarnet.com/sn/gadsden/9331.

[115] The subsequent treaties, conventions minutes and agreements have established a structure for the administration of rivers and other water bodies along the common border of the United States and Mexico. These include the Convention of July 29, 1882; the Convention of November 12, 1884, 24 Stat. 1011; the Boundary Convention of March 1, 1889, 26 Stat. 1512; the Convention of November 21, 1900, 31 Stat. 1936; the Convention of May 21, 1906; the Convention for the Rectification of the Rio Grande (Rio Bravo) in the El Paso-Juarez Valley of February 1, 1933, 48 Stat. 1621; the Treaty for Utilization of Waters of the Colorado and Tijuana Rivers and of the Rio Grande in 1944, USTS 944, signed at Wash., DC, Feb. 3, 1944 (*hereinafter* "1944 Water Treaty"); the Chamizal Convention of August 29, 1963; and the November 1970 Treaty.

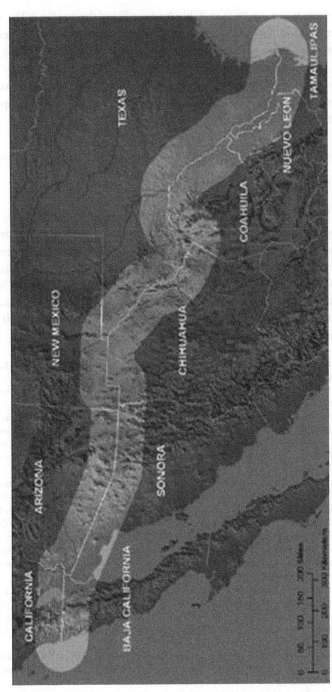

FIGURE 6.1 The Extent of the Mexico-United States Border (After IBWC http://www.ibwc.state.gov/About_Us/history.html)

between these two states.[116] (See Table 6.1 for a list of the treaties.) The water use and allocation portions of these instruments were borne over a century of increasingly thorny transboundary water disputes over the Colorado, Rio Conchos,[117] and the Rio Grande (Rio Bravo in Mexico) Rivers. They were also shaped by recent droughts,[118] increasing border population and economic activity that have, from time to time, required the development and improvement of management rules.

B *The International Boundary and Water Commission's Jurisdiction*

1 The Establishment of a Bi-Lateral Commission

The two State-Parties realized early on that the need for an ongoing system of management rules would be best dealt with by a bilateral administrative body. Consequently, as part of the Boundary Convention of 1889, Mexico and the United States established the bilateral International Boundary Commission ("IBC").[119] Indeed, in 1898 the Commission's work was hailed by United States President William McKinley, in his State of the Union Address. He observed that the Mexican Water Boundary Commission has adjusted all matters submitted to it to the satisfaction of both Governments.[120]

For a fuller discussion of these instruments *see generally,* Alyssa M. Neir and Michael E. Campana, The Peaceful Resolution of US–Mexican Transboundary Water Disputes, 2 *Econ of Peace & Security J* (2007) 41, *available at* http://aquadoc.typepad.com/waterwired/files/eps_v2n2_Neir_Campana.pdf.

[116] The boundary excludes "the maritime boundaries of 18 miles in the Pacific Ocean and 12 miles in the Gulf of Mexico." The International Boundary & Water Commission United States and Mexico, United States Section, Est. 1889, The International Boundary and Water Commission, Its Mission, Organization and Procedures for Solution of Boundary and Water Problems (undated), *available at* http://www.ibwc.state.gov/About_Us/About_Us.html.

[117] The Rio Conchos has been included in the international environmental organization the World Wildlife Fund ("WWF") Global 200 Freshwater Ecoregions Assessment. The WWF's appraisal is made-up of globally designated bodies of water that contain exceptionally biodiverse environments which must be conserved. Moreover, the WWF's assessment rates the Rio Conchos as biologically distinctive and as "globally outstanding" and its conservation status as critically endangered, placing this river within an extremely high priority requiring conservation care. See e.g., Robin A. Abell, *et al., Freshwater Ecoregions of North America: A Conservation Assessment* (2000) 93, 103, 188–189.

[118] McKinney, *CE* 397 *Transboundary Water Resources, ibid.* "During the [ten year period] (1992–1997 and 1997–2002), Northern Mexico experienced the most acute drought on record... [Similarly,] that the situation in southern Texas was pressing, and according to the State Government of Texas, the drought had originated the loss of 30,000 jobs and one-billion-dollar income."

[119] International Boundary and Water Commission United States and Mexico, United States Section, Strategic Plan, FY 2011–2016 (undated), at 46, *available at* http://www.ibwc.state.gov/files/strategic_plan.pdf.

[120] State of the Union Address: William McKinley (December 5, 1898), *available at* Infoplease.com http://www.infoplease.com/t/hist/state-of-the-union/110.html.

TABLE 6.1 *Treaties and Conventions between the USA and Mexico (T: treaty, C: convention)*[121]

T	February 2, 1848	Established the United States–Mexico international boundary
T	December 30, 1853	Modified the boundary, as it exists today.
C	July 29, 1882	Established another temporary commission to resurvey and place additional monuments along the western land boundary from El Paso, Texas/Ciudad Juárez, Chihuahua to San Diego, California/Tijuana, Baja California.
C	November 12, 1884	Established rules for determining the location of the boundary when the meandering rivers transferred tracts of land from one bank to the other.
C	March 1, 1889	Established the International Boundary Commission (IBC) to apply the rules in the 1884 Convention
C	March 20, 1905	The 1889 convention was modified by this Convention to retain the Rio Grande/Rio Bravo and the Colorado River as the international boundary.
C	May 21, 1906	Provides for the distribution between the United States and Mexico of the waters of the Rio Grande/Rio Bravo in the international reach of the river between the El Paso-Juárez Valley and Fort Quitman, Texas.
C	February 1, 1933	The two governments agreed to jointly construct, operate and maintain, through the IBC, the Rio Grande/Rio Bravo Rectification Project, which straightened, stabilized, and shortened the river boundary along the El Paso – Juárez border.
T	February 3, 1944	Distributed the waters of the Colorado River, Tijuana River, and the Rio Grande from Fort Quitman, Texas to the Gulf of Mexico. Authorized the two countries to construct operate and maintain dams on the main channel of the Rio Grande. Changed the name of the IBC to the International Boundary and Water Commission IBWC (in Spanish *Comisión Internacional de Límites y Aguas CILA*) and entrusted the IBWC to give preferential attention to the solution of all border sanitation problems (in Article 3).
C	August 29, 1963	The Chamizal Convention resolved an old boundary problem at El Paso, Texas/Ciudad Juárez, Chihuahua, known as the Chamizal Dispute. The Commission relocated and concrete-lined 4.4 miles (7.1 km) of the channel of the Rio Grande to transfer 437 acres (176.8 ha) to Mexico.
T	November 23, 1970	Resolved all pending boundary differences, and provided for maintaining the Rio Grande/Rio Bravo and the Colorado River as the international boundary. It provides procedures designed to avoid the loss or gain of territory by either country incident to future changes in the river.

[121] McKinney, CE 397 Transboundary Water Resources, *ibid.*

C *The Expansion of Administrative Jurisdiction*

The IBC was replaced by the International Boundary and Water Commission ("IBWC")[122] or the Comisión Internacional de Límites y Aguas, in Spanish, as part of the 1944 Treaty for the Utilization of Waters of the Colorado and Tijuana Rivers and of the Rio Grande.[123] The IBWC, like its predecessor, "is responsible for applying the boundary and water treaties between the two countries and settling differences that arise in their application."[124] Since the IBWC is a bilateral organ, it is composed of two separate sections: a Mexican Section and a United States Section. Each section is chaired by an engineer-commissioner that is appointed by his/her country's respective president.

Furthermore, each country's section is governed independently of the other. The United States Section, known by the acronym USIBWC, is an arm of the State Department, and is headquartered at El Paso, Texas, while the Mexican Section, referred to in English as the MIBWC, is headquartered in El Paso's sister city Ciudad Juárez, Chihuahua. The latter is administered by the Secretariat of Foreign Relations of Mexico. Despite occasional disagreements the IBC–IBWC administrative system has achieved many of its goals. For example, the Chamizal dispute, discussed *infra* is the only conflict that the parties have had since the nineteenth century.

Many of the water-related issues have arisen due to a persistently growing population and concomitant economic activity on both sides of the Parties' common border. Moreover, the prodigious rate of growth[125] and the

---

[122] 59 Stat. 1219; Treaty Series 994, at Art. 2, which in pertinent part provides that:

> The International Boundary Commission established pursuant to the provisions of the Convention between the United States and Mexico signed in Washington March 1, 1889 [footnote omitted] to facilitate the carrying out of the principles contained in the Treaty of November 12, 1884 [footnote omitted] and to avoid difficulties occasioned by reason of the changes which take place in the beds of the Rio Grande (Rio Bravo) and the Colorado River shall hereafter be known as the International Boundary and Water Commission, United States and Mexico, which shall continue to function for the entire period during which the present Treaty shall continue in force.

The treaty is available at http://www.usembassy-mexico.gov/bbf/b.fboundwater.pdf.

[123] *Ibid.*

[124] International Boundary and Water Commission United States and Mexico, 2006 Annual Report, (2006) ii.*t.*

[125] For example, the Phoenix-Mesa-Scottsdale, Arizona, Metropolitan Statistical Area grew from 2.24 million people in 1990 to 3.25 million people in 2000, a 69% growth rate over that ten-year period. However, from 2000–2010 the population increased from 3.25 million to 4.2 million, an increase of 25.5%. This includes the 2008–2012 real estate downturn. *See* Paul J. Mackun, Current Population Reports, United States Census Bureau, Population Change in Metropolitan and Micropolitan Statistical Areas 1990–2003: Population Estimates and Projections (Sept. 2005), http://www.census.gov/prod/2005pubs/p25–1134.pdf. "By the year 2030, Arizona's population will nearly double, totaling more than 11 million residents. Arizona's metropolitan areas

concomitantly substantial water usage on the United States side of the border has caused a strain on the region's water resources, as well as on the relations between the two parties' governments. One example is a dispute over the water quality of the Colorado River. The 1944 Treaty[126] allocates a guaranteed yearly quantity to Mexico from the Colorado, Rio Grande and Tijuana Rivers. It does not, however, specifically address water quality.[127]

D *The Commission's Responsibilities and Jurisdiction*

The IBWC is responsible for enforcing the water and boundary treaties between the two states-parties and for settling disputes between them. The Commission's jurisdiction extends to the limotrophe, the line or segment of the Rio Grande River that serves as the international boundary.[128]

The IBWC's administrative obligations include:

(1) distributing the waters of the Colorado and Rio Grande Rivers between the two States-Parties;
(2) the preservation of the Colorado and Rio Grande Rivers as the international boundary;
(3) the demarcation of the transboundary border;
(4) the regulation and conservation of the Rio Grande's waters for use by the two states' mutual building, maintenance, operations and of the storage reservoirs and dams for the generation of hydroelectric energy at these dams;
(5) managing sanitation and other border water quality ills; and
(6) the protection of the terrain adjacent to the Rio Grande River from floods and floodway development.

The Mexican and United States commissioners meet at least weekly. They alternate the meeting place and are generally in daily contact. Both sections

will continue growing, ultimately leading to a merger of Phoenix and Tucson metropolitan areas." John Wright, Planning Arizona's Future Begins with Education, *Arizona Daily Star*, Mar. 4, 2008, http://arizonaea.org/pdfs/news/AEA_Budget_paper08.pdf. Note that due to the housing collapse the foregoing numbers have likely been reduced.
126 United States–Mexico Treaty for Utilization of Waters of the Colorado and Tijuana Rivers and of the Rio Grande, *ibid.*
127 This situation differs markedly from the Canadian–United States Boundary Waters Treaty of 1909, which in Art. IV provides that "[i]t is further agreed that the waters herein defined as *boundary waters and flowing across the boundary shall not be polluted on either side to the injury of health or property on the other."* Treaty Between the United States and Great Britain Relating to Boundary Waters between the United States and Canada, Art. IV, US–Gr. Brit., Jan. 11, 1909, 36 Stat. 2448.
128 1944 Water Treaty, Art. 2. "The jurisdiction of the Commission shall extend to the limitrophe parts of the Rio Grande (Rio Bravo) and the Colorado River, to the land boundary between the two countries..."

maintain their own engineering staffs, a secretary, and other personnel, as each commission requires, *e.g.*, legal advisers, expert engineers and hydrogeologists. These "personnel" have been called upon several times when the Commission was confronted with controversies concerning contaminates such as salt and sediment, water quality, as well as the delivery of water. The latter has been critical during times of drought[129] or floods.[130]

High levels of saline runoff and silt from irrigation have also greatly reduced the quality of the water that Mexico receives from the United States. Furthermore, in recent years droughts in the southwest have caused Mexico to fail to uphold its quota of water to be returned to the United States. This deficit has resulted in a water debt that was paid off in September 2005. However, the droughts in the second decade of the twenty-first century have crippled agriculture in Texas[131] and, the Southwest United States generally.[132]

These issues have been dealt with by the adoption of an instrument called a "Minute." Article 25 of the 1944 Treaty includes the concept of "Minutes."[133] They constitute decisions by the IBWC that implement broad provisions of the 1944 treaty and other international accords which often require specific binational understandings for planning, operation, and maintenance of joint projects, as well as, to outline how costs will be shared.[134] For example, to

---

[129] Priscila Mosqueda, On the Border, a Struggle over Water: As the Rio Grande runs dry, Texas and Mexico fight for a diminishing resource, *Tex. Observer*, June 10, 2013, https://www.texasobserver.org/on-the-border-a-struggle-over-water.

[130] National Weather Service, Record Flooding along the Rio Grande River in Laredo on July 8–9th 2010. (Last modified: Aug. 16, 2010), http://srh.noaa.gov/crp?n=riograndeflood.

[131] *See e.g.*, Texas A&M News & Information Services, *Texas Drought Officially Over*, Feb. 10, 2010, http://tamunews.tamu.edu/2010/02/18/texas-drought-officially-over.

> The Texas drought – one of the worst the state has ever experienced . . . 'began in fall 2007, as an unusually wet year for Texas suddenly turned dry . . . The lack of rainfall led to the first drought impacts in late fall and winter of 2007–2008. In the summer of 2008 much of the state experienced drought relief with two tropical cyclones, Dolly and Ike, but core areas of the drought in south-central and southern Texas missed out on much of the tropical rainfall. A second straight dry winter followed, and while spring rains shrunk the area of drought in Texas considerably, core areas of the drought continued to degrade.'

[132] Massachusetts Institute of Technology, Mission 2012: Clean Water, International Cooperation (undated), available at http://web.mit.edu/12.000/www/m2012/finalwebsite/problem/international.shtml.

[133] 1944 Treaty on Utilization, *ibid.* at p. 45, Art. 25.

[134] Art. 25 of the 1944 Treaty, *ibid.* requires that

> "[d]ecisions of the Commission shall be recorded in the form of Minutes done in duplicate in the English and Spanish languages, signed by each Commissioner and attested by the Secretaries . . . [They are] subject to the approval of the two Governments . . . signed by each Commissioner and attested by the Secretaries. [Once they] are approved by both Governments, the Minutes enter into force as binding obligations . . ."

date, the Minutes have addressed such issues as Boundary Mapping, Minutes 253, 268, 275; Colorado River Salinity, Minutes 218, 241, 242, 248, 284; and Rio Grande Pollution, Minutes 276, 288.[135] Similarly, the water use and allocation sections of the conventions and minutes were promulgated over a century of increasingly complex transboundary water disagreements over the Colorado, Rio Conchos,[136] and the Rio Grande (Rio Bravo del Norte in Mexico) Rivers.

In closing this section, I would like to emphasize that in negotiating the series of treaties and establishing the IBC/IBWC, Mexico and the United States, sought to create a binational body that would reconcile their differences by negotiation, only resolving them by adjudication as a last resort.

III THE INTERNATIONAL JOINT COMMISSION (CANADA/USA)

A *Introduction*

The North American Great Lakes[137] – Superior, Michigan, Huron, Erie, and Ontario – are the most prominent feature of the Canadian–United States transboundary border. Representing the largest surface freshwater system on earth, they contain roughly 21 percent of the world's fresh water supply and approximately 84 percent of North America's surface fresh water.[138] Only the polar ice caps – at least at this juncture – contain more fresh water. Today, over 30 million people live in the Great Lakes Basin – in excess of 30 percent of the Canadian population and roughly 10 percent of that of the

[135] The International Boundary & Water Commission United States and Mexico, *Minutes between the US and Mexican Sections of the IBWC by Project* (2013), http://www.ibwc.state .gov/Treaties_Minutes/Minutes_ByProject.html.

[136] The Rio Conchos has been included in the international environmental organization the World Wildlife Fund ("WWF") Global 200 Freshwater Ecoregions assessment. This assessment is, in fact, a list of globally designated bodies of water that contain exceptionally biodiverse environments that must be conserved. Moreover, the WWF's assessment rates the Rio Conchos as biologically distinctive and as "globally outstanding" and its conservation status as critically endangered, placing this river within an extremely high priority of requiring conservation care. *See e.g.*, Robin A. Abell, *et al.*, *Freshwater Ecoregions of North America: A Conservation Assessment* (2000) 93, 103, 188–189.

[137] United States Environmental Agency, *Great Lakes: Basic Information* (Last Updated Aug. 29, 2016), *available at* http://www.epa.gov/glnpo/basicinfo.html.

> The Great Lakes are the largest surface freshwater body on Earth, and are a major element of the North American geological and social fabric. The Lakes are equally situated between Canada and the United States of America and extend over 750 miles (1,200 kilometers) from east to west. These vast inland freshwater seas have for centuries supplied water for transport, drinking, agriculture, manufacturing, hydropower, recreation and numerous other uses. The daily activities of these people, from the water consumed to the waste returned, directly affect the Great Lakes environments.

[138] *Ibid.*

United States.[139] Jurisdiction for these Lakes is mutually allocated between the two federal governments, two Canadian provinces – Ontario and Quebec – and eight US states, including New York, Pennsylvania, Michigan, Ohio, Illinois, Indiana, Wisconsin, and Minnesota, as well as hundreds of local governments. (See Figure 6.2).

At present, practically 25 percent of Canada's agricultural production and over 7 percent of the United States' farm production are situated in the basin.[140] The everyday activities of these people, from the consumption of water to the waste returned, directly affect the Great Lakes' various ecological environments. Then, of course, there are the other lakes and rivers along the two states' common border, *e.g.*, the St. Mary's River, the Niagara River, and the Red River. Some of these rivers were and are the subjects of disputes over water allocation, between the USA and Canada.[141]

Although today, relations between Canada and the United States are rooted in comity and amiability, particularly, as concerns these transboundary waters that was not always the case. During the nineteenth century, as the population along the Canadian–US border swelled, and mining and other industries burgeoned around the Great Lakes region, the Saint Lawrence Seaway,[142] and along other waterways of their common border, the two countries were involved in a string of disputes over their joint sharing of several these transboundary water bodies. Many of these conflicts concerned water allocation issues as well as their pollution. This state of discord raged until 1909, when the two states executed the Boundary Waters Treaty.[143] That accord's aim was and continues to be, to provide rules and procedures designed for studying water-related issues along the common border and, to assist the two states in resolving disputes, principally those involving water quantity and water quality, along their common five-thousand-mile frontier.

The convention defines "boundary waters" as

> the waters from main shore to main shore of the lakes and rivers and connecting waterways, or the portions thereof, along which the international boundary between the United States and the Dominion of Canada passes,

---

[139] *Ibid.*   [140] *Ibid.*

[141] *See e.g.*, The Dispute over the St. Mary's River. Alberta Environment, Text, History and Geography of the 1909 Boundary Waters Treaty and the 1921 Order of the International Joint Commission: A supplement to Sharing the Waters (July 2004), *available at* http://environment.gov .ab.ca/info/library/7022.pdf.

[142] The St. Lawrence Seaway, *la Voie Maritime du Saint-Laurent*, in French, named after the Saint Lawrence River, is the common name for the 3,700-kilometer (2,300-mile) marine highway that runs between Canada and the United States, and empties into the Atlantic Ocean.

[143] Treaty Between the United States and Great Britain Relating to Boundary Waters Between the United States and Canada, US–UK, Jan. 11, 1909, 36 Stat. 2448 (1909). Signed at Washington January 1909. 36 Stat. at 2448 (1910). (Hereinafter "Boundary Water Treaty" or "BWT".)

including all bays, arms, and inlets thereof, but not including tributary waters which in their natural channels would flow into such lakes, rivers, and waterways, or waters flowing from such lakes, rivers, and waterways, or the waters of rivers flowing across the boundary.[144]

Note that the Boundary Waters Treaty exempts tributaries and distributaries. This fact is a conspicuous flaw in the accord, particularly regarding the non-Great Lakes Basin Rivers and lakes. Indeed, these other bodies of water have repeatedly received less attention in subsequent agreements and bilateral programs. That flaw aside, one of the Boundary Waters Treaty's far-reaching and prescient provisions, was many decades ahead of its time: Article IV of the accord states that the two states-parties agree "that the boundary waters *shall not be polluted on either side to the injury to health or property to the other side.*"[145] Another sweeping provision of the 1909 treaty was the creation of a joint body to carry out the accord's mandate.

B *The Commission: Composition and Mandate*

This joint body was named the International Joint Commission ("IJC").[146] It is composed of six members, known as Commissioners:[147] three nationals are appointed by Canada and three nationals are selected by the United States. The respective Commissioners are appointed as follows: in the United States by the President of the United States with the advice and consent of the US Senate, and in Canada by the Governor in Council on the advice of the Prime Minister. The IJC can be characterized as a *quasi*-adjudicative body, and may be employed for non-binding investigations as well as for binding arbitration,[148] albeit most of its work is investigative.

The IJC's role in averting and resolving transboundary environmental and water resource disputes, between the two states, is like that of the IBWC. Indeed, the IJC's success over the past 108 years reflects the foresight and sound judgment of the negotiators who developed the Boundary Waters Treaty, as well as the professionalism of the numerous Commissioners, who have executed its provisions over the decades. It may also reflect the fact that Canadians and Americans are culturally and ethnically similar, and therefore, are more attuned to each other's needs.

The IJC's mission statement declares that it "prevents and resolves disputes between the United States of America and Canada under the 1909 Boundary Waters Treaty and pursues the common good of both countries as an

[144] *Id.* at Preamble. 36 Stat. at 2449.
[145] *Ibid.* at Art. IV. (Emphasis supplied.)   [146] *Ibid.* at Art. III.
[147] For the current commissioners, *see* http://www.ijc.org/en/The_Commissioners.
[148] *The Trail Smelter Arbitration* (US v. Canada), 3 RIAA 1965 (1941).

independent and objective advisor to the two governments."[149] Furthermore, the IJC assists the two governments in avoiding transboundary disputes,[150] principally those concerning water and environmental issues, by embarking upon inquiries and analyses.[151] The IJC also provides an awareness of emerging transboundary matters to both governments.[152] However, in order for it to act, it must receive a "reference," pursuant to Article IX of the Treaty, from either or both countries.[153] These references involve both environmental and non-environmental disagreements.

1 The Referral Process

Since its founding in 1911 the IJC[154] has received over 120 referrals[155] from both governments.[156] A reference is an "application,"[157] by one or both

---

[149] The International Joint Commission, *Mission Statement, available at* http://www.ijc.org/en_/ IJC_Mandates (2016)

[150] The joint border includes some 150 lakes and rivers, which comprise ninety percent of the surface fresh water in North America, as well as over twenty percent of the earth's useable surface fresh water. *See generally,* Noah Hall, Bilateral Breakdown: US–Canada Pollution Disputes, 21 *Nat Resources & Envt* (2006) 18, 19.

[151] For example, United States Commissioner Allen Olson and Canadian Commissioner Jack Blaney used their "good offices" during 2008–09, on behalf of the IJC to seek a resolution to a problem between North Dakota and the Province of Manitoba over North Dakota's Devil's Lake. Interview with Allen I. Olson, IJC Commissioner, in Detroit, Mich. (Feb. 5, 2009).

[152] International Joint Commission, Canada and United States, 2003 Annual Report, *available at* http://www.ijc.org/php/publications/pdf/ID1555.pdf (last visited Aug. 29, 2015).

[153] Referrals to the IJC for non-binding recommendations may occur "whenever either the Government of the United States or the Government of the Dominion of Canada shall request." Boundary Waters Treaty, *ibid.,* art. IX. Due to the requirement of a reference, individuals cannot request the IJC to act. *Ibid.* Nevertheless, a solitary citizen or groups may petition their respective governments for a reference. *Ibid.,* art. X. However, such requests may, in some cases, raise delicate political questions.

[154] The United States members were appointed on March 9, 1911 and the Canadian members were appointed on November 10, 1911. The Commission's first organizational meeting, under Article XII of the treaty, took place in Washington, DC, January 10, 1912. The Commission's adoption and publication of its Rules of Procedure in accordance with Article XII occurred on February 2, 1912. Rules of Procedure of the International Joint Commission, Adopted Pursuant to Art. XII of the Treaty Between the United States and Great Britain, Signed January 11, 1909, Promulgated February 2, 1912, Washington, DC.

[155] Interview with Frank Bevacqua, Public Information Officer for the IJC's Section, Washington office, at 2401 Pennsylvania Avenue, N.W., Fourth Floor, Washington, DC 20440.

[156] Article IX states:

> The High Contracting Parties further agree that any other questions or matters of difference arising between them involving the rights, obligations, or interests of either in relation to the other or to the inhabitants of the other, along the common frontier between the United States and the Dominion of Canada, shall be referred from time to time to the International Joint Commission for examination and report, whenever either the Government of the United States or the Government of the Dominion of Canada shall request that such questions or matters of difference be so referred.

[157] *See* Rules of Procedure of the International Joint Commission, *ibid.* at 5, Applications.

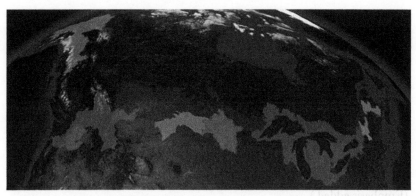

FIGURE 6.2 Map of the Water Bodies Under the Jurisdiction of the International Joint Commission, as Established by the Boundary Waters Treaty of 1909 (After the IJC, 2016, http://www.ijc.org/en)

governments, requesting that the IJC undertake an analysis or study on vital issues, about which the parties disagree or on which they seek the Commission's counsel. Additionally, "the IJC presently supervises 17 boards of control, investigative and surveillance boards, task forces and accredited officers who operate from the Gulf of Maine to the Pacific Northwest. Boards and task forces are established with equal US and Canadian membership. Like the Commission itself, members represent the agencies and institutions from which they come."[158]

2 The Commission's Procedural Rules

As required by the Boundary Waters Treaty's Article XII, the IJC promulgated its internal rules of procedure on February 12, 1912.[159] The Commission, also pursuant to the Treaty, has two permanent offices located in each of the states-parties' capitals: one in the District of Columbia, and the other in Ottawa. Each section has its own secretary, who is in complete charge of the respective office, subject of course to the orders of Commission.

The IJC's procedural rules provide for reference applications to abide by the following protocols, which for our purposes, provide in the pertinent section:

---

[158] Murray Clamens, The International Joint Commission: A Model for Inter-American Cooperation? (L'eau en Amérique du Nord: facteur de coopération, outil de développement ou enjeu de conflit?) (Sept. 1, 2005), available at http://vertigo.revues.org/1885.

[159] Rules of Procedure of the International Joint Commission, *ibid.* at 4, Permanent Offices 4.

Applications

6. In all cases to be submitted to the Commission ... the method of bringing such cases to the attention of the Commission and invoking its action shall be as follows:

(a) Where one or the other of the Governments on its own initiative seeks the approval of the Commission for the use, obstruction or diversion of waters with respect to which under Articles III and IV of the Treaty the approval of the Commission is required, it shall file with the Commission *an application setting forth as fully as may be necessary for the information of the Commission the facts upon which the application is based, and the nature of the order of approval desired.*[160]

(Emphasis added.)

Once an application is filed by a state-party, the secretary of the non-filing state is required to provide notice of the filing of the reference to her government as well as notice to the public.[161]

C The International Joint Commission's Investigative Powers

The IJC's ability to conduct in-depth studies of each referral, to hold public hearings,[162] and to afford parties the opportunity to submit amicus briefs,[163]

---

[160] Rules of Procedure of the International Joint Commission, *ibid.* at 5–6 (emphasis added to ¶ 6). Moreover, the filing of a reference necessitates that a party file:

> 7. One duplicate original and 25 copies of the application shall be filed with each of the secretaries, and there shall be filed with each of the secretaries such drawings, profiles, and plans of survey on tracing linen, and such specifications and maps, as may be necessary to illustrate clearly the matter of the application.
>
> 8. In cases where either of the respective Governments shall have authorized the use, obstruction or diversion of navigable waters, *all plans filed as aforesaid shall be accompanied with the approval thereof by the Government or proper department of the Government within whose jurisdiction such waters lie.*

Ibid. at ¶¶ 7–8. Emphasis added.

[161] *Ibid.* at ¶ 9. "As soon as practicable after an application is made as hereinbefore in rule 6 provided for, the secretary of the section of the Commission appointed by the other Government shall forthwith send to such Government a notice in writing that the application has been made and a copy thereof."

[162] *See, e.g.*, Mimi Larsen Becker, The International Joint Commission and Public Participation: Past Experiences, Present Challenges, Future Tasks, 33 *Nat Res J* (1993) 235, 237. *See also*, The Right Honourable Herb Gray, Proceedings of the Canada-United States Law Institute Conference on Understanding Each Other Across the Largest Undefended Border in History, 31 *Can-US L J* (2005) 287, 299 (observing that only when the public is "vigilant" can international agreements be successful).

[163] At a February 5, 2009, Conference on the One Hundredth Anniversary of the Boundary Waters Treaty, the author directed a question to then US Commissioner Allen I. Olson regarding a party's ability to submit an amicus brief. He responded that in his view the submission of amicus briefs is just another form of public participation.

provides it with powers that courts simply lack. The latter may only deal with narrow legal issues, and in the United States, when certain constitutional touchstones are met, such as when those issues raise a "case or controversy."[164] Other issues such as standing[165] are required by the courts of both countries.[166] In addition, once the Commission receives a reference, its jurisdiction is extremely broad, and unlike courts, it is unconstrained by constitutional provisions or legislative mandates.

Moreover, as noted above, the Commission may be utilized for binding arbitral adjudication. However, both countries must issue a reference to the IJC before it can entertain the enterprise of a binding arbitration. Such a reference, per the Treaty, requires the consent of the United States Senate on the one hand, and the consent of Canada's Governor General in Council, on the other.[167]

D *Consultation and Consensus Building*

The IJC and their association of consultants, counselors, and regulatory boards make every effort for consensus building as a means of reflecting the parties' common interests. In practice, most of the Commission's decisions are undertaken in this fashion, and if the respective board members are incapable of reaching a consensus, the IJC obliges them to submit issues to it for resolution.

1 Opportunity to be Heard: Providing a Forum for Public Participation

Article XII of the Boundary Waters Treaty requires that "[t]he Commission shall have [*sic*] power to administer oaths to witnesses, and to take evidence on oath whenever deemed necessary in any proceeding, or inquiry, or matter within its jurisdiction under this treaty, and all parties interested therein

---

[164] US CONST. art. III, § 2, cl. 1.

[165] Standing, or *locus standi*, is capacity of a party to bring suit in court. *See e.g.*, *Lujan v. Defenders of Wildlife*, 504 US 555 (1992). Standing law has its roots in Article III's case and controversy requirement. *Summers v. Earth Island Institute*, 555 US 488, 492–93 (2009).

[166] *Canadian Council of Churches v. Canada (Minister of Employment and Immigration)*, [1992] 1 SCR 236. ("It has been seen that when public interest standing is sought, consideration must be given to three aspects. First, is there a serious issue raised as to the invalidity of legislation in question? Second, has it been established that the plaintiff is directly affected by the legislation or if not does the plaintiff have a genuine interest in its validity? Third, is there another reasonable and effective way to bring the issue before the court?")

[167] Treaty Between the United States and Great Britain Relating to Boundary Waters between the United States and Canada, US–Gr. Brit., Jan. 11, 1909, 36 Stat. 2448, at Art. X.

shall be given convenient opportunity to be heard."[168] In practice, according to Murray Clamens, formerly of the IJC's Canadian Section, the Commission has always emphasized the importance of public participation and advice.[169]

The drafters of the Treaty built a framework, into the IJC, anticipating that the Commissioners would seek practical solutions that would be in the common interests of the two State-Parties and would take into account the interests of the affected public. To that end, each Commissioner "make[s] and subscribe[s] a solemn declaration in writing that he will faithfully and impartially perform the duties imposed upon him under [the treaty]."[170] Similarly, members of IJC boards are expected to serve the Commission in their personal and professional capacities. This allows board members to explore all options, which help promote the development of novel solutions and consensus.

Moreover, an important feature of the IJC's work – "some would say the most important"[171] – has been described as: (1) its elastic nature, that is so intrinsic to its mandate and process; and (2) its adaptability to the vagaries of the issues that can arise in addressing transboundary situations. Consequently, the flexibility inherent in the Boundary Waters Treaty has allowed the Commission to develop pioneering solutions when working with the two governments, in the interest of solving problems, and for soliciting public participation.

E Dispute Resolution

The IJC's role in preventing and resolving transboundary water and environmental disputes is a unique institutional attribute. Consequently, the Commission provides the state-parties with two vital tools: (1) a flexible set of mechanisms whose purpose is to assist the Commissioners in managing their liaison across the five-thousand-mile boundary region; and (2) the assurance that decision-making will reflect the shared system of principles and values recognized in the Boundary Waters Treaty.

1 Jurisdiction and Management

The IJC's jurisdiction is set forth in the 1909 Treaty, and extends to authorizing international water uses; limiting water flows so that shoreline properties can be protected; and granting applications for canals or dams in each of the

---

[168] Boundary Waters Treaty *ibid.* at Art. XII.   [169] Clamens *ibid.* at ¶ 13.
[170] Boundary Waters Treaty *ibid.* at Art. XII.   [171] Clamens, *ibid.*

countries that will affect flows; water quality; and water levels.[172] The particular water projects at issue when the Boundary Waters Treaty was ratified included those on the Niagara River in New York State, which would influence the water levels of Lake Erie, and on the Milk and St. Mary's rivers in Montana.[173] Finally, in fashioning the 1972 Great Lakes Agreement,[174] the Commission helped to transform an enormous likely source of discord into a model of bi-national transboundary water and environmental collaboration.

In conclusion, the IJC, like its southern sister, the IBWC, was established as a binational body that would largely address disputes between the two states, by non-adversary means. Nevertheless, since 1909, two *ad hoc* adjudications have taken place – the *Trail Smelter Arbitration* and the *Gut Dam Arbitration*. The Commission also provides advice and counsel to both governments on environmental and natural resource issues, including water allocation, including formulating the Great Lakes Water Quality Agreement of 1972, which was amended in 1978,[175] and updated in 2009,[176] and in 2012.[177]

Moreover, as part of its other counselling responsibilities the Commission is charged with the administration of numerous rivers, *e.g.*, the Souris River, which begins its flow in the Province of Saskatchewan, crosses the border into the state of North Dakota, and subsequently flows north back into Manitoba,[178] or, Red River, which flows into Devil's Lake, and has for

---

[172] Boundary Waters Treaty, *ibid.* at Arts. II, III, VIII, and XII.

[173] Boundary Waters Treaty, *ibid.*, at Art. VI: "The High Contracting Parties agree that the St. Mary and Milk Rivers and their tributaries (in the State of Montana and the Provinces of Alberta and Saskatchewan) are to be treated as one stream for the purposes of irrigation and power..."

[174] *See e.g.*, Great Lakes Water Quality Agreement of 1972, US–Can., Apr. 15, 1972, 23 UST 301; Great Lakes Water Quality Agreement of 1978, US–Can., Nov. 22, 1978, 30 UST 1384; Protocol Between the United States of America and Canada, Amending the Agreement of November 22, 1978, US–Can., Nov. 18, 1987, TIAS No. 11551.

[175] *See e.g.*, International Joint Commission, Treaties and Agreements: About the Great Lakes Water Quality Agreement (Last updated, Dec. 14, 2009), http://www.ijc.org/rel/agree/quality .html.

[176] *USA, Canada to Modernize Great Lakes Water Quality Pact*, Environment News Service June 15, 2009, *available at* http://www.ens-newswire.com/ens/jun2009/2009-06-15-01.html.

[177] Great Lakes Water Quality Agreement – 2012 Protocol (2016), *available at* http://www.ijc.org/ en_/Great_Lakes_Water_Quality.

[178] International Joint Commission, International Souris River Board, *Welcome, Background Information: The Souris River Basin* (last updated, December 14, 2009), http://www.ijc .org/conseil_board/souris_river/en/souris_home_accueil.htm. (The International Souris River Board also works "[t]o ensure a more ecosystemic approach to transboundary water issues and to achieve operational efficiencies in the conduct of IJC responsibilities, the IJC has combined the ongoing responsibilities of the International Souris River Board of Control and

several years diverted toxic chemicals from North Dakota into Manitoba's Lake Winnipeg.[179] Finally, the IJC also manages a range of programs and, develops procedures designed to enhance the water quality in the water bodies across the 8,851-kilometer (5,500-mile) frontier.

IV THE NORTH AMERICAN FREE TRADE AGREEMENT (NAFTA)

A *Introduction*

The North American Free Trade Agreement *(hereinafter* "NAFTA")[180] is a trilateral convention entered into between the governments of Canada, the United Mexican States and the United States of America. The agreement, which entered into force on January 1, 1994,[181] created a multilateral trading bloc in North America. NAFTA has two supplemental components, the North American Agreement on Environmental Cooperation *(hereinafter* "NAAEC")[182] and the North American Agreement on Labor Cooperation *(hereinafter* "NAALC"). The focus here will be on NAFTA's Chapter 11, its investor–state dispute resolution mechanism. Much has been written about NAFTA's, history,[183] negotiations,[184] political economy,[185] and the Agreement's environmental negotiations.[186] This section departs from these previous works; its focus is on the agreement's dispute resolution provisions.

the Souris River aspects of the International Souris-Red Rivers Engineering Board mandates into the International Souris River Board." *Ibid.*)

[179] Duncan B. Hollis, Disaggregating Devils Lake: Can Non-State Actors, Hegemony, or Principal–Agent Theory Explain the Boundary Waters Treaty? http://ssrn.com/abstract=976829.

[180] Can–Mex–US, 32 I.L.M. 289 (1993). The Agreement is also known in Spanish as the Tratado de Libre Comercio de América del Norte, and in French as Accord de libre-échange Nord-Américain.

[181] NAFTA supplanted the Canada-United States Free Trade Agreement between the USA and Canada, which was finalized in October of 1987 and entered into force on October 4, 1988.

[182] North American Agreement on Environmental Cooperation, Sept. 14, 1993, 32 I.L.M. 1480.

[183] *See generally,* Kevin Gallagher, *Free Trade and The Environment: Mexico, NAFTA, and Beyond* (2004); Alexandre Kiss, Dinah Shelton & Kanami Ishibashi (eds.), *Economic Globalization and Compliance With International Environmental Agreements* (2003); Pierre-Marc Johnson & André Beaulieu, *The Environment and NAFTA: Understanding and Implementing the New Continental Law* (1996).

[184] John R. MacArthur, The Selling of Free Trade: NAFTA, Washington and the Subversion of American Democracy (2001).

[185] Daniel C. Esty, Making Trade and Environmental Policies Work Together: Lessons from NAFTA, 49 *Aussenswirtshaft* (1994) 59; John J. Audley, *Green Politics and Global Trade: NAFTA and the Future of Environmental Politics* (1997); I. M. Destler & Peter J. Balint, *The New Politics of American Trade: Trade Labor and the Environment* (Policy Analyses in International Economics) (1999).

[186] Gallagher *ibid.*; Carolyn L. Deere and Daniel C. Esty (eds.), Greening the Americas: NAFTA's Lessons for Hemispheric Trade (2002).

B *Background*

1 Adjudicating NAFTA

NAFTA's Chapter 11 (investor–state) disputes are generally adjudicated at the World Bank's International Centre for Settlement of Investment Disputes ("ICSID"), in Washington, DC. The adjudications are before arbitral tribunals, consisting of three arbitrators, and are governed by ICSID's rules,[187] or at the discretion of the parties, its additional facility rules, or the rules of the United Nations Commission on International Trade Law ("UNCITRAL").[188] The next section addresses NAFTA's dispute resolution provisions. However, prior to dealing directly with these provisions I focus on the critical issue of discovery.

2 Discovery Issues

From a litigation perspective NAFTA has several problems, one of which is discovery. Discovery problems also routinely arise in municipal courts. However, in the domestic legal arena courts can compel or sanction the litigants to produce documents, employing the hammer of sanctions. Alternatively, NAFTA tribunals do not have the jurisdiction to compel parties to exchange discovery. Moreover, neither ICSID's nor UNCITRAL's rules have provisions that provide for sanctions against a party that does not comply with a discovery order. Furthermore, my research was unable to identify any cases where a panel sanctioned a party for non-compliance with a discovery order. NAFTA non-compliance may be solely subject to trade sanctions imposed by the prevailing States-Party.

For example, in *United Parcel Service of America Inc.* v. *Government of Canada*, UPS asserted that the Canadian government breached its NAFTA obligations.[189] The Claimant also argued that Canada was subsidizing the

---

[187] *See generally*, International Centre for Settlement of Investment Disputes, ICSID Convention, Regulations and Rules (Apr. 2006), https://icsid.worldbank.org/ICSID/StaticFiles/basicdoc/CRR_English-final.pdf; *see also*, ICSID Rules of Procedure for Arbitration Proceedings (Arbitration Rules) 4 *Berkley J Int'l L* (1986) 362.

[188] *See generally*, UNCITRAL, International Commercial Arbitration & Conciliation, (2014), http://www.uncitral.org/uncitral/uncitral_texts/arbitration.html. *See also*, David Caron and Lee M. Caplan, *The UNCITRAL Arbitration Rules: A Commentary (Oxford Commentaries on International Law)* (2013).

[189] *United Parcel Serv. of Am., Inc.* v. *Canada*, ICSID (W. Bank), Award on the Merits in an Arbitration under Chapter 11 of the North American Free Trade Agreement, at P 1 (issued May 24, 2007 and provided to the parties on June 11, 2007), available at http://www.international.gc.ca/trade-agreements-accords-commerciaux/assets/pdfs/MeritsAward24May2007.pdf.

Canada Post Corporation ("Canada Post") and Purolator Courier Ltd. ("Puro-lator") (a subsidiary of Canada Post) in the non-monopoly courier market, which produced a discriminatory result against UPS, as a consequence American nationality.[190] During the discovery phase of the NAFTA proceeding UPS was unsuccessful in causing Canada to reveal certain distinct details and characteristics of the latter's contractual connection with Canada Post. UPS's sole remedy therefore was to file suit in Canada's municipal courts. That proceeding initiated before the Federal Court of Canada,[191] sought relief under Canada's municipal laws.[192]

Similarly, in *Glamis Gold, Ltd.* v. *United States*,[193] another arbitration under NAFTA's Chapter 11, employing the UNCITRAL's arbitration rules, "the Tribunal [stated that it] has endeavoured to ensure that any documents which it compels a Party to produce should be of a 'narrow and specific' nature, 'reasonably believed to exist', and likely 'material to the outcome of the case.'"[194] However, because the panel held that the document request was premature, it did not address the sanctions issue.[195] These flaws in NAFTA's procedural rules likely have negative impacts during the litigation of investor–state dispute.

C NAFTA's Dispute Resolution Provisions

NAFTA is composed of eight parts, consisting of twenty-two chapters and eight annexes. These include three formal dispute settlement procedures, each addressing a different trade issue. As noted earlier, the focus here is on Chapter 11, which concerns investments in a Party's territory, by external parties.

NAFTA's Chapter 11, denominated "Investment," incorporates "Part Five: Investment, Services and Related Matters" is the dispute resolution provision for Investor–State disputes. It contains three sections. Section B, comprising Articles 1115–1138 is devoted solely to the claims of investors and the "Settlement of Disputes between a Party and an Investor of Another Party." It also

---

[190] *Ibid.* at 11–17.
[191] *Dussault* v. *Can. Customs and Revenue Agency*, [2003] F.C. 973 (Can. Fed. Ct.), *available at* http://decisions.fct-cf.gc.ca/en/2003/2003fc973/2003fc973.html.
[192] *Ibid.* at ¶ 1. The claims were brought "under section 41 of the *Access to Information Act*, R.S.C. 1985, c. A-1 ("Act").
[193] *See* Documents from *Glamis Gold, Ltd.* v. *United States*, http://www.state.gov/s/l/c10986.htm. Panel Decision on Objections to Document Production (July 20, 2005), http://www.state.gov/documents/organization/54365.pdf.
[194] *Ibid.* at ¶ 10.
[195] *Ibid.* at ¶ 34 ("After reviewing the documents made available to it by the Claimant, the Respondent will either be able to renew its broad request or narrowly tailor its request to compel production of documents that are likely material to the outcome of this case.").

makes a pioneering contribution to the dispute settlement regime by providing individuals, corporate entities and other investors with standing to sue
member states, *i.e.*, direct access to an international dispute settlement mechanism, regardless of the position of their national government, a characteristic
common to bilateral investment treaties (BITs).

According to the NAFTA's Secretariat, Chapter 11 "establishes a mechanism for the settlement of investment disputes that assures both equal treatment among investors of the Parties to the Agreement in accordance with
the principle of international reciprocity and due process before an impartial
tribunal."[196] Accordingly, a NAFTA investor who alleges that a host government has breached its investment obligations under Chapter 11 may, at its
option, have recourse to a number of arbitral mechanisms, (under ICSID's
and UNCITRAL Rules. Alternatively, the investor may choose remedies available in the host country's domestic courts.

An important feature of the Chapter 11 arbitral provisions is the enforceabil-
ity in domestic courts of final awards issued by arbitration tribunals.[197] Pursuant to the Agreement, investors have the option of filing their claims against
States-Parties in four separate venues. Thus, the NAFTA ICSID mechanism
is not the sole adjudicative device for resolving disputes, as is the case with
the World Trade Organization. Nevertheless, an investor who seeks to file a
claim in a municipal forum must do so within the statute of limitations of
three years,[198] from the date when the investor first learned or should have
learned of an alleged breach, and within the same number of years that she
gained knowledge that a loss or damage was incurred.[199]

For example, in *The Loewen Group, Inc. v. United States*,[200] the Investor,
Loewen, was free to file a claim under Chapter 11 immediately. Nonetheless,
it was not required to do so. Indeed, the language of Article 1121 suggests that
"an investor may challenge a court judgment or other 'measure' in domestic
court." *See* Art. 1121(1) (b). However, the investor must waive "their right to initiate or continue before any administrative tribunal or court under the law of
any Party, or other dispute settlement procedure,"[201] in order to continue those

---

[196] NAFTA Secretariat, Legal Texts *ibid.* at Art. 1115.
[197] NAFTA Secretariat, *ibid.* at *Overview of the Dispute Settlement Provisions Chapter 11, available at* http://www.nafta-sec-alena.org/en/view.aspx?x=226.
[198] NAFTA Secretariat *ibid.* at Art. 1116 (2). Art. 1116(2) is the specific provision that addresses
questions of jurisdiction.
[199] *Ibid.* at Art. 1116.2, Claim by an Investor of a Party on Its Own Behalf.
[200] *The Loewen Group, Inc. v. United States*, (ICSID Case No. ARB(AF)/98/3), Decision on
Hearing of Respondent's Objection to Competence and Jurisdiction 9–16 (Jan. 5, 2001).
[201] NAFTA, Art. 1121(1)(b).

proceedings once it files a NAFTA claim.[202] In reviewing the *The Loewen Group* litigation, Professor William Dodge suggests that in order for the arbitral panel to maintain jurisdiction over a case "Chapter 11 contains a statute of limitations provision requiring a foreign investor to file its claim within three years of the alleged breach and loss . . . But this means Loewen had the option of pursuing appeals in the United States court system for up to three years without foregoing its right to seek redress under NAFTA."[203]

On the other hand, in *Mondev International, Ltd.* v. *United States* the tribunal suggested that the investor's claims would have been time-barred by the three-year time limitation.[204] The panel also observed that pursuant to Article 1116(2): "An investor may not make a claim if more than three years have elapsed from the date on which the investor first acquired, or should have first acquired, knowledge of the alleged breach and knowledge that the investor has incurred loss or damage."[205]

In this regard, Dodge has observed that

> [t]here are several aspects of Chapter 11, however, that will tend to discourage a foreign investor from exhausting its domestic appeals. First, Chapter 11 does not expressly toll its three-year statute of limitations while those appeals are exhausted. [Footnote omitted]. A foreign investor might therefore expend substantial time and resources pursuing its domestic appeals, only to be forced to abandon either of those appeals or its potential Chapter 11 claim if the appellate process takes more than three years.[206]

He also argues that Chapter 11 implicitly tolls its statute of limitations while an investor exhausts its domestic remedies. The three-year period set forth in Articles 1116 (2) and 1117 (2) does not begin running until the investor or enterprise acquired, or should have acquired, knowledge "of the alleged breach and knowledge that the investor [or enterprise] has incurred loss or

[202] William S. Dodge, *Loewen Group, Inc.* v. *United States: Trials and Errors Under NAFTA Chapter Eleven*, 52 *DePaul L R.* (2002) 563, 567-68.

[203] *Ibid.* at 568. *See* NAFTA Art. 1116(2), Canada–Mexico–United States: North American Free Trade Agreement, 32 ILM 289 (1993) (stating that "[a]n investor may not make a claim if more than three years have elapsed from the date on which the investor first acquired, or should have first acquired, knowledge of the alleged breach and knowledge that the investor has incurred loss or damage.")

[204] *Mondev International Ltd.* v. *United States of America*, Case No. ARB (AF)/99/2, Award (Oct. 11, 2002), 42 ILM 811 (2003) at paras. 57–75.

[205] NAFTA Art. 1116(2) *ibid.* For a good discussion regarding Art. 1162, *see* Bradford K. Gathright, Comment, *Step in the Wrong Direction: The Loewen Finality Requirement and the Local Remedies Rule in NAFTA Chapter Eleven*, 54 *Emory L J* (2005) 1093, 1133.

[206] Dodge *ibid.* at 568.

damage."[207] To date, no panel has adopted Dodge's proposal. Nevertheless, the disputing parties "should first attempt to settle a claim through consultation or negotiation."[208]

1 Submission to Arbitration

Where the disputing parties are unable to settle their claim via consultation or negotiation the investor must deliver to the State-Party a written notice of its intention to tender a request for arbitration, at least 90 days prior to submitting the claim.[209] The notice must include the name and address of the disputing investor. However, where the claim is made pursuant to Article 1117, "Claim by an Investor of a Party on Behalf of an Enterprise," the enterprise's name and address must be set forth,[210] and it must include which provisions are alleged to have been breached and whatever other provisions are relevant to the claim;[211] the issues and facts;[212] and the relief as well as the damages sought.[213]

a NAFTA'S NOTICE PROVISION

NAFTA's notice provision is contained in Article 1119. In order, for ICSID to maintain jurisdiction, the filing party must meet the requirements contained in Article 1119 (2). That provision declares that the notice of a party's intention to submit a claim for arbitration, must mention, which NAFTA provisions are alleged to have been breached, as well as any relevant procedures. Moreover, a disputing investor may submit its claim for arbitration only six months after the occurrence complained of.[214] Finally, a filing party is required to meet the conditions precedent cited in Article 1121.[215]

That condition requires that: (1) the complaining investor must agree to be bound by NAFTA's arbitration procedures; and (2) that the investor is required to waive her right to either commence or maintain any action at

---

[207] *See e.g.*, *United Parcel Serv. of Am., Inc.* v. *Canada ibid.* In addition, once commentator has observed that "Given the nature of disputes under NAFTA, it would seem reasonable to predict that the cause of delay in filing a claim would not (and *should* not) elicit sympathy from tribunals."

[208] *Ibid.* at NAFTA Article 1118: Settlement of a Claim through Consultation and Negotiation.

[209] *Ibid.* at Art. 1119: Notice of Intent to Submit a Claim to Arbitration.

[210] *Ibid.* at (a).   [211] *Ibid.* at (b).   [212] *Ibid.* at (c).   [213] *Ibid.* at (d).

[214] NAFTA Article 1120: "Submission of a Claim to Arbitration

> 1. Except as provided in Annex 1120.1, and provided that six months have elapsed since the events giving rise to a claim, a disputing investor may submit the claim to arbitration."

[215] Article 1121. *See also, Waste Management, Inc.* v. *United Mexican States* (ICSID Case No. ARB(AF)/00/3), Decision on Mexico's Preliminary Objection, June 26, 2002, at ¶ 8.

law under that Party's home courts or any other dispute settlement forum.[216] The investor, moreover, may not employ any dispute settlement procedures that have not been incorporated into NAFTA.[217] However, an investor may file a claim or employ in her "home's" municipal courts the laws of equity, *i.e.*, actions for injunctive, declaratory or other extraordinary relief, which does not address or involve the recompense of damages. The foregoing also applies to investors who claim a loss or damage to a corporate interest in an enterprise of another Party that the investor owns or controls either directly or indirectly.[218]

For example, in *Waste Management, Inc. v. United Mexican States*,[219] NAFTA's arbitration regime applied where the investor and the enterprise: (1) consented to arbitration in accordance with the procedures set out in the NAFTA; and (2) waived their rights to commence or maintain litigation regarding that claim before any dispute settlement regime. These fora included the respective Parties' municipal courts, other tribunals, or laws and procedures that govern those fora.[220] Finally, the disputing state-party must be served by the contesting investor with a written agreement and waiver, which is compulsory pursuant to Arts. 1116 and 1117.[221]

2 The Mechanics of Filing a Claim

Initially, each disputing party is required to submit its Consent to Arbitration, as per Art. 1122.[222] The number of arbitrators, usually three, and the method of their appointment are governed by Art. 1123, unless the disputing parties agree to a different number. The disputing investor and the disputing state-party, are each to appoint one arbitrator and the third, who is to be the president of the panel, is to be selected by agreement of the two parties.[223] Where a Party fails to appoint an arbitrator or the disputing parties are unable to agree on a presiding arbitrator, NAFTA's provides several possibilities, pursuant to Art. 1124.

---

[216] *Ibid.* at ¶ 2. (Citing *Waste Management, Inc. v. United Mexican States*, Arbitral Award of 2 June 2000, 40 ILM 56, 69–70 (2001); also in 15 ICSID Review-Foreign Investment L J (2000) 211.

[217] NAFTA Secretariat Legal Text, *ibid.* at Art. 1121.1 (a)-(c), Conditions Precedent to Submission of a Claim to Arbitration.

[218] *Ibid.*   [219] Arbitral Award of 2 June 2000, 40 ILM 56, 69–70 (2001).   [220] *Ibid.*

[221] *Mondev International Ltd., ibid.* at ¶10. ("As required by NAFTA Article 1119, the Claimant notified the Respondent on 6 May 1999 of its intention to submit its dispute with the United States to arbitration under Section B of Chapter 11 of NAFTA.")

[222] *Ibid.* at Art. 1122.1: Consent to Arbitration.

[223] *Ibid.* at NAFTA Art. 1123 (emphasis added).

Choice of Venue is governed by prescribed rules.[224] Likewise, once the tribunal is seated it may need to decide issues of law. Art. 1131, "Governing Law," sets forth the choice of law selection, where the parties cannot agree as to what law applies. NAFTA also provides for *interim measures*. The question of when these apply is governed by Art. 1134. A NAFTA tribunal may, at its discretion, order an interim measure of protection, to safeguard the rights of a disputing party, "or to ensure that the Tribunal's jurisdiction is made fully effective, including an order to preserve evidence in the possession or control of a disputing party or to protect the Tribunal's jurisdiction."[225]

D Criticism of NAFTA's Chapter 11

"Chapter 11, as it has operated, has been one of the most controversial of NAFTA's provisions. It has taken all three governments and their citizens by surprise with how it has been used."[226] The detractors argue that Chapter 11 has not been utilized, as intended, "to protect property rights against government measures 'tantamount to expropriation' but has *legalized a peculiar American conception of property rights*, giving foreign corporations rights not available to nationals, and has also been used to attack a wide array of national government regulation aimed at the social, environmental and other public goods."[227]

In conclusion, NAFTA's investor–state dispute resolution system has established a rule-based system that has yielded several norms. However, that system, and NAFTA itself, have not been free of criticism and rebuke. It is not clear to this author whether the Agreement's mandate providers would be satisfied with how Chapter 11's dispute resolution system has and is functioning. However, the three member-states have not moved to amend it. But the lack of enhancement of NAFTA is not surprising, since most treaties are not amended or rewritten.

[224] *Ibid.* at NAFTA Article 1130, Place of Arbitration.
[225] NAFTA Convention, Chapter 11, *ibid.* at Art. 1134, Interim Measures of Protection.
[226] John Kirton, *NAFTA* Dispute Settlement Mechanisms: An Overview, Paper prepared for an Experts Workshop on *"NAFTA and its Implications for ASEAN's Free Trade Area,"* Asian Inst., Munk Centre for International Studies, Toronto, Canada (May 27, 2004).
[227] *Ibid.* (Emphasis added.)

7

Factors Used in Analyzing Effectiveness

I INTRODUCTION

Direct measurement of the effectiveness of international courts and tribunals, including those assessed here, is difficult at best. This fact has been established by Yuval Shany, in his recent book, *Assessing the Effectiveness of International Courts.*[1] Therefore, the determination of the effectiveness of an adjudicative body must be done via proxies.

Prior to discussing and selecting proxies, one must confront a more fundamental issue: "When can adjudication be said to be 'effective'?"[2] This question is particularly compelling when measuring the effectiveness of individual courts or tribunals that adjudicate transboundary water disputes. Since the issues raised by the effectiveness question rapidly becomes enmeshed with bigger jurisprudential questions that include "the nature of law and the sources of compliance."[3] Moreover, in seeking to define a tribunal's effectiveness one is required to ask, "effective for what purpose?"[4]

Indeed, such an inquiry is contingent upon an erstwhile perception of what the specific role or purpose of a particular court or tribunal is, within specific legal systems.[5] For example, such tasks may incorporate "dispute resolution, 'social control'...lawmaking...articulating social and political ideals...and securing social change."[6] All-important undertakings when applied to the adjudication of transboundary water disputes. However, each of these tasks may conflict with one or more of the others, and may produce different measures of "effectiveness."[7] For instance, since transboundary water disputes are

---

[1] Yuval Shany, *Assessing the Effectiveness of International Courts* (2014) (Oxford Univ. Press, Oxford).
[2] Laurence R. Helfer & Anne-Marie Slaughter, Toward a Theory of Effective Supranational Adjudication, 107 *Yale L J* (1997) 273, 282.
[3] *Ibid.*   [4] *Ibid.*   [5] *Ibid.*   [6] *Ibid.*   [7] *Ibid.*

resolved by recourse to equitable principles,[8] attempting to assess their overall normative impact or, measuring a court's effectiveness may prove to be difficult or may provide inconclusive results because of the case-by-case adjudication. How then can we characterize court and tribunal effectiveness within the universe of the adjudicatory process?

Laurence Helfer & Anne-Marie Slaughter propose a very stripped-down or basic definition of effective adjudication. For them, "the effectiveness of a particular court [or tribunal] rests on its power to compel a party to a dispute to defend against a plaintiff's complaint and to comply with the resulting judgment. This power [they note] is the characteristic that typically distinguishes courts from other dispute resolvers such as go-betweens, mediators, and arbitrators."[9] Indeed, under Helfer's & Slaughter's rubric every adjudicative body analyzed here is "effective" since the respondent in each case defended the claims against it.

Alternatively, Yuval Shany argues that effectiveness for the majority of international courts and tribunals is measured by evaluating whether these adjudicative bodies satisfy four goals established for them by their mandate providers, i.e., those who created them. These objectives are: (1) promoting compliance with the prevailing international norms; (2) resolving disputes; (3) supporting applicable international regimes; and (4) legitimizing the legal regime and its norms.[10] Employing these characteristics, legitimacy may correspondingly serve to reinforce other goals and assist an international court or tribunal in fulfilling them. Furthermore, these factors demonstrate that courts must pursue or, assume trade-offs between diverse goals.[11] In fact, we can state with certainty at this juncture, that each of the adjudicative bodies assayed herein, except for the IBC/*Chamizal Dispute*, have met Shany's first two objectives and most likely his third. I will return to this subject below, during the assessment section.

One of the key measures or proxies for the effectiveness of international courts and tribunals is their power to compel parties to appear before them and to abide by their judgments or awards, particularly when participation

---

[8] *See e.g., Kansas v. Colorado*, 206 US 47 (1907). Equity has also been used in boundary delimitation cases. See e.g., *Delimitation of Maritime Boundary in Gulf of Maine Area* (Can/US), 1984 I.C.J. 246, 278. ("The Chamber is, furthermore, convinced for the purposes of such a delimitation operation as is here required, international law, as will be shown below, does no more than lay down in general that equitable criteria are to be applied . . . "). (Emphasis added.)

[9] Helfer & Slaughter, *ibid.* at 283.

[10] Yuval Shany, Assessing the Effectiveness of International Courts – A Goal-Based Approach, 106 *AJIL* (2012) 225, 244–47.

[11] *Ibid.* at 246.

is mandatory. Nevertheless, it should be clear that although compliance and questions of effectiveness are distinct from one another they are still linked. That is, these two characteristics or proxies do not share a one to one relationship. For example, international legal regimes could have high rates of compliance with low and ineffectual standards.[12] Yuval Shany has suggested that in some cases this type of court or tribunal is a "low aiming" one, *i.e.*, it issues "minimalist remedies [that] may generate a high level of compliance but have little impact on the state of the world."[13] None of the courts or tribunals analyzed here appears to fit the characterization of a "low aiming" adjudicative body. Therefore, that measure is not utilized here as a proxy for effectiveness. However, the issue of effectiveness also raises questions regarding the legitimacy of an international court's or tribunal's power – another proxy – which is discussed next.

A Court and Tribunal Legitimacy

Laurence Helfer and Anne-Marie Slaughter posit that legitimacy is a notion or characteristic that has no clear-cut or objective meaning; rather, it is a concept that is more predisposed to a subjective definition than an objective one. These two authors note that there are several articulations of the bases of judicial legitimacy. They include the following characteristics, that are associated with the structural and procedural attributes of a court's or tribunal's authority: "impartiality; principled decisionmaking; reasoned decisionmaking ... consistency of judicial decisions over time ... and provision of a meaningful opportunity for litigants to be heard."[14] Although the foregoing list is not exhaustive, it does provide a general idea of the "judicial attributes that undergird the 'compliance pull' of judicial decisions."[15] Similarly, Shai Dothan has observed that international courts strive to enhance their legitimacy, *i.e.*, they seek to have their judgments perceived as just, correct and unbiased, by the international community.[16]

A more nuanced view of legitimacy is expressed by Thomas Franck, who contended that it is "that quality of a rule which derives from a perception on the part of those to whom it is addressed that it has come into being in

---

[12] *See e.g.*, Par Engstrom, Effectiveness of International and Regional Human Rights Regimes, *The Int'l Studies Encyclopedia* (Robert A. Denemark ed., 2010) 5.

[13] Shany *ibid.* at 227.   [14] *Ibid.* at 284.   [15] *Ibid.*

[16] Shai Dothan, How International Courts Enhance their Legitimacy, 14 *Theoretical Inquiries L* (2013) 455, 456 ("International courts try to enhance their legitimacy and behave strategically to pursue this goal. They seek legitimacy both for its own sake and as a way to fulfill other goals, such as improving compliance with their judgments.")

accordance with the right process."[17] But there are also other elements of legitimacy. For example, any democratic governmental institution, particularly a court, seeks to protect its institution, authority, and authenticity, as well as abiding by its mandate. A court's legitimacy is therefore both its foundation stone and its stock and trade.

Finally, Andreas Follesdal has coined the term "social legitimacy,"[18] defined as a measure of the public's support for the judiciary, and which hinges upon whether the judiciary is worthy of the public's support, *i.e.*, "does the judiciary command general public belief that it has *rightful authority* to secure general *compliance?*"[19] Moreover, he suggests that there have been and continue to be challenges to the legal legitimacy of some international courts and tribunals, and some of their judgments.[20] Follesdal then asks two pointed questions: (1) does a given court or tribunal have the legal authority or jurisdiction that it claims over a specific issue(s)? and (2) are a court's or tribunal's judgments in keeping with the proper principles of the law?[21]

Each court and tribunal assessed herein fits within the Helfer & Slaughter's, Dothan's, Franck's, and Follesdal's proxies or factors, that is: each is impartial; each makes or provides principled, consistent, and reasoned decisions that are perceived as just, fair, correct, and unbiased. Additionally, each court or tribunal provides the parties with procedural due process, including the opportunity to be heard. The courts and tribunals assessed here also reinforce Follesdal's two requirements. First, they possess the legal authority over a specific issue or claim presented to them – since the jurisdiction of the adjudicative bodies assessed here was not challenged by any party; and second, in every case the judgments or awards of the respective courts and tribunals was in keeping with the proper principles of law.[22]

Another attribute of legitimacy is a key attribute of international courts and tribunals: that they are institutions that issue judgments and awards, but rely

---

[17] Thomas M. Franck, Legitimacy in the International System, 82 *AJIL* (1988) 705, 706.
[18] Andreas Follesdal, The Legitimacy Deficits of the Human Rights Judiciary: Elements and Implications of a Normative Theory, 14 *Theoretical Inquiries L* (2013) 339, 345.
[19] *Ibid.*   [20] *Ibid.*   [21] *Ibid.*
[22] One issue that is not addressed herein, but that may have some implications for measuring effectiveness, is the political environment that courts and tribunals find themselves in. For example, Ariel Dulitzky has pointed out with regards to the Inter-American Commission on Human Rights (*hereinafter* IACHR) that "[a]ny attempt to comprehend the functioning of the Commission's procedure must therefore take into account the hostile environment in which it operates. As such, the context in which the Commission operates *supports a goal-based approach to measure its effectiveness as it demonstrates the constraints that hinder international adjudicatory bodies in their particular political and institutional environment.* Ariel Dulitzky, Too Little, Too Late: The Pace of Adjudication of the Inter-American Commission on Human Rights, 35 *Loy. L.A. Int'l & Comp L R* (2013) 131, 207. (Emphasis added.)

on the goodwill of the parties and political pressures, to enforce those rulings, because they lack the means of enforcing them. Moreover, international courts and tribunals serve broad audiences, with more varied stakeholders and constituencies than those of national tribunals. Consequently, they are more likely to issue rulings that are unpredictable, which may produce serious repercussions.[23] Accordingly, if litigants file their disputes and adhere to a given court or tribunal's judgment or award, they likely find that institution to be legitimate.

International adjudicative bodies can also make lasting and systemic contributions to the development of international law and to the legitimacy of international governance, which may display itself in state enhanced compliance.[24] Indeed, Andrew Guzman has argued that one of the reasons for founding international tribunals is that they may develop or illuminate the substantive rules of international law.[25]

B *Analyzing the Relationship between Effectiveness and Usage Rates*

One proxy for measuring effectiveness that has been utilized by many scholars who study international courts and tribunals is the usage rate of a court or tribunal. Prior to utilizing this proxy in assessing the courts and tribunals selected for this study, I want to expand on the discussion in Chapter 2, where I observed that Yuval Shany suggests that "usage rates are . . . a poor proxy for judicial effectiveness for two . . . reasons." The first is the fact that disputing parties limit their use of adjudication, may simply reflect their perception that the court or tribunal in question is either perceived as useless in resolving their dispute, *e.g.*, the choice by India and Pakistan to employ the Permanent Court of Arbitration rather than the ICJ in their dispute over the *Indus Waters Kishenganga* dispute. Alternatively, adjudication is sometimes not completed, because the court or tribunal casts a "long shadow," *i.e.*, it provokes parties to settle their dispute out of court, which avoids adjudication altogether, *e.g.*, the *Gut Dam Arbitration*. Conversely, a high usage rate of an adjudicating body, may point to legal stability. Nevertheless, an adjudicatory body that lacks judgment or award predictability, *e.g.*, the ICJ's conflicting delimitation judgments, during the 1980s, will generally not be utilized.

[23] *See e.g.*, Yonatan Lupu, International Judicial Legitimacy: Lessons from National Courts, 14 *Theoretical Inquiries L* 2103 (437).

[24] Shany, *ibid.* at 229.

[25] Andrew T. Guzman, International Tribunals: A Rational Choice Analysis, 157 *U Pa L R* (2008) 171.

The latter would certainly have very little impact on State conduct. One cannot, however, dismiss the large volume of disputes that are adjudicated by the World Trade Organization, or those of ICSID: they certainly do have significance. That being said, as per their treaties, trade disputes for member states cannot be adjudicated before any other forum. Nor can NAFTA investor–state disputes be adjudicated beyond the four walls of ICSID. Thus, the WTO and ICSID have a "monopoly" on these types of disputes. All the same, in assessing disputes where the litigating parties have some freedom to select their forum, *i.e.* forum shopping, one was unable to find anything in the literature that demonstrates a causal relationship between usage rates and why a particular adjudicative forum was utilized.

Indeed, for the suite of courts and tribunals evaluated here, an analysis of usage rates as a proxy for effectiveness did not yield any clear trend, and, in some cases, produced no usable data at all. For example, with recourse to tribunals: the arbitral arm of the International Joint Commission (Canada/USA) has been utilized twice in one hundred years: once in the *Gut Dam Arbitration* and once in the *Trail Smelter Arbitration*. The first case settled and the second was fully litigated. Consequently, due to the small sample size, one cannot say with any degree of confidence that usage rate is linked to effectiveness.

Similarly, the IBC/IBWC has been called upon only once in its 125-year history to adjudicate a dispute, the *Chamizal Tract Arbitration*. Therefore, usage rates for this body are of no moment, since one data point cannot provide any conclusion whatsoever. That is also the case for the NAFTA/ICSID arbitral process, involving Chapter 11 Investor–State disputes. Certainly, the usage rate for disputes like the *Bayview Irrigation Case* disclose little; as this type of water rights conflict has only come before ICSID once, and in that case the arbitral panel dismissed Bayview's claim for lack of jurisdiction. Moreover, to the best of this author's knowledge there has been no study of usage rates and effectiveness for the forty-three[26] NAFTA cases adjudicated to date.

C *Efficiency, Effectiveness, and Judgment Compliance*

Another proxy that is utilized in analyzing effectiveness is efficiency, defined here as the time it takes a court or tribunal to adjudicate a dispute, *i.e.*, the

[26] As of August 18, 2017, 25 cases against Canada, 18 cases against Mexico, and 16 cases against the United States for a total of 59. *See generally*, Geoffrey Gertz, Global Views: Renegotiating NAFTA: Options for Investment Protection (Mar. 2017) 1, http://www.brookings.edu/wp-content/uploads/2017/03/global-20170315-nafta.pdf.

shorter the time period that an adjudicative body requires to resolve a dispute, the more efficient it is. As is demonstrated below this proxy is a poor or weak measure for effectiveness. Indeed, measuring efficiency is difficult, particularly, since international courts and tribunals are likely to possess multiple goals, some of which contradict one another, and therefore efficiency may fall by the wayside in their calculus. For example, in *California* v. *Arizona* and *Kansas* v. *Colorado* the SCOTUS can be said to have been managing, rather than resolving the disputes. I posit that managing these two disputes may not have been efficient, or necessarily effective, due to the length of time that the Court took to fashion remedies, which ultimately resolved the cases. Further, there is the issue of litigation/dispute creep, *i.e.*, the parties routinely and sometimes obsessively file new disputes before the Court, which may go beyond their original goals and expands the litigation,[27] or which may unnecessarily expand the dispute.

That said, the Court may have had other institutional goals in mind in taking decades to adjudicate the entirety of these disputes. These goals may include remaining relevant in this dispute and in similar disputes in the future. Other goals may include the following: (1) attempting to be true to the Constitution's mandate to resolve disputes between the states; (2) demonstrating that even in complex inter-state disputes the Court can successfully complete cases and see them through to the end, no matter (a) how entangled the facts and/or the law are and (b) how many years are required to resolve a dispute in its entirety. Consequently, the Court's importance and legitimacy may increase in the eyes of the litigants, the legal community at large – meaning states attorney generals, who litigate these types of disputes, lower court judges, lawyers and the general public, who will learn all about the Court's judgment from the media.

Other goals in such long-term adjudications may demonstrate the Court's view that it must provide information and demonstrate how it develops norms. The latter may be seen as an attempt to either encourage compliance with the Court's judgments, whether interim, or long-term, *e.g.*, the formula developed and established in the 1963 Allocation Order in *Arizona* v. *California*; or in the alternative, to encourage parties to settle their dispute, essentially, under the Court's shadow. A representative example of the latter type is the Court's

---

[27] I utilize the term litigation/dispute creep, as a takeoff of the term "mission Creep," which is defined as "the gradual broadening of the original objectives of a mission or organization." Merriam Webster Dictionary (2015), http://www.merriam-webster.com/dictionary/mission%20creep.

1943 *Colorado* v. *Kansas* judgment, which essentially compelled the parties to enter into a Compact, under the Court's shadow. Moreover, there may be a push by the Court to promote a particular legal agenda or norm. An example of the latter is the Court's 1907 decision in the *Kansas* v. *Colorado* dispute, where it established the doctrine of equitable allocation – which I believe colored the case for over forty years, until the parties themselves entered into a compact.

Still other goals that the justices may be aiming for could embrace the simple task of resolving the parties' dispute, and may also include other aspects that may touch upon the object and purpose of the Court's legal regime and its operation, *e.g.*, the justices may be seeking to advance not only the norms of interstate disputes but also others, as well as, ones that the federal government – and other parties – may be involved in, since these too may come before this Court. Two other possible goals that the Court may be striving to fulfil are the prevention of: (1) deterioration in the parties' relationship, which could lead to a digging in of the heels by one party, which would discourage that party from cooperating in discovery or providing relevant evidence, thereby halting the litigation, particularly before the master; and (2) the parties' citizens from becoming violent. The foregoing situations can be seen as the Court's efforts to protect its core interests during the pendency of the dispute. The decades-long adjudication of these two disputes then may be a built-in part of the original jurisdiction structure.

In assessing the Court's goals, a note of caution is warranted, since no one factor or goal can circumscribe or encompass the totality of a goal-based approach to measuring the effectiveness of this or any other interstate adjudicative body. This is particularly true for State compliance with judgments or norms. Indeed, Yuval Shany has observed that acute attention to specific goals such as "norm-compliance or, even 'state conduct' may discount or completely overlook [the] longer-term and systemic impact of [inter-State] courts to international law development or the legitimacy of [inter-State] governance, which do not directly manifest themselves in state compliance."[28] He also cautions that simply measuring a single-set of impacts "may fail to capture the actual organizational features or dynamics leading to those impacts, and thus provide us with a limited understanding of those aspects of international courts in need of reform."[29]

In contrast, Ariel Dulitzky has observed that when the Inter-American Commission on Human Rights seeks to balance "its efficiency and

---

[28] Shany, Assessing the Effectiveness *ibid.* at 228–229.　　[29] *Ibid.* at 228.

TABLE 7.1 *Total Length of Time to Resolve*
Each Dispute

Case Name	Time to Resolution
Kansas v. *Colorado*	104 years
Arizona v. *California*	86 years
Nebraska v. *Wyoming*	37 years
Chamizal Dispute	1 year 9 days
Gut Dam Arbitration	1 year 351 days
Bayview Arbitration	2.4 years

effectiveness...[it] must consider its broader goals, while also realizing that the growing delays may thwart its ability to actually address the problems of petitioners."[30] One of the broader goals of most, if not all, courts and tribunals, is to satisfy the party-litigants, and their counsel. Thus, efficiency, as utilized here, translates to quickly and effectively resolving disputes. For example, Table 7.1 shows the length of time that each adjudicative body assessed here took to resolve the dispute before it.

Scholars have observed that the "pace of adjudication is closely tied to the goals of the adjudicatory body...and expediency does not always contribute to effectiveness. [Certainly,] [t]ime may be required to accommodate the needs of the"[31] parties. "At the same time, excessive delays could hamper the overall effectiveness of the System."[32] A lack of response to the filing of petitions or the resolution of cases, including issuing judgments and awards, respectively, "creates distrust in the System."[33] Nevertheless, as noted above, at times a court's goals may trump issues related to efficiency.

[30] Dulitzky, Too Little, Too Late, *ibid.* at 208.   [31] *Ibid.*

[32] *Ibid.* Dulitzky cites data that he and his colleagues have collected from cases filed with the IACHR that

> indicates that the average time between filing and settlement approval was almost five months shorter than the average time between filing and merits decisions, and almost two years shorter than the average time between filing and receiving a decision from the Court...Additionally, friendly settlements increase the effectiveness of the Commission. In a study of compliance with decisions in the Inter-American System, 54% of friendly settlements had total compliance by States, while only 29% of Court decisions and 11% of Commission reports were fully complied with...Additionally, like any method of alternative dispute resolution, friendly settlements can be more flexible than Commission and Court decisions.

  Ibid. at 165.

[33] *Ibid.*

1 The Identification of Goals of International Courts

One of the missing pieces in the effectiveness puzzle is the identification of the goals of international courts and tribunals, *i.e.*, what are the preferred results that a given adjudicative body seeks to obtain. Yuval Shany, recently asserted that

> an action is effective if it accomplishes its specific objective aim... Satisfaction of this performance-based standard is assessed over predefined units of time. Consequently, in order to measure the effectiveness of an international court using this approach, one has to identify the court's aims or goals... that is, the desired outcomes that it ought to generate – and ascertain a reasonable time frame for meeting some or all of these goals.[34]

The difficulty with this formulation is that there are few, if any, studies that have either identified or analyzed the goals, or measured the effectiveness of any international court's or tribunal's goals.[35] Indeed, one encounters both theoretical and practical challenges in seeking to define the objectives of adjudicative bodies. The theoretical impediment, as noted above, is a lack of data or analysis of goals, within the international judicial or arbitral system. As for the practical obstacle, there is a lack of unanimity among the various actors regarding these goals.

Furthermore, each international tribunal has its own diverse goals, that reflect the expectations of its different constituencies – which may include its mandate providers, counsel, parties, its arbitrators or judges – that operate within the organization. Indeed, we are once again confronted with Helfer and Slaughter's query regarding effectiveness: "effective for what purpose?"[36]

Shany also points to other weak links in the relationships between effectiveness and other proxies. For instance, he declares that "measuring the impact of international courts on state conduct... may help us in assessing what courts actually do, *but it lacks a normative baseline, which would enable us to evaluate actual performance (or lack thereof)* against some preconceived idea about what it is that courts should be doing."[37] Indeed, he notes that demarcating a causal associations between judicial performance and state behavior could still be problematic.[38] Similarly, Andrew Guzman contends that in discussing international judicial effectiveness, the focus needs to be on the extent to

---

[34] Shany, Assessing the Effectiveness *ibid.*
[35] *But see*, Yuval Shany, *Assessing the Effectiveness of International Courts* (2014). Applying the goal-based approach to the ICJ, the WTO, the ICC, the ECHR and the ECJ).
[36] Helfer & Slaughter, *ibid.* at 282.   [37] Shany, *ibid.* at 228. (Emphasis added.)
[38] *Ibid.*

which international courts and tribunals produce a given and desirable result, *viz.*, enhanced compliance by states and other stakeholders with the legal standards that these adjudicative bodies enforce.[39] In assessing this argument, Shany observes that while Guzman's approach to evaluating the effectiveness of international courts and tribunals is superior to determining compliance with judgments or awards alone, "we should focus on the degree to which international courts generate one particular set of effects (whose desirability can be assumed) – namely, improved compliance by states and other relevant actors with the legal norms that such courts enforce."[40] Shany also observes that it is debatable whether this type of methodology can offer a specific means for grasping and analysing explicit approaches through which tribunals are able to further norm compliance.[41]

That is, "since measuring effects may fail to capture the actual organizational features or dynamics leading to those effects, such measures may provide a limited understanding of those aspects of international courts in need of reform."[42] As can be seen from the foregoing, measuring a court's or a tribunal's effectiveness can be difficult. That is why proxies are employed.

Indeed, the difficulty of measuring a court's or tribunal's effectiveness is exemplified by the International Court of Justice. As the longest-standing international judicial body, now approaching its eighth decade of continued operation, one would expect that the Court has had an impact on primary norm compliance. Nevertheless, the ICJ's implementation of its adjudicative tasks and the resulting accomplishments regarding the evaluation of norm compliance are somewhat problematic. This proxy, within the realm of the goal-based approach for measuring this court's effectiveness, persists as an incomplete proxy.

One of the reasons that this proxy is imperfect is because the methods for measuring a party's compliance with a court's or tribunal's judgment are challenging. For instance, there exists no longitudinal study that demonstrates whether the state-parties to a dispute have continued to comply with the judgment in the long term. Nevertheless, a number of scholars have posited that overall, the ICJ's final judgments have experienced comparatively high rates of compliance. For example, Colter Paulson,[43] has observed that

> [c]ommentators on the International Court of Justice (ICJ) note that cases of noncompliance with final judgments are very rare. The ICJ registrar Philippe Couvreur, however, recognized that compliance is often hard to

---

[39] Guzman, *ibid.* at 188.   [40] Shany, *ibid.* at 228.   [41] *Ibid.*   [42] *Ibid.*
[43] *See e.g.*, Colter Paulson, Compliance with Final Judgments of the ICJ Since 1987, 98 *AJIL* (2004) 434, 434.

determine because judgments are varied, declarations may not reflect actual conduct, effects may only become apparent long after the judgment is given, and the legal or political situation may substantially change after the judgment...[44]

Similarly, Tom Ginsburg and Richard H. McAdams,[45] have found that

[a] detailed analysis of the caseload of the ICJ...[demonstrates] that it has been effective when it focuses on resolving coordination problems among states...[Indeed], the primary function of the [ICJ] is to resolve situations in which states are in mixed games of coordination and conflict

a THE USE OF PROXIES What can we learn from utilizing proxies to measure effectiveness? Each of these proxies has both positive and negative attributes. Both figure into the interpretation of the correlation between the proxy and a prospective direct measurement. For example, if we examine a given proxy that assesses whether the parties perceived that a given court or tribunal as being fair, just, and independent forum, an initial issue that is raised is how can this proxy be measured? Unless we have direct evidence, *e.g.*, a statement from, or acknowledgment by a Party, that it was satisfied, we are required to read between the lines.

Similarly, assume another proxy. It seeks to evaluate whether there was an overall impact of a resolution of the dispute on international legal norms. This surrogate too may be difficult to measure because in some cases it may take years for a norm to have an impact on international law. For example, although today we accept equitable allocation as a principle of international law that was not always the case.[46] Indeed, it took many years for the doctrine to take hold. Likewise, assessing whether a specific judgment or award, or even a settlement, has any effects on international legal norms may be problematic, since the "[r]ecognition of international law itself as a valid corpus of rules has been a gradual process."[47]

---

[44] *Ibid.*

[45] *See also*, Tom Ginsburg and Richard H. McAdams, Adjudicating in Anarchy: An Expressive Theory of International Dispute Resolution, 45 *Wm & Mary L R* (2004) 1229, 1304, 1308.

[46] *See e.g.*, Dante A. Caponera, Patterns of Cooperation in International Water Law: Principles and Institutions, 25 *Nat. Res. J.* (1985) 563; Joseph Dellapenna, Building International Water Management Institutions: The Role of Treaties and Other Legal Arrangements, in *Water in the Middle East: Legal, Political, and Commercial Implications* (1995) 55.

[47] *See generally*, L. Oppenheim, *Oppenheim's International Law*, (9th ed. Robert Jennings and Arthur Watts eds. 1992), Vol. 1, pp. 3 *et seq*. In contrast, "[i]n systems of municipal law the concept of formal source [of law] refers to the constitutional machinery of law-making and the status of the rule is established by constitutional law." Ian Brownlie, *Principles of Public International Law* (5th ed. 1998) 1.

Additionally, other legal concepts, including polycentricity, the tribunal's "long shadow," the development of new norms and regimes, and the effective resolution of disputes are also evaluated. These doctrinal, legal constructs, and aspects of adjudication, are then utilized in the analysis of the disputes investigated herein. Also assessed, is the impact of each dispute examined here, by assaying its normative impact on international law. Furthermore, the overall impact that each dispute had/has on the legitimacy of each adjudicative body is likewise evaluated.

D *Courts as Political Actors*

One aspect of the effectiveness of international courts that is currently difficult to measure, is the impact of the political leanings of judges on the judgments that they issue, and on the two courts discussed here: the ICJ and the US Supreme Court. Robert A. Dahl, the father of political science,[48] observed in a path-breaking study of the US Supreme Court, that

> [t]o consider the Supreme Court of the United States strictly as a legal institution is to underestimate its significance in the American political system. For it is also a political institution, an institution, that is to say, for arriving at decisions on controversial questions of national policy. As a political institution, the court is highly unusual, not least because Americans are not quite willing to accept the fact that it *is* a political institution and not quite capable of denying it; so that frequently we take both positions at once. This is confusing to foreigners, amusing to logicians, and rewarding to ordinary Americans who thus manage to retain the best of both worlds.[49]

In one of the most political cases in the history of Supreme Court, the political stripes of the Justices were never clearer than in its judgment in the *Bush v. Gore*,[50] case. That 5–4 decision decreed that George W. Bush defeated Albert Gore, Jr., in the presidential election of 2000. The dissent, authored by then Associate Justice John Paul Stevens, on behalf of the four dissenting justices, asserted that "although we may never know with complete certainty the identity of the winner of this year's presidential election, the identity of

---

[48] *See e.g.,* Linda Greenhouse, Law and Politics, N.Y. *Times*, Feb. 20, 2014, *available at* http://www.nytimes.com/2014/02/20/opinion/greenhouse-law-and-politics.html?hp&rref= opinion&_r=o.

[49] Robert A. Dahl, Decision-Making in a Democracy: The Supreme Court as a National Policy-Maker Policy Making in a Democracy: The Role of the United States Supreme Court, 6 J Public L (1957) 279, 279. (Emphasis in original.)

[50] 531 US 98 (2000).

the loser is perfectly clear: *It is the nation's confidence in the judge as the impartial guardian of the rule of law.*"[51]

The ICJ has likewise been described as a political body.[52] The fact that the five permanent members of the Security Council always occupy five of the fifteen of the Court's seats, while the remaining 187 UN member states[53] divide between them the remaining seats every three years, means that many states have yet to and will likely never have their candidate assume a seat. Indeed, data from a recent study "suggest that national bias has an important influence on the decision making of the ICJ. Judges vote for their home states about 90 percent of the time. When their home states are not involved, judges vote for states that are similar to their home states – along the dimensions of wealth, culture, and political regime."[54]

As noted above, the political proclivities of judges are hard to tease out of a given judgment. But, a corollary to the political influence of and upon judges is that in some cases arbitrators may also be selected for their political views or leanings. That is apparent in the choice of Edwin Meese, III, as an arbitrator[55] by the *Bayview Irrigation District*, in its NAFTA case against Mexico. Mr. Meese is known to be extremely conservative, as are the south Texas irrigators. However, in that case Mr. Meese voted with his colleagues and against the interest of his selectors. These issues are more fully discussed in the analysis of that case.

Moreover, each adjudicative body assessed here, whether the *ad hoc* arbitral tribunals of the IBWC, the IJC or the NAFTA/ICSID, all have power to adjudicate a dispute, either via a treaty or *compromis*, States Supreme Court,

---

[51] *Ibid.* at 128–129. (Emphasis added.) In a second dissent Justice Souter noted that

> [i]f this Court had allowed the State to follow the course indicated by the opinions of its own Supreme Court, it is entirely possible that there would ultimately have been no issue requiring our review, *and political tension* could have worked itself out in *the Congress*... The case being before us, however, its resolution by the majority is another erroneous decision.

Ibid. at 129.

[52] *See e.g.*, Eric A. Posner & Miguel F. P. de Figueiredo, Is the International Court of Justice Biased? 34 J *Legal Stud* (2005) 599; David Schultz, Book Review of Constanze Schulte, *Compliance with Decisions of the International Court of Justice* (2004), 15 *Law & Politics Book R* (2005) 282 ("the International Court of Justice (ICJ) is also a major player in world politics"), *available at* http://www.gvpt.umd.edu/lpbr/subpages/reviews/schulte405.htm; Thomas J. Bodie, *Politics and the Emergence of an Activist International Court of Justice* (1995).

[53] According to the UN's website the General Assembly is composed of 192 member-states. *See*, http://www.un.org/en/members.

[54] Posner & de Figueiredo *ibid.* at 624.

[55] One of the three lawyers that represented Bayview, Roger J. Marzulla, of the law firm of Marzulla & Marzulla, worked in Mr. Meese's Justice Department.

TABLE 7.2 *Proxies to be Utilized in Assessing Effectiveness*

---

(1) **Compliance:** did this court promote compliance with the governing
international norms (primary norm compliance), was there an impact on state
conduct, and was there improved compliance by states and other relevant actors?
(2) **Resolution and Satisfaction:** did the court or tribunal resolve this particular
dispute and the specific problem it was asked to solve, and if so, did that
institution satisfy these litigants with the judgment or award it handed down?
(3) **Normative Impact:** did the court resolve this international dispute while
providing new remedies (law making), and was there an overall impact that the
resolution had on international legal norms, furthermore, did the court
contribute to the operation of related institutional and normative regimes?
(4) **Fairness and Legitimation:** was this court perceived as a being fair, just and
independent forum, and did the judgment or award add to the legitimization of
the regime and its norms?
(5) **Efficiency:** was the Court efficient in issuing its judgment?

---

which adjudicates common law, legislative or interstate agreements. Nevertheless, the three *ad hoc* tribunals, those that adjudicated the *Chamizal Arbitration*, the *Gut Dam Arbitration* and the *Bayview Irrigation Arbitration*, did
not add a great deal or, at all to the normative impact of international law[56] – a
proxy which although elusive or difficult to quantify is one that has an "impact
on the internal laws and practices of . . . state parties."[57]

In closing this section, it should be noted that other legal concepts, including: (1) temporality; (2) the development of new laws or norms; and (3) the
effective resolution of disputes, are also important vectors. These doctrinal,
legal constructs and aspects of adjudication are utilized in the analysis of the
disputes investigated herein. I also assess the impact of each dispute examined
here, by assaying their normative impact on international law. Moreover, the
overall impact that each dispute had on international legal norms is also evaluated. Finally, the proxies for measuring effectiveness are listed in Table 7.2.

The underpinnings for measurements of the effectiveness of courts and
tribunals were discussed in a previous chapter; therefore, I will only briefly
address the issue of effective resolution. International courts and tribunals
exist for resolving disputes. As noted above, sometimes they are unable to do
so, whether for lack of jurisdiction or some other reason. Moreover, these

---

[56] Arguably, the *Chamizal Tract Arbitration* added to the law of river boundaries including the
principle of thalweg.
[57] Yuval Shany, Assessing the Effectiveness of International Courts: A Goal-Based Approach, 106
AJIL (2012) 225, 249.

adjudicative bodies are also guided by the maxim, *ubi non jus, ibi remedium nullum*, where there is no right there is no remedy. Therefore, one must seek a right and have an obligation to "do something" within the legal framework, *e.g.*, owe a duty under a treaty or *compromis*, follow a court's judgment or a tribunal's award or, heed customary international law.

Indeed, some years ago, Joseph Vining observed, "[t]hat which evokes no sense of obligation is not law. It is only the appearance of law."[58] Accordingly, in analyzing the effective resolution of disputes one must determine whether a party has a "sense of obligation" or, not. We now move on to the analysis of the disputes.

[58] Joseph Vining, *From Newton's Sleep* (1995) 34.

8

Analyzing the Disputes – The Supreme Court

Sitting, as it were, as an international as well as a domestic tribunal, we apply Federal law, state law, and international law, as the exigencies of the particular case may demand . . . [1]

The United States Supreme Court has heard 137 cases under its Original Jurisdiction.[2] I will discuss three of these in this chapter: the *Kansas v. Colorado* case (Original No. 105); the *Arizona v. California* case (Original No. 8); and the *Nebraska v. Wyoming* dispute (Original No. 16). Like a number of the original jurisdiction cases these three address interstate water disputes. Indeed, each involves a problem that has bedeviled the American West for over one hundred years: the apportionment of river water, for mostly agricultural purposes, in a desert to semi-desert environment.

The Supreme Court's first legal duty and challenge – like that of all international courts and tribunals – is to balance the competing interests of state sovereignty.[3] In the *Kansas v. Colorado, Arizona v. California*, and *Wyoming v. Nebraska* disputes, we see these competing interests in the guise of water allocation and the rough and tumble wrangling between the litigants. We are also witness to the lengths to which States situated in the arid West will go to for a greater share of the existing pool of water. An excellent example of this "hunger" for water is demonstrated by California's decades-long rancorous dispute with Arizona, over 548 ac-ft of water/day,[4] or 200,000 acre-feet (approximately 247 million m³) of water annually.

---

[1] *Kansas v. Colorado*, 206 US 46, 97 (1907). (Emphasis added.)

[2] The most recent case, *Kansas v. Nebraska*, judgement issue Mar. 9, 2015.

[3] *See e.g.*, Itzchak E. Kornfeld, Is News of "Sovereignty's Death" Exaggerated? 18 *ILSA J International & Comparative L* (2012) 315; Noah Hall, Bilateral Breakdown: US–Canada Pollution Disputes, 21 *Nat. Resources & Envt* (2006) 18, 68.

[4] An acre-foot of water is the quantity of water required to cover an acre to a depth of one foot, which converts to 43,560 cubic feet. 548 ac-ft/day converts to 222 hectares/day. The following conversion rates were used: one acre = 0.405 hectares. That is: 178,566,567 gallons, or 678,552,122 liters.

The issue of state sovereignty was also commented upon by Justice Oliver Wendell Holmes in 1931, in *New Jersey* v. *New York*.[5] This, of course, was the same year that the first opinion in *Arizona* v. *California*[6] was issued. *New Jersey* v. *New York* was another water dispute case, involving the diversion of water from non-navigable tributaries of the Delaware River. There, Holmes, writing for the Court, addressed the competing interests of state sovereignty with regards to the Delaware River and its tributaries, observing that New York has the physical power to cut off all the water within its jurisdiction, and further noting

> But clearly the exercise of such a power to the destruction of the interest of lower States could not be tolerated. And on the other hand equally little could New Jersey be permitted to require New York to give up its power altogether in order that the river might come down to it undiminished. Both States have real and substantial interests in the River that must be reconciled as best they may be.[7]

What we can learn from the foregoing quote is that the Court is looking at "a community of interests" between these two sovereign states. In a federal system, such as that of the United States, state sovereignty, given American history, can be confusing. Suffice it to say that the original thirteen states joined at the Federal Convention convened in Philadelphia's Independence Hall on May 14, 1787,[8] to create a federal entity. Moreover, the Tenth Amendment declares that "[t]he powers not delegated to the United States by the Constitution, nor prohibited by it to the States, are reserved to the States respectively, or to the people."[9] Thus, the states are *quasi*-sovereign entities whose own water laws govern water use within their political jurisdictions.

The paramount importance of the sovereignty issue[10] means that it casts a long shadow over the Court's adjudication. Consequently, that historical artefact is always in the background of the Court's adjudication of inter-state disputes. One example, from the latter part of *Arizona* v. *California* case, is

---

[5] 283 US 336 (1931).   [6] 283 US 423 (1931).   [7] *Ibid.* at 342–343. (Emphasis added.)

[8] Exploring Constitutional Conflicts, The Constitutional Convention of 1787 (undated), http://law2.umkc.edu/faculty/projects/ftrials/conlaw/convention1787.html.

[9] US Const., Art. X.

[10] The sovereignty issue plays out as follows inside a federal state: The US Constitution's 10th Amendment states that: "The powers not delegated to the United States by the Constitution, nor prohibited by it to the States, are reserved to the States respectively, or to the people." Thus, there exists a continuous interplay between state and federal sovereignty, and in Congress the issue of state's rights versus federal rights.

the issue of whether under the 11th Amendment[11] the Native American Tribes involved in the dispute could sue a state, since individuals may not. However, because the Tribes are seen as separate sovereigns the majority held that they could.

THE AMERICAN WEST AND THE WATER PARADOX

The following section addresses three separate disputes that were adjudicated by the Supreme Court of the United States. Each of them addresses water allocation issues in the western United States, which is an arid region of the country. In order to understand the reasons for the disputes that erupted, some historical perspective is necessary.

In 1893, Maj. John Wesley Powell, the explorer who opened up the West, declared

> When all the rivers are used, when all the creeks in the ravines, when all the brooks, when all the streams are used, when all the reservoirs along the streams are used, when all the canyon waters are taken up, when all the artisan waters are taken up, when all the wells are sunk or dug that can be dug in all this arid region, there is still not sufficient water to irrigate all this arid region . . . Not one more acre of land should be granted to individuals for irrigating purposes.[12]

Powell underscored that in the western United States water is life. However, for over 170 years both the federal and state governments have been attempting to fool Mother Nature. In some ways, they have succeeded. Today, however, the piper is asking to be paid.

Beginning in the 1840s the United States Government gave land patents to people who were willing to farm the land. Although most eastern politicians and government officials had never been west of St. Louis, they believed that eastern and west European farming methods were appropriate for the areas west of the 100th meridian. But the prospective farmers were fooled by the federal government, which advertised that the land was fertile and would grow anything. Many immigrants were recruited to move west and make

---

11 The 11th Amendment provides the following: "The Judicial power of the United States shall not be construed to extend to any suit in law or equity, commenced or prosecuted against one of the United States by Citizens of another State, or by Citizens or Subjects of any Foreign State."

12 Maj. John Wesley Powell speaking extemporaneously at the Second International Water Irrigation congress in Los Angeles, in mid-October 1893, quoted in Jonathan Waterman, *Running Dry: A Journey from Source to Sea Down the Colorado River* (2010) 242. (Emphasis added.)

their fortune.[13] Of course, these people were entirely unaware of the fact that the region encompassing Colorado, Kansas, Nebraska and Wyoming, among other states, was extremely arid, receiving from 15 inches (38 cm) to 19 inches (48 cm) of annual rainfall,[14] in contrast to the 40–60 inches average (102–152 cm) that fall from Virginia northwards,[15] and what many of these settlers were used to in Europe.

When these states were settled, the settlers quickly learned that the farming methods they brought from Europe were utterly unsuitable because of the lack of water. Accordingly, to cultivate crops they needed to be irrigated; as in ancient Mesopotamia, water had to be channelled and diverted from its only source: rivers. When these cases were filed in the Supreme Court, as is true today, in these agrarian lands, water equalled money, in state revenue and revenue for the citizens who farmed the land and those that provided service to the farmers, *i.e.*, *water was and is the lifeblood of the economy*. Therefore, states were extremely jealous and combative about their apportionment of water. Accordingly, Kansas has had water disputes with Colorado, Nebraska, its neighbor to the north,[16] as well as Wyoming, its neighbor to the northwest, over water allocation. Similarly, Wyoming has sued Colorado, its neighbor to the south, over appropriative rights.[17]

Moreover, the first in time, first in right, or the prior appropriation doctrine of water use, was developed in Nevada and then extended to western Kansas. Accordingly, given a new legal regime of water allocation and the fact that water was an imperative in this semi-desert agricultural environment, rather than outright war, the law was tested as a means of pacific dispute resolution. Today, as has been true for decades, the importance of water as a resource is demonstrated by the fact that every southwestern and western state has a water

---

[13] The Homestead Act of 1862, Act of May 20, 1862, Public Law 37–64, enacted during the Civil War, provided, among other benefits, that any adult citizen, or future citizen, *i.e.*, European settlers, who had never borne arms against the United States, which excluded Confederate soldiers, would be granted plots of 160 acres of government surveyed land, if he or she paid a $10 fee, lived on the land for five years, "improved" the parcel by constructing a dwelling building and cultivating the plot. After five-years the original patent holder or filer, was entitled to a fee simple deed. Homestead Act (1862), Ourdocuments.gov (1995), https://www.ourdocuments .gov/doc.php?flash=true&doc=31.

[14] United States Department of the Interior, United States Geological Survey, Nationalata- las.gov, *Colorado, Precipitation* (2011), http://www.nationalatlas.gov/printable/images/pdf/ precip/pageprecip_co3.pdf. ("The average annual precipitation for Colorado is 15.47 inches.")

[15] The average rainfall in Virginia for the period 1895–1998 was 42.7 inches. *See* Bruce P. Hayden and Patrick J. Michaels, *Virginia's Climate*, University of Virginia Climatology Office (Jan. 20, 2000), http://climate.virginia.edu/description.htm.

[16] *Nebraska v. Wyoming*, 325 U.S. 589 (1945).   [17] *Wyoming v. Colorado*, 259 US 419 (1922).

court[18] and a state water engineer.[19] These types of disputes will continue to flare up as a consequence of climate change and, the routine cycles of drought. The latter will result in the apportionment of water under a new set of rules. Finally, this chapter analyzes three dispute adjudicated by a court. The next chapter assesses three arbitrations.

I KANSAS V. COLORADO

A *Introduction*

Kansas v. Colorado involved a long-term two-state dispute over the transboundary apportionment of the waters of the Arkansas River. The case can be divided into two temporal periods: (1) the first, encompassing the period from 1901–1949, addressed apportionment issues that preceded a compact executed by the two states – a compact is equivalent to a treaty between two US states, pursuant to the Constitution's Compact Clause;[20] and (2) the second period from 1949–2009, which post-dates the compact.

These two temporal periods can also be divided into a common law, equitable apportionment period, followed by a compact/treaty era. In the Court's 1907 decision, its second in the case,[21] Justice Brewer introduced the concept of equitable apportionment, as a means of pacifically resolving the dispute between two States of the Union. He also noted that the concept of "equality of right" does not refer to an equal division of the water between states disputing an allocation along the same transboundary river, but rather, to the equal standing, in their sovereign power and right, within the constitutional system of the United States.[22] Brewer similarly observed the following, with regards to the common law, international law, and dispute resolution:

---

[18] *See e.g.*, Colorado State Judicial Branch, *Water Courts* (2011), http://www.courts.state.co.us/Courts/Water/Index.cfm.

[19] *See generally*, Kansas Dept. of Agriculture, Division of Water Resources (2011), http://www.ksda.gov/dwr. ("The Division of Water Resources administers 30 laws and responsibilities including the Kansas Water Appropriation Act which governs how water is allocated and used; statutes regulating the construction of dams, levees and other changes to streams; the state's four interstate river compacts; as well as coordinating the national flood insurance program in Kansas.")

[20] US Const. art. 1 § 1. ("No State shall, without the Consent of Congress, lay any duty of Tonnage, keep Troops, or Ships of War in time of Peace, enter into any Agreement or Compact with another State, or with a foreign Power, or engage in War, unless actually invaded, or in such imminent Danger as will not admit of delay.")

[21] *Kansas v. Colorado*, 206 US 46 (1907).   [22] *Ibid.* 206 at 97.

For after all, the common law is but *the accumulated expressions of the various judicial tribunals in their efforts to ascertain what is right and just between* [parties]...We have exercised that power in a variety of instances, determining in the several instances the justice of the dispute. *Nor is our jurisdiction ousted, even if, because Kansas and Colorado are States sovereign and independent in local matters, the relations between them depend in any respect upon principles of international law.* International law is no alien in this tribunal.[23]

The foregoing set the stage for many of the Court's subsequent equitable apportionment cases, including two of its most recent ones, the 2010 *North Carolina v. South Carolina*,[24] and the 2015 *Wyoming v. Montana*.[25] Indeed, there was an essential need for a structure to replace "the waging of war and to negotiating treaties,"[26] which would allow for the pacific resolution of disputes, while according the respect and dignity due to the sovereignty and equality of each State.[27] Moreover, some years later, in *Wyoming v. Colorado*,[28] Justice Van Devanter hailed the doctrine of equitable allocation as "a pioneer in its field."[29]

The gravamen of the pre-compact claim by Kansas was that Colorado acting as *parens patria* and on behalf of a number of corporate irrigation companies, deprived and threatened to deprive the State of Kansas and its citizens of the water that naturally and habitually flowed in the Arkansas river from Colorado to Kansas.[30] *See* Figure 8.1.

The case began on May 20, 1901, when Kansas, by leave of the Supreme Court, pursuant to the Court's original jurisdiction, filed its complaint. Since that time the Court has issued opinions in 1902, 1907, 1943, 1995, 2001, 2004, 2009, and it has separately also had to address certain procedural aspects of the case. Table 8.1 lists the dates of each decision.

B *The Subject Matter of the Dispute*

Colorado's Rocky Mountains are the source for the arid West's four major rivers: the Arkansas, the Colorado, the Platte, and the Rio Grande. Without these rivers' watersheds, the American West would remain the arid region that

---

[23] *Ibid.* (Emphasis added.)
[24] No. 138 Original, *South Carolina v. North Carolina*, 558 US 256 (2010).
[25] No. 137 Original, 577 US ____, 131 S.Ct. 1765 (2011).
[26] Kristin Linsley Myles, *South Carolina v. North Carolina* – Some Problems Arising in an East Coast Water Dispute, 12 *Wyoming LR* (2012) 3, 5.
[27] *Ibid.* [28] 259 US 419 (1922). [29] *Ibid.* 259 at 464.
[30] *Kansas v. Colorado*, 206 US 46, 47–48 (1907).

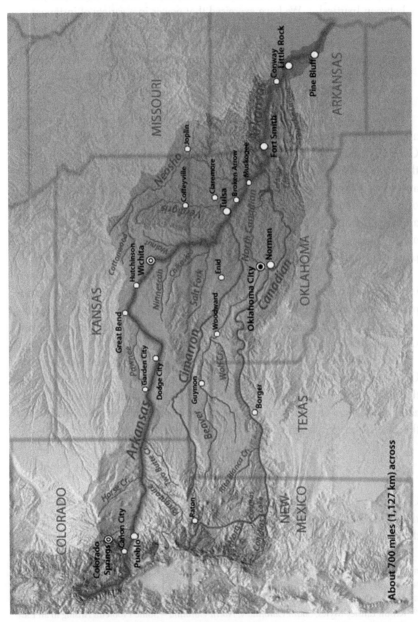

FIGURE 8.1 The Arkansas River (Flowing eastwards) from its Headwaters in Colorado through Arkansas

TABLE 8.1 *Procedural History of the* Kansas v. Colorado *case*

*1902 – *Kansas v. Colorado*, 185 US 125	2001 – *Kansas v. Colorado*, 531 US 1122. Colorado's Motion for leave to reply to the brief of the USA. Granted, and the exceptions to the Special Master's Report are set for oral argument in due course
*1907 – *Kansas v. Colorado*, 206 US 46.	2001 – *Kansas v. Colorado*, 532 US 902, Motion of the Acting Solicitor General for divided argument granted
*1943 – *Colorado v. Kansas*, 320 US 383.	2001 – *Kansas v. Colorado*, 537 U.S. 1230, Motion of Special Master for Interim Fees and Costs Granted
1944 – *Colorado v. Kansas*, 321 US 803, Petition for rehearing denied.	2004 – *Kansas v. Colorado*, 541 US 1071, Motion of Kansas for leave to file sur-reply granted. Exceptions to the Special Master's Report are set for oral argument in due course.
*1995 – *Kansas v. Colorado*, 514 US 673.	*2004 – *Kansas v. Colorado*, 543 US 86, Exceptions to Special Master's pre-judgment interest calculation overruled and other findings.
1997 – *Kansas v. Colorado*, 522 US 803, The Second Report of the Special Master Received and Filed	2008 – *Kansas v. Colorado*, 552 US 1229, Special Mater's Fifth Report received and ordered filed. Briefing schedule ordered. Motion of Special Master for Interim Fees & Costs granted
1998 – *Kansas v. Colorado*, 522 US 1073, Colorado's exceptions to the Special Master's Second Report overruled w/o prejudice.	*2009 – *Kansas v. Colorado*, 129 S. Ct. 1294, Opinion re: Kansas' exceptions to Special Master's Fifth and Final Report, contending that the Special Master erred in setting expert witness fees
1999 – *Kansas v. Colorado*, 526 US 1048, Motion of Special Master for Interim Fees and Costs Granted	2009 – *Kansas v. Colorado*, 129 S. Ct. 2423, Motion of the Special Master to be discharged is granted.
2000 – *Kansas v. Colorado*, 529 US 1015, Motion of Special Master for Interim Fees & Costs Granted.	

* Denotes Case Discussed in this Section

America's natives discovered when they arrived on the continent. But for these four rivers irrigation would not be possible. Consequently, any water projects that are developed in Colorado will affect water flow into bordering states.

The Arkansas River,[31] one of those rivers, flows along the eastern flanks of the Rocky Mountains. Its headwaters are located near Leadville, Garfield County, Colorado and its mouth is located at Napoleon, Arkansas.[32] (Figure 8.1). "Once proudly known as the 'Nile of America,'"[33] it is 2,364 kilometers (1,469 miles) long, making it the sixth-longest river in the United States and the second-longest tributary in the Mississippi-Missouri River system.[34] The River's drainage basin envelops approximately 440,300 square kilometers (170,000 square miles).[35]

The area in dispute, in this case, is the upper 280 miles [450 km] of the Arkansas[36] and its tributaries in Colorado, which drain an area of "approximately 22,000 square miles [56,979 km²] . . . All [of which drains] east of the summit of the Rocky mountains and a large portion thereof in the mountains . . . "[37] and the "length of the river in Kansas [which] is about 310 miles [499 km].[38]

C *The Initial Salvo: The 1902 Action, Kansas v.* Colorado,
185 US 125 (1902)

The state of Kansas, by leave of Court, filed its complaint on May 20, 1901. Kansas' complaint sought an injunction enjoining and restraining Colorado

---

[31] The history of the Arkansas River follows the Europeans' colonialism and development of the United States. The river was discovered in 1541 by Francisco Vasquez de Coronado, who traversed it near what today is Dodge City, Kansas. *See generally,* The Arkansas River Historical Society Museum, An Outline History of the Arkansas River from Early European Explorations to the Development of the McClellan-Kerr Arkansas River Navigation System (1997), http://www.tulsaweb.com/port/history.htm; Francis Parkman, *La Salle and the Discovery of the Great West* (1999).

[32] United States Geological Survey, Geographic Names Information System, *Feature Detail Report for: Arkansas River* (last updated Apr. 2, 2011), http://geonames.usgs.gov/pls/gnispublic / f?p = gnispq:3:1932465391042904::NO::P3_FID:78956.

[33] *Kansas v. Colorado,* 543 US 86, 90 (2004) (Breyer, J.).

[34] J.C. Kammerer, US Geological Survey, *Largest Rivers in the United States* (Rev. May 1990), http://pubs.usgs.gov/of/1987/ofr87-242.

[35] *Ibid.*

[36] "The river has its origin in central Colorado, and is a mountain torrent for 130 miles to a point near Canon City where it enters a foothill region ending near Pueblo. Thence it traverses the high plains of eastern Colorado and western Kansas. In the areas mentioned the stream is non-navigable." *Colorado v. Kansas,* 320 US 383, 385 (1943).

[37] *Kansas v. Colorado,* 185 US 125, 126 (1902).   [38] *Ibid.* at 126–127.

from diverting, or permitting any corporation or other private person from diverting, any of the Arkansas River's waters, including any of the river's tributaries that course through the state of Colorado. Kansas also sought to enjoin Colorado from permitting any natural or corporeal persons, from lengthening or enlarging any of the canals or ditches that were then in existence.[39]

In its complaint Kansas likewise, claimed that Colorado began to systematically appropriate and redirect the river's waters for the purpose of irrigating *non-riparian* arid lands, adjacent to the river, for a distance of 190 miles – from Cañon City, Colorado to the Kansas border. Moreover, Kansas alleged that, by 1891, Colorado appropriated the entire natural flow of the Arkansas and a considerable amount of its flood waters.[40] Thus, the average flow (between the two) was reduced considerably.[41]

In response, Colorado filed a demurrer, which contained ten points.[42] Two of these are relevant here. The first asserted that the Supreme Court had no jurisdiction over either the parties nor did it have subject matter over the suit, because Kansas' claims on their face did not constitute a colorable controversy between the two states, that is supported by the United States' Constitution.[43] The second, asserted that Kansas' allegations do not arise between it and the state of Colorado, rather they arise, "if at all, between the state of Kansas and certain private corporations and certain persons in the state of Colorado who are not made parties herein, and which matters so stated, if true, do not concern the state of Colorado as a corporate body or state."[44]

The Court, by Chief Justice Fuller,[45] held that Colorado's filing of a demurrer cannot dispose of a case between two states, even though it could between two private parties. Ultimately, Justice Fuller observed that too many issues were unanswered at that juncture, including: (1) whether Colorado was apportioning too much water from the Arkansas River; and (2) whether certain Colorado corporations needed to be made defendants because they were indispensable parties. Accordingly, he held that there were too many "intricate questions arising on the record [and therefore the Court was] constrained to forbear proceeding until all the facts are before us on the evidence."[46] The demurrer was overruled, without prejudice, and the Court postponed its

---

[39] *Ibid.* at 137.   [40] *Colorado v. Kansas ibid.* 320 at US 385 (1943).

[41] *Colorado v. Kansas ibid.* 320 at US 385 (1943).

[42] *Kansas v. Colorado, ibid.* 185 US at 137–139.   [43] *Ibid.* at 138.   [44] *Ibid.*

[45] "Mr. Justice Gray did not hear the argument, and took no part in the decision." *Ibid.* at 147.

[46] *Ibid.*

decision regarding any relief until a more complete factual record could be developed.[47]

D Round Two: The 1907 Decision and the Introduction of the Concept of Equitable Apportionment, Kansas v. Colorado, 206 US 46, 49 (1907)

The case next came before the Court on August 17, 1903, when Kansas filed an amended complaint, naming "as defendants Colorado and a quite a number of corporations, who were charged to be engaged in depleting the flow of water in the Arkansas River."[48] Here, Kansas again asserted that Colorado and the corporate defendants were illegally diverting water from the Arkansas River to the detriment of Kansas, and once more requested the Court to enjoin the defendants from diverting the water of the Arkansas River. But before taking any steps the Court required the parties to conduct discovery and "take evidence." This process concluded on June 16, 1905, and Supreme Court's decision was issued on May 13, 1907.

There was, however, a new twist, during the period when the parties gathered their evidence. On March 21, 1904, the United States filed a petition for intervention, which the Court granted.[49] The United States' intervention petition claimed that the amount of the flow of the river was subject to its "superior authority and supervisory control."[50]

In a decision issued on May 13, 1907, the Court noted the State of Colorado and several of the defendant corporations answered the Complaint. It nevertheless did not consider the defenses of the corporations separately from those asserted by Colorado. Initially, Justice Brewer, writing for the majority, stated that the Court's jurisdiction, is granted it under the Constitution's Article III Section 2, which provides that "the judicial power shall extend to all cases, in law and *equity*, arising under this Constitution."[51] The majority then dismissed the claim of the United States since the case involved a conflict between two states. Moreover, the Court noted that under the Constitution the states have the power to prescribe laws regarding the appropriation and distribution of waters from rivers in their territory. Furthermore, it is the states that establish

---

[47] *Ibid*. Indeed, "[t]he court added that, before the developments in Colorado consequent upon irrigation were to be destroyed or materially affected, Kansas must show not merely some technical right but one which carried corresponding benefits." *Colorado v. Kansas, supra* note 16, 320 at US 385–386.

[48] *Kansas v. Colorado*, 206 US 46, 49 (1907).

[49] *Ibid*. at 86.   [50] *Ibid*. at 85.   [51] *Ibid*. at 82.

their own water law regime, not the federal government.[52] Consequently, the Congress' power to prescribe laws[53] under these facts was wholly irrelevant.

The Court also held that Kansas' attempt at enjoining Colorado's diversion of the Arkansas River were insufficient, although the diversions had a "perceptible injury to portions of the Arkansas valley in Kansas, particularly to those portions closest to the Colorado line."[54]

Moreover, this was the decision where Justice Brewer introduced a newly fashioned doctrine: "equitable apportionment." In so doing, he observed that

> [a]s Kansas thus recognizes the right of appropriating the waters of a stream for the purposes of irrigation, subject to the condition of an equitable division between the riparian proprietors, she cannot complain if the same rule is administered between herself and a sister state. And this is especially true when the waters are, except for domestic purposes, practically useful only for purposes of irrigation.[55]

The Court was confronted with two water law regimes. Kansas adopted and still maintains the common law or, Eastern riparian water rights. That system allocates water among riparians those who possess land along its path. It has its origins in English common law. Riparian water rights exist in many jurisdictions with a common law heritage, such as Canada, Australia, and states in the eastern United States.

Alternatively, Colorado adopted the prior appropriation doctrine, or "first in time – first in right", developed in the western United States in response to the scarcity of water in the region. In contrast to a riparian right, an appropriative right exists without regard to the relationship between the land and water.

---

[52] Amy Kelly, Federal Preemption and State Water Law, 105 *J Contemp Water Res and Educ* (1996) 4. ("One cannot fairly say that federal rules dominate in the field of water law... In this absence of any congressional interest in establishing a legal regime for water allocation during the decades of western expansion in the 1800's, the States took it upon themselves to choose which theory of water rights, riparianism or prior appropriation, best suited their needs; a practice that Congress did not choose to disrupt retroactively, and that the Supreme Court approved in *California Oregon Power Co. v. Beaver Portland Cement Co.*, 295 US 142 (1935).")

[53] Pursuant to the Constitution's Article I, § 1 ("All legislative powers herein granted shall be vested in a Congress of the United States, which shall consist of a Senate and House of Representatives.")

[54] *Kansas v. Colorado, ibid.* at 206 US 117. Accordingly, Justice Brewer's opinion holds that whatever injury Kansas suffered it is minimal when seen through the prism of the entire Arkansas river valley, "and regarding the interests of both states, and the right of each to receive benefit through irrigation and in any other manner from the waters of the Arkansas, Kansas has not made out a case entitling it to a decree..." *Ibid.*

[55] *Ibid.* at 206 US 105.

In order to resolve the dispute Brewer had to balance these two competing regimes and thus, he formulated the equitable remedy of equitable allocation.

Accordingly, Kansas' complaint was dismissed without prejudice. Nevertheless, the Court held that Kansas had the right to institute a new suit at any point when that state believed that its interests in the Arkansas River's waters would be substantially injured "to the extent of destroying the equitable apportionment of benefits between the two states resulting from the flow of the river."[56]

E 1943, *Round Three:* Colorado v. Kansas, 320 US 383 (1943)

For over twenty years following the 1907 ruling, various private irrigation and ditch companies in Kansas engaged their counterparts in Colorado in the lower courts. The primary initiator of these suits was the Finney County (Kansas) Water Users' Association ("Finney Association"). It filed numerous suits against a host of defendants, claiming that its allocation of water was wanting due to an over allocation by various Colorado ditch companies.[57] A good deal of the dispute concerned the diversion of water from the Purgatoire River,[58] a tributary, which flows north into the Arkansas.

Subsequently on January 24, 1928, the State of Colorado filed an action in the Supreme Court, against the State of Kansas and the Finney Association. Colorado's suit first referred to the Court's two previous decisions in *Kansas* v. *Colorado*.[59] Relying on those decisions Colorado averred that, it had invested capital in improving the irrigation systems along the Arkansas River. It then described the pending private litigation against its appropriators, and asserted "that the establishment of an interstate priority schedule sought in the pending suits would disrupt and destroy Colorado's administration of the waters of the Arkansas basin and result in a conflict of state authority... "[60] Colorado also argued that a proper settlement of the relative rights of the two states could not result via the private suits by each state's appropriators.

---

[56] *Ibid.* at 118.

[57] The Finney Association filed suits in 1909, rejected a settlement in 1911, sought to intervene in a suit filed by the Colorado-based United States Irrigating Company filed suit against among other Kansas ditch companies, the Graham Ditch Company, which was settled on February 19, 1916. Rejecting this settlement, as well, Finney filed suit against another set of Colorado defendants on November 27, 1916, seeking the same relief as that in the 1916 settlement. Then on January 29, 1923, the Finney Association filed another suit in the same court against other Colorado defendants seeking the same relief.

[58] The Purgatoire River originates in southeastern Colorado and flows northeasterly to a confluence with the Arkansas River near Las Animas, Colorado. US Geological Survey, Geographic Names Information System, "Purgatoire River" (Last modified Jan. 3, 2011), http://nhd.usgs .gov/gnis/html.

[59] *Colorado* v. *Kansas, ibid.,* 320 US at 388.   [60] *Ibid.*

Furthermore, Colorado delineated other injuries to its state interests which would be susceptible by the continued litigation. It then requested the following relief: (1) the Finney Association withdraw the pending actions; and (2) that both Kansas "and her citizens be enjoined from litigating, or attempting to litigate, the relative rights of the two states and their citizens to the waters of the river on claims similar to those made by the [Finney] Association in its pending suits;" and (3) that Colorado's rights and those of her citizens, as decided by the 1907 judgment in *Kansas v. Colorado* be protected.[61]

In response, Kansas filed an answer, in which it admitted a number of the allegations in the complaint, denied others, and then claimed certain rights in the Arkansas River's waters. It also, enumerated a litany of appropriations by "Kansas residents and citizens, [and pursuant to the doctrine of prior appropriation] diversions by Colorado citizens under appropriations junior in time and inferior in right to those made in Kansas."[62] The respondent's answer also claimed that since the filing of the complaint in the previous case, Colorado users have greatly increased their appropriations and diversions, and threaten further to increase them, to the injury of Kansas users.[63]

Consequently, Kansas requested the following relief: that the Court "protect and quiet her rights and those of her citizens and residents, including the Finney County Association, to their appropriations";[64] and that the Court should issue a decree that would establish the volume of water in feet per second that the state's citizens can divert for irrigation from the Arkansas River.[65] Kansas similarly requested the Court to issue an order requiring that Colorado, "her officers, agents, and citizens be perpetually enjoined from diverting any waters from the river or its tributaries in Colorado until the rights of Kansas, her citizens and residents, are satisfied."[66] Defendant Finney Association also filed an answer to Colorado's complaint.[67]

The Court ordered that a Commissioner be appointed to take evidence. Thereafter, the case was referred to a Master, who was asked to make further evidentiary findings, including to make findings of fact and conclusions of law and finally, to recommend a written order.[68] In his report to the Court, the Master stated that the "evidence is voluminous and conflicting on many of the material issues of fact."[69] However, his report contained no discussion or analysis of the proofs, only some recitals and a form of decree, and three recommendations.[70] Each party filed exceptions to the Master's report.

---

[61] *Ibid.*   [62] *Ibid.*   [63] *Ibid.*   [64] *Ibid.*
[65] *Ibid.* at 388–389.   [66] *Ibid.* at 389.   [67] *Ibid.*
[68] *Ibid.* ("The evidence consists of some seven thousand typewritten pages of testimony and 368 exhibits covering thousands of pages.")
[69] *Ibid.*   [70] *Ibid.*

In his opinion for the Court, Justice Owen Roberts found that the case presented three issues:

(1) Is Colorado entitled to an injunction against the further prosecution of litigation by Kansas users against Colorado users?
(2) Does the situation call for allocation of the waters of the basin as between Colorado and Kansas in second-feet or acre-feet?
(3) Has Kansas proved that Colorado has substantially and injuriously aggravated conditions which existed at the time of her earlier suit?[71]

Neither party took exception to the Master's first or third recommendations. Therefore, the Court adopted them.[72] These recommendations concluded that the first question should be answered in the affirmative, *i.e.*, that Colorado was indeed entitled to an injunction against the further prosecution of litigation by Kansas' users against Colorado's users. Accordingly, the Court issued an injunction in favor of Colorado.

With regards to the third question, the Master found that since the Court's 1907 decision Colorado had materially increased its consumption of the Arkansas River's water for irrigation and therefore "diminished the flow of water into the State of Kansas."[73] This increased consumption, he established, had caused injury to Kansas' substantial interests.[74] Nevertheless, Kansas did not take exception to the Master's recommendation that the Court issue an injunction against any further prosecution of the Finney Association's suits against Colorado users.[75] Consequently, here too the Court found that the issuance of an injunction was appropriate and therefore should issue.

The second question was the one that posed the greatest difficulty for the Master and one that the Court was therefore required to fully address. The Court disagreed with the Master's recommendation and consequently had to determine what allocation formula it should employ. One of the critical facts that Kansas pointed to, was the amount of storage of flood waters contained in two reservoirs: one by Colorado, and one by the federal government. Under natural flow, these waters would have been captured by the Arkansas River and would thus flow into the river across the Colorado–Kansas state line, thereby benefiting Kansas.

Initially, Justice Roberts observed that the Master did not endeavor to formulate a definition for flood waters or, the extent to which they were unusable by either state.[76] Moreover, he noted that the Master did not propose a

---

[71] *Ibid.* at 389–390.   [72] *Ibid.* at 390.   [73] *Ibid.* at 391.   [74] *Ibid.*
[75] *Ibid.*   [76] *Ibid.* at 390.

method for measuring the flood waters' occurrence nor did he define Colorado's obligation to deliver water to Kansas.[77] Finally, Roberts stressed that the Master's form of decree, would require measurement of water flow by two gauges: one at Cañon City – east of the Colorado–Kansas state line – and one at the mouth of the Purgatoire River,[78] which is located in southeastern Colorado – east of the Colorado–Kansas state line. Moreover, the Master's decree stated that water deliveries to Kansas were required to be prorated at the two-gauge stations.[79] In assessing the Master's apportionment of water between the two states Justice Roberts observed that

> 'the average annual natural flow of the river and its tributaries' is 1,240,000-acre feet [1.5 billion cubic meters], and the 'average annual dependable and fairly continuous water supply and flow' of 1,110,000-acre feet [1.3 billion cubic meters]. He recommends that the dependable flow be allocated 925,000-acre feet [1.1 billion cubic meters] to Colorado and 185,000-acre feet [22.3 million cubic meters] to Kansas, 150,000 [18.5 million cubic meters] thereof between April 1 and October 1, and 35,000 [4.3 million cubic meters] between October 1 and April 1 of each year, that is, five-sixths to Colorado and one-sixth to Kansas.[80]

It was to these two elements of the Master's order that both Colorado and Kansas filed exceptions. They asserted that the Master's recommendations were both ambiguous and impossible to administer. Moreover, Kansas claimed that the Master's award to it was deficient, but acknowledged her willingness to accede to the Master's recommended allocation, although insisting that the order should require Colorado to deliver the quantity of water awarded to Kansas when and as demanded by her.[81] Alternatively, Colorado asserted that the Master's proposed order, as well as Kansas' suggested modification, would necessitate severe and unwarranted harm to Colorado's interests, if the state would be required to comply with the order's terms.[82] Note

---

[77] *Ibid.*

[78] The Purgatoire River begins its course at the confluence of the North Fork Purgatoire and Middle Fork Purgatoire rivers near Weston, Las Animas County, Colorado (approximately 185 miles (300 km) almost due south of Denver)) and flows mostly in an easterly-northeasterly direction, roughly 196 miles (315 km) to a confluence with the Arkansas River and the John Martin Reservoir, between Las Animas and Fort Lyon, Colorado. *See* Google Maps at https://www.google.com/maps/@38.014219,-103.2654661,40724m/data = !3m1!1e3.

[79] *Colorado v. Kansas, ibid.* 320 US at 390.

[80] *Ibid.* (An acre-foot is defined as a column of water one foot high that covers an area that is one acre 43,560 square feet or about 4,050 square meters or 0.405 hectares in size. One acre-foot = 1,233 cubic meters.)

[81] *Ibid.*   [82] *Ibid.* at 390–391.

that both states sought to protect their sovereign interest in what can be described as stressing the Harmon Doctrine.

Justice Roberts referred to the Court's previous decisions in the case, where it ruled that Kansas was not entitled to a *specific share of the total quantity of water*, even if it flowed freely, in its natural state. Furthermore, given the evidence and the data, it did not appear that Colorado had appropriated more than her equitable share of the flow. Therefore, if Kansas was to be accorded relief, she would have to demonstrate that additional allocations by Colorado, of the Arkansas River, had worked serious injuries to her substantial interests.[83]

Moreover, the Court declared the following, in what is now a classic view of the prudence that it takes in addressing allocation issues between states:

> The reason for judicial caution in adjudicating the relative rights of states in such cases is that, while we have jurisdiction of such disputes, [footnote omitted] they involve the interests of quasi-sovereigns, present complicated and delicate questions, and, due to the possibility of future change of conditions, necessitate expert administration rather than judicial imposition of a hard and fast rule. Such controversies may appropriately be composed by negotiation and agreement, pursuant to the compact clause of the Federal constitution. We say of this case, as the court has said of interstate differences of like nature, that such mutual accommodation and agreement should, if possible, be the medium of settlement, instead of invocation of our adjudicatory power...[84]

The Court, Justice Roberts observed, cannot interfere in every case requiring recourse to equity by one citizen against another, let alone actions between states, because the burden upon a complaining state is much greater than that generally required to be borne by private parties.[85] Therefore, before the court intervenes, the case must be of considerable significance and completely and clearly proved,[86] noting that this case was not. Moreover, when asked to determine whether one state is using, or threatening to use, more than its equitable share of the benefits of a stream, all the factors which create equities in favor of one state or the other, must be weighed as of the date when the controversy is mooted.[87]

The Court then ruled that Colorado's request for an injunction would be granted, since Kansas was unable to prove that Colorado's use of the Arkansas River *materially* increased, and that the increase has worked *a serious detriment* to the substantial interests of Kansas.[88]

---

[83] *Ibid.* at 391.   [84] *Ibid.* at 391. (Emphasis added.)   [85] *Ibid.*
[86] *Ibid.* (*Citing Missouri v. Illinois*, 200 US 496, 520, 521 (1906); *New York v. New Jersey*, 256 US 296, 309 (1921); and *North Dakota v. Minnesota*, 263 US 365, 374 (1923), among others).
[87] *Ibid.* at 394.   [88] *Ibid.* at 395.

F 1949: A New Era, The Compact Years

Following the Court's 1943 decision, the two states, taking seriously the Court's "advice" to settle the case, entered into a three-year-long series of negotiations to resolve their conflict. In 1949, these negotiations yielded a result: the approval by Kansas and Colorado of the Arkansas River Compact, which was subsequently ratified by Congress.[89] Article VIII of the Compact established the Arkansas River Compact Administration (ARCA) and conferred upon it the authority and duty of administering the Compact.[90]

The compact's primary purpose was to settle the two states' Arkansas River allocation dispute, and to apportion those waters equitably. Another of the compact's objectives was to account for water quantity gains arising from the construction, operation, and maintenance by the United States' Bureau of Reclamation of the John Martin Reservoir, situated at the confluence of the Arkansas and Purgatoire rivers.[91] However, the compact failed to allocate to Kansas either a defined quantity of Arkansas River water, or a specific share of the river's flow.[92] This flaw, opened a new chapter of disputes between the two states. The error is startling, given the fact that "both states had sought... to attain a definitive solution to their perennial problem of apportionment of the waters of the Arkansas River."[93]

G The Next Phase: Kansas v. Colorado, 1985–1994

Some conflicts don't die easily. In the early 1980s Kansas' water officials again began to suspect that Colorado was over pumping its groundwater wells, and was therefore exceeding its volume pursuant to the compact. Consequently, in 1983 Kansas performed an independent analysis of potential Compact violations – which were occasioned by the intensified post-Compact well pumping in Colorado – as well as the federal governments operation of its Pueblo and Trinidad reservoirs.[94] As a result, in December 1985, Kansas filed a new original action against Colorado, seeking a resolution to these problems, which it suggested were in violation of the Compact.[95] Kansas alleged that Colorado had violated the Compact by drilling new irrigation wells, which, in the words of Art. IV-D of the Compact, "materially depleted" the Arkansas

---

[89] 63 Stat. 145.

[90] *Kansas v. Colorado*, 514 US 673, 678 (1995) (Rehnquist, C.J.). ("The Administration is composed of a nonvoting presiding officer designated by the President of the United States, and three voting representatives from each State. Each State has one vote, and every decision, authorization, or other action by the Administration requires a unanimous vote...(Article VIII-D))."

[91] *Ibid.* at 678–679.   [92] Special Master's Report, *ibid.* at footnote 8.

[93] *Kansas v. Colorado*, 514 at US 678-9.   [94] *Ibid.* at 679.   [95] *Ibid.*

River's "usable flow" of water that would otherwise be available for use by Kansas' water users.

In March 1986, the Court granted Kansas its motion for leave to file a bill of complaint, which Colorado had to answer within sixty days.[96] It then appointed a Special Master to hear the case. Kansas' complaint proceeded on three grounds. First, it charged that Colorado, along with its water users, materially depleted the usable and available Stateline flows of the Arkansas River in violation of the compact.[97] Specifically, Kansas asserted that post-compact groundwater wells in Colorado depleted the flow of water across the Colorado–Kansas border into Kansas,[98] in violation of Article IV-D of the Compact.

Next, Kansas alleged that Colorado's Winter Water Storage Program (WWSP) – a program in which Colorado and the United States Department of the Interior's Bureau of Reclamation (BOR) use excess water capacity at the Pueblo Reservoir to collect a share of the winter flow of the Arkansas River – similarly breached the Compact.[99] Finally, Kansas asserted that Colorado impeded an administrative investigation by the Arkansas River Compact Administration into Colorado's compact violations, which included: the impact of post-Compact wells; the operation of the federal Bureau of Reclamation's Trinidad Reservoir located on the Purgatoire River;[100] and the consequences of future increases in the consumption of return flows[101] from water imported by Colorado into the Arkansas River Watershed, among others.[102] These actions were claimed to be violative of Colorado's obligation to abide by the Trinidad Reservoir Operating Principles (Operating Principles) and

---

96 *Kansas v. Colorado*, 475 US 1079 (1986). In turn, Colorado opposed Kansas' filing and filed a "Brief in Opposition to Motion for Leave to File Complaint," *Kansas v. Colorado*, 1986 WL 1178161 (US).

97 Special Master's Report, *ibid.* at * 6.

98 *Ibid.* at * 6. Special Master's Report, *supra* note 63 at * 6. "Kansas alleged that these wells pumped approximately 150,000 acre-feet [185,023,350 cubic meters] of groundwater related to flows in the Arkansas River on an annual basis."

99 *Ibid.* at 680.

100 *See generally, Purgatoire River Water Conservancy Dist. v. Kuiper*, 197 Colo. 200, 593 P.2d 333 (Colo., 1979). ("The Trinidad Project consists of an on-stream dam and a114,000-acre foot reservoir (TRINIDAD RESERVOIR) on the Purgatoire River approximately four miles upstream from the City of Trinidad. This is a multi-use flood control, reclamation and recreation project authorized by Congress in 1958 [footnote omitted] under the Flood Control Act of 1944.").

101 "Return flow is water that is diverted from a source that is not consumed and can be reused. This could be water from a river or aquifer system that is not consumed and can be reused and essentially recaptured by the local hydrologic system." Phillip King, Return Flow Efficiency, Surface Water Opportunities in New Mexico, New Mexico Water Research Institute (Oct. 2008), http://www.wrri.nmsu.edu/publish/watcon/proc53/king.pdf.

102 Special Master's Rept. *Ibid.* at * 6.

also constituted a violation of the Compact.[103] Kansas' complaint sought a decree directing Colorado, its officers, citizens and political subdivisions to deliver the waters of the Arkansas River in accordance with the provisions of the compact.[104]

Following the conclusion of the liability phase, the Special Master filed his Report with the Court, setting forth his findings of fact and recommendations of law.[105] The Court issued the following findings:

(1) the post-Compact well pumping in Colorado had 'materially depleted' the 'usable' flow at the Colorado-Kansas border (stateline) in violation of Article IV-D of the Compact... ;

(2) 'Kansas has failed to prove that operation of the [WWSP][106] program has violated the [C]ompact'... and

(3) 'dismiss[ed] the Kansas claim arising from the operation of Trinidad Reservoir.'[107]

H 1995: *Round 5, Back Before the Court*

The case next came to the Court in 1995, when the two states filed exceptions to the Special Master's most recent recommendation.[108] Procedurally, the Court generally accepts the Master's findings of fact unless they are clearly erroneous.[109] Therefore, writing for a unanimous court Chief Justice Rehnquist adopted the Special Master's recommendations and overruled Colorado's and Kansas' exceptions. He also noted that the Compact's Article IV-D, was the provision of the Compact most relevant to this dispute. Article IV-D states:

> This Compact is not intended to impede or prevent future beneficial development of the Arkansas River basin in Colorado and Kansas by Federal or State agencies, by private enterprise, or by combinations thereof, which may involve construction of dams, reservoir, and other works for the purposes of water utilization and control, as well as the improved or prolonged functioning of existing works: *Provided*, that the waters of the Arkansas River... shall not be materially depleted in usable quantity or availability for use to the

---

[103] *Kansas v. Colorado, ibid.* at 514 US 678.   [104] Special Master's Rept. *Ibid.* at * 6.

[105] This was the Special Master's first report. *Kansas v. Colorado*, 533 US 1, 5 (2001). He subsequently filed four more over the next eight years.

[106] The Winter Water Storage Program (WWSP). The program was developed by the Bureau of Reclamation and Colorado to store a portion of the Arkansas River's winter-time flow in the Pueblo Reservoir. *See* discussion *infra*.

[107] *Kansas v. Colorado, ibid.* at 514 US 680.   [108] *Ibid.*

[109] The Supreme Court accepts the master's findings of fact unless clearly erroneous.

water users in Colorado and Kansas under this Compact by such future development or construction."[110]

Turning to the parties' exceptions the Court ruled that for Kansas to demonstrate a violation of Article IV-D it was required to establish that development in Colorado resulted in material depletions of "usable" river flow.[111] Because the term "usable" is not defined in the Compact the Court cited language from its 1943 decision, wherein it stated: "[t]he critical matter is the amount of divertible flow at times when water is most needed for irrigation. Calculations of average annual flow, which include flood flows, are, therefore, not helpful in ascertaining the dependable supply of water usable for irrigation."[112] At trial before the Special Master, Kansas presented three methods for determining depletions of usable flow.

In examining these exceptions, the Court began with an analysis of Kansas' claim regarding the operation of Trinidad Reservoir. The Chief Justice surveyed the history of the Trinidad, noting that the Bureau of Reclamation established Operating Principles whereby the Trinidad Project could be administered "without adverse effect on downstream water users and the inflow into John Martin Reservoir."[113] These Principles, he noted, were reviewed and approved by the Governor of Kansas, following some minor additions, and by the Compact's Administration in June 1967.[114]

Thirteen years hence, in 1979, Colorado began storage of water at the Trinidad Reservoir. "Kansas immediately complained that the Operating Principles were being violated. [Then i]n 1988, at the request of the [Compact's] Administration, the Bureau of Reclamation conducted a study of the Trinidad Reservoir. It concluded that two storage practices at the Trinidad Reservoir constituted a 'departure from the intent of the operating principles.'"[115]

Kansas contended that the BOR's Operating Principles were binding on Colorado and that any deviation therefrom signified a violation of the Compact regardless of injury.[116] However, Kansas, offered no evidence, apart from the Bureau's studies, to show that the actual operation of the Trinidad project caused it to receive less water than under historical, pre-project

---

[110] *Kansas v. Colorado, ibid.* at 514 US 678. (Emphasis in the original.)

[111] *Ibid.* at 685. Article IV-D's precise language is "the waters of the Arkansas River...shall not be materially depleted in usable quantity or availability for use to the water users in Colorado and Kansas under this Compact by such future development or construction."

[112] *Colorado v. Kansas, ibid.* 320 US at 396–397.

[113] *Kansas v. Colorado, ibid.* 514 US at 681. (*Citing* Special Master's Rept. at 390 (internal quotation marks omitted).)

[114] *Ibid.* at 681–682. [115] *Ibid.* at 682. [116] *Ibid.* at 682.

conditions.[117] The Master concluded that in order to prove a violation of the Compact, Kansas was required to establish that the Trinidad Reservoir's operations caused *a material depletion* within the meaning of Article IV-D.[118] Kansas did not meet that burden per the Special Master's findings. Accordingly, he recommended that the Court dismiss Kansas' Trinidad claim.[119]

In its exceptions and before the Court Kansas argued that "[d]eparture from the Operating Principles is *ipso facto* a violation of the Compact, and it [is] entirely sufficient, for purposes of quantifying the effects of the violation, to compare the actual operation with simulated operation as it should have been under the Operating Principles."[120] However, once again, other than that assertion, Kansas could not meet its burden of proof under Article IV-D. The relevant portion of that article provides that the "Compact is not intended to prevent future beneficial development of the Arkansas River basin-including dams and reservoirs-provided that the river flow shall not be materially deplete…"[121] Moreover, the fact that the Compact enables the expansion of projects such as the Pueblo Reservoir – so long as these operations do not result in a material depletion of usable flow to Kansas users,[122] – also belied Kansas' allegation. Accordingly, the Court adopted the Special Master's recommendation and dismissed this exception.[123]

In so doing, Justice Rehnquist observed that to establish a Compact violation "based upon failure to obey the Operating Principles, [Kansas] was required to demonstrate that this failure resulted in a material depletion under Article IV-D." Kansas could not. Therefore, the Court upheld the Master's recommendation.[124]

Kansas' second exception dealt with the Winter Water Storage Program (WWSP). That program was developed to store a portion of the Arkansas River's winter-time flow in the Pueblo Reservoir, which had excess capacity during the winter. This excess water was to be utilized for beneficial uses.[125] Previously, this water was utilized to flood uncultivated cropland.[126] Although Kansas alleged violations of the Compact, once again, it could not prove injury,[127] and, once again, the Court upheld the Master's rejection of the state's objection.

---

[117] *Ibid.* at 682 (*citing* Special Master's Rept. at 412).   [118] *Ibid.* (Emphasis added.)
[119] *Ibid.*   [120] *Ibid.*   [121] *Ibid.* at 683.   [122] *Ibid.*
[123] *Ibid.* ("The theory advocated by Kansas is inconsistent with Article IV-D, which allows for the development and operation of dams and reservoirs so long as there is no resultant material depletion of usable flows at stateline.")
[124] *Ibid.* at 682.
[125] "An inherent and necessary limitation." *Schodde* v. *Twin Falls L. & W. Co.*, 224 US 107, 120 (1911).
[126] *Ibid.* at 684.   [127] *Ibid.*

Indeed, the Chief Justice observed that the "Master examined the computer models submitted by Kansas and Colorado and determined that the depletions shown by the Kansas model are well within the model's range of error. [As a result, o]ne [could not] be sure whether impact or error [was] being shown."[128] The Court also found that the Master gave Kansas every reasonable opportunity to meet its burden of proving its WWSP claim, which it could not.[129]

As for the third exception, here Kansas also claimed that Colorado depleted stateline flows "in *usable* quantity or availability."[130] At trial, Kansas presented three experts, who produced separate methods for measuring the depletion of "usable" flow.[131] Kansas' first expert analyzed the river's flow data for the time period between 1951 and 1985, and came up with a number. Colorado found errors in this expert's analysis. Kansas then presented a second expert, who used the same methodology as the first one, but revised some exhibits and corrected some of the data, modifying the first expert's flow factors.[132] Finally, well after trial before the Master began, Kansas hired a third expert, who proposed a third method of calculating the depletion of usable stateline flow.[133] The Special Master concluded that the second expert's approach was the better one. However, rather than employing his factors, the Master found that, on the basis of the evidence, the third expert's factors were more reliable.[134]

The Court agreed with the Special Master's conclusions. In support of that decision Chief Justice Rehnquist pointed out that the hydrological model that Kansas employed to calculate the depletion of usable flow, as pointed out by the first expert, was only 'a good predictor' when 'looking at long periods of time.'[135] In contrast, the third expert's method required Kansas' model to do something that it was not designed to do, *i.e.*, predict accurately depletions on a monthly basis.[136] And since the third expert's model best matched Kansas' model, the Court upheld the Master's rejection of the latter method.

Colorado's exceptions were quickly disposed of, and will therefore, not be addressed.

---

[128] *Ibid.*   [129] *Ibid.*   [130] *Ibid.* at 685 (emphasis added).   [131] *Ibid.*
[132] *Ibid.*   [133] *Ibid.* at 686.
[134] The Special Master concluded that "the Durbin [the first expert's] approach, using Larson's [the second expert's] coefficients, is the best of the several methods presented for determining usable flow" and that it provided "a reasonable way in which to determine depletions of usable flow." *Ibid.*
[135] *Ibid.* (quoting the expert's testimony).   [136] *Ibid.*

I 1988: *The Master's Second Report*

On September 9, 1997, the Master issued his Second Report. He found that Colorado had over depleted more than 400,000 acre-feet (493 million cubic meters) of usable river flow from 1950 through 1994.[137] The Master, therefore, recommended that Kansas be awarded damages as well as pre-judgment interest for this over-depletion.[138] However, since this issue does not address the issue of apportionment it will not be discussed here.

J 2001: *Exceptions to the Master's Third Report*

On August 31, 2000, the Master issued his third report.[139] Here too he dealt with the issue of damages. Indeed, the report and the Court's disposition completed the remedy phase of the trial for past violations of the Arkansas River Compact.[140] Nevertheless, as above, since this issue does not address apportionment it will not be discussed here.[141]

K 2004: *Exception to the Master's Fourth Report*

On January 17, 2003, both sides rested their respective cases. Thus, the final phase of the trial that began in 1986 was completed. On November 13, 2003, the Master issued his final set of recommendations, which are embodied in his Fourth Report. Kansas filed exceptions to these. The exceptions were argued to the Court in October 2004 and the justices handed down their decision on December 7, 2004. Kansas filed four exceptions, which the Court, by Justice Breyer, overruled. Only the third exception is relevant here, and so it will be the only one addressed.

Recall that in 1995, Chief Justice Rehnquist in addressing Kansas' second exception, dealt with hydrological experts. Subsequently, the parties agreed to employ a hydrological modelling program – the Hydrologic-Institutional Model (H-I Model), a highly complex computer model – that would calculate Colorado's future compliance and to calculate whether there was a material depletion, as required by the Compact. The Special Master recommended that a ten-year measurement period be used to determine compliance. However, in this set of exceptions Kansas asserted that the Compact's

---

[137] *Kansas v. Colorado, ibid.* 543 US at 91. (*Citing* the Special Master's Second Report at 112.)

[138] Report of Special Master, *Kansas v. Colorado*, No. 105, Original 1997, WL 33796878 (US Sept. 9, 1997).

[139] Report of Special Master, *Kansas v. Colorado*, No. 105, Original 2000, WL 34508307 (US Aug. 31, 2000).

[140] *Ibid.* at * 5.   [141] *Kansas v. Colorado*, 533 US 1 (2001).

language only allowed a one-year measuring period, contrary to the Master's recommendation.

The H-I Model was utilized to ascertain what the precise water flow into Kansas *would have been* had Colorado not allowed increased consumption of groundwater after 1949.[142] The Court noted that the model is more accurate when it considers a suite of data that extends out over several years, as opposed to one year. It therefore rejected Kansas exception seeking a one-year period of measurement and thereby upheld the Special Master's recommendation.

L 2009: *The Curtain Falls*

On February 4, 2008, the Master filed his Fifth and Final Report, which included a proposed judgment and decree. Kansas once again, filed an exception. This time, regarding the expenses of its expert witnesses. Thus, this issue will not be addressed here.

M *Assessing the Court's Effectiveness*

In assessing the Court's effectiveness in the adjudication of the *Kansas* v. *Colorado* dispute we will utilize the five proxies that were contained in, above. Prior to delving into an evaluation of these proxies, there are several points that I would like to highlight.

1 A Court Confronted: Two Diverging Water Regimes

Initially, it is important to emphasize that the *Kansas* v. *Colorado* Court was required to grapple with two opposing water rights regimes – the eastern, or common law riparian rights regime in Kansas, and the western prior appropriation regime in Colorado. The Court, therefore, was required to decide between two legal rules that would have yielded entirely differing results.[143] Given this circumstance, the justices were confronted with a practical consideration: which system to select in resolving the dispute? As the Court observed "[i]f the two states were absolutely independent nations [the dispute] would be settled by treaty or by force."[144] However, "[n]either of these ways being practicable, it must be settled by decision of this court."[145] As a result the Court conducted a very broad inquiry, leading it to explain, some years later, in *Nebraska* v. *Wyoming*[146]:

---

[142] *Ibid.* at 93. (Emphasis in original.)
[143] *Ibid.* at 6.   [144] *Kansas v. Colorado*, 206 US at 98. *See also*, Myles, *ibid.* at 6.
[145] *Ibid.* 206 US at 98.   [146] 325 US 589 (1945). (Douglas, J.).

We stated in *Colorado v. Kansas, supra,* [320 US 383, 393–394] that in determining whether one State is "using, or threatening to use, more than its equitable share of the benefits of a stream, all the factors which create equities in favor of one State or the other must be weighed as of the date when the controversy is mooted."... Apportionment calls for the exercise of an informed judgment on a consideration of many factors.[147]

In taking account of the consumptive use[148] of the water of the Arkansas River, the SCOTUS sought to find a middle ground that would satisfy both litigants; particularly, since consumptive use results in the depletion of available allocable water to the user. Whether the parties were completely satisfied with this result is at best conjectural. However, the fact that they did not return to the Court until 1943, suggests that they accepted the judgment. Thus, the Court appears to have been effective in this phase of the dispute.

Recall the earlier discussion of the equality of rights, which appears to urge either the principle of limited territorial sovereignty or the view that these states had a community of interest in the Arkansas River's waters. This dichotomy provided the Court with the opportunity to fashion an equitable common law remedy where no law existed previously. It also allowed the Court to fill a *lacuna*[149] in transboundary water law. The filling of voids in the law, can be seen to fit into the second and fourth proxies for effectiveness: resolving this dispute, and resolving it while providing a new remedy. In this regard, one author recently noted that "[t]he objectives of international adjudicative bodies today include the advancement of particular normative goals like... the maintenance of cooperative arrangements."[150] Consequently, in fashioning the doctrine of equitable allocation and filling a gap in the law, the Court likely also sought to maintain harmony and concordant relations between Colorado and Kansas, as "separate communities of interest."

In addition to the above, I posit that given the absence of other remedies, the Court saw that as an institution, it needed to mold a norm that: (1) would allow it to resolve this dispute; and (2) demonstrate that its judgments are not mechanical. Rather, they are institutional constructs created by judges who possess an understanding of the problem at hand, and who are adept at the

---

[147] *Ibid.* 325 US at 618. (Emphasis added.)

[148] "Consumptive use of water typically refers to uses that make that water unavailable for immediate or short-term reuse within the same watershed." Peter H. Gleick and Meena Palaniappan, Peak Water Limits to Freshwater Withdrawal and Use, 107 *Proc of the Nat Acad of Sci of the U S* 11155 (2010), *available at* http://www.pnas.org/Scontent/107/25/11155.full.

[149] *See generally,* Nienke Grossman, The Normative Legitimacy of International Courts, 86 *Temple L R* 62, 62 (2013). ("International courts and tribunals are deciding more disputes involving sovereign states than ever before. They find facts, identify and interpret relevant rules, *fill gaps and ambiguities in the law,* and apply rules to facts.") (Emphasis added.)

[150] *Ibid.* at 64.

politics and regional conflicts over transboundary water.[151] Indeed, the Court realized that it could not fashion an appropriate non-equitable remedy for two states whose water law regimes were dissimilar.

In defining and utilizing equitable principles to resolving this dispute, Justice Brewer strove to accomplish two fundamental goals. First, he sought, on behalf of the Court, to limit the federal government's reach and its influence into governing interstate rivers – that is why the United States was not allowed to intervene in the 1907 case. Second, Justice Brewer likely sought to extricate the Court from the position of having to declare which water doctrine, the prior appropriation of Colorado, or Kansas' riparian rights doctrine, governed the Arkansas River. As a result, his solution was the use of equity, wherein he weighed the cost and benefit of water use by one state alongside the other. Thus, in Brewer's view equity did not compel the Court to divide the Arkansas River's flow equally. Rather, it meant the most efficient allocation of water in aid of development in the two adjoining states.[152]

We now move on to the justices' employment of these principles vis-à-vis the Report of the Special Master, and whether the Court was effective in this phase of its adjudication.

2 The Court's Approach to the Master's Findings of Fact and Conclusions of Law

The Master's apportionment of water between the two states was reviewed by the Court in 1943. There, Justice Owen Roberts attempted to "reapportion" the allocation of the Arkansas River's waters between Colorado and Kansas. Prior to discussing that issue, it is critical to an understanding of this phase of the adjudication, to examine how the Court assessed the Parties' respective positions. We will then consider whether the Court's adjudication was effective.

Recall that both Colorado and Kansas filed exceptions to the calculations in the Master's order. They asserted that the Master's recommendations were ambiguous and impossible to administer. Furthermore, Kansas claimed that the Master's award to her was deficient,[153] while Colorado asserted that if it was required to comply with the terms of the Master's proposed order, as well as Kansas' suggested modification, it would have to bear severe and unwarranted harm to its interests.[154]

---

[151] Grossman, *ibid.* at 62. ("International court judges are of diverse citizenship, and they are charged with discerning the international responsibility of sovereigns and awarding remedies as mandated by international law.")

[152] Latent Influence of Equity *ibid.* at 15.   [153] *Colorado v. Kansas ibid.* 320 US at 390.

[154] *Ibid.* at 390–391.

In assessing the Master's proposed order and the parties' positions, the Court harkened back to previous evidence demonstrating that during 1907 Colorado significantly increased its use for irrigation of the Arkansas River's water, thereby causing a diminution of the water flowing into Kansas. That action had a "perceptible injury to portions of the Arkansas valley in Kansas, particularly to those portions closest to the Colorado line." It therefore, had a detectible injury upon the interests of Kansas, as the *parens patria* of its irrigators.[155] Nevertheless, that Court held that Kansas' attempt at enjoining Colorado's diversion of the Arkansas River were insufficient. Similarly, in his 1943 judgment, Justice Owen Roberts, on behalf of a unanimous court, held that Kansas' request for an alteration of its water flow allotment could not be permitted.[156] Here, again, the Court sought to resolve this transboundary water dispute while providing a new remedy (law making), by both finding a middle ground and applying its previously established norms.

Two lessons may be drawn from the foregoing. The first, bears on the effectiveness of the Court. In the pre-Compact era, we saw that even when the Court has an imposing docket, as was true in 1943, the Justices carefully examined and assessed the Master's Report – voluminous as it was.[157] This is obviously a credit to the Court as an institution, but also speaks to how it strove to grasp the facts of the case, and to be fair and just to the litigants. The latter point can be used as a comparison with other adjudicative bodies, and may also be utilized as a proxy for effectiveness.

The second lesson, is that in evaluating the Master's report, the Court, is, in some respects, analogous to the European Court of Justice ("ECJ").[158] The ECJ and its Advocate Generals, and this Court with its Master, sit in a reviewing or appellate capacity. Similarly, the WTO's Appellate Body,[159] reviews the recommendations of the arbitral panels, when they are challenged by a party. That is not, however, the case with the International Court of Justice ("ICJ"), as it, like the US Supreme Court, is the final arbiter of inter-state disputes. From an institutional perspective, a second set of eyes, or a review, of a Master's, Advocate's or panel's recommendation/decision, is likely beneficial both to the parties, norm development and the legitimacy of the court or tribunal, since, like the ECJ and the WTO's Appellate Panel, in this dispute the Court is the institution that is ultimately responsible to the Parties, not the Master.

---

[155] *Ibid.*   [156] *Ibid.* at 391–392.

[157] ("The evidence consists of some seven thousand typewritten pages of testimony and 368 exhibits covering thousands of pages."). *Ibid.* at 389.

[158] On the structure and history of the ECJ, *see generally*, Eurofound, European Court of Justice (2013), *available at* http://www.eurofound.europa.eu/areas/industrialrelations/dictionary/definitions/europeancourtofjustice.htm.

[159] World Trade Organization, Dispute Settlement: Appellate Body (2017), *available at* http://www.wto.org/english/tratop_e/dispu_e/appellate_body_e.htm.

With regards to the court's legitimacy, the issue, is how can one evaluate whether it: (1) promotes compliance with the governing international norms; (2) resolves problems and disputes; (3) supports the relevant international legal regime; and (4) legitimizes the legal regime and its norms? In considering these four factors concerning the Court and its use of Masters reports, years of experience demonstrate that each of the foregoing elements is met. For instance, as a *quasi*-international court adjudicating transboundary water problems, the Court (1) has a record of a 100 per cent compliance rate with its decisions and the norms that it has established; (2) routinely resolves disputes; (3) there were no relevant legal regimes to support; and (4) did legitimate its new norms.

One other issue that may be included within the sphere of a court's or tribunal's "function" is how it deals with polycentric issues. Recall that in 1943 the Court observed that the "reason for judicial caution in adjudicating the relative rights of states in such cases is that... they... *present complicated and delicate questions*, and, due to the possibility of future change of conditions, necessitate expert administration rather than judicial imposition of a hard and fast rule."[160] This position means that the Court is disinclined from undertaking polycentric issues related to transboundary water disputes.

The foregoing notwithstanding, the Master's analysis of the H-I model demonstrates that he could address such questions. Moreover, in reviewing the Court's prior judgments, Justice Owen Roberts and the majority in the 1943 phase of the case appear to be applying previous judgments to the most recent problem. Is the Court inclined then to follow its precedents rather than deal with polycentric issues? Certainly, a number of the Court's transboundary disputes have had polycentric issues. For example, Chief Justice Rehnquist's adjudication of the complex hydrological model. That analysis demonstrates that the Court is, at times, willing to address polycentric issues.[161]

3 Multiple Bites of the Apple and the Management of Disputes

Another issue that is raised by the Supreme Court's multiple adjudications, in the same dispute, is its role in managing the entirety of the case. These multiple adjudications set the Court apart from other international courts. In

---

[160] *Kansas v. Colorado*, 320 US at 391 (emphasis added).

[161] The US Supreme Court's multiple judgments in one overall dispute prove somewhat problematical; every new case or judgment within the *Kansas v. Colorado, Arizona v. California*, or *Nebraska v. Wyoming* line of cases, reviews previous judgments. In true international fora, the court or tribunal adjudicates the case and issues its judgment or award, and that is it, for that dispute. *See generally*, the ICJ judgments or those of the ECJ or ECHR, or the WTO and ICSID.

"true" international fora the court or tribunal adjudicates the dispute, issues its judgment or award, and the dispute ends. *See e.g.,* the *Case Concerning the Gabcikovo Nagymaros Project.* No two parties have returned to the IJC, for example, to relitigate other or new issues in a dispute, although there is no reason why that Court would not do so.

Indeed, I posit that one of the flaws of the original jurisdiction interstate cases, is that in "managing" a dispute over decades, the SCOTUS must address new problems in every phase of the litigation and determine whether the new round fits within the framework of the overall dispute's previous facts and remedies. Such a review likely requires the Justices to invest a great deal of time in re-examining both the current and past records made by both an earlier court and its Special Master(s). But, as demonstrated by the Court's 1943 decision, the justices do thoroughly review the evidence presented to the Master – and in the 1943 phase, they specifically examined the factual record, the expert witness testimony, and the expert calculations – and they are able to spot the flaws in the testimony.

Finally, in its post-1943 judgment the Court used its "long shadow" to push the Parties to negotiate a compact. It followed the language that Justice Owen Roberts employed in "nudging" Colorado and Kansas to the negotiating table. The Court, as was pointed out previously, observed, that

> [t]he reason for judicial caution in adjudicating the relative rights of states in such cases is that, while we have jurisdiction of such disputes, *they involve the interests of quasi-sovereigns, present complicated and delicate questions, and, due to the possibility of future change of conditions, necessitate expert administration rather than judicial imposition of a hard and fast rule.* Such controversies may appropriately be composed by negotiation and agreement, pursuant to the compact clause of the Federal constitution. We say of this case, as the court has said of interstate differences of like nature, that such mutual accommodation and agreement should, if possible, be the medium of settlement, instead of invocation of our adjudicatory power.[162]

This is an important aspect of the dispute and the Court, because it suggests a view of adjudicative process, as only one stage on the path of dispute resolution, rather than a one-stop shop. Nonetheless, it still leaves open the question of whether institutionally the Court and the parties benefit from being a multi-stop shop. Certainly, one argument in favor of this system is that the state litigants are able to ask the Court to adjudicate various aspects of their dispute that they are unable to resolve; or alternatively to have the justices "nudge" them to settle certain aspects of the case, or the dispute in its entirety.

---

[162] *Colorado v. Kansas*, 323 US at 392 (emphasis added).

There may also be a boost to the Court's authority and a view of its fairness, with the multi-stop shop, since it offers the states an adjudicatory avenue for dispute resolution, and prevents armed conflict.

Nevertheless, Justice Owen Roberts' language demonstrates the frustration and difficulty that the Court finds itself in when requested to adjudicate original jurisdiction transboundary water disputes. The Court's vexation with original jurisdiction cases is more fully discussed *infra*, in the next two cases.

4 Criticism of the Doctrine of Equitable Allocation

For all of the benefits of the doctrine of equitable allocation, it does have its critics. One of the major ones was the renowned water scholar Charles J. Meyers. In his classic study of the Colorado River,[163] Meyers condemned both the equitable apportionment method and the Supreme Court's principle as unwieldy and inefficient. In fact, he echoes Justice Owen Roberts' frustration. Moreover, Meyers reasoned that either a compact or a congressional mandated apportionment are better than an equitable apportionment since Supreme Court's adjudications are (1) time consuming; and (2) the "Court lacks the ability to deal with the technical information that is a predicate to a good decision, and federalism considerations prevent the Court from adopting the right standard of apportionment."[164] He advocated for the execution of compacts pursuant to the Constitution's Article I, Section 10, Clause 3, Compact Clause. This is akin to a treaty being executed by two independent states, as opposed to allowing courts or tribunals to implement an equitable apportionment.

Despite these criticisms and the Court's 1943's judgment, wherein it declared the following regarding its original jurisdiction in transboundary water disputes:

> [these] controversies may appropriately be composed by negotiation and agreement, pursuant to the compact clause [as the ideal way to resolve these conflicts]. We say of this case, as the court has said of interstate differences of like nature, that *such mutual accommodation and agreement should, if possible, be the medium of settlement, instead of invocation of our adjudicatory power.*[165]

Nevertheless, the SCOTUS has yet to decline to hear an inter-state water dispute, and continues to hear equitable apportionment cases "and to develop

---

[163] Charles Meyers, The Colorado River, 19 *Stan. L. Rev.* (1967) 1.

[164] *Ibid.* at 48–50. Meyers, however, did not account for the inaction of Congress and those states that will not or are unable to enter into compacts.

[165] *Colorado v. Kansas*, 323 US at 392. (Emphasis added.)

the law."[166] For example, in its 1982–83 term the Court expanded the doctrine to other types of water disputes,[167] and "as is the Court's current practice, [it] broke a long tradition of not announcing substantive standards ... " Furthermore, at least three former members of the Court,[168] Justices O'Connor, Brennan, and Stevens have said that they would be willing to abandon the Court's historic reluctance to adjudicate interstate rights.

5 The Post-Compact Era

In its 1995 judgment,[169] the Court noted that the Parties negotiated the Arkansas River Compact, which Congress approved in 1949.[170] This judgment was in response to a request by both Colorado and Kansas for the justices to construe the Parties' Compact – specifically Article IV-D[171] – because of a challenge to the Master's Report, particularly his interpretation of that Article.

Here, as was the case in the earlier adjudication, and in the Court's 1943 judgment, Chief Justice Rehnquist, on behalf of a unanimous court, dissected Kansas' experts' testimony and their reports, agreeing with the Master's assessment of the evidence. The Chief Justice, who was a strict constructionist, plainly construed the language of the Compact's Article IV in overruling both sides' exceptions. Moreover, it appears that in this phase of the dispute, the Court sought to have its judgment further the existing transboundary water law norm. Indeed, when a norm exists, unless it is woefully inadequate or against current legal standards, courts have generally followed the precedent, thereby reinforcing or sustaining it.

a NORM DEVELOPMENT In the Court's 1995 judgment's[172] interpretation of the Compact's Article IV-D, Chief Justice Rehnquist reached back to resurrect language from Justice Roberts' 1943 majority opinion, wherein he declared that "[t]he critical matter is the amount of divertible flow at times when water *is most needed for irrigation*. Calculations of average annual flow, which include flood flows, are, therefore, not helpful in ascertaining the

---

[166] A. Dan Tarlock, The Law of Equitable Apportionment Revisited, Updated, and Restated, 56 *Colo L R* (1985) 381, 382.

[167] *Ibid. Citing Idaho ex rel. Evans v. Oregon*, 462 US 1017 (1983) ("equitable apportionment applies to anadromous fish"). *Ibid.* at n. 3.

[168] *Ibid.*

[169] *Kansas v. Colorado*, 514 US 673 (1995). The cause to the Court "[o]n Exceptions to Report of Special Master No. 105, Orig."

[170] 63 Stat. 145.   [171] *Ibid.* at Art. IV-D.

[172] *Kansas v. Colorado*, 514 US 673, 678 (1995) (Rehnquist, C.J.).

dependable supply of water usable for irrigation."[173] There is a likely reason
why the Court held firm to a concept of divertible flow. Floods do not occur
every spring, and when they do occur, their volume is not reliably the same in
any given year. Thus, flood flows, cannot be reliably added to a river's divertible flow.

The parties' dispute always centered upon the diversion of water for irrigation from the Arkansas and Purgatory Rivers. Consequently, when the Court
was asked to interpret the Compact's Article IV-D, in light of the irrigation
issue, it chose to strictly construe that portion of the article. Recall that Article
IV-D states in pertinent part that "the waters of the Arkansas River . . . shall not
be materially depleted in usable quantity or availability for use to the water
users in Colorado and Kansas under this Compact by such future development or construction."[174] Thus, any other uses, including for drinking, were
irrelevant. That lack of importance placed on other uses was most likely due
to the fact that at the time of this dispute (from 1901 to the 1980s), there was
little or no concern over water for fisheries, wildlife habitat, including wetland enhancement, domestic or industrial uses, recreational uses, instream
flow, recharge of groundwater, water quality or other transboundary water
related uses. All uses that will gain greater concern given the advent of climate change.

6 Judgment Legitimation

The Supreme Court, like other adjudicative bodies, seeks to add to its institutional legitimacy. Indeed, in fashioning a new norm as a remedy, the Court
likely understood that the "equitable allocation" formulation would do just
that. Moreover, in developing the new equitable norm, Justice Brewer's majority likely sought, not just to resolve the dispute before them, but also, whether
consciously or not, also to enhance the Court's legitimacy as a dispute-
resolving institution; in its unique role as the sole Court that had the jurisdiction to resolve transboundary water issues. Consequently, in developing and
adopting the doctrine of equitable apportionment, the justices also launched
a new transboundary water norm that would be amenable for use in similar
inter-state adjudications in the future. And, as a precedent, the norm has been
employed, numerous times, not only by this court, but by United Nations
bodies and other tribunals, *see, e.g., Wyoming* v. *Colorado*, 259 US 419 (1922);
New Jersey v. *New York*, 283 US 286 (1931); United Nations Convention on the

---

[173] *Colorado v. Kansas, ibid.* 320 US at 396–397 (emphasis added).
[174] *Kansas v. Colorado, ibid.* 514 US at 685.

Law of Non-Navigational Uses of International Watercourses (1997), at Art. 5, Equitable and Reasonable Utilization and Participation.[175]

The Court was, of course, cognizant in 1907 of other water law rules. For instance, the Harmon Doctrine hung behind the scenes of this dispute.[176] It has been said to be "perhaps the most notorious theory in all of international natural resources law"[177] and holds that an upstream State is absolutely sovereign over an international river/watercourse that partly flows within its boundaries.[178] Although the doctrine was never employed as a legal tool, by either the United States or, in an international setting, it was likely fresh in the American legal psyche in 1907.

Justice Brewer's majority could, of course, have easily adopted this doctrine of absolute territorial sovereignty, and dismissed the case, by declaring that Colorado, as a *quasi*-sovereign and the upstream state, had exclusive rights to the Arkansas River. However, such a decision would not have been reasonable for either party, nor would it have been equitable, particularly, given the West's on-again and off-again series of droughts.[179] Indeed, as has been previously noted "[w]hen drought returns to Colorado, as it surely will, it will be challenging to see just how far we can stretch our water."[180] Accordingly, in disregarding these doctrines, the justices were more faithful to the Court's role as an adjudicative body: designed by its founders to dependably resolve disputes between states, rather than to any single principle of law.

---

[175] *See also*, Krishna Water Tribunal II, Report and Decision: *In the Matter of Water Disputes Regarding the Inter-State River Krishna and the River Valley Thereof, Between 1. The State of Maharashtra; 2. The State of Karnataka; and 3. The State of Andhra Pradesh* (2010), *available at* http://www.indiawater portal.org/sites/indiawaterportal.org/files/Krishna %20Water%20 Disputes%20 Tribunal _II_ Report_2010.pdf. (p. 40 "(2) In equitable allocation, future uses requiring diversion of water outside the basin are relevant, but more weight may be given to uses requiring diversion of water inside the basin.")

[176] As noted in an earlier, the Harmon Doctrine was developed by the then United States Attorney General, Judson Harmon, in an opinion authored to questions posed to him by Secretary of State, Richard Olney, in November and December 1895, regarding an issue related to the 1844 Treaty of Guadalupe–Hidalgo, brought to the Secretary's attention by Mexican Foreign Minister Romero. 21 Op. Att'y Gen. 274 (1895).

[177] On the Harmon Doctrine, *see generally*, Stephen C. McCaffrey, The Harmon Doctrine One Hundred Years Later: Buried, Not Praised, 36 *Natural Resources J* (1996) 549.

[178] *Ibid.*

[179] *See e.g.*, Thomas B. McKee, *et al.* A History of Drought in Colorado: Lessons Learned and What Lies Ahead (Feb. 2000), http://www.cwi.colostate.edu/publications/wb/9.pdf. ("1898-1904 DRY Sustained and very severe drought over southwestern Colorado. Worst drought on record in Durango area. Some dry years elsewhere in Colorado, but not as severe or sustained. Very wet 1900 northeast Colorado . . . 1905-1929 WET Longest recorded wet period in Colorado history with greatest areal extent in 1905- 1906.")

[180] Carl Ubbelohde, *et al.*, *A Colorado History*, 10th ed. (2015) 387.

The Court may have similarly understood that given the facts and circumstances of the case before them, they could not adjudicate the case by adopting the Harmon Doctrine, since that would have resolved nothing.[181] And they may have also been aware of the 1870 award in the *Helmand River Delta Case*,[182] where the arbitrators found that a river's water must be *equitably apportioned* between two co-riparians there, Afghanistan and Iran. Moreover, the American West was growing and it needed water for irrigation and the building of cities and towns.

Additionally, this dispute was one guided by the first impression, and the justices likely were cognizant of the fact that this type of transboundary water conflict might occur again, as more western states joined the Union. Indeed, numerous interstate water disputes came rushing at the Court over the next few decades.[183] Thus, since no appropriate law existed with which to resolve the dispute, it was incumbent on the Court to create it.

7 Using the Proxies to Assess the Court's Effectiveness

In assessing the *Court's effectiveness* in this dispute, utilizing's **proxy number 2, Resolution;** the Court did resolve the problem before it. It also managed the litigation over a period of a few decades. The parties also seem to have been satisfied with the Court's numerous rulings. If they were not I was unable to find a record that demonstrated that this was the case.

Similarly, with regards to proxy number 3 – normative impact – in fashioning the law of equitable allocation, the Court certainly provided a new remedy. Moreover, the affirmance of the Master's findings – based on his assessment of the H-I Model and ten-year measurement period – could also be said to be a new remedy. Because any future time that model is before a court, it will have to employ the Court's precedent.

Furthermore, in founding the doctrine of equitable allocation, the justices also applied the principle of a "shared commons" or a shared "communal interest," another novel remedy, for interstate water norms. It also fit well into the "primary norm compliance" proxy. Moreover, the construction of a

---

[181] The Court may also have been aware that in negotiating a 1906 treaty with Mexico the State Department abandoned the logic of the Harmon doctrine.

[182] *See* Text in, Mayors St. John, Lovett, and Evan Smith and Mayor-General Sir Frederick John Goldsmid, *Eastern Persia, An Account of the Journeys of the Persian Boundary Commission, 1870–71–72,* (London, 1876), Vol. I, p. 413.

[183] *See e.g., Missouri v. Illinois,* 200 US 496 (1906); *Wyoming v. Colorado,* 259 US 419 (1922); *New Jersey v. New York,* 283 US 336 (1931); and *Arizona v. California,* 283 US 423 (1931).

TABLE 8.2 Kansas *v.* Colorado, *Efficiency – Time from Date of Argument to Judgment*

---

(1) 1902 – *Kansas v. Colorado*, 185 US 125. Argued Feb. 24–25; Decided April 7, 1902. = **1 month and 23 days**.

(2) 1907 – *Kansas v. Colorado*, 206 US 46. Argued Dec. 17–20, 1906; Decided May 13, 1907. = **4 months and 26 days**.

(3) 1943 – *Colorado v. Kansas*, 320 US 383. Argued Oct. 11–12, 1943; Decided Dec. 6, 1943. = **1 month and 24 days**.

(4) 1995 – *Kansas v. Colorado*, 514 US 673. Argued Mar. 21, 1995; Decided May 15, 1995. = **1 month and 23 days**.

(5) 2001 – *Kansas v. Colorado*, 533 US 1. Argued Mar. 19, 2001; Decided June 11, 2001. = **2 months and 23 days**.

(6) 2004 – Argued Oct. 4, 2007; Decided Dec. 7, 2007 = **2 months and 3 days**.

(7) 2009 – *Kansas v. Colorado*, 129 S. Ct. 1294. Argued Dec. 1, 2008; Decided Mar. 9, 2009. = **3 months and 8 days**.

Average = 2 months and 19 days.

---

treaty-like instrument, such as the Compact, may have a conclusive influence on future courts' interpretation of the language of other compacts, or international treaties.

In concluding this section, it appears that the Court was effective in resolving this dispute, as measured by proxies 1–4 in Table 7.2 (at p. 130).

Nevertheless, with regards to the institution's efficiency, proxy 5, given the 104 years the Court invested in this dispute: a century-long conflict over transboundary water is, in this author's view, completely inefficient. So many bites of the apple are clearly an institutional construct created by the Supreme Court for its original jurisdiction disputes. Nevertheless, the Court has yet to explain why it has continued along this path. The downside of this "management" of a dispute allows the parties to dictate the litigation. That function, I suggest, should be the Court's. Albeit, an examination of the individual phases or adjudications of this dispute demonstrates that for each episode/phase, they were efficient, *i.e.*, the cases took little time to adjudicate, as is clear from Table 8.2, above. Yet one must stress that for a dispute to last or extend for over a century is not only unusual but requires a good deal of judicial time and intervention. This cannot serve the institution well, and likely departs from the framers intention for the Court.

With the foregoing in mind, we move to the analysis of the effectiveness of the SCOTUS in its adjudication of the dispute in *Wyoming* v. *Colorado*.

II WYOMING V. COLORADO

A Wyoming *v.* Colorado, 259 *US* 419 *(1922)*

Wyoming v. *Colorado* was also a dispute over the allocation of a river origi-
nating in Colorado: the Laramie River. The Laramie flows down the eastern
flank of Colorado's Front Range and then turns north, entering Wyoming.
The Laramie's headwaters originate in Chambers Lake, in Colorado's Roosevelt National Forest, in western Larimer County, Colorado. It is an unnavi-
gable river, which flows north-northwest from the Roosevelt Forest for 25 miles
in Colorado into Wyoming, where it flows for some 150 miles[184] through the
City of Laramie turning east-northeast south of Garrett, and empties into the
North Platte River near Casper, Wyoming.

This dispute also turned on the doctrine of prior appropriation – first in
time, first in right – that governed water law in both states. It began in
1900, when irrigators in southern Wyoming became aware that irrigators in
Colorado, the upstream state, were using the waters of the Laramie River.
The Coloradans utilized the waters along the river's alpine valley to irrigate their hay meadows and for grazing for their livestock. However, to the
east of these meadows, near Greeley, Colorado, there was a paucity of water
for irrigation. Thus, in 1902, a Colorado corporation began to build a tunnel, the Laramie–Poudre tunnel, to divert water from the northerly-flowing
Laramie to the easterly-flowing Cache La Poudre River, so that the lands east
of the Laramie in the high plains near Greeley, could also be utilized for
irrigation.

At approximately the same time, north of Laramie, Wyoming, that state's
irrigators began building the Wheatland project, an irrigation district fed by
water diverted from the Laramie River, into the twenty-mile-wide Wheatland
flats. The project planned for irrigation of the flats, which were for the most
part owned by then Judge Joseph M. Carey – who subsequently became a
United States Senator from Wyoming – his son and other partners.[185] The
judge and his co-owners also sought to divert water from the Laramie into
two adjacent creeks, the Blue Grass and Sybille creeks. These creeks flowed
onto the Wheatland Flats, and Carey's company's 50,000 acres.[186] The proposal consisted of building a dam and canals to transport water to farmers,

---

[184] *Wyoming v. Colorado*, 259 US 419, 456 (1922).
[185] Nicole Lebsack, Platte County, Wyoming (undated), http://www.wyohistory.org/encyclopedia/
platte-county-wyoming.
[186] James E. Sherow, The Latent Influence of Equity in *Wyoming v. Colorado* (1922), 2 *Great
Plains Res. A J. Nat. & Soc. Sci.*, Paper 44 (1992) 7, 10.

who purchased land from the Carey partners, and who would then be obliged to pay Carey's company for irrigation water. In aid of his company, in 1892, now Senator Carey drafted and introduced the Federal Desert Land Act, also known as the Carey Act, which was enacted in 1894.[187]

The Act provided for private entities in the United States to construct irrigation systems in Idaho, Wyoming, and other western semi-arid states, and profit from the sales of water. The Carey Act was a new approach to the federal government's disposal of public lands, in its efforts to attract new western settlers. Rather than undertake the advertising and other efforts required to dispose of these public lands, the government "farmed out" this task to private companies, who would entice new settlers to the land. Needing water to irrigate their crops, these settlers would then have to pay these companies a fee for the water they utilized for irrigation. Thus, in 1904, Carey's company advertised and attracted farmers unto its 50,000 acres, which at this point was watered by the Wheatland Project.

By 1910, Carey's company had built a considerable storage reservoir on the Laramie River and launched two new irrigation areas.[188] Concomitantly, along Colorado's portion of the Laramie, the Laramie–Poudre tunnel was being built.[189] The Carey Company's investors and its farmers caught wind of these developments, and realized that they could ill afford the competition for water by the Coloradans' diversion of the Laramie River.

Cognisant that other irrigators in Wyoming were complaining to Douglas A. Preston, the State's Attorney General, about other Colorado water users who were allegedly drying Wyoming's Sand Creek, Carey pushed the Attorney General to file suit against Colorado, on the grounds the latter was "stealing" Wyoming irrigators' water. Thus, the State of Wyoming brought an original action, in 1911, against the State of Colorado, as well as two Colorado Corporations. The gravamen of the suit, was to thwart the defendants' proposed diversion of part of the interstate Laramie River.[190] Discovery and the collection of evidence were conducted during 1913 and 1914, and the parties presented their arguments on three separate occasions, December 6, 7, and 8, 1916, reargued them on January 9, 10, and 11, 1918, and then reargued them again, on January 9 and 10, 1922. The case was decided on June 5, 1922.[191] The

---

[187] Act of August 18, 1894 (28 Stat. 422), as amended by PL 114–38 (codified at 43 USC § 641 et seq.). The Act allowed private companies to construct irrigation structures in the western semi-arid states, such as Wyoming, and profit from the sales of water, used to "reclaim" desert lands "therein, and [aid in] the settlement, cultivation and sale thereof in small tracts to actual settlers ... ").

[188] Sherow, *ibid.* 188 at 10.   [189] *Ibid.*   [190] *Wyoming v. Colorado*, 243 US 622 (1917).

[191] *Wyoming v. Colorado*, 259 US 419 (1922).

1922 arguments occurred (1) because the justices believed that the issues were important and novel; (2) due to the death of Chief Justice Edward D. White, in 1921; and (3) because of the appointment of Chief Justice William H. Taft, following White's death.[192] Additionally, the Court asked the United States to intervene.[193]

At the outset of its opinion, the Court observed that both Colorado and Wyoming are situated in an "arid region where flowing waters are, and long have been, commonly diverted from their natural channels and used in irrigating the soil and making it productive. For many years some of the waters of the Laramie River have been subjected to such diversion and use, part in Colorado and part in Wyoming."[194]

Wyoming's allegations were based on the fact that it was seeking to prevent corporate entities in Colorado, who were purportedly acting under the authority and permission of the State of Colorado. Under that color of law, Wyoming purported that the Coloradans were diverting, a considerable volume of water from the Laramie, via the Laramie–Poudre tunnel, into the Cache La Poudre River watershed, which was also wholly in Colorado. As the Court described it, the purpose of the diversion was to irrigate lands that were situated "more than fifty miles distant from the point of diversion. The topography and natural drainage are such that none of the water can return to the stream or ever reach Wyoming."[195]

Wyoming specifically claimed that the diversion was unlawful on two grounds: (1) that, without her authorization, the Laramie's waters could not rightfully be removed from their watershed and diverted into another, so that Wyoming would never receive any benefit from those waters; and (2) that through many costly prior appropriations, which were prior in time and therefore senior and superior in right to the proposed Colorado diversion, the State of Wyoming and her citizens were entitled to use a greater portion of the Laramie's waters, for the "irrigation of lands in that State . . . [Furthermore,] the proposed Colorado diversion will not leave in the stream sufficient water to satisfy these prior and superior appropriations, and so will work irreparable prejudice to Wyoming and her citizens."[196] Wyoming was thus invoking a Harmon Doctrine argument.

The State of Colorado and her co-defendants answered the complaint and "[sought] to justify and sustain the proposed diversion on three distinct grounds":[197] (1) that it was Colorado's right as a State to utilize, as she sees fit, "any part or all of the waters flowing in the portion of the river within her borders, 'regardless of the prejudice that it may work' to Wyoming and her

---

[192] *Ibid.* at 456.   [193] *Ibid.*   [194] *Ibid.*   [195] *Ibid.*   [196] *Ibid.* 456–57.   [197] *Ibid.*

citizens."[198] Also a Harmon assertion; (2) that as a state, Colorado was permitted to an equitable division of the waters of the Laramie and that the proposed diversion, together with all existing appropriations within the state, did not exceed Colorado's rightful share; and (3) that following the proposed diversion, Wyoming's portion of the Laramie, along with its tributaries, would leave sufficient water to fulfil its appropriations, which originated prior in time to the effective commencement of Colorado's proposed 1902 diversion, *i.e.*, prior in time to 1902.

Before beginning the analysis of the case, it is important to note that the opinion's author, Associate Justice Willis Van Devanter, had moved to Cheyenne in the Wyoming Territory, at the age of twenty-five, held numerous positions on commissions that drafted statutes for the Territory, served as the City Attorney of Cheyenne, was elected to the Territory's legislature, served as the Chief Justice of the Wyoming Territorial Supreme Court, among other positions in the Territory, and, once Wyoming became a state, became its Attorney General.[199] Additionally, "[t]here was far more to [Devanter's] prejudice than simply hailing from Wyoming and having served as a state and federal judge there. He and Judge John W. Lacey, Wyoming's lead counsel during the suit, had been former law partners in Cheyenne, and they were also brothers-in-law,"[200] who were well known to jointly host parties and spend holidays with each other's families. Furthermore, Ralph Meeker, Wyoming's consulting engineer, remained in Washington, DC, to hear the final arguments presented to the Court, and then became Van Devanter's "confidential adviser in the areas of hydrology and engineering."[201] It is also possible that Van Devanter may have lobbied the Chief Justice to author the opinion. I believe that he should have recused himself, however, I leave it to others to address that issue.

Colorado's attorneys were aware that they could not do much about what certainly amounted to Justice Van Devanter's conflict of interest.[202] However, as one author has noted, they had a big concern about a case that they had won, *Kansas v. Colorado*. In that case's decision, authored by Justice David J. Brewer, a Kansan, found primarily for Colorado, on the grounds that an expanding economy, in Colorado, was entitled to more water than was

[198] *Ibid.*

[199] The Supreme Court Historical Society, Timeline of the Justices, Willis Van Devanter, 1911–1937 (undated), http://supremecourthistory.org/timeline_devanter.html.

[200] Sherow, *ibid.* at 17.

[201] *Ibid.* (*Citing* Letter from Delph E. Carpenter, Counsel to Colorado, in *Kansas v. Colorado*, to Colorado's Attorney General, Clarence L. Ireland, July 1, 1931.)

[202] Sherow, *ibid.* at 17.

potential development in his home state of Kansas. Brewer had passed away in 1910.[203] Although neither the Court nor historians state the obvious, I posit that Colorado's attorneys hoped that Van Devanter would follow Brewer's logic, and hold that Wyoming was the less developed state. Accordingly, Colorado's counsel contemplated filing a motion for recusal, but believed that such a request would be "'bad policy' in light of the precedent established by Justice Brewer. So, from 1917 to 1922, a time which included three sets of arguments before the Court, Colorado's attorneys waited anxiously for the Court's opinion."[204]

Writing for the Court, Van Devanter spent a good deal of time reciting the history of the prior appropriation doctrine, ultimately upholding it, but curiously declared that it also applies to the federal government, regardless of state boundaries.[205] This latter point – regardless of state boundaries – is inexplicable, as priority in time is a state doctrine not a federal one. Indeed, it has never again been utilized for the federal government and, Van Devanter did not explain how he reached this conclusion. He also noted that although the 1907 dispute between *Kansas v. Colorado*[206] involved two states whose water laws were different in the case *sub judice* the two antagonists both subscribed to the rule of prior appropriation.[207]

Van Devanter also observed that Wyoming sought to determine the two states' relative rights in the Laramie. And then Colorado's worse fears were realized, when Van Devanter, employing Brewer's balancing test, declared that "here the complaining State is not seeking to interfere with a diversion which has long been practiced and under which much reclamation has been affected but to prevent a proposed diversion for the benefit of lands as yet unreclaimed."[208] Which was not totally correct.

1 Allocation

The Court then moved on to the issue of allocation. Initially, Justice Van Devanter noted that "[t]he decision in *Kansas v. Colorado*, 206 US 46, was

---

[203] The Supreme Court Historical Society, Timeline of the Justices, David J. Brewer, 1890–1910 (undated), http://supremecourthistory.org/timeline_brewer.html.
[204] Sherow, *ibid.* at 18.
[205] *Ibid.* at 462.

"Obviously by these acts, so far as they extended, Congress recognized and assented to the appropriation of water in contravention of the common law rule as to continuous flow"; and again, "the obvious purpose of Congress was to give its assent, so far as the public lands were concerned, to any system, although in contravention to the common law rule, which permitted the appropriation of those waters for legitimate industries."
[206] 206 US 46 (1907).   [207] *Wyoming v. Colorado ibid.* at 465.   [208] *Ibid.*

a pioneer in its field."[209] He then cited *Kansas* for the proposition that in a dispute between states over the diversion and use of waters of their transboundary river the upper riparian state has neither ownership or control of the waters flowing within its border, and therefore it has no entitlement to divert and use these waters in a manner that injures or prejudices the lower riparian state,[210] *i.e.*, no state has absolute sovereignty over the waters that pass through her boundaries. The foregoing, can be viewed from two perspectives: (1) a favorable one for Wyoming, *i.e.*, it was simply a reiteration of the law laid down by Justice Brewer's 1907 decision; or (2) an unfavorable one for Colorado, *i.e.*, was the extent of the injury perceptible, as was the case in *Kansas v. Colorado*. Citing Wyoming's Attorney General's argument, Van Devanter, found that the Court's 1907 *Kansas v. Colorado* opinion expressed disapproval of Colorado's position of "complete sovereignty" over its water.[211] Thus, he disposed of Colorado's first objection, on the grounds that it was contrary to the then existing equitable apportionment law.

Van Devanter next referred to the concept of "equality of rights," noting that it did not mean an equal division of transboundary water; rather, it denoted an equal level or plane upon which all the States stand.[212] He likewise overruled Wyoming's objection to Colorado's proposed diversion, on the grounds a state may transfer its appropriated water across any of its watersheds.[213] Indeed, he found that diversions "from one watershed to another are commonly made in both States and the practice is recognized by the decisions of their courts."[214] It is entirely possible that this sentence was a concession to one or more justice on the court, in order to have a unanimous judgment.

Nevertheless, Van Devanter adopted the entirety of the rest of Wyoming's argument. Of critical importance in his decision was that Wyoming's priority dates were earlier than Colorado's, thereby negating the parties' state boundaries. Crucially, Wyoming's lawyers repudiated Colorado's 1902 priority of the

---

[209] *Ibid.* at 463–464.   [210] *Ibid.* at 464.

[211] *Wyoming v. Colorado*, 259 US 419 (1922), at Wyoming's 1916 Bill of Complaint, Abstract of Record, Volume I, at 128 (as *cited* in Sherow).

[212] *Kansas v. Colorado*, 206 US at 97.

[213] *Wyoming v. Colorado ibid.* at 466.

> The objection of Wyoming to the proposed diversion on the ground that it is to another watershed, from which she can receive no benefit, is also untenable. The fact that the diversion is to such a watershed has a bearing in another connection, but does not in itself constitute a ground for condemning it. In neither State does the right of appropriation depend on the place of use being within the same watershed. Diversions from one watershed to another are commonly made in both States and the practice is recognized by the decisions of their courts.

[214] *Ibid.*

tunnel and maintained that the tunnel's appropriation should date to 1909, "the year when the project actually began diverting water into the Cache la Poudre River."[215]

Although Van Devanter found that "[s]ome of [Colorado's] appropriations were made as much as fifty years ago and many as much as twenty-five,"[216] he ignored these appropriations, and asked why, under the circumstances of the case, appropriations from the Laramie should not be respected, "as between the two States, according to their several priorities, as would be done if the stream lay wholly within either State"?[217] In response to this question Colorado asserted that "this is not a suit between private appropriators."[218] However, Van Devanter, while declaring that this was true, asserted that it does not necessarily follow that the respective appropriators on either side of the border are on equal footing in their accomplishments. He then announced that

> As respects Wyoming the welfare, prosperity and happiness of the people of *the larger part of the Laramie valley, as also a large portion of the taxable resources of two counties, are dependent on the appropriations in that State.* Thus, the interests of the State are indissolubly linked with the rights of the appropriators. *To the extent of the appropriations and use of the water in Colorado a like situation exists there.*[219]

One assumes, since Van Devanter does not say so, that the two counties in Wyoming are Laramie and Platte. However, more critical to the appropriation issue, is that a state's interests may diverge from its appropriators. Indeed, the eminent water law scholar, A. Dan Tarlock

> argues that priority is an efficient rule of water allocation, but it is often more rhetoric than rule. Like all drastic rules, the rule's importance lies more in the threat of its application rather than the application.[220] ... The fact that priority enforcement is more bluff than substance does not undermine the need for consistent and fair allocation rules, but it does call into question the sole reliance on enforcement of priorities to allocate water in temporary and chronic shortages. [Moreover,] ... experience will demonstrate that priorities are seldom enforced in practice. In many situations, the strict enforcement of prior appropriation would raise substantial fairness and efficiency concerns.

Wyoming's AG's next argument was contrary to the law established by the Court in its 1907 *Kansas v. Colorado* decision. The Court adopted the claim, which asserted that "[i]n a contest for property of any kind we have never known a case where it was held material that one of the parties could make

---

[215] *Ibid.*   [216] *Ibid.* at 468.   [217] *Ibid.*   [218] *Ibid.*

[219] *Wyoming v. Colorado ibid.* at 468. (Emphasis added.)

[220] A. Dan Tarlock, Prior Appropriation: Rule, Principle, or Rhetoric? 76 N. D. L. Rev. (2000) 881, 883.

better use of the property involved than the other."[221] Recall that in *Kansas v. Colorado*, Justice Brewer declared that although water diversions in Colorado had clearly injured Kansas' irrigators, as part of the equitable apportionment of the Arkansas River's water, he determined that given the higher yields from water uses by Coloradans they would receive the greater allocation.[222] Thus, if Brewer's opinion was to serve as a precedent in this dispute, Wyoming's AG position was on infirm ground.

a COLORADO'S ARGUMENT WITH RESPECT TO EQUITABLE ALLOCATION
Colorado's counsel sought to construct their argument based on the principle of equitable allocation. Since that doctrine did not dictate an equal allocation of a transboundary river's flow, but, rather, the most efficient allocation that would enable economic growth in both states, these attorneys fully expected and argued that this equitable precedent would be employed in Colorado's favor. Indeed, given this precedential interpretation of equitable allocation, Colorado's counsel sought to contrast the priority of uses in their state with those of Wyoming's, in order to demonstrate that Coloradans worked harder at conserving water, and, thus, could make more efficient use of, and be more cost-effective and profitable than Wyoming's irrigators.[223]

Colorado's attorneys founded their argument based on the testimony of two expert engineers, who testified about their comparisons of irrigation practices, performance, and crop yields in Colorado and Wyoming. They sought, via expert testimony, to exhibit the superior economic returns of Colorado's irrigators. That evidence described how wasteful Wyoming's irrigators were in their use of the Laramie's waters, thereby suggesting that if Wyoming's irrigators were thriftier in their water uses, there would be no shortages whatsoever.[224] Accordingly, the major issue was the greater economic returns of the Cache la Poudre Valley irrigators as compared to those of the Laramie Plains and the Wheatland tracts. The Court rejected the expert testimony, even though there was no testimony on Wyoming behalf and responded as follows to Colorado's argument:

---

[221] Wyoming's 1916 Bill, *ibid.* at 94.
[222] *Kansas v. Colorado*, 206 US at 117.

> ("The result of that appropriation has been the reclamation of large areas in Colorado, transforming thousands of acres into fertile fields, and rendering possible their occupation and cultivation when otherwise they would have continued barren and unoccupied; that, while the influence of such diminution has been of perceptible injury to portions of the Arkansas Valley in Kansas . . . it has worked little, if any, detriment, and regarding the interests of both states").

[223] Sherow at 16 (*Citing* Delph Carpenter's 1931 to Colorado's Attorney General).
[224] Sheorw *ibid.* at 16 (*Citing* Louis G. Carpenter and John E. Field, 1916 Testimony, in *Wyoming v. Colorado*: Abstract of Record, Volume I).

It is true that irrigation in the Poudre valley has been carried to a higher state of development than elsewhere in the Rocky Mountain region and that the lands of that valley lies at a lower altitude than do those in the Laramie Plains and generally are better adapted to agriculture. In some parts, they also require less water. It may be assumed that the lands intended to be reclaimed and irrigated in the Poudre valley conform to the general standard, *although this is left uncertain*. But for combined farming and stockraising those of the Laramie Plains offer opportunities and advantages which are well recognized. It is to this use that they chiefly are devoted. It is a recognized and profitable industry, has been carried on there for many years and is of general economic value.[225]

Thus, Justice Van Devanter made short shrift of Colorado's argument, suggesting that it was speculative. He then, without citing any sources whatsoever, asserted that Wyoming's stockraising and farming present economic prospects that "are well recognized." Recognized by whom, Van Devanter failed to say. He then continued along the same vein, declaring that

Many of the original ranchmen still are engaged in it, – some on the tracts where they first settled. With the aid of irrigation, native hay of a high quality, *alfalfa*, oats and other forage are grown for winter feeding, the livestock being grazed most of the year on unirrigated areas and in the neighboring hills and mountains. In this way not only are the irrigated tracts made productive, but the utility and value of the grazing areas are greatly enhanced. The same industry is carried on in the same way in sections of Colorado. In both States this is a purpose for which the right to appropriate water may be exercised, and no discrimination is made between it and other farming.[226]

Note that the Court cites alfalfa, which it notes grows with the "aid of irrigation." Indeed, alfalfa requires high water usage to grow. For example, the University of Wyoming Extension Service stated unequivocally, in 2013, that alfalfa has "[r]elatively high water use requirements."[227] Similarly, a recent study in California found that the crop is the single-largest agricultural water user. The study's authors also noted that

[s]easonal alfalfa water applications generally range from 4,000,000 to 5,500,000 acre-feet. Because of the high-water usage, interest exists in better defining the seasonal water use of fully irrigated alfalfa for different climatic

[225] *Wyoming v. Colorado*, 259 US at 469. Note that the Court's discussion of these issues is in the section that addresses the doctrine of appropriation. (Emphasis added.)
[226] *Ibid.*
[227] Axel Garcia y Garcia, Irrigation Scheduling for Forage Crops, University of Wyoming Extension (2013) 8, http://www.uwyo.edu/uwexpstn/centers/sheridan/_files/2013-field-days-pdfs/irrigation-scheduling-of-forage-crops.pdf.

areas of California and in midsummer deficit irrigation (no irrigation in July, August, and September) of alfalfa as a strategy for coping with limited water supplies . . . [228]

Van Devanter was likely aware of alfalfa's thirst, from his experience representing farmers, and as Attorney General and as the Chief Justice of the Wyoming Supreme Court. However, he again ignored Colorado's two experts' testimony regarding how wasteful Wyoming's irrigators were, and the fact that if they were thriftier in their water uses, there would be no shortages whatsoever. Nevertheless, later in the opinion he declares that "[b]oth States recognize *that conservation within practicable limits is essential in order that needless waste may be secured.* This comports with largest feasible use may be secured."[229]

2 Appropriating the Laramie River

Van Devanter then found that the critical issue to be adjudicated concerned the flow of the Laramie River. He declared that because the Laramie's flow varies over the course of each year and from year to year, the allocation of water between the two states is not a simple matter.[230] The justice rejected Colorado's evidence that the Laramie's flow was the average of the yearly flow, which included the total quantity of available water; due to the large variation of flow during the year. Indeed, he observed that for the water supply to be practically "available" it "must be fairly continuous and dependable."[231] Why the flow must be continuous or even dependable is not elaborated upon.

Accordingly, under Van Devanter's view, the river's natural flow can be substantially conserved and levelled by constructing reservoirs. However, such construction, he noted, is limited by both financial and physical limitations.[232] The justice once again focused on Colorado's evidence, now, regarding the average yearly flow of the Cache La Poudre River for the period 1884–1913, as a method for measuring the available supply of water. Again, he rejected this method because of the variability in the flow.[233] He then sought to replicate Justice Brewer's use tables to demonstrate data,[234] constructing a table of selected data from a Colorado exhibit of the annual flow for the La Poudre River and its Valley and for high water flow years, as measured from April to October. As part of that table – which to this author does not

[228] Blaine Hanson *et al.*, How Much Water Does Alfalfa Really Need? (2008), http://alfalfa.ucdavis.edu/+symposium/proceedings/2008/08-265.pdf.
[229] *Wyoming v. Colorado*, 259 US at 484.
[230] *Ibid.* at 471.   [231] *Ibid.*   [232] *Ibid.* at 472.   [233] *Ibid.* at 472.
[234] *Kansas v. Colorado*, 206 US 46, 108–112 (1907).

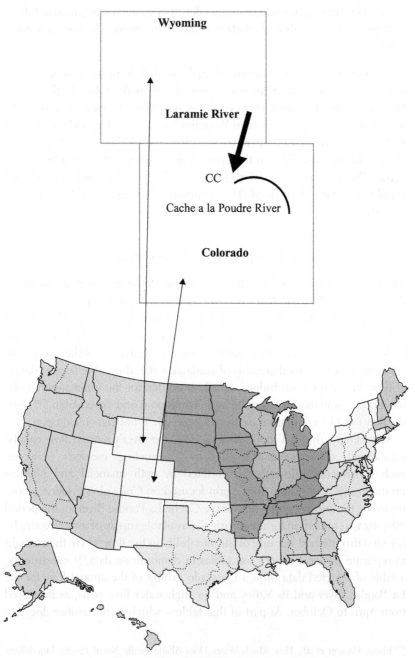

FIGURE 8.2 The Laramie & Cache la Poudre Rivers

make sense and is meaningless in the context of the case – the Justice showed that in 1884 the flow was 403,883 acre-feet with a runoff figure of 666,466 acre-feet, while the flow for 1885 was 202,892 acre-feet and the runoff was 290,392 acre-feet, and in 1900 flow was 211,990 acre-feet, while runoff was 474,573 acre-feet.[235]

He then averaged the water flow for the thirty-year period, 1884–1913, and arrived at an average flow in the Cache La Poudre Basin of 297,322 ac-ft for all years and an average of 262,583 ac-ft, omitting the excessively wet years of 1884, 1885, 1900, and 1909.[236] From his table, he indicated the following:

> that during the thirty years – 1884 to 1913 – the yearly flow of the Cache La Poudre ranged from 151,636 to 666,466 acre-feet, that in sixteen of the thirty it fell below the average, and that eight of the sixteen were in immediate succession. Obviously it is not financially practicable, even by means of reservoirs, to equalize the flow of a stream subject to such variation so that it will have a fairly constant and dependable flow at the average of all years.[237]

However, Van Devanter did not fully explain why equalizing the flow in a region that is arid and has variable rains is critical to what Colorado sought to do: divert water from the Laramie River via a tunnel to the Cache La Poudre River. Since the bulk of the flow occurred during the seasonal flood period, that flow could have been allocated, along with the remaining yearly flow, to satisfy both states' needs, were the doctrine of prior appropriation followed. After examining the flow for each of the thirty years and making a number of calculations, the Court found that the Laramie's flow at Woods, Wyoming, just north of the parties' border, is a "fairly constant and dependable"[238] 170,000 acre-feet, "which is after the recognized Colorado [diverted] appropriations are satisfied."[239] Van Devanter then added the flow of the Little Laramie River, whose course was wholly in Wyoming, and the flow of some minor tributaries and arrived at an "available supply" of 288,000 acre-feet.[240] Of that, he calculated the annual amount of flow held by Wyoming's senior appropriators was 272,500 acre-feet, with a remaining 15,500 acre-feet held by junior appropriators in Colorado.[241] Nevertheless, he noted that the latter figure is far short of what Colorado sought to divert via the Cache La Poudre tunnel.

3 Equitably Allocating the Laramie River's Flow

The Court, nevertheless, observed that the available supply of 288,000 acre-feet was not adequate to satisfy both the Wyoming appropriators that are

---

[235] *Wyoming v. Colorado*, 259 US at 475.   [236] *Ibid.*   [237] *Ibid.* at 473.
[238] *Ibid.* at 485.   [239] *Ibid.*   [240] *Ibid.* at 496.   [241] *Ibid.*

dependent upon the flow and the proposed Colorado appropriation, "so it becomes necessary to consider their relative priorities."[242] This is where Van Devanter begins his equitable allocation. Initially, he notes that there were several existing appropriations in Colorado that held priorities entitling them to preference over some of those in Wyoming.[243] Again, one must point out that pursuant to the doctrine of prior appropriation, the date of appropriation is only considered in an intra-state situation and not in an inter-state one.

According to the Court, the documented appropriations in Colorado were as follows: 18,000 acre-feet for the Skyline Ditch tract and 4,250 acre-feet utilized for irrigating native-hay meadows in Colorado's Laramie valley.[244] Van Devanter found that 4,250 acre-feet were reasonably required for irrigation, based on the testimony of Louis G. Carpenter, Colorado's chief witness, although the state's answer claimed a larger volume.[245] Thus, the total volume of Colorado's recognized divertible appropriation of 22,250 acre-feet, were, according to the Court, not deductible from the total of 288,000 ac-ft available, but only after the 22,500 ac-ft/year were fulfilled. Additionally, Van Devanter noted that Colorado's appropriation from the Sand Creek could not be deducted from the entire volume of 288,000 ac-ft, since that creek was not a tributary of the Laramie River.[246]

Next, the Justice ascribed an appropriation date of October 1909 to Colorado's Laramie–Poudre tunnel – which was incorrect, of course, since it had a priority date of 1902 (but that is where, I posit, Van Devanter's bias came into play – expediently post-dating the Wheatland District extensions).[247] He then totalled the pre-1909 diversions in Wyoming, and arrived at an amount of 272,500 ac-ft/year.[248] This latter figure, according to the Court, established Wyoming' allotment, while the remaining 15,500 ac-ft was apportioned to the Cache La Poudre tunnel diversion (recall that Colorado originally sought 56,000 ac-ft). Consequently, it appears that the 1909 priority date of 15,500 ac-ft water entitlement played a central role in the Justice's calculations.

Finally, note that Van Devanter did not allocate any divertible water to Wyoming's irrigators. Accordingly, before Wyoming's irrigators would receive their 272,500 ac-ft/year Colorado would first receive its Laramie River allocation of 22,250 ac-ft/year (the Skyline Ditch = 18,000 + 4,250 = 22,250)[249] Moreover, once each state received its allotment it could appropriate it in any manner it saw fit. Finally, as to the gravamen of the dispute, on June 5, 1922, the Court entered a decree enjoining Colorado from diverting more than 15,500 ac-ft/year "from the Laramie River by means of or through the so-called Laramie-Poudre project."[250]

[242] *Ibid.* at 489.   [243] *Ibid.* 489–90.   [244] *Ibid.* 490.   [245] *Ibid.*   [246] *Ibid.*
[247] *Ibid.* at 490 and 495.   [248] *Ibid.* at 496.   [249] *Ibid.* at 490.   [250] *Ibid.* at 496.

A Wyoming *v.* Colorado, 260 US 1 (1922). R'hng

Following the entry of the decree on June 5, 1922, Colorado petitioned for a rehearing, seeking an increase in the 15,500 ac-ft allocation for the Laramie Poudre project. In a *per curium* order, dated October 9, 1922, the Court once again enjoined Colorado from diverting any more water than it was allowed in the decree. However, the Court awarded Colorado an additional 2,000 ac-ft/year, appropriated prior to 1902 through the Wilson Supply ditch via the headwaters of a tributary of the Laramie, the Deadman Creek[251] and the petition for rehearing was denied.

B Wyoming *v.* Colorado, 286 US 494 (1932)

In 1932, Wyoming again sued Colorado. Here, it alleged that Colorado was departing from the 1922 decree's terms, by allowing diversions and uses within its borders, of quantities from the Laramie River that were in excess of the decree. It also charged that the water gauges used by Colorado did not correctly measure the amount of divertible water. Accordingly, Wyoming sought the protection and quieting of its rights, and requested that it be allowed to place "more accurate" gauges in Colorado's territory to monitor the amount of water that was being diverted.[252]

With regards to the diversions, Wyoming asserted that (1) in 1926 Colorado allowed water to be diverted from the Laramie through the Laramie–Poudre tunnel that was substantially in excess of the decree's required 15,500 acre-feet;[253] (2) that in the years 1926, 1927, and 1928, with Colorado state officials' cooperation, water was diverted from the Laramie River and its tributaries through the Skyline ditch[254] in amounts that substantially exceeded the 18,000 acre-feet specified in the decree;[255] (3) that in 1926, 1927, 1928, and 1929, with Colorado's state officials assent, diversions were made that materially exceeded the decree's 4,250 acre-feet;[256] and (4) that in defiance of the decree, Colorado allowed diversions from the Laramie and its tributaries, via a creek named Bob Creek, as well as other ditches, none of which were acknowledged or identified in the decree. Finally, Wyoming claimed that as far as it

---

[251] *Wyoming v. Colorado*, 260 US at 2.   [252] *Wyoming v. Colorado*, 286 US 494, 495 (1932).
[253] *Ibid.* at 509.
[254] "The Skyline Ditch, one of the first successful transbasin diversions in the Cache la Poudre River Basin, distributes water from the Laramie River and its tributaries to the north end of Chambers Lake." Colorado State University, Public Lands History Center, Skyline Ditch (2018), https://publiclands.colostate.edu/digital_projects/dp/poudre-river/moving-storing/ditches-dams-diversions/skyline-ditch.
[255] *Wyoming v. Colorado*, 286 US at 509.   [256] *Ibid.* at 510.

was concerned the decree was the instrument that governed the water rights and responsibilities of the two States.[257]

Colorado filed a motion to dismiss the complaint. In its response, Colorado argued that that the entire matter was adjudicated by the former decree. Next, Colorado stated three principal grounds for dismissal of the suit: (1) that the complaint advances the theory that the decree determined and governed the full amount of water that Colorado and it's water users may divert from the Laramie within the State's borders; (2) the decree governed the quantity which Wyoming and it's water users were entitled to divert from the Laramie and, used within its borders;[258] (3) that the acts Wyoming complained of were not those undertaken by Colorado, or under the state's authorization. Rather, they were carried out by individuals and private corporations, who were not parties to the suit, and therefore, no remedy can be ascribed to Colorado;[259] and (4) that, in any event, Wyoming's complaint lacked any specificity or alleged of any clear violation of the Court's decree, nor demonstrated any harm to Wyoming or, her water users.[260]

The case was once again assigned to Justice Van Devanter. In his opinion for the Court, he recalled the Court's 1922 judgment, citing Colorado's response that Wyoming's suit was not between private appropriators, but, rather, between two states. In that judgement, the Court agreed, but noted that what the appropriators accomplished for their respective state cannot be disregarded.[261] Indeed, Van Devanter noted that as regards the appropriations and diversions of the Laramie's waters in Wyoming, both the prosperity of the people of the Laramie Valley, and the concomitant generation of tax revenues, were contingent upon water appropriation in that State.[262] Similarly, an analogous situation occurred in Colorado.[263] Consequently, the Court found, "the interests of the State are indissolubly linked with the rights of the appropriators."[264]

The Court rejected Colorado's motion to dismiss. In so doing, Van Devanter observed that its contention that some of Wyoming's allegations may have been speculative was not enough. Nor was Colorado's claim that Wyoming's Complaint failed to demonstrate with certainty any violation of the 1922 decree, or any harm to Wyoming or the state's water users; since the latter was essentially contradicted by Wyoming's allegations. Furthermore, Colorado's contention was refuted by the plaintiff's allegation that its water users had access to less than their allocated 272,500 ac-ft/annum. Thus, Wyoming was given thirty days to amend her complaint, by making some of the claims more definite and certain.

[257] *Ibid.* at 496. [258] *Ibid.* [259] *Ibid.* at 497. [260] *Ibid.* [261] *Ibid.* at 502.
[262] *Ibid.* [263] *Ibid.* at 503. [264] *Ibid.*

C Wyoming v. Colorado, 298 US 573 (1936)

This action was the follow-up suit by Wyoming to the 1932 case. Wyoming's chief complaint in this action, was as before, that Colorado and its water claimants were continuing to deviate from the Court's 1922 decree and, that these claimed divergences were causing material damage to Wyoming and its water claimants. The petition highlighted two deviations from the decree: The first comprised diversions that were not part of the decree, while the second consisted of diversions of more water than the decree allowed. Wyoming, once again sought an injunction enforcing adherence to that decree.

In response, Colorado denied that certain diversions, particularly the Wilson supply ditch, were in excess or otherwise in violation of the decree, but, admitted that the decree's meadowlands diversions did violate the decree. Nevertheless, it asserted that these departures were made in good faith and in accord with what the state's officers understood the terms of the decree to be.[265]

Once again, Van Devanter was assigned to author the opinion. With regards to the Wilson ditch, he noted that the evidence regarding the excessive deviations were contradictory. Nevertheless, the Court was persuaded that the deviations were done as a matter of repair, rather than an expansion, and therefore the amount of water utilized by Colorado was not in excess of the decree's appropriation.[266] As to the meadowlands diversion, which the Court set at 4,250 ac-ft per annum, Wyoming claimed that the actual diversions ranged from 36,000 to 62,000 acre-feet per year, or 8.45 to 14.6 times in excess of the decree.[267]

In response to the second allegation, Colorado admitted that it greatly exceeded the 4,250 ac-ft per annum fixed in the decree. This water was diverted from the Laramie into ditches and was thereafter applied to the meadowlands by continuous flooding, but, Colorado asserted that, after the water was applied, most of it was returned to the river by way of surface drainage and percolation.[268] Moreover, it argued, that the portion of the water that was consumed was not in excess of the amount set in the decree.[269]

The Court noted that the evidence before it demonstrated that water was applied by a process called "continuous flooding, whereby 10 or more acre-feet [of water] are put on each acre during the irrigating season of 50 or 60 days. That this is a distinctly wasteful process is obvious."[270] Agreeing with Colorado that when water is applied by continuous flooding a substantial quantity ultimately returns to the river, as was the case here. Van Devanter observed, however, "that a material percentage of the water is lost by evaporation and

---

[265] *Wyoming v. Colorado*, 298 US 573, 578 (1936).   [266] *Ibid.* at 581.
[267] *Ibid.*   [268] *Ibid.*   [269] *Ibid.*   [270] *Ibid.*

other natural processes, and that there is no way of determining with even approximate certainty how much of the water returns to the stream."[271]

Colorado contended that the 4,250 ac-ft/annum fixed in the decree, referred to an amount of water that was used consumptively, and not to the amount that it was permitted to divert from the Laramie into the ditches and ultimately to the fields.[272] The Court rejected that argument, observing that the right "to divert and take" from the river and its tributaries was clearly the total quantity of water at the point of diversion, and not to the variable and uncertain part of it that is consumptively used. Moreover, Van Devanter's opinion declared that the 4,250 ac-ft was fixed as the measure for the meadowlands, as it was deemed to be sufficient for that use, "when the water is rightly, and not wastefully applied."[273] Thus, Van Devanter held that Colorado, in fact, exceeded its allocation, and accordingly an injunction issued prohibiting the state from deviating from the decree.

Another part of Wyoming's complaint was that Colorado was transferring and diverting water between watersheds and, that the diversions under the Skyline ditch's 18,000 ac-ft appropriation, as well as those pursuant to the Laramie–Poudre tunnel's 4,250 ac-ft appropriation, exceeded the decree's amount. Colorado's answer implied that all diversions were made under the state's authority and then admitted that it did exceed the Skyline ditch appropriation, but denied that the Laramie–Poudre tunnel's appropriation was exceeded, and stressed that, possibly excepting for 1929, the total diversions were always consistent with the decree. Furthermore, it argued that as to the aggregate of all appropriated water, these too were consistent with the decree, and that so long as the aggregate comports with the decree, it should not matter where the diversions occur.

Assessing the evidence the Court found that indeed the Skyline ditch appropriation was confusing. However, upon further consideration, it established that the decree's quantity was exceeded by 1,000–5,000 ac-ft/year,[274] although the tunnel diversions were not exceeded.[275] Thus, the injunction included a prohibition on surpassing the decree by the Skyline ditch.

Van Devanter then considered whether Colorado was within her rights, under the decree, to transfer or divert water out of one watershed into another under the decree. He declared that the Court saw no material reason why Wyoming should concern itself with what Colorado did, under that state's appropriation law, so long as there was no interference with petitioner's rights and the decree was not exceeded.[276] Indeed, Van Deventer noted that intra-state transfers were incidental to the doctrine of appropriation. Impliedly

[271] *Ibid.*   [272] *Ibid.* at 582.   [273] *Ibid.* at 581.
[274] *Ibid.* at 583.   [275] *Ibid.*   [276] *Ibid.* at 584–85.

in that observation is that Wyoming had no right to interfere with Colorado's sovereignty. Note the Justice's tailoring of his opinion. I believe that the other justices realized that Van Devanter had gone "too far" in his previous judgments and therefore circumscribed Wyoming's relief. Finally, the Court was also asked for other relief which is immaterial for our purposes.

D Wyoming v. Colorado, 309 US 572 (1940)

Wyoming again sought leave to file a complaint charging Colorado with violating the decree.[277] Specifically, it alleged that from May 1, 1939, to June 18, 1939, Colorado diverted in excess of 39,865.43 ac-ft from the Laramie River, which exceeded the decree's amount of 37,500 ac-ft, by 2,365.43 ac-ft ±; and that on June 19, 1939, Colorado shut the headgates[278] of several ditches involved in diverting the Laramie's waters. Thereafter, from June 22, 1939 to July 11, 1939, Colorado opened the headgates, allowing water diversions of 12,673 ac-ft above the decree's 37,500 ac-ft, and more precisely with regards to the meadowland ditches, from May 1, 1939 to July 11, 1939, Colorado allowed diversions of 24,775 ac-ft beyond the 4,250 ac-ft permitted by the 1922 decree.

In its response brief, Colorado requested that it be allowed to measure the quantity of return flow to the Laramie from the headgates diversions of the meadowland ditches. It further asserted that it had Wyoming's permission to make these diversions and appended correspondence from Wyoming and affidavits from its governor, among others.[279] Colorado also averred that Wyoming was not injured by its actions. With regards to the latter response, the Court – by Chief Justice Hughes, as Van Devanter retired in 1937 – found that Colorado's claim that it caused no injury was inadmissible, as the amount that could be diverted was fixed by the 1922 decrees.[280]

Wyoming denied Colorado's assertions and provided its own affidavits in support of its position.[281] Faced with opposing affidavits the Court found it

---

[277] *Wyoming v. Colorado,* 309 US 572, 573 (1940). "Wyoming sought leave to file its petition for a rule requiring the State of Colorado to show cause why it should not be adjudged in contempt for violation of the decree in this suit, restraining diversions of water from the Laramie river." *Ibid.*

[278] A headgate is a gate used to control the flow of irrigation water from a river or stream into a ditch or some other canal.

[279] *Wyoming v. Colorado,* 309 US 572, at 581–82.

[280] *Ibid.* at 581. The Court reasoned that

> Colorado is bound by the decree not to permit a greater withdrawal and, if she does
>
> so, she violates the decree and is not entitled to raise any question as to injury to Wyoming when the latter insists upon her adjudicated rights. If nothing further were shown, it would be our duty to grant the petition of Wyoming and to adjudge Colorado in contempt for her violation of the decree.

[281] *Ibid.* at 582.

unnecessary to undertake a detailed analysis of the disagreement. Consequently, it held that in light of all the circumstances, it appeared that there was "a period of uncertainty and room for misunderstanding which may be considered in extenuation,"[282] and therefore dismissed Wyoming's petition. Note that without a stake in the outcome, Chief Justice Hughes assigned the authorship of the opinion to himself, likely to make a point: Wyoming's repeated claims were taxing the Court for small amounts of diversions by Colorado, and he, as Chief Justice, would not get into the weeds of the apportionment of acre-feet of water. There may have been another consideration. That was the case of *Nebraska* v. *Wyoming and Colorado*,[283] which began during the 1930s. That was a controversy over the North Platte River, where Colorado was impleaded, and in a 1935 decision Wyoming was charged with wrongfully permitting its appropriators to divert water belonging to Nebraska's appropriators.[284] Similarly, the Court at the time also had the *Colorado* v. *Kansas*[285] dispute on its docket. Accordingly, the Court may have simply sought to lend finality to the case. Another possibility, is that the Chief Justice may have been attempting to use the Court's long shadow to force a settlement, which indeed came in 1957.

E Wyoming v. Colorado, 353 US 953 (1957)

In this phase of the dispute, the parties settled their differences and submitted a joint motion to vacate to the Court the two 1922 decrees.[286] The Court issued a new decree whose terms, without its caveats are as follows: Colorado's divertible appropriation was increased to 49,375 acre-feet of water in each calendar year, while Wyoming had the right to divert and use the remainder of the Laramie's water and its tributaries, following Colorado's diversion and use. Moreover, of the 49,375 acre-feet, Colorado could divert up to 19,875 acre-feet of water from the Laramie, outside of the Laramie River basin, in any calendar year.

Furthermore, Colorado agreed that its appropriators would not divert more than 29,500 ac-ft/calendar year, from the Laramie, for use within the Laramie's basin. However, Colorado's appropriators would not be permitted to divert more than 1,800 ac-ft/annum after July 31, provided, that if any of the 19,875 ac-ft were not diverted outside the basin. However, that surplus quantity of water could be added to the 1,800 ac-ft. Additionally, the terms of the stipulation were to remain in force unless modified or restricted by the Court. Moreover, the portion of the Laramie inuring to Colorado's benefit was to be

---

[282] *Ibid.*   [283] 295 US 40.   [284] *Ibid.* at 42. Wyoming's motion to dismiss was denied.
[285] 320 US 383, which was before at a Master at the time.
[286] 259 US 496 (1922), *as amended by* 260 US 1 (1922).

governed by the state's rules of appropriation and administered by its water officials.

Finally, both parties' appropriators were to continue to use the water from the Sand Creek, without prejudicing either state's rights. The decree had two unspoken aspects to it. The first was that the Court respected each state's sovereignty, while second, was the Court's equitable apportionment decree, which demonstrated a legal expectation that each state may restrict water use within its borders, without interference from an upstream or downstream state,[287] thus creating a community of interest.

G Analyzing this Court's Effectiveness

The proxies outlined in Table 7.2 will again be utilized to measure the Court's effectiveness. With regards to the first proxy, **compliance**, the Court did promote compliance with the doctrine of equitable allocation developed in *Kansas* v. *Colorado* and its decree. The fact that the two states followed the Court's rulings demonstrates that there was an impact on these two states' conduct. However, one does not believe that there was any improved compliance by other states or relevant actors.

As concerns the second proxy, **resolution and satisfaction**, did the court or tribunal resolve this dispute and the specific problem it was asked to solve? The answer is affirmative, particularly since it likely encouraged the parties to settle their dispute during the 1950s, with Colorado gaining more water than it was allotted at the start of the dispute. I believe that in the 1940 dismissal of Wyoming petition, Chief Justice Hughes' likely utilized the Court's "long shadow" to bolster the settlement.

The third proxy, **Normative Impact**, inquires whether the court resolved this dispute while providing new remedies (law-making), and whether there was an overall impact that the resolution had on legal norms. In the Court's 1922 decision, Justice Van Devanter combined the appropriations of two states, to determine which state's appropriators had priority. This was a new norm, albeit, it was altered, some years later, by Justice Douglas, in Nebraska v. Wyoming and Colorado, 325 U.S. 589, 618 (1945). There, the rule was re-stated as follows:

> But if an allocation between appropriation States is to be just and equitable, strict adherence to the priority rule may not be possible. For example,

---

[287] *See generally, Sporhase v. Nebraska ex rel Douglas*, 484 US 491, 956 (1982). ("Our law therefore has recognized the relevance of state boundaries in the allocation of scarce water resources.")

TABLE 8.3 Wyoming *v.* Colorado, *Efficiency – Time from Date of Argument to Judgment (Total = 35 Years)*

(1) **1922** – *Wyoming* v. *Colorado*, 259 US 41. Argued in Dec. 1916, 1917, 1918, 1921, and reargued Jan. 9–10, 1922; Decided June 5, 1922 = **4 years and 5 months.**	(4) **1936** – *Wyoming* v. *Colorado*, 298 US 573. Argued Feb. 11–12, 1936; Decided June 11, 1936 = **3 months and 13** days.
(2) **1922** – *Wyoming* v. *Colorado*, 260 US 1. Petition for a rehearing submitted sometime in July, 1922; Decided Oct. 9, 1922 = **4 less than 3 months.**	(5) **1940** – *Wyoming* v. *Colorado*, 309 US 572. Pet. Submitted Mar. 23; Decided Apr. 22 = **1 month.**
(3) **1932** – *Wyoming* v. *Colorado*, 286 US494. Argued Dec. 3, 1931; Decided May 31, 1932 = **approximately 6 months.**	(6) **1957** – *Wyoming* v. *Colorado*, 353 US 953. Decree issued on May 13, 1957.

the economy of a region may have been established on the basis of junior appropriations. So far as possible, those established uses should be protected though strict application of the priority rule might jeopardize them. Apportionment calls for the exercise of an informed judgment on a consideration of many factors. Priority of appropriation is the guiding principle. But physical and climatic conditions, the consumptive use of water in the several sections of the river, the character and rate of return flows, the extent of established uses, the availability of storage water, the practical effect of wasteful uses on downstream areas, the damage to upstream areas as compared to the benefits to downstream areas if a limitation is imposed on the former – these are all relevant factors. They are merely an illustrative, not an exhaustive, catalogue. They indicate the nature of the problem of apportionment and the delicate adjustment of interests which must be made.

Nevertheless, this norm, has not been utilized in any subsequent decision. The Court, however, may have reinforced the prior appropriation doctrine and by reutilizing the doctrine of equitable allocation bolstered it.

With regards to the fourth proxy, **Fairness and Legitimation**, I would argue that given Van Devanter's predisposition toward his home state of Wyoming, the Court in 1922, cannot be perceived as being a fair, just and independent forum. Moreover, his bias, I suggest detracted from the Court's legitimacy. In contrast, Chief Justice Hughes judgment did uphold the view of the Court as a fair and legitimate institution.

As to the fifth proxy, **Efficiency**, was the Court efficient in issuing its judgment? The tabulations for the time of filing of a petition to decision are shown in Table 8.3. For the most part, the Court was efficient. The initial 1922 decision was years in the making. However, this can be chalked up to procedural issues. Nevertheless, multiple arguments cost these parties attorneys' fees and time, while Colorado's and Wyoming's appropriators may have suffered, due to lack of water diversion.

III ARIZONA V. CALIFORNIA

"The problem of irrigating the arid lands of the Colorado River basin has been confronted by the peoples of that region for two thousand years and by Congress and this Court for many decades." *Arizona v. California*, 460 US 605, 608 (1983).

A *Introduction*

The conflict between Arizona and California, although bloodless, was nevertheless hard fought, and endures. It also turns on water greed. The reason: because in these two deserts states water is accurately characterized as life itself. It is also for this reason that although to some the demand for an additional 4.5 percent extra water – that is, 548 acre-feet/day (or 200,000 ac-ft/annum (247 million cubic-meters/annum)) out of 4.4 million acre-feet, may appear to be insignificant, in the scheme of the total amount of water that Arizona and California were fighting over, it was obviously not so for the two protagonists in this case. What also appears perplexing is that the Colorado River's source states, Wyoming, Colorado, Utah, and New Mexico, were not as "jealous" about their appropriation, as was California.

This may be a consequence of the fact that California is the most downstream riparian, as well as the most populated.[288] That situation also exists in the Nile River System and in Mesopotamia. For example, in the Nile River Basin, Egypt routinely threatens armed conflict with the very uppermost riparians – Rwanda, Burundi, Congo, and Uganda – if they allocate for themselves more than Egypt believes they should.[289]

Arizona v. California is also one of the longest and most contentious cases in United States Supreme Court history[290] – transboundary or otherwise. Like

---

[288] The population of these states, according to the United States Census Bureau, is as follows: Wyoming 584,153 (2014 estimate), http://quickfacts.census.gov/qfd/states/56000.html; Colorado, 5,355,866 (2014 estimate), http://www.census.gov/quickfacts/table/PST045214/08,00; Utah 2,942,902, http://www.census.gov/quickfacts/table/PST045214/49,08,00; and New Mexico, 2,085,572, http://www.census.gov/quickfacts/table/PST045214/35,49,08,00. Whereas California has a total population of 38,802,500 (2014 estimate), http://www.census.gov/quickfacts/table/PST045214/06,35,49,08,00.

[289] *See generally*, P. Godfrey Okoth, The Nile River Question and the Riparian States: Contextualising Uganda's Foreign Policy Interests, 11 *African Soc R* (2007) 81.

[290] Jack L. August, Jr., *Dividing Western Waters: Mark Wilmer and Arizona v. California* xvi–xvii (2007). Although the case began in 1930 and ended in 2006, the contentious and longest part

Kansas v. *Colorado*, this dispute can be divided into two stages 1930–36 and 1950–2006. The longest active portion of the case lasted for eleven years, from its inception in 1952, until its initial resolution in 1963. The case generated 14 separate opinions, which are summarized below. These opinions have populated hundreds and hundreds of pages. Additionally, the Court also issued approximately two dozen memorandum opinions.

Initially, this transboundary water dispute involved the apportionment of water from the Colorado River primarily between Arizona and California. It then also concerned several California irrigation districts and related agencies. Subsequently, the dispute incorporated a number of adjacent states: including Colorado, Wyoming, Utah, New Mexico, and Nevada, as well as the United Sates Government, and five Indian Tribes. This case is replete with numerous allocation formulae, priorities of ownership, and calculations of how much water each set of acreages should be granted. It also made new law.

From 1931 to 1952, the dispute centered on Arizona's challenge to the interpretation of the Colorado River Compact,[291] ("Compact") and the Boulder Canyon Project Act ("BCPA"),[292] both of which are elaborated upon below. The Compact and the BCPA constitute what has been termed the "Law of the River."[293] This series of cases will be discussed briefly, and then the focus will turn to the 1953–1979 phase.

At issue in the dispute was Arizona's aspiration and claim of putting to "beneficial use,"[294] its "fair share" of the Colorado River's mainstream[295] water, as

---

of the case was before the Court from 1952–1963. Indeed, August asserts that cases that are considered "The Case of the Century," *e.g.,* the *Scopes Monkey Trial,* and *Brown v Board of Education* "pale in comparison to *Arizona v. California . . . " Ibid.* at xvii.

[291] Act of Aug. 9, 1921, c. 72, 42 Stat. 171, Ratified by Proclamation of June 25, 1929, 46 Stat. 20.

[292] Act of Dec. 21, 1928, c. 42, 45 Stat. 1057, codified at 43 USC §§ 617 *et seq.* Obviously, from an international law perspective, the BCPA is not very relevant, since there is no international legislature. However, it may be of significance when discussing the European Union's regulations or directives. *See e.g.,* European Union, Regulations, Directives and Other Acts (Last updated Aug. 5, 2015), *available at* https://europa.eu/european-union/law/legal-acts_en.

[293] *See generally,* US Department of the Interior, Bureau of Reclamation, Lower Colorado Region, The Law of the River (Last updated Mar. 2008), http://www.usbr.gov/lc/region/g1000/lawofrvr.html.

[294] "One of the most basic premises of . . . Water Law [in the western states] is that beneficial use is the basis, the measure and the limit of the right to the use of water . . . " *United States v. Orr Water Ditch, Co.,* No. CV-N-73-0012-LDG, 2005 WL 3767091, at * 12 (D. Nev. May 20, 2005). (Trial Motion, Mem. and Aff.) *See also, Montana v. Wyoming,* ___ US ___131 S.Ct. 1765, 1774–75 (2011). *See* generally, Barton Thompson, Jr. John Leshy, & Robert Abrams's Legal Control of Water Resources, Cases and Materials, (6th ed. 2016).

[295] As referred to herein "the mainstream" of the Colorado River refers exclusively to the water in the river itself, without including the water that is contained in its tributaries. That is, once a tributary feeds into the river that water is part of the mainstream.

well as the water contained in state's tributaries, including the Gila,[296] and Salt Rivers. Indeed, for Arizona and California, both desert states, the Colorado River held the key to sustaining their civilization, life, and economy.[297] California had from the date of the passage of the Reclamation Act of 1902[298] and well into the 1960s battled aggressively for as much water as the state could acquire. It also took every opportunity to develop and use the water resources of the lower Colorado River, to Arizona's and the other Colorado River states' consternation.[299]

The Colorado River is the lifeline of the desert southwest.[300] But for the river's diversion and damming, cities such as Las Vegas and Phoenix would have remained mere hamlets. Similarly, Los Angeles would not have experienced the growth in population that it sees today. Indeed, the huge agricultural economy, which requires irrigation, particularly in Arizona and California,[301] would not be possible without the series of dams and their reservoirs that were built during the era encompassing the period from 1930 through the 1960s.[302] Control of the river meant potential riches and wealth.[303] In fact, but for the Colorado's waters Arizona and California may have been destined to desolation and impoverishment.[304] The roots of the present dispute stretch back to at least 1892, when a number of Californians realized that California's Imperial Valley "could be a vast year-round garden if water could be diverted to the land."[305]

---

[296] August *ibid.* at 15.   [297] *Ibid.*

[298] The Newlands Reclamation Act of June 17, 1902, P. L. 57–161, 32 Stat. 388. Its purpose is to "[a]ppopriat[e] the receipts from the sale and disposal of public lands in certain States and Territories to the construction of irrigation works for the reclamation of arid lands." Congress' intent when it passed the Act was to exploit the intermittent precipitation in the western states, because settlers in the American west outstripped the supply of river water that they had diverted. See generally, US Department of the Interior, Bureau of Reclamation, *The Bureau of Reclamation: A Very Brief History* (Last Updated July 5, 2011), http://www.usbr.gov/history/2011NEWBRIEFHISTORY.pdf.

[299] *Bureau of Reclamation: A Very Brief History, ibid.*

[300] Charles J. Meyers, The Colorado River, 19 *Stanford L R* 1 (1966) 1. ("The Colorado River has been the cause of bitter and protracted struggles. Control of the river means potential wealth and prosperity; without water from the river, a state may be condemned to desert and destitution."); Norris Hundley Jr., *Water and the West: The Colorado River Compact and the Politics of Water in the American West* (2009).

[301] *See e.g.,* California's 2010 crop output amounted to approximately $28 billion, while its animal output was approximately $10 billion. United States Department of Agriculture, Economic Research Service, State Fact Sheets: California (Last updated October 27, 2011), http://www.ers.usda.gov/statefacts/ca.htm.

[302] Ellen Hanak, *et al. Managing California's Water: From Conflict to Reconciliation* (2011) *available at* http://www.ppic.org/content/pubs/report/R_211EHR.pdf.

[303] Meyers *ibid.* at 1.   [304] *Ibid.* at 1–2.

[305] August *ibid.* 1 at 27. The Imperial Valley is a large agricultural area in southeastern California, which is bordered on the east by Arizona, to the south by Mexico and on the north by the

There was also an international dimension to the allocation of the Colorado's waters. In 1906 the United States and Mexico negotiated a treaty aimed at allocating water from the river by the USA to northern Mexico. Although that treaty was not consummated until 1944, the parties arrived at a draft agreement that awarded Mexico 60,000 acre-feet[306] annually from the Rio Grande River. Secretary of State Robert Lansing, for example, argued that "equity and comity" entitled Mexico to some of the Colorado's flow and consequently demurred in 1920 to congressional bills that would "develop" the Colorado River.[307]

Finally, returning to the subject of state sovereignty, as it relates to this dispute, the Supreme Court in *Arizona v. California*, as it was required to do,[308] was very cognizant of each state's sovereign right, to allocate water internally, or to do within its borders as it saw fit.

B *The Geographic Setting*

The Colorado River rises along the continental divide in Colorado and flows approximately 1,293 miles (2,081 km) to its mouth in Baja California, draining into Mexico's Gulf of California.[309] *See* Fig. 8.3. It is a navigable stream,[310] a fact that will become relevant in the Court's various rulings, as it is a jurisdictional issue.[311] The Colorado River system, consisting of its main stream and tributaries, drains 242,000 square miles (389,461 sq. km) in the United States and 2,000 square miles (3,219 sq. km) in Mexico.[312] The River flows 245 miles (394 km) through Colorado, then 285 miles (459 km) through Utah, continuing to flow 292 miles (470 km) through Arizona.[313] It then courses 145 miles (233 km) along the boundary between Arizona and Nevada, and continues 235 miles (378 km) along the boundary between Arizona

---

Salton Sea. Its main water source is the Colorado River. "In the early 1900's the region was a barren desert. Early developers saw that Colorado River could be diverted to supply irrigation water. By 1915, three hundred thousand acres were under cultivation producing vegetables, agronomic crops and livestock to feed the nation." *Ibid.*

[306] 1 acre-foot = 1,234 m³. An acre-foot is the quantity of water required to cover an acre to a depth of one foot. An acre-foot equals 326,851 gallons or 43,560 cubic feet.

[307] August *ibid.* at 31.

[308] Recall that under US law the states regulate water within their borders, borders and are free to do so, within the bounds of federalism.

[309] Meyers *ibid.* at 1–2.   [310] *See generally, Arizona v. California*, 283 US 423 (1931).

[311] US Const. Art. 1 § 8 ("The Congress shall have Power . . . To regulate Commerce with foreign Nations, and among the several States, and with the Indian Tribes.").

[312] American Section of the Int'l Water Comm'n, *United States and Mexico*, HR Doc. No. 359, 71st Cong., 2d Sess. 17 (1930).

[313] *State of Arizona v. State of California*, 298 US 558, 561 (1936), *Rhng den.*, 299 US __ (1936).

and California, and finally flows southwardly into Mexico.[314] For over 688 miles (1,177 km), more than half its length, the Colorado flows in Arizona (Figure 8.3).[315] Average precipitation in the river's basin is 15 inches (38.1 cm.) annually "and evaporation reduce[s] runoff by ninety percent."[316]

As noted previously, apportionment of water from the Colorado River has been the source of acrimony and prolonged struggles.[317] Indeed, the Colorado "had been the most litigated, regulated, politicized, and argued-about river in the world."[318] From a dispute resolution perspective, given the Boulder Canyon Project Act, the Colorado River Compact, as well as other agreements and treaties over the River's water allocation, litigation has been the predominant trend over a span of seventy-five years. (*See* Table 8.4 for a listing of the cases.)

The history of the development of the Colorado River began in 1902, when Arthur Powell Davis – who in 1906 became the Chief Engineer of the United States Bureau of Reclamation, and subsequently its Director[319] – "devised a 'plan for the gradual comprehensive development of the Colorado River by a series of storage reservoirs.'"[320] He convinced then President Theodore Roosevelt to ask Congress "to enter into a broad comprehensive scheme of development for all irrigable land"[321] along the river. Subsequently, Davis persuaded President Woodrow Wilson's secretary of the interior, Franklin K. Lane, to fund a survey of these irrigable lands. In 1914, Davis became the Director of the Reclamation Service and undertook the assessment. Imperial Valley residents and other Southern Californians were elated at the prospect of the federal government's broad irrigation and flood control plans.[322] Moreover, the recently formed California's Imperial Irrigation District's lawyers saw the district advancing its grip on its prior rights and enlarging its share of Colorado River water.[323]

---

[314] *Ibid.*   [315] *Ibid.*   [316] August *ibid.* at 26.
[317] Meyers *ibid.* at 1.   [318] August *ibid.* at 26.
[319] United states Department of the Interior, Bureau of Reclamation, Arthur P. Davis, Director, Reclamation Service, 1914–1923 (last updated, July 13, 2009), http://www.usbr.gov/history/CommissBios/davis.html.
[320] August *ibid.* at 29.   [321] *Ibid.*
[322] *See generally* Joe Gelt, Sharing Colorado River Water: History, Public Policy and the Colorado River Compact, 10 *Arroyo*, Aug. 1997, No. 1, *available* at http://ag.arizona.edu/azwater/arroyo/101comm.html. (By the early 1920s the Colorado Basin states were anxious about their share of the Colorado River. Then, as now, California's growth was viewed with concern. Burgeoning growth meant increased water demand, and the other Colorado Basin states feared California would establish priority rights to Colorado River water. That California contributed the least amount of runoff to the river added gall to the situation.)
[323] August *ibid.* at 33.

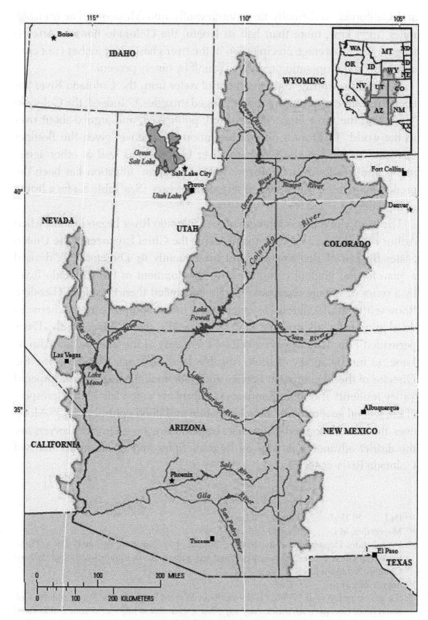

FIGURE 8.3 The Colorado River Basin

TABLE 8.4 *Procedural History of the* Arizona v. California *case*

*1931 – *Arizona v. California*, 283 US 423.	*1979 – **Arizona v. California**, 440 US 59. California filed motion for leave to file a complaint against Arizona and the United States to quiet title. Motion for leave granted. Defendants allowed 45 days in which to respond.
*1934 – **Arizona v. California**, 292 US 341.	1982 – *Arizona v. California*, 456 US 912. Report of Special Master is received and ordered filed. Exceptions, if any, must be filed within 45 days.
*1935 – *US v. Arizona*, 295 U.S. 174.	1982 – *Arizona v. California*, 459 US 811. Motion of Pyramid Lake Indian Tribe for leave to file a brief as *amicus curiae* is granted. Exceptions to the Special Master's Report are set for oral argument in due course. Motion of Arizona, *et al.* for leave to file a brief in response to the reply briefs of the U.S. *et al.* is granted.
1936 – *Arizona v. California*, 298 US 558, *Reh'g denied*, 299 US 618.	*1979 – **Arizona v. California**, 439 US 995. Joint motion to enter supplemental decree by the U.S., Arizona and Private California Defendants, and Nevada is granted.
*1954 – *Arizona v. California*, 347 US 986. Appointment of Special Master, George I. Haught.	*1983 – **Arizona v. California**, 460 US 605. Motion to intervene of Indian tribes, who had previously been represented by the USA for greater water rights, granted; and exceptions of States' pursuant to principles of *res judicata* also granted.
1961 – *Arizona v. California*, 364 US 940. Report of the Special Master is Received and Filed.	*1984 – **Arizona v. California**, 466 US 144. Second Supplemental Decree.
1963 – *Arizona v. California*, 373 US 546.	*2000 – **Arizona v. California**, 530 US 392. Intervention by United States on behalf of five Indian Tribes and States' request to reopen decree.
1964 – *Arizona v. California*, 376 US 340. Decree Issued.	*2000 – **Arizona v. California**, 531 US 1. Supplemental Entry of decree with respect to Fort Mojave and Colorado River Indian Reservations.
1978 – *Arizona v. California*, 439 US 812. Motion of Donald D. Stark for leave to file a brief, as *amicus curiae*, granted.	*2006 – **Arizona v. California**, 547 US 150. Approval of Joint Motion for entry of final consolidated decree.

* Denotes Case Discussed in this Section.

California's "water greed"[324] caused a great deal of anxiety among the other Colorado River states, but particularly so, in Arizona, where politicians, farmers and miners were afraid that California would steal "their" Colorado River water.[325] Similarly, the leaders of the upper-Colorado states, Wyoming, Colorado, Nevada and New Mexico, were so apprehensive about California's desire for more and more water, that at a meeting of southwestern leaders, Oliver Shoup, Colorado's Governor, issued some provocative remarks regarding California's water greed.[326] Subsequently, Shoup asked his legal advisor, Delphus E. Carpenter,[327] to devise a plan which ultimately led to the formation of the Colorado River Commission, and subsequently to negotiations over the Colorado River Compact. The latter has been said to be "one of the most significant developments not only of the legal and political history of the river, but also the history of the American West."[328]

With the formation of the Commission in 1921, which required Congressional authorization, each of the seven[329] Colorado River states appointed a commissioner to formulate a joint agreement, for managing the basin. Moreover, these states requested Congress to provide its assent and, to authorize the nomination of a federal government representative, who would act on behalf of the United States, and jointly with the state commissioners.[330] On November 24, 1922, these commissioners and the federal representative signed an agreement, which was to become effective when ratified by Congress and the Legislatures of each of the seven states. That agreement became the Colorado River Compact.[331] It governs the allocation of water rights of the Colorado River among the signatory parties.[332] The Compact was finally ratified

---

[324] *Ibid.* Similarly, in 1997 "Pat Mulroy, the general manager of the Southern Nevada Water Authority, commented, 'Things have changed, but what remains the same is that California was the problem back then, and California is the problem today.'" Gelt *supra*.

[325] *Ibid.*   [326] *Ibid.*

[327] Mr. Carpenter was one of Colorado's lawyers in *Wyoming v. Colorado* 259 US 419 (1922).

[328] August *ibid.* at 33. In 1920 Congress passed the Kincaid Act (41. Stat 600). In the Act Congress directed the Secretary of the Interior to undertake a full and comprehensive investigation and to report back to the Congress on the possibility of diverting the water for beneficial use.

[329] These states respectively include, from the River's headwater to its drainage in the Gulf of California: Wyoming, Colorado, Utah, New Mexico, Nevada, Arizona, and California.

[330] Act of August 19, 1921, c. 72, 42 Stat. 171.

[331] 43 USC § 617L (1922). Article I of the Compact, provides that "[t]he major purposes of this compact are to provide for the equitable division and apportionment of the use of the waters of the Colorado River System; to establish the relative importance of different beneficial uses of water, to promote interstate comity; to remove causes of present and future controversies..."

[332] *Ibid.* at (a) Approval by Congress. "The States of Arizona, California, Colorado, Nevada, New Mexico, Utah, and Wyoming, having resolved to enter into a compact under the Act of the Congress of the United States of America approved August 19, 1921 (42 Statutes at Large, page 171), and the Acts of the Legislatures of the said States ... who, after negotiations participated

by Congress in 1928, as a part of the passage of the Boulder Canyon Act, and on June 25, 1929, President Hoover signed it into law. Arizona did not ratify the Compact until 1944.[333]

Pursuant to the Compact each basin is entitled to 7.5 million acre-feet of consumptive use annually, and the Lower Basin was entitled to an additional 1 million acre-feet in annual consumptive use. In addition, the Compact specifies how water would be allocated to Mexico should a treaty be signed. Finally, the Upper Basin states agreed not to cause the flow at Lee's Ferry, Arizona (the midpoint between the upper and lower basins), to drop below 75 million acre-feet every 10 years. The Boulder Canyon Project Act approved this agreement subject to certain limitations and conditions.[334]

C The Boulder Canyon Project Act

The Boulder Canyon Project Act ("BCPA") authorizes the Secretary of the Interior to expend the necessary funds to construct a dam, a storage reservoir, and a hydroelectric plant on the Colorado River at Black Canyon[335] (which is located on the Nevada–Arizona border). In addition, the Congress provided funding for their operations, control, and management, via the United States Department of Interior's Bureau of Reclamation. The Act further declares that that authority is conferred "subject to the terms of the Colorado River compact... for the purpose of controlling the floods, improving navigation and regulating the flow of the Colorado River, providing for storage and for the delivery of the stored waters thereof for reclamation of public lands and other beneficial uses exclusively within the United States, and for the generation of electrical energy as a means of making the project herein authorized a self-supporting and financially solvent undertaking."[336]

Finally, the Act authorized the construction of the Hoover Dam. It also allocated the Lower Basin's share of 7.5 million acre-feet among its three states, with Arizona entitled to 2.8 million acre-feet (maf), California entitled to 4.4 maf, and Nevada entitled to 300,000 acre-feet.

---

in by Herbert Hoover appointed by The President as the representative of the United States of America, have agreed upon the following..."

[333] Meyers *ibid.* at text accompanying notes 67 and 68.

[334] Proclamation of June 25, 1929, 46 Stat. 20.

[335] *See generally,* 43 USC § 617, Colorado River Basin; Protection and Development; Dam, Reservoir, and Incidental Works; Water, Water Power, and Electrical Energy; Eminent Domain; *specifically,* 43 USC § 617a. The Colorado River Dam Fund.

[336] *Ibid.*

D A Summary of the Cases

1 Arizona v. California, 283 US 423 (1931)

On October 13, 1930, Arizona filed a motion for leave to file an original complaint, in the Supreme Court of the United States, against the Secretary of
the Interior Ray Wilbur, as well as the states of California, Nevada, Utah,
New Mexico, Colorado, and Wyoming.[337] Arizona's motion charged that Secretary Wilbur authorization the construction of a dam at Black Canyon on
the Colorado River,[338] was in violation of Arizona's state laws and in violation
of its *quasi*-sovereign rights. Arizona further alleged that half the dam and its
reservoir were on Arizona's territory. Accordingly, Arizona asked the Court to
declare that the Colorado River Compact and the Boulder Canyon Project
Act are unconstitutional, void and of no effect."[339]

Additionally, Arizona sought a permanent injunction against each of the
defendants. The injunction would prohibit the defendants from enforcing or
carrying out the terms of the Compact or the BCPA. Petitioner, also requested
the Court to enjoin Secretary Wilbur, from the performance of a number of
contracts for the storage of water and for hydropower development – executed
by the Secretary, on behalf of the United States – as well as from taking any
action in furtherance or under color of the Act.[340] Arizona similarly requested
that Mr. Wilbur be enjoined from executing contracts which he negotiated
on behalf of the United States, for the use of the waters stored in the Black
Canyon Dam's reservoir (now known as the Hoover Dam and Lake Mead).
Moreover, Arizona sought an Order directing Secretary Mr. Wilbur not to
deliver electricity/power following the project's completion, and from undertaking any other efforts that the United States sought to fulfil under the BCPA.

Finally, Arizona challenged the United States' position that the Colorado
River was a navigable river, and therefore claimed that the United States
government had no jurisdiction over the river.[341] The defendants/respondents
filed a motion to dismiss, which the Court ultimately granted.

Responding to Arizona's claims, the Court held that based on the evidence
before it, the Colorado River is navigable.[342] It also observed that under

---

[337] *Arizona v. California*, 283 US 423, 449 (1931).

[338] The Black Canyon is situated on the Colorado River at the state line between Nevada and
Arizona, slightly south of Las Vegas. The canyon is the location where the Boulder Canyon
Dam, later renamed the Hoover Dam, was constructed.

[339] *Arizona v. California ibid.* 283 at 450.   [340] *Ibid.*

[341] Contrary to *Gibbons v. Ogden*, 22 US 1, 190 (1824), where the Court held that under the
Constitution's Commerce Clause, Art. I § 8, cl. 3, commerce includes navigation of rivers,
and therefore the federal government regulates them.

[342] *Arizona v. California*, 283 at 453–454. (*Citing* Report Upon the Colorado River of the West,
June 5, 1860.) "It is true that whether a stream is navigable in law depends upon whether it is

its previous decisions, the federal government may lawfully perform its congressionally mandated functions without yielding to the police powers of a state.[343] Moreover, Justice Brandeis, writing for the Court, noted that Congress can approve the construction of the dam and reservoir, and that Secretary Wilbur was under no duty to submit the plans and specifications for that construction to the state for approval. In addition, the Court observed that the federal government has the authority and jurisdiction to construct any obstruction in the river for improving navigation, since the Colorado is navigable.[344]

The majority also disagreed with Arizona's assertion that Secretary Wilbur's authorization to construct a dam at Black Canyon was in violation of Arizona's laws and in violation of its *quasi*-sovereign rights to appropriate additional water. First, Justice Brandeis calculated the total amount of the Colorado's available water for appropriation as 18,000,000 acre-feet.[345] He then found that the claims by Arizona that any "additional appropriations will be prevented because Wilbur proposed to store the entire unappropriated flow of the main stream of the Colorado River at the dam . . . "[346] were without merit. Finally, in denying Arizona's motion the Court found that the state's contention cannot prevail since it was grounded, "not on any actual or threatened impairment of Arizona's rights, but upon assumed potential invasions."[347]

2 *Arizona v. California*, 292 US 341 (1934)

On February 14, 1934, Arizona, once again, filed a motion for leave to file a complaint against California, the federal government and other defendants. The motion requested the Court to allow Arizona to file a suit, by which the state sought to perpetuate testimony "in an[y future] action or actions arising out of the Boulder Canyon Project Act which 'at some time in the future' it will commence . . . "[348] Although Arizona's contention was that she sought to perpetuate testimony, I read the case as the state's challenge to the interpretation by California and the United States, in particular, and the states of the upper and lower basins of the Colorado River generally, to the allocations

---

navigable in fact . . . Commercial disuse resulting from changed geographical conditions, and a congressional failure to deal with them, does not amount to an abandonment of a navigable river or prohibit future exertion of federal control."

[343] *Citing Johnson v. Maryland*, 254 US 51 (1920).

[344] The Court noted that "[t]he act declares that the authority to construct the dam and reservoir is conferred, among other things, for the purpose of 'improving navigation and regulating the flow of the Colorado River.' As the river is navigable and the means which the act provides are not unrelated to the control of navigation . . . " *Arizona v. California, ibid.* 283 at 455–56.

[345] *Ibid.* at 460. *See also*, the definition of an acre-foot, *ibid.* An acre-foot is the quantity of water required to cover an acre to a depth of one foot.

[346] *Ibid.* at 461.   [347] *Ibid.* at 461.   [348] *Ibid.* 292 US at 345.

agreed to by the defendant states and the United States, in the Colorado River Compact (Compact) and the BCPA, neither of which it entered into. Indeed, the Court spends most of its decision addressing the various allocations. These are discussed below.

On February 20, 1934, the Court issued a rule to the defendants to show cause why Arizona should not be granted leave to file its motion for the taking of any testimony. The defendants divided along those that opposed the motion and those that did not.

Justice Brandeis, writing for a unanimous court, first pointed out that Arizona's expected action may rest upon an assertion that "the stored water [in the Boulder Dam Reservoir] is used in such a way as to interfere with Arizona's enjoyment by Arizona, or those claiming under it, of any rights already perfected."[349] Moreover, petitioner averred that its rights in making "additional legal appropriations" and to enjoy the use of the stored water would be "limited."[350]

Specifically, the Court noted that Arizona claimed rights under section 4(a) of the BCPA.[351] These rights, it was claimed, were governed by the terms of the Compact.[352]

Arizona further alleged that the potential interference by California, the United States, and the other Basin states would result from their refusal to

---

[349] *Ibid.* "Under the law of Arizona, *the perfected vested* right to appropriate water flowing within the state cannot be acquired without the performance of physical acts through which the water is and will in fact be diverted to beneficial use." *Arizona v. California*, 283 US 423, 459 (1931). (Emphasis added.)

[350] *Ibid.* 283 US at 459.

[351] Section 4. (a) of the BCPA provides in the relevant section:

> The States of Arizona, California, and Nevada are authorized to enter into an agreement which
>
> shall provide (1) that of the 7,500,000 acre-feet annually apportioned to the lower basin by paragraph (a) of Article III of the Colorado River compact, there shall be apportioned to the State of Nevada 300,000 acre-feet and to the State of Arizona 2,800,000 acre-feet for exclusive beneficial consumptive use in perpetuity, and (2) that the State of Arizona may annually use one-half of the excess or surplus waters unapportioned by the Colorado River compact, and (3) that the State of Arizona shall have the exclusive beneficial consumptive use of the Gila River and its tributaries within the boundaries of said State, and (4) that the waters of the Gila River and its tributaries, except return flow after the same enters the Colorado River, shall never be subject to any diminution whatever....

[352] *Arizona v. California*, 292 US 341, 348 (1934). Recall that the Compact "apportions the waters of the Colorado River between a group of states, termed the upper basin, north of Lee Ferry, and a group south thereof, the lower basin, among which are Arizona and California." *Ibid.* at 348.

accept its interpretation of article III (b) of the Colorado River Compact,[353] which Arizona argued is the correct one. Furthermore, the motion asserted that contracts executed between the United States and California, would appropriate an extra, but illegal, 1,000,000 acre-feet of water for California users. These contracts, it was argued, would materially affect Arizona's rights under the Colorado River Compact. Specifically, Arizona was concerned that a future decision would construe the Compact's § 4(a) against it. That section provides in pertinent part that

> (a) Inasmuch as the Colorado River has ceased to be navigable for commerce ... the use of its waters for purposes of navigation shall be subservient to the uses of such waters for domestic, agricultural, and power purposes.

The Court observed that the 1,000,000 acre-feet/annum were allotted exclusively to California by article III (b) of the Compact. Therefore, the lower basin would receive a total of 8,500,000 acre-feet/annum, which, under the terms negotiated during the Compact, would be allocated as follows in acre-feet: 300,000 to Nevada, 2.8 million to Arizona, 4.4 million to California, plus the additional one million that was appropriated exclusively to California. One will recall that Arizona rejected these terms.

In essence, Arizona sought to change the allocation formulae in its favor, using the terms of agreements it rejected. It therefore argued that the one million acre-feet apportioned to California was to compensate Arizona for the equivalent loss from the Gila River and its tributaries. The latter are tributaries of the Colorado River system wholly located within Arizona.

Consequently, Arizona argued that it sought to perpetuate testimony, in support of its construction of the Compact's article III (b). That testimony was to be taken from persons connected with the negotiations over the Compact in 1921 and 1922, and would be used as evidence in any future proceeding(s) before the Court. Arizona also asserted other rights under the BCPA that were unrelated to the Compact, which the Court again noted, the state refused to ratify.[354] The Court found that Arizona's claims could not stand, since both

---

[353] Article III states the following:

> (b) In addition to the apportionment in paragraph (a), the Lower Basin is hereby given the right to increase its beneficial consumptive use of such waters by one million acre-feet per annum ... [In turn III(a) states] (a) There is hereby apportioned from the Colorado River System in perpetuity to the Upper Basin and to the Lower Basin, respectively, the exclusive beneficial consumptive use of 7,500,000 acre-feet of water per annum, which shall include all water necessary for the supply of any rights which may now exist.

[354] *Arizona v. California*, 292 US 341, 352 (1934).

Arizona and California ostensibly agreed that the one million acre-feet incorporated into the BCPA's article III(b), were already apportioned.[355]

Furthermore, Justice Brandies found that the oral evidence requested to be perpetuated was not of the type that would be sufficient to prove Congressional intent re: the Compact or, the BCPA. Additionally, in addressing whether Arizona's proposed evidence would be admissible, the Court treated the Compact as it would any treaty. It then declared that when the meaning of a treaty is ambiguous, "recourse may be had to the negotiations, preparatory works, and diplomatic correspondence of the contracting parties to establish its meaning."[356] That rule, the Court noted, cannot be applied to oral statements made by the persons who took part in the negotiations over the treaty. Accordingly, Arizona was not entitled to file its original complaint.

3 *United States* v. *Arizona*, 295 US 174 (1935)

This suit was initiated by the United States against Arizona. Nevertheless, the case fits within the history of the *Arizona* v. *California* dispute, and so it will be briefly reviewed here. The facts are as follows: on September 10, 1934, the United States, initiated the construction of the Parker Dam "in the main stream of the Colorado River."[357] The dam and its reservoir were to straddle the Arizona-California border, which is located northeast of Vidal Junction, California.[358] Arizona objected to the dam's construction, claiming that it was unlawful to "be built without her consent, and threaten[ed] the use of military force to stop the"[359] project. Accordingly, on January 14, 1935, the US government filed a complaint in the Court seeking an injunction permanently enjoining Arizona from interfering with the dam's construction.

The Court issued a show cause order to Arizona, to demonstrate why it should not be restrained, pending the final determination of the suit. In turn, Arizona filed a motion to dismiss the United States' action, containing an affidavit executed by its Governor, Benjamin Baker Moeur, in which he laid out the grounds upon which the State relied upon, in its objections to the dam's construction.[360]

---

[355] *Ibid.* at 357.   [356] *Ibid.* at 359–360 (*citing Nielsen v. Johnson*, 279 US 47, 52(1929)).

[357] 295 US 174, 179 (1935).

[358] *Ibid.* The dam was ultimately built and is located in La Paz County, Arizona and San Bernardino County, California.

[359] *Ibid.*

[360] Governor Mouer previously called "out the Arizona National Guard to stop the construction of Parker Dam. The dam was to be a diversion point to send water to the Metropolitan Water District of Southern California." *See* Tempe Historical Society, *The Cowboy Who Came to*

The gravamen of the complaint was that on February 10, 1933, the Secretary of the Interior entered into a contract with the Metropolitan Water District of Southern California (MWD). As part of that agreement the MWD consented to pay to the United States the full cost of the dam's construction, not to surpass $13 million. Pursuant to the agreement the MWD and the Department of the Interior were to each receive rights to one-half of the power generated by the Parker Dam, and the MWD would acquire the right to divert a specified amount of water from the dam's reservoir. It was implicit that the federal government had the jurisdiction to construct the dam under a number of federal laws,[361] including the Boulder Canyon Act. The Secretary alleged that Arizona's interference was illegal under the federal laws.

In the complaint, the United States also alleged that heavy flash floods caused by Arizona's Bill Williams River,[362] were "a menace to the Colorado River Indian Reservation, to United States public lands, and to navigation below Parker." Consequently, the dam "[w]as designed to promote reclamation of the [Indian] reservation lands and of [the] public lands of the United States."[363] Moreover, the United States asserted that the stretch of the Colorado between Arizona and California was navigable, providing it with jurisdiction pursuant to the Commerce Clause of the Constitution. Finally, the federal government argued that only Congress has the power to regulate navigation[364] and the construction of dams.[365] Furthermore the Parker Dam's construction was authorized by Congress and over several decades it allotted $1.36 million for the construction of irrigation and diversion works.[366]

Tempe as a Doctor and Ended Up Being Governor, Benjamin B. Moeur (undated), http://tempehistoricalsociety.org/page13.html.

[361] The other laws asserted by the USA were the Reclamation Act, June 17, 1902, 32 Stat. 388, and supplemental acts, particularly those of April 21, 1904, 33 Stat. 224, March 4, 1921, 41 Stat. 1404.

[362] The Bill Williams River flows roughly 45 miles to the Colorado River, north of Parker Arizona. The Nature Conservancy, *Arizona: The Bill Williams River* (2011), http://www.nature.org/ourinitiatives/regions/northamerica/unitedstates/arizona/placesweprotect/bill-williams-river.xml.

[363] *United States* 295 US at 182.

[364] *Gibbons v. Ogden*, 22 US 1, 3 (Wheat.) (1824) ("The power of regulating commerce extends to the regulation of navigation. The power to regulate commerce extends to every species of commercial intercourse between the United States and foreign nations, and among the several States.")

[365] The Rivers and Harbors Act, 33 USC § 401 ("It shall not be lawful to construct or commence the construction of any bridge, causeway, dam, or dike over or in any port, roadstead, haven, harbor, canal, navigable river, or other navigable water of the United States until the consent of Congress to the building of such structures shall have been obtained . . . ")

[366] Act of March 2, 1867, 14 Stat. 514, where Congress appropriated $50,000 "[f]or expense of collecting and locating the Colorado River Indians in Arizona, on a reservation set apart for them by" § 1 *Ibid. at* 182.

Arizona's motion to dismiss claimed that it owned the portion of the riverbed that lies east of the Colorado's channel.[367] Accordingly, the State reasoned the United States did not have a right to build on its portion of the river. Essentially, this meant that the Parker Dam could not be built. The issue before the Court, then, was whether Congress had specifically authorized the construction of the Parker Dam; and if not did the executive branch have the authority to do so under the National Industrial Recovery Act ("NIRA"),[368] the depression era program of public works.

In addressing the parties' contentions, the Court once again stressed that Arizona was not a signatory to the Compact, which was made "to provide an equitable apportionment of the waters of the Colorado River system among the interested States, establish relative importance of different beneficial uses, and secure the development of the Colorado River basin, the storage of its waters, and protection against floods."[369] Moreover, the Court held that the "Colorado ha[d] ceased to be navigable for commerce and that the use of its waters for purposes of navigation should be subservient to uses for domestic, agricultural, and power purposes."[370] Thus, it dispensed with the United States' navigability argument.

Furthermore, the Court observed that Arizona's jurisdiction with respect to the apportionment, use, and equitable distribution of its share of the Colorado River's waters that flow within its territory are entirely unaffected by the Compact or the federal Reclamation Act of 1902.[371] Nevertheless, Justice Butler, writing for the majority, noted that the State's title to any portion of its streams is held conditionally to Congress's power under the commerce clause.[372] Under that clause, Congress has authority "to cause to be built a dam across the river in aid of navigation. The Boulder Canyon Project Act is an example of the exertion of that power."[373]

However, following an extensive review of various laws and apportionments, the Court held that the Congress did not, as required, specifically authorize the construction of the dam in question. Analyzing NIRA, it also found that Parker Dam was not approved by President Roosevelt, as required by a 1910 law. Accordingly, the Court dismissed the suit.

Arizona's victory against the United States was fleeting, however. Having won its case against the United States on April 29, 1935, it saw that triumph

---

[367] *Ibid.* at 183. The Court refers to the channel as the "thread of the stream," a common-law term, *see e.g., Kinkead v. Turgeon*, 74 Neb. 580, 109 N.W. 744 (1906); *Arizona v. Bonelli Cattle Co.*, 107 Ariz. 465, 489 P. 2d 699 (1971). *See also, New Jersey v. Delaware*, 291 US 361, 379 (1934).
[368] § 202, National Industrial Recovery Act, 48 Stat. 201.
[369] *United States* 295 US at 180.   [370] *Ibid.*   [371] *Ibid.* at 183.   [372] *Ibid.*
[373] *Ibid.* (*Citing Arizona v. California*, 283 US 423, 451 (1931).)

vanish four months later, when on August 30 of that year, Congress authorized the construction of the Parker Dam and ratified the contracts that the Department of the Interior had entered into previously.[374] By 1938, the dam and its reservoir, Lake Havasu, were completed.

4 *Arizona* v. *California*, 298 US 558 (1936)

Following its victory in the previous case, Arizona immediately filed another petition for leave to file a complaint against California and others. In this matter, Arizona again sought a rule to be issued directing the defendants to show cause why the filing of the complaint should not be granted.[375] Relitigating the Compact, Arizona's proposed complaint requested the following relief:[376] a judicial apportionment of the Colorado River's waters, among the seven states in the Colorado River Basin, while limiting California's share solely to the amount established by the BCPA, with the proviso that any increase in the apportionment that the United States agrees to supply to the Republic of Mexico should be furnished from California's overall allotment.

The defendants' replies raised numerous objections to the sufficiency of the proposed complaint. However, the Court considered only two of them, both procedural. The Supreme Court's consideration, at this stage in the proceedings – it was assessing whether the motion was legally sufficient for the complaint to be filed – was restricted to an examination of the facts alleged in the proposed complaint. In addressing these claims, the Court – contrary to its decision in *US* v. *Arizona* – again found that the Colorado River was a navigable stream. Justice Harlan Stone, writing for the Court, also noted that at the time Arizona filed its petition two dams existed on the Colorado: Boulder Dam and Laguna Dam. Additionally, the Bureau of Reclamation planned to construct two new dams: the Parker and the Imperial.

The court also made the following findings:

(1) That the average annual flow[377] of the Colorado River in Arizona, at Imperial Dam was approximately 16. 8 million acre-feet/annum. Of that

---

[374] 49 Stat. 1039.

[375] *See* 296 US 552 (1935).

> "A rule is ordered to issue requiring the defendants to show cause on or before January 13, next [1936], why leave to file the Bill of Complaint herein should not be granted. Complainant shall have three weeks from the date of service of the returns to the rule within which to reply thereto if so advised."

[376] *Arizona* v. *California*, 298 US 558, 559–560 (1936).

[377] These figures did not contribute to the Court's analysis of this particular case. However, Justice Stone appears to want to lay out a roadmap for how the Court will ultimately resolve this case.

number, approximately 6.1 million acre-feet of water per annum was appropriated and put to beneficial use in the United States and the Mexican Republic. Of the remaining amount, approximately 2.5 million acre-feet were diverted above Lees Ferry, Arizona, the boundary between the upper and lower basins – per the Compact, as adopted by the BCPA – and were utilized and consumed in Utah, New Mexico, Colorado, and Wyoming. Moreover, another 3.6 maf were diverted annually below Lees Ferry – to Arizona, California, and Nevada.[378] The annual average water rerouted from the Colorado below Utah's southern boundary was as follows in ac-ft: "Arizona, 585,000; California, 2,475,000; Nevada 40,000; Mexican Republic, 500,000,"[379] for a total of 3,600,000 acre-feet.

(2) Once the existing appropriations were deducted from the 16.8 maf annual average flow, a net average annual flow of at least 9.7 maf remained for future appropriations.[380]

(3) that municipal corporations, and water districts in California contracted for storage of Colorado River waters in the Boulder Dam and as compensation would have delivered to them 5.4 maf annually.

(4) That Arizona argued that the contracts between the United States and the California entities would annually consume, all the unappropriated water, except for approximately 1 maf, and therefore Arizona would be incapable of reclaiming/irrigating additional land that it wanted to develop.

Justice Stone also observed that Arizona and five of the other defendant states agreed in their pleadings that each of them employs the doctrine of prior appropriation. California did not. However, it did so as far as was material to the present case.

Initially, the Court examined whether it had jurisdiction over the case. Justice Stone, writing for the Court, initially observed that Arizona's proposed complaint does not claim any rights that arise from the state's "own appropriation of the waters of the Colorado river."[381] The proposed complaint also did not assert any violation or encroachment of Arizona's rights acquired by appropriation, nor did the state seek any relief for the protection of those rights.

The importance of these figures will become more evident, particularly in the analysis of the very next case that the Court addressed.

[378] *Arizona v. California*, 298 US at 562, n. 2.   [379] *Ibid*.

[380] *Ibid*. at 562. It is not at all clear how the Court arrived at this number, as can be seen by the following calculation. Total available is 16.8 million acre-feet. If we subtract the amount that, according to the Court was appropriated, 6.1 million acre-feet, one arrives at 10. 7 million acre-feet, not 9.72 million acre-feet.

[381] *Ibid*. at 566.

Indeed, although the Arizona proposed complaint alleged that it had made "definite plans for the irrigation of 1,000,000 acres of unirrigated land in the state, and a right to share in the water for that purpose is asserted,"[382] there was no sign that the state took any steps to appropriate any water for the project. The majority also observed that Arizona's proposed complaint did not challenge California's corporate entities' right to withdraw the annual amount of 5,362,000 acre-feet as part of its contracts with the United States, except as far as its request for relief related to the Colorado River's unappropriated water.[383]

Justice Stone, thus, dismissed Arizona's claims, noting that, given the allegations in the proposed complaint, without joining the United States as a party, the Court was unable to adjudicate any of the state's rights to the Colorado's unappropriated water. The Court reasoned that the federal government's construction of its dams and reservoirs, which contained unappropriated water from the Colorado, meant that the United States had a stake in the outcome, and, therefore, had to be joined in the litigation. Justice Stone also held that the Colorado River Compact and the BCPA were a valid exercise of Congress' Commerce Clause authority and, therefore they governed the case.[384] Consequently, since the BCPA calls for the construction of a series of dams and reservoirs on the Colorado, providing for the storage of water, hydropower and directed the Secretary of the Interior to enter into a series of contracts to provide water in exchange for funds which would be used for operating these structures, the Secretary acted within the rights delegated to him by Congress, to provide the California corporations with the delivery of 5.4 million acre-feet of stored water. The decree sought by Arizona was therefore, dismissed as it had "no relation to any present use of the water thus impounded which infringes rights which Arizona may assert subject to superior but unexercised powers of the United States."[385]

5 The Post-1936 Period

Following its loss in the Supreme Court, Arizona found itself on the losing end of three cases. Moreover, the state did not gain access to any more water than it had in 1930, when it filed its initial suit. Indeed, the fight was just beginning. California's growing congressional delegation, which, since the 1920s, sought to gain more and more water for the Imperial Valley, had pushed through a law that provided the authorization and funds for the construction of the Parker Dam, and more was to come.

---

[382] *Ibid.*   [383] *Ibid.*   [384] *Ibid.* at 569.   [385] *Ibid.* at 570.

In 1940 Arizona elected Sidney P. Osborn, Governor. With that election, the state's political class changed its approach to water policy. In 1944,
Osborne ended the state's drawn out battle over Arizona's membership in the
Colorado River Compact, and convinced the legislature to sign onto it.[386] He
also announced that with the passage of the Boulder Canyon Project Act, "the
era of philosophizing and theorizing about the River had ended: 'Whatever
our previous opinions about the best place or planned, we can only recognize
that decisions have been made and the dam constructed.'"[387]

In the post-World War II era more and more people were moving to both
Arizona and California. And, as populations and industry grew, water became
an extremely critical resource. California's congressional delegation, particularly its members in the House of Representatives, whose numbers were much
larger than those of Arizona, continued their push for greater water allocation
for their state.

6 *Arizona* v. *California*, 373 US 546 (1963) (Arizona I)

Consequently, in 1952 Arizona once again filed suit in the Supreme Court
against California, as well as seven of its public agencies.[388] Later, Nevada,
New Mexico, Utah, and the United States were joined as parties. This new
suit involved a change in strategy and was a seminal element of the dispute.
It was the most protracted case before the Court, lasting over a decade. Here,
the Court set a water allocation formula, which governs to the present day.
That apportionment involved an extremely exhaustive analysis of allocation
schemes, water rights and priorities dating back to the 1800s. These are discussed below in the most basic and curtailed manner.

The essence of the dispute was over "how much water each State ha[d] a
legal right to use out of the waters of the Colorado River and its tributaries,"[389]
which had been set, of course, by the Compact. Following the filing of the
initial set of pleadings, the Court referred the case to a Special Master. Subsequently, the Court noted that

> Master [Judge Simon Rifkind] conducted a trial lasting from June 14, 1956, to
> August 28, 1958, during which 340 witnesses were heard orally or by deposi-
> tion, thousands of exhibits were received, and 25,000 pages of transcript were

---

[386] "Arizona did ratify the Compact in 1944, after it had already become effective by six-state
ratification as permitted by the Boulder Canyon Project Act." *California* v. *Arizona*, 373 US
546, 558, n. 24 (1936).

[387] Katharine L. Jacobs & Bonnie G. Colby (eds.), *Arizona Water Policy: Management Innovations in an Urbanizing, Arid Region* (2006) 17.

[388] *Arizona* v. *California*, 373 US 546, 551, n. 2 (1963).   [389] *Ibid.* 373 US 551.

filled. Following many motions, arguments, and briefs, the Master in a 433-page volume reported his findings, conclusions, and recommended decree, which he submitted to the Court on January 16, 1961.[390]

Additionally, following Master Rifkind's report and the filing of exceptions by the parties, the case was extensively briefed and the Court heard oral arguments for 22 hours, on two separate occasions.[391] Justice Hugo Black framed the issue before the Court as follows: "the question of each State's share of the waters of the Colorado and its tributaries turns on the meaning and the scope of the Boulder Canyon Project Act passed by Congress in 1928."[392]

The Court agreed with and adopted the majority of the Master's recommendations. Judge Rifkind found that the law of prior appropriation, the Colorado River Compact, and the doctrine of equitable apportionment did not apply in this case, since Congress apportioned the Colorado River's waters in the BCPA. California disagreed with the entirety of the Master's Report, arguing that the BCPA was inapplicable, since it governed the complete Colorado River System, not just the mainstream, *i.e.*, according to California, the BCPA also included all of the Colorado River's tributaries.[393] California also argued "that the Act neither allocates the Colorado River waters nor gives the Secretary authority to make an allocation"[394] and it further asserted that the doctrine of equitable apportionment, should govern the parties rights to the water.

California also argued that Master Rifkind wrongfully found that since the three Lower Basin States failed to execute a compact among themselves, for the allocation of the Colorado's waters as authorized by section 4(a)[395] of the

---

[390] *Ibid.* at n. 5. (*Citing* 364 US 940 (1961).)   [391] *Ibid.* at 551.   [392] *Ibid.* at 551–552.

[393] *Ibid.* at 563. "This would mean that diversions within Arizona and Nevada of tributary waters flowing in those States would be charged against their apportionments, and that, because tributary water would be added to the mainstream water in computing the first 7,500,000 acre-feet available to the States, there would be a greater likelihood of a surplus, of which California gets one-half." *Ibid.*

[394] *Ibid.*

[395] Sec. 4(a) of the Boulder Canyon Project Act provides in the relevant section that

The States of Arizona, California, and Nevada are authorized to enter into an agreement which

shall provide (1) that of the 7,500,000 acre-feet annually apportioned to the lower basin by paragraph (a) of Article III of the Colorado River compact, there shall be apportioned to the State of Nevada 300,000 acre-feet and to the State of Arizona 2,800,000 acre-feet for exclusive beneficial consumptive use in perpetuity, and (2) that the State of Arizona may annually use one-half of the excess or surplus waters unapportioned by the Colorado River compact, and (3) that the State of Arizona shall have the exclusive

BCPA, the Congressional scheme established in the Act must govern. Furthermore, it asserted that the Master was incorrect in finding that the BCPA authorized the Secretary of the Interior to enter into contracts to supply water for various types of beneficial uses.

a THE ARGUMENT BEFORE THE COURT, AND ITS FINDINGS Justice Hugo Black noted that, with a few exceptions, Arizona, Nevada, and the United States supported the Master's analysis, conclusions, and recommendations. They also agreed that Congress did not permit the division of the Colorado's waters by the Court's use of equitable apportionment. Rather, the Court found that in the BCPA, Congress fashioned a broad statutory scheme for the appropriation of the Colorado's mainstream waters.

Black also noted that Arizona's claim that the apportionment formula created by the Secretary's contracts was in fact the formula prescribed by the BCPA. Alternatively, the United States, and California, reasoned that the Master erroneously nullified the conditions of Arizona's and Nevada's water contracts, while compelling these two States to deduct from their appropriations any diversions of water east or above the Boulder Canyon Dam's (n/k/a the Hoover Dam) reservoir, Lake Mead.

The Golden State challenged the Court's jurisdiction, and asserted that the Project Act, like the Colorado River Compact, addresses the entire Colorado River System, including its tributaries, not solely the mainstream. Under California's theory, any diversion of waters from the tributaries within Arizona and Nevada would be charged against their allotments. In addition, California reasoned that these internal tributary waters were to be added to the Colorado's mainstream waters, in calculating the first 7.5 maf available to the Lower Basin States under the Compact. Consequently, the likelihood that a surplus would occur increased, and California should receive one-half of this surplus, which would mean "much more water for California and much less for Arizona."[396]

In exercising its jurisdiction, the majority stated that the Court was mindful of its oft-articulated preference that, where feasible, States ought to settle their disputes by "mutual accommodation and agreement,"[397] and that Congress gave the Lower Basin states the opportunity to execute a compact between

> beneficial consumptive use of the Gila River and its tributaries within the boundaries of said State...

(Emphasis supplied.)

[396] *Ibid.* at 563.

[397] *Ibid.* at 564. (*Citing Colorado v. Kansas*, 320 US 383 (1943); and *Nebraska v. Wyoming*, 325 US 589 (1945).)

themselves on any terms they wished. Nevertheless, the Court made it clear that it had a solemn duty to adjudicate cases where a genuine controversy existed over how interstate rivers are to be apportioned among the states. This cause, Justice Black observed, is but the most recent chapter of an ongoing dispute over the waters of the Colorado, which Arizona and California, notwithstanding repeated efforts, have been unable to resolve.[398]

The settlement of this controversy, the Court observed, required a determination of what apportionment, if any, was made by the BCPA and what authority was granted by the Act to the Secretary of the Interior. Justice Black also noted that unless many of the issues presented were adjudicated, the parties' diverging claims would persist, and would raise considerable doubts regarding the extent of each of these States' rights to appropriate the waters of the Colorado for both existing and new uses. Accordingly, "In this situation we should and do exercise our jurisdiction."[399]

Once the Court established that it had jurisdiction it moved to the merits. Justice Black conducted a probing analysis. The majority then concluded that when Congress passed the Boulder Canyon Project Act it created a discrete comprehensive plan for the apportionment between the three Lower Basin states, Arizona, California, and Nevada. That scheme, Justice Black found, allotted to the three States their respective shares of the Colorado's mainstream waters, leaving for each State the waters from its own tributaries.[400] Furthermore, he observed, when Congress exercises its constitutional authority and has spoken, the Court cannot interject its own apportionment formulae.[401]

Congress, the Court found, determined that a reasonable division of the first 7.5 maf of the river's mainstream waters would provide 4.4 maf to California, 2.8 maf to Arizona, 300,000 ac-ft to Nevada and that Arizona and California would each equally divide any surplus.[402] Moreover, "the Act explicitly approve[d] the Compact and thereby fixe[d] a division of the waters between the [upper and lower] basins which must be respected,"[403] regardless of how the Compact apportioned the Colorado's waters. Additionally, the Court found that the BCPA dealt solely with the mainstream water, reserving for each state the exclusive use of its tributaries.[404] Consequently, the majority assumed an apportionment of 7.5 maf or more water in the Colorado's mainstream and 2.0 maf in its tributaries. Finally, the Court also observed that since Congress provided the Secretary of the Interior with the authority to achieve the division, he had the jurisdiction to execute contracts for the delivery of water.[405]

[398] *Ibid.*   [399] *Ibid.*   [400] *Ibid.* at 565.   [401] *Ibid.*   [402] *Ibid.*
[403] *Ibid.* at 566.   [404] *Ibid.*   [405] *Ibid.*

California next argued that under § 8 of the Reclamation Act[406] the Secretary of the Interior was bound by state law priorities, for water delivery. The Court summarily dismissed this contention, holding that "We do not suggest that where Congress has provided a system of regulation for federal projects it must give way before an inconsistent state system ... We read nothing in § 8 that compels the United States to deliver water on conditions imposed by the State."[407]

Justice Black also noted that before the BCPA was passed the flow of the Colorado River's waters were uncertain and too free, causing droughts and floods. These tribulations proved much too immense and the solutions beyond the financial ability of any one State or all the States together. The Court observed that the seven States were unable to settle the water allocation issues, notwithstanding their recurring attempts. Then, the federal government stepped in, responded to the States' pleas and came to their aid, resulting in the BCPA "and the harnessing of the bountiful waters of the Colorado to sustain growing cities, to support expanding industries, and to transform dry and barren deserts into lands that are liveable and productive."[408]

This vast system of dams, reservoirs, diversion conduits, and pipelines, for which Congress set allocations could only function efficiently, according to the Court, under one manager, who is able to plan and administer a coordinated strategy that would take into account the varied, frequently opposing, and inconsistent interests of the citizens and communities of the three Lower Basin States.[409] Indeed, Congress was surely aware of this fact, and accordingly charged the Secretary with the authority under § 5 of the BCPA to manage and direct these works' operation, as well as to contract power, and to allocate water.

b ALLOCATION IN TIMES OF SHORTAGE The next issue that the Court addressed was whether the Master correctly decided that under the BCPA the Secretary must allocate water during times of shortage or drought on a pro rata basis.[410] Justice Black reasoned that neither the Master nor the Court itself could bind the Secretary to a set allocation formula, when Congress did

---

[406] *Ibid. Citing* sec. 8, of the Newland Reclamation Act of June 17, 1902, PL 57–161, 32 Stat. 388 43 USC § 383.

[407] *Ibid.* at 586. (*Citing Nebraska v. Wyoming*, 325 US 589, 615 (1945).)

[408] *Ibid.* at 588–589.   [409] *Ibid.* at 589.

[410] *Ibid.* at 592–593. The Court also points out that "Proration of shortage is the method agreed upon by the United States and Mexico to adjust Mexico's share of Colorado River water should there be insufficient water to supply each country's apportionment." *Ibid.* at 593 n. 96.

not. Consequently, the Court decided that it was not its place to interfere with Congress' delegation of authority.[411]

C CLAIMS MADE BY THE UNITED STATES ON BEHALF OF INDIAN TRIBES
As a party to the proceedings, the United States asserted claims to waters within the main stream of the river and in several of its tributaries for use in National Forests, Indian Reservations,[412] Recreational and Wildlife Areas as well as on other government lands and works.[413] The Master either passed on or declined to address these claims, principally those concerning the tributaries.[414] He also held that the cumulative amount of water set aside for the five Indian reservations at issue, was approximately 1,000,000 acre-feet, to be used on about 135,000 irrigable acres of land.

The Court found that several of the relevant Indian tribal territories reserved by the federal government were made nearly 100 years ago, and all of them were at least 45 years ago. For over 50 years, the majority observed, both the Executive and Congress recognized the Indian Reservations. Congress also made frequent appropriations to the Tribes, including ones for projects related to irrigation.[415] Indeed, Justice Black noted that the bulk of the land on the reservations had been arid since time immemorial. Consequently, in order to live and to grow crops, water is an imperative, and that water must come from the Colorado.[416] In furtherance of its position the Court cited approvingly testimony given before Congress by delegates from the territory of Arizona, in 1865, and a seminal case involving "reserved" water rights that it decided in 1908.[417]

The majority found that the allocated quantity of water was meant to assure both the present and future requirements of the Indian Reservations. It therefore established that an adequate amount of water was set aside or reserved to irrigate the entirety of the irrigable acreage on the Arizona reservations. Conversely, Arizona contended that the extent of the water to be reserved

---

[411] *Ibid.* at 593–594.
[412] The two significant reservations in Arizona, at issue, were the Colorado River Indian Reservation and the Fort Mohave Indian Reservation.
[413] *California v. Arizona*, 373 US at 595–596.   [414] *Ibid.* at 595.   [415] *Ibid.*
[416] Moreover, the majority observed, that it is impossible to comprehend that when Congress and the Executive created the reservations, that they had no knowledge of the fact that the lands that comprised most of the territory was not "of the desert kind – hot, scorching sands – and that water from the river would be essential to the life of the Indian people and to the animals they hunted and the crops they raised." *Ibid.* at 599.
[417] *Ibid.* (*Citing* Statement made to Congress by the delegate from the Territory of Arizona, at Cong. Globe, 38th Cong., 2d Sess. 1321 (1865), and *Winters v. United States*, 207 US 564 (1908).)

must be calculated by the Indians' "reasonably foreseeable needs,"[418] which, the majority noted, meant by their population. However, the Court rejected Arizona's formulation as too speculative and held that the only reasonable method by which water can be reserved was by calculating the amount of irrigable acreage.[419]

The next issue that the Court confronted was a challenge to Master Rifkind's ruling that the United States planned to reserve water, adequate for the future supplies of several national recreation areas, national refuges and national forests along the Colorado River in Arizona.[420] It ruled that the federal government indeed did reserve these waters. Justice Black reasoned that the rule underlying the "reservation of water rights for Indian Reservations was equally applicable to other federal establishments such as National Recreation Areas and National Forests."[421]

Finally, the majority found that under the BCPA all consumptive uses must be calculated in the following manner: the net water use must be the sum of all diversions minus returns to the river, by both consumptive and non-consumptive uses. Therefore, the entire suite of uses of the Colorado's mainstream waters inside each State "are to be charged against that State's apportionment, which of course includes uses by the United States."[422] The Court did not issue a decree along with its opinion. Rather, it gave the parties the opportunity to submit a form of decree, consistent with its opinion, prior to September 16, 1963. Although, if the parties failed to do so, the Court stated that it would do so "at the next Term of Court."[423] It is to that decree that we move to next.

7 Arizona v. Colorado, 376 US 340 (1964)

On March 9, 1964, the Court issued its decree. That 13-page order was exceptionally detailed.[424] The decree set an allocation scheme based on formulas of acreage, water use and water need. It also enumerated the number of acre-feet for each state, specific owners and tracts within each State, various irrigation districts, and use of groundwater for individual/private landowners. Similarly, the Court set appropriations for river regulation, improvement of navigation, flood control, as well as for irrigation and domestic uses. Also included was the satisfaction of present perfected rights, and for electric power. Moreover, the Court ordered that the United States may release water in satisfaction of its

---

[418] *Ibid.*   [419] *Ibid.* at 601.   [420] *Ibid.*   [421] *Ibid.*   [422] *Ibid.*   [423] *Ibid.* at 602.
[424] In 1964, Associate Justices had only one law clerk, as opposed to today's four.

obligations to Mexico under the Treaty dated February 3, 1944, without regard to the priorities.[425]

Of relevance here, are the decree's articles II, IV and VI. The relevant part states that:

II. The United States was enjoined from releasing water that it controlled except: "(1) For river regulation, improvement of navigation, and flood control; (2) For irrigation and domestic uses, including the satisfaction of present perfected rights; and (3) For power..."

IV. The State of New Mexico and its employees were enjoined from diverting "water from San Simon Creek, its tributaries and underground water sources for the irrigation of more than a total of 2,900 acres during any one year, for a term for four years from the date of the decree. The New Mexicans were also enjoined from exceeding a total consumptive use of the surface and subsurface water, for whatever purpose, of 72,000 acre-feet during any ten year consecutive period; and from exceeding a total consumptive use of such water, for whatever purpose, of 8,220 acre-feet during any one year."

VI. Within two years from the date of the decree, the States of Arizona, California, and Nevada were to furnish to the Court and to the Secretary of the Interior a list of the then present perfected rights, with their claimed priority dates, in waters of the mainstream within each State, respectively, in terms of consumptive use, except those relating to federal establishments.[426]

As will be seen *infra*, the Court in future decisions made numerous amendments to these articles. From a dispute settlement perspective, other than its detail, the terms of the decree do not appear to be relevant, since they comport with the Court's 1963 opinion. Therefore, they will be not detailed here.

8 *Arizona v. California*, 383 US 268 (1966)

In this stage of the dispute, the Parties submitted to the Court a joint motion to amend Article VI of the Decree. The amendment read as follows:

VI. Within three years from the date of this decree [March 9, 1964], the States of Arizona, California, and Nevada shall furnish to this Court and to the Secretary of the Interior a list of the present perfected rights [to water], with their claimed priority dates, in waters of the mainstream within each State,

---

[425] *Arizona v. California*, 376 US 340, 341–342 (1964).
[426] *Ibid.* at 376 US 340, 341, 347–348, 351–352.

respectively, in terms of consumptive use, except those relating to federal establishments.[427]

However, if the parties and the Secretary fail to agree at the end of the three-year period, to utilize the Colorado's mainstream water in each of the Lower Basin states, they could request that the Court make a judicial finding of the determination of such rights by the Court.[428]

9 *Arizona v. California*, 439 US 419 (1979)

This part of the case involved a joint motion by the Intervenors, the United States and Nevada, the Complainant, Arizona, and a host of California Defendants. These parties, sought to amend article IV of the 1964 Decree. Here, the state parties and the United States sought a supplemental decree, which would incorporate "perfected rights in each State and their priority dates."[429] The Court first listed the perfected rights of several Arizona Indian Tribes, including: (1) the Cocopah Indian Reservation; (2) the Colorado River Indian Reservation; and (3) the Fort Mojave Indian Reservation, as well as the amount of annual diversion in acre-feet.

Next, the Court listed other water projects in Arizona, and in California,[430] including on Indian Reservations, located exclusively in California or, those extending across the border from Arizona,[431] and the various irrigation districts. The supplemental decree also included a paragraph, which noted that the determinations in the decree would in "no way affect future adjustments resulting from determinations relating to settlement of Indian reservations."[432] It also provided the Secretary of the Interior with the authority, in the case of water shortage, to first satisfy in full the rights of the Indian Reservations, without regards to state boundaries, so long as he also exercised his judgment in meeting adjustments to water appropriated throughout the Lower Colorado Basin. The latter would be undertaken either, by agreement of the parties or by court decree "in the event that the boundaries of the respective reservations are finally determined."

Moreover, the Court provided that any additional perfected rights were to be apportioned and adjusted in annual acre-feet quantities. However, these were not to exceed the mainstream water quantities necessary to source the

[427] *Arizona v. California*, 383 US 268 (1966).
[428] *Arizona v. California*, 383 at 269.   [429] *Ibid.* at 422–424.   [430] *Ibid.* at 428–428.
[431] *Ibid.* at 428. These included the Chemehuevi Indian Reservation, the Yuma Indian Reservation, the Colorado Indian Reservation and the Fort Mojave Indian Reservation.
[432] *Ibid.* at 421–422 (5).

consumptive use required for irrigation or to satisfy other related beneficial uses.[433] Finally, the majority expressly noted that the amount fixed in Article II (D) of its 1964 Decree "shall continue to be subject to appropriate adjustment by agreement or decree of this court in the event that the boundaries of the respective reservations are finally determined."[434] This supplemental decree also included the appointment of a new master.

10 *California* v. *Arizona*, 440 US 59 (1979) (This case was argued on February 9, 1979, the day the previous opinion was issued)

In this phase, California filed a motion seeking to invoke the Court's original jurisdiction in a suit to quiet title to a 229-mile tract along its southeastern boundary, *i.e.*, its border with Arizona. The central issue in this stage of the dispute, was whether the Government of the United States surrendered its sovereign immunity to be sued in actions to quiet title filed by one of its states. The court found that it had. Since this action does not directly address the apportionment of water from Colorado River, it will not be elaborated upon.

11 *Arizona* v. *California*, 460 US 605 (1983) (Arizona II)

In this segment of the case, the Court was asked to determine whether five Indian tribes who were previously represented in the litigation by the United States, as Intervenor, could intervene in their own behalf. The Tribes sought to intervene in order to have their water allocation increased to account for at least 18,500[435] irrigable acres, situated within the boundaries of their reservations, which the United States omitted in the calculations that led to the 1964 decree. Initially, the United States opposed the intervention, but then joined the Tribes in their motion. California objected to the intervention.

At the outset of its opinion, the Supreme Court observed that "[i]n earlier proceedings in this case, the United States . . . acquired water rights for five Indian Reservations that are dependent upon the [Colorado] River for their water. The United States, and the Tribes which ask to intervene in the action, now seek to have those water rights increased."[436] The majority also noted that "[t]he principal dispute that became increasingly pressing over the years concerned the respective shares of the lower-basin states, particularly the shares of California and Arizona."[437]

---

[433] *Ibid.* at 421 (2).   [434] *Ibid.*

[435] *Arizona* v. *California*, 460 US 605, 643 (1983) (Brennan J., dissenting).

[436] *Arizona* v. *California*, 460 US at 608.   [437] *Ibid.*

It similarly observed that the Court entered a supplemental decree on January 9, 1979, in which the justices identified "the present perfected rights to the use of the mainstream water in each state and their priority dates as agreed to by the parties."[438]

Ultimately, the majority concluded that the 1964 Decree should be amended "by providing to the respective Reservations appropriate water rights to service the irrigable acreage the Master found to be contained within the tracts adjudicated by court decree to be Reservation lands."[439] Similarly, in 1984,[440] the Court entered a second supplemental decree. In this amendment to Arizona I, and the 1979 Decree, the Court supplemented Article II (D) ¶¶ (2) and (5), which increased the allocation to the Five Indian Tribes, as well as to three of the five tribes that were either partially or totally situated in Arizona.[441]

12 *Arizona* v. *California*, 530 US 392 (2000)

The present stage of this litigation focused on additional claims made by the Quechan Indian Tribe, whose reservation borders the states of Arizona, California and Baja California, Mexico. Encompassing 45,000 acres – which are largely agriculture. Indeed, the Tribe leases its thousands of acres for farming to both Indian and non-Indian farmers. Accordingly, the United States on the Tribe's behalf, sought increased water rights for the Quechan's Fort Yuma Reservation. These claims were grounded on the assertion that the Fort Yuma Reservation included approximately 25,000 acres of disputed boundary lands not credited to that reservation in earlier phases of the case. The territory in question was ostensibly ceded to the United States under an 1893 treaty with the Tribe.

Here, the main issue before the Court was whether a settlement that the Tribe entered into with the United States in 1983, was precluded by *res judicata* principles. The majority overruled the State parties' exception, and sustained the exceptions of the Quechan Tribe and the United States. Finally, the Court, once again, remanded to the Master the remaining water rights contentions, which were coupled with the disputed Fort Yuma Reservation boundary lands.

13 *Arizona* v. *Colorado*, 531 US 1 (2000) (Third Supplemental Decree)

On October 10, 2000, less than four months following the Court's latest decision, and its remand to the Master, for an assessment of the remaining water

---

[438] *Arizona* v. *California*, 460 US at 611.   [439] *Ibid.*
[440] *Arizona* v. *California*, 466 US 144 (1984).   [441] *Ibid.* at 146.

rights contentions vis-à-vis the Fort Yuma Reservation boundary lands, the Court entered an order again amending

> a number of sections of Arizona I's Article II (D), including a modification yielding an increased allocation to the Colorado River's Indian Reservation's annual mainstream diversion of the Colorado's mainstream water.[442] That section was modified so that the Fort Mojave Indian Reservation would also see an increase in its annual quantities of diversions from the river's mainstream.[443] Other adjustments included paragraphs that listed numerical limits for water diversion and their concomitant priorities. Finally, the supplemental decree declared that the Court would maintain jurisdiction over this case.

14 *Arizona v. Colorado*, 547 US 150 (2006) (Final & Consolidated Decree)

In this concluding portion of the case the Court approved the parties' final settlement agreements. It also granted their joint motion for the entry of a final decree, and entered the Master's proposed consolidated decree. Following the Court's remand of the outstanding issues related to the remaining water rights claims, as well as, the disputed Fort Yuma Reservation boundary lands, in *Arizona v. California*, 530 US 392 (2000), the Master held a series of hearings. At their conclusion, on June 14, 2005, he submitted his report to the Court. In it, he recommended (1) that the Court approve the parties' water rights claim settlements, with respect to the Fort Yuma Indian Reservation; and (2) proposed a fourth supplemental decree so that those settlements would be realized.

At the direction of the Court, the parties filed a joint motion to enter a consolidated decree, which confirmed the substantive provisions in the previous decrees, and implemented the settlements of the water rights pressed by the Quechan Tribes for their Fort Yuma Indian Reservation. The Court then declared that this specific decree was "entered in order to provide a single convenient reference to ascertain the rights and obligations of the parties adjudicated in this original proceeding, and reflects only the incremental changes

---

[442] *Arizona v. California* 531 US 1 (2000). The amendment increased the diversion of mainstream water to a maximum of 719,248 acre-feet/annum or, in the alternative, a quantity of mainstream water required to supply the consumptive use necessary for irrigating 107,903 acres or whichever of the two is less. *Ibid.*

[443] *Ibid.* The Fort Mojave Indian Reservation's allotment was increased resulting in annual quantities that "would not exceed (i) 132,789 acre-feet of diversions from the mainstream or (ii) the quantity of mainstream water necessary to supply the consumptive use required for irrigation of 20,544 acres and for the satisfaction of related uses, whichever of (i) or (ii) is less."

in the original 1964 decree by subsequent decrees and the settlements of the federal reserved water rights claim for the Fort Yuma Indian Reservation."[444]

Moreover, in setting the water allocation priorities for the Lower Basin, among the numerous other elements, the Court's Consolidated Decree enjoined the United States from acting other than in accordance with the following sequence: (1) for river regulation, improvement of navigation, and flood control; (2) for irrigation and domestic uses, including the satisfaction of present perfected rights; and (3) for power. The foregoing notwithstanding, the Court obliged the Government of the United States to above all, honor its international commitment to satisfy the water allocation contained in its 1944 Treaty with Mexico.

The Decree also reiterated that if the Secretary of the Interior determines that there was sufficient water in the Colorado River's mainstream he could release enough to satisfy the Lower Basin's requirement of 7,500,000 acre-feet of annual consumptive use, which is to be apportioned in the following manner: (1) 2,800,000 acre-feet for use in Arizona; (2) 4,400,000 acre-feet for use in California; and (3) 300,000 acre-feet for use in Nevada. Note that these allocations are identical to the ones contained in the Colorado River Compact, which was executed in 1922, 84 years earlier.

In addition, the Court upheld the portion of its 1964 Decree which, declared that

(3) If sufficient mainstream water is available for release, as determined by the Secretary of the Interior, to satisfy annual consumptive use in the aforesaid States in above 7,500,000 acre-feet, and any surplus, would be split 50% to Arizona and 50% to California; provided, however, if the United States contracts to deliver water to Nevada, then Arizona's share falls to 46% and the remaining 4% would be used by Nevada.

F Analysis

1 What Law to Apply?

As an initial matter, the Supreme Court was confronted with a choice of law issue: what law to apply? Recall that in *Kansas v. Colorado* the Court originally employed the doctrine of equitable apportionment, because there was no existing law in place to resolve the dispute. However, in this dispute the justices were governed by the congressionally enacted Boulder Canyon Project

---

[444] *Arizona v. California*, 547 US 150, 152 (2006).

Act, and to a lesser extent, the Colorado River Compact. Consequently, the common law governs unless a statute or rule is extant, then the latter is the guidepost for the Court.

2 Measuring the Court's Effectiveness

In measuring the Court's effectiveness, we once again will utilize the proxies listed in Table 7.2.

In assessing **proxy number 1**, we seek to learn whether the Court promoted compliance with the governing norms (primary norm compliance). If so, was there an impact on state conduct, and improved compliance by states and, other relevant actors with the legal norms that the court developed or was asked to enforce.

As there was no pre-existing norm to comply with at the outset of the dispute, the Court could not promote its compliance. However, once it established the order of interpretation: congressional act and then compacts, and construed the BCPA, to include any excess over the 7.5 maf allocated to the Lower Basin; as well as, Arizona's entitlement to those tributaries flowing wholly within its territory, the Court established a norm, which was complied with. Moreover, neither the Court nor the parties deviated from the 1964 decree or its supplementation. This dispute also established new norms regarding the allocation of water for Indian reservations, and recognized the Indian Tribes' territorial rights to water. Each of these norms and the Court's judgments were all complied with by the parties, which, of course had an impact on their conduct – albeit their continued litigation – and ultimate settlement.

As for **proxy number 2, dispute resolution**, plainly, the SCOTUS resolved each phase of the dispute. However, it did so over many, many years. Moreover, the Court also resolved the specific problem(s) that it was asked to determine. As noted previously, it is difficult to assess, without direct testimony, whether the parties were satisfied with the Court's various judgments. However, we do know that they complied with them.

With respect to **proxy number 3, normative impact**, we seek to learn, whether the court resolved this international dispute while providing new remedies (law making). Furthermore, was there an overall impact that the resolution had on international legal norms? And, did the court contribute to the operation of related institutional and normative regimes? I do not believe that this dispute had an overall impact on transboundary water legal norms. It did, however, set a procedure for this Court. As noted above, that procedure is as follows: The Court will use the common law doctrine of equitable apportionment when it has no direction from Congress or from a Compact. Where water allocation is established by another scheme or instrument, however, the Court does not, and will not, interfere with that selection.[445] Thus, the Court's 1963 majority found that where Congress exercises its constitutional authority, under the Commerce Clause, the courts must abide by that choice.

Finally, there was an institutional quirk in the 1963 judgment. The dispute arrived at the Court's doorstep during its 1962 term, and Justice Frankfurter authored the Court's opinion. Justice Black and a few other justices were dissatisfied with that opinion. Aware that Justice Frankfurter would be stepping down after suffering a stroke, Black rewrote the judgment and garnered a majority for his version of the judgment.[446] One wonders whether a Justice Frankfurter opinion might have added to the Court's norms or, the parties subsequent conduct. But we do see in Justice Black's actions a manipulation of the institution's norms.

With recourse to **proxy number 4, fairness and legitimation,** one is required to query whether the court was perceived as being a fair, just, and an independent forum, and whether its various judgments added to the legitimization of the regime and its norms? The Supreme Court has been consistently rated as fair, albeit the incident by Justice Van Devanter in *Wyoming v. Colorado*. Here the Court's successive Judgments construed the law, the BCPA and the Colorado River Compact, which may have added to the transboundary "law of the river." Similarly, with each of which the various rulings regarding the water allocation for the various Indian tribes, and the treaty interpretations, likely, had both at least some normative impact, at least as far as the Court is concerned.

With recourse to the Court's **legitimacy,** although I discussed Thomas Franck's definition previously, here I adopt Joseph Raz's definition for the term. Raz theorizes that legal systems supply legal norms in order to provide guidance for how the law's subjects are to conduct themselves. These rules similarly assert a type of legitimate authority over those governed by them.[447] Assuming that we accept Raz's theory, one ought to also accept the notion that

---

[445] *Arizona v. California ibid.* at 565–566.

[446] *See* Roger K. Newman, *Hugo Black: A Biography* 531–32 (1994), stating that Justice Black spent much time condensing Justice Frankfurter's memorandum from 142 to 52, written the previous term, which by internal understanding of the other justices would serve as the basis for a forthcoming opinion in *Arizona v. California,* 373 US 546 (1963).

[447] Joseph Raz, *The Authority of Law* (1979) 116–120; see also Joseph Raz, *Ethics in the Public Domain* (1995) 214.

legal legitimacy is the acceptance of an authority, usually a governing law or a régime. That was accomplished in this dispute.

Nevertheless, whether the litigants considered the judgments to be fair or just is another issue. History certainly proves that Arizona, as the ultimate "victor" in this conflict, was very satisfied with judgment,[448] California was not. However, being satisfied or pleased with a judgment does not necessarily mean that the parties automatically felt that it was unfair. Acceptance of a judgment or ruling may in itself be a form of legitimacy.

Finally, with respect to **proxy Number 5**, the **Court's efficiency**; in issuing its judgments, it is apparent that in handing down its individual rulings the Court was efficient. For example, in *Arizona v. California*, 373 US 546 (1963), the Court heard argument between January 8 and 11, 1962, and reargument on November 13 and 14, 1962; it then issued its judgment on June 3, 1963:[449] a maximum period of one and a half years. However, if one measures the amount of time, from November 13 and 14, 1962, to the issuance of the judgment in June 1963, that timeline is approximately 6.5 months long. Table 8.5, lists the cumulative amount of time from the date of argument to the date of Judgment for each phase.

However, I return to the fact that the problem with the Court's piecemeal decision-making is that there appears to be no finality – the dispute goes on and on and on (as discussed previously). Such a situation not only wastes judicial resources, it also requires the litigants, who are paying their lawyers as well as the master's fees, to almost endlessly provide funds from their citizens' treasuries, for the continual litigation and for the various experts. This is neither an efficient nor a salubrious state of affairs.

This dispute and the others analyzed here, appear to belie Posner & Yoo's contention that dependent courts and tribunals are more effective;[450] although these authors did state that they excluded domestic courts, like the Supreme Court. Nevertheless, one will recall that Helfer & Slaughter,[451] in

---

[448] See e.g., Jack L. August, Jr. *Dividing Western Waters: Mark Wilmer and Arizona v. California* (2007).

[449] *Arizona v. California*, 373 US 546 (1963).

[450] Posner & Yoo *ibid.* at 6. Moreover, as noted in chapter 3 *supra*, these authors reasoned that dependent tribunals, *i.e.*, ad hoc tribunals, are more effective since they "render judgments that reflect the interests of the states at the time that they submit the dispute to the tribunal." *Ibid.* They also posited that if their judges or arbitrators failed to please the State-party that engaged them they would not be rehired by other parties in the future.

[451] Laurence R. Helfer & Anne-Marie Slaughter, Why States Create International Tribunals: A Response to Professors Posner and Yoo, 93 *Calif L R* (2005) 899, 901 "A recent article... by Professors Eric Posner and John Yoo, Judicial Independence in International Tribunals, argues that the only effective international tribunals are 'dependent' tribunals, by which the authors

TABLE 8.5 Arizona *v.* California *Efficiency – Time from Date of Argument to Judgment*

(1) **1931** – *Arizona v. California*, 283 US 423. Argued Mar. 9–10, 1931; Decided May 18, 1931. **= 3 months and 8 days.**

(2) **1934** – *Arizona v. California*, 292 US 341. Argued Feb. 14, 1934; Decided May 21, 1934. **= 3 months and 7 days.**

(3) **1935** – *US v. Arizona*, 295 US 174. Argued Mar. 4, 1935; Decided Apr. 29, 1935. **= 1 month and 25 days.**

(4) **1936** – *Arizona v. California*, 298 US. Argued Apr. 28, 1936; Decided May 25, 1936. **= 27 days.**

(5) **1963** – *Arizona v. California*, 373 US 546. Argued Jan. 8–11, 1962; Reargued Nov. 13–14, 1962; Decided June 3, 1963. **= 1 year 5 months and 23 days.**

(6) **1964** – *Arizona v. California*, 376 US 340. Decided June 3, 1963; Decree entered Mar. 9, 1964. **= 9 months and 6 days.**

(7) **1983** – *Arizona v. California*, 460 US 605. Argued Dec. 8, 1982; Decided Mar. 30, 1983. **= 3 months and 22 days.**

(8) **2000** – *Arizona v. California*, 530 US 392. Argued Apr. 25, 2000; Decided June 19, 2000. **= 1 month and 24 days.** **Average = 158 days/5 months and 8 days.** (If we remove the 1963 result, which was an aberration, due to the death of Justice Frankfurter, requiring a rehearing then the) **average = 3 months and 12 days.**

response to Posner & Yoo, not only argued but demonstrated that from a normative perspective independent judges are more effective.[452] Since I am treating the SCOTUS as a *quasi*-international court, I believe that the latter authors view is the more valid one.

Alternatively, recall Richard Epstein's finding that "judicial independence [or dependence] offers no guarantee that judicial decisions will serve the public interest, even if we could all agree as to how it should be defined."[453] In apportioning the Colorado River's waters and interpreting the BCPA, the

mean ad hoc tribunals staffed by judges closely controlled by governments through the power of reappointment or threats of retaliation."

[452] *Ibid.* at 938–939.

Independent tribunals are also more likely to help states resolve cooperation problems arising from treaties that regulate public goods or the global commons… This problem arises when one state generates negative externalities that are not fully absorbed by other states. In these situations, contrary to what Posner and Yoo assert… it is not merely appropriate but necessary to consider the interests of nonparties.

[453] Richard Epstein, *ibid.* at 827.

Court functioned as a pacific adjudicative body, and may have served the public interest in delivering a fair, just and equitable resolution.

Nevertheless, ultimately, these judgments do not meet Epstein's test of acting in the public interest (and doing justice, *i.e.*, making fair or equitable decisions, as defined herein). Why is that so? If the main job of an effective international court is to resolve disputes, then a possible failing of this court has to do with the length of time that it took to resolve this dispute *in toto* – forty-six years – and, as noted above in *Kansas* v. *Colorado*, the fact that it did so incrementally, *e.g.*, requiring the appointment of three sets of Special Masters, at a great cost to both the parties and to judicial resources. Of course, as noted in the analysis of the *Kansas* v. *Colorado* dispute, sometimes the Court's role is to manage a dispute. However, taking over four decades to resolve one dispute – no matter how many phases – cannot, in this author's opinion, be said to be efficient or timely. Consequently, this variable affects the temporal proxy.

When one utilizes the term "manage" or "management" one does not do so in the same manner as defined by Judith Resnick[454] or Maximo Langer.[455] They use these terms to describe a procedural model that has been adopted in the federal civil procedure of United States courts. This system's rules require the trial judge to be an active participant during the pre-trial phase, *e.g.*, managing discovery, when settlement discussions take place, and during the post-trial stage, as opposed to the classic view of the common law judge as a passive decision maker. The system described above is not what the US Supreme Court does when it adjudicates interstate water disputes or other original jurisdiction cases. The procedure outlined by Resnick and Langer is undertaken by the Master.

In contrast, my use of the term "managing" is to describe the Court's function in shepherding along or guiding the litigation. That is, every time a new issue or phase of the dispute comes before the Court, one of its chief goals is to resolve it as quickly as possible, *i.e.*, the Court's goal under these circumstances is to clear its docket of the dispute. In managing the dispute, I mean that each phase is steered along, and becomes another link in a long chain of events. That is, the Court adjudicates each discrete portion in this case in a piecemeal fashion, where the litigants prosecute anew each issue.

---

454 Judith Resnick, Managerial Judges, 96 *Harv L R* (1982) 374.
455 Maximo Langer, The Rise of Managerial Judging in International Criminal Law, 53 *Am J Comp L* (2005) 835.

The foregoing raises the following query: why did the Court allow this dispute to progress on and on? I have no direct answer to the question, and a review of the case files at the Library of Congress, did not aid me in my attempt to find a response to that query. Nor have other scholars hazarded a guess regarding this issue. It is just taken for granted that the Court's "job" is to resolve disputes, whether that task is efficient or not. Nevertheless, it appears that the multiple adjudications of a dispute are part of the Court's institutional design. That is, the justices may be quite cognizant of the fact that transboundary water disputes that don't settle, are extremely significant and involve critical issues because they involve a critical resource – water – and numerous communities of interest.

Moreover, the Court's constitutional mandate, via its original jurisdiction, may require the justices to be more forbearing of the state litigants in their adjudication of transboundary disputes; as opposed to its standard appellate jurisdiction, where, all issues and claims must be contained in one filing. Otherwise, in the Court's appellate cases, the parties cannot raise new issues, all issues must be raised at one time. Consequently, States that are unable to resolve their dispute and the Court's long shadow does not compel them to settle a given phase of the dispute, are provided with the opportunity to have each separate issue adjudicated. Returning to the subject of goals, the possibility exists that the opportunity for States to have multiple bites of the proverbial apple may be a goal that the Court's mandate providers – the authors of the Constitution – sought to establish in practice, although the Constitution is silent on that point.

Alternatively, if one of the Court's roles is to manage a dispute, then the temporal element of this dispute across its 54-year litigation history, and at its various stages or adjudications, can be framed by the Court's own language in its 1963 *Arizona* judgment. There it declared:

[a]s we see this case, the question of each State's share of the waters of the Colorado and its tributaries turns on the meaning and the scope of the Boulder Canyon Project Act passed by Congress in 1928. That meaning and scope can be better understood when the Act is set against its background – the gravity of the Southwest's water problems; the inability of local groups or individual States to deal with these enormous problems; the continued failure of the States to agree on how to conserve and divide the waters; and the ultimate action by Congress, at the request of the States, creating a great system of dams and public works nationally built, controlled, and operated for the purpose of conserving and distributing the water.

Another of the Court's shortcoming, in hindsight, as I see it, is the fact that the justices ignored Master Rifkind's recommendation, in his 1961 Report.[456] In that report Judge Rifkind recommended that the Tribal Reservation issue should be resolved then and there. In rejecting the Master's recommendation, the Court proclaimed the following:

> We disagree with the Master's decision to determine the disputed bound-aries of the Colorado River Indian Reservation and the Fort Mohave Indian Reservation. *We hold that it is unnecessary to resolve those disputes here. Should a dispute over title arise because of some future refusal by the Sec-retary to deliver water to either area, the dispute can be settled at that time.*[457]

Of course, the SCOTUS, like any court or tribunal, may reject a conclusion that is made by an inferior forum. Nevertheless, that deferral – by Justice Hugo Black's majority, which switched and baited Justice's Frankfurter's opinion – caused the Parties to relitigate the issue, as well as the expenditure of additional judicial resources. Although one can be accused of 20–20 hindsight, this phenomenon may be an institutional problem. This difficulty, I believe, is rooted in a number of possibilities. These include: (1) the Court's unwillingness to go beyond a certain point in its judgments, which may be due to caution regarding certain norms; (2) a concern regarding how a commitment to a legal point may handcuff the Court in future disputes; (3) the fact that a bare majority, *e.g.*, here a 5–3 decision (with the Chief Justice recusing himself),[458] may have been too frail to extend its jurisdiction; (4) commit the Court to a given norm; (5) or, the Court simply did not wish to look ahead, to further phases of the case. Each of these facets may be viewed as the justices' concern for the Court's legitimacy or its normative impact. Alternatively, it may suggest a political or regional bias, or laziness on the part of the Court.

---

[456] Recall that the Court in *California v. Arizona*, 373 US 546, 551, at n. 5. (*Citing* 364 US 940 (1961)), observed that the

> Master conducted a trial lasting from June 14, 1956, to August 28, 1958, during which 340 witnesses were heard orally or by deposition, thousands of exhibits were received, and 25,000 pages of transcript were filled. Following many motions, arguments, and briefs, the Master in a 433-page volume reported his findings, conclusions, and recommended decree, received by the Court on January 16, 1961.

[457] *California v. Arizona, ibid.*, 373 US at 601. (Emphasis added.)

[458] Chief Justice Earl Warren recused himself because he was a former governor of California. See *California v. Arizona*, 373 US at 546 (1963).

Indeed, the Court has often deferred action in all manner of cases, stating that one issue or, another, should be left "for another day,"[459] as it did here, and as asserted: "[w]e hold that it is unnecessary to resolve those disputes here."[460] Then again, there may be political considerations, including cobbling together a majority. And, of course, there is the overarching fact that the Court ignored the voluminous record compiled by Special Master Rifkind, in a trial that lasted twenty-six months.

Similarly, Master Rifkind also observed that the three Lower Basin States, Nevada, Arizona, and California, had the opportunity to, but failed, to conclude a compact between themselves for the allocation of the Colorado's waters, as required by sections 4(a) and 8(b) of the BCPA. The Court, of course, could have used its "long shadow" to "nudge" the Parties to enter into the Compact, as it did in *Kansas* v. *Colorado*,[461] or ordered them to comply with the BCPA. Nevertheless, none of the judgments in this case suggest that the Court attempted to do either.

A Court's decision of when to use its "long shadow" may, of course, depend upon the justices who occupy it at any given time – since the SCOTUS' composition in 1943 differed from those sitting in 1963 (only two of the nine, Justices Black and Douglas, were on each of the respective courts). Conversely, it may depend on the facts of a given case. The use of the Court's "long shadow" may also be governed by other factors, including the posture of the parties, the "read" that the Court may gain from counsel, or how much leverage the Justices believe they have, in order, to convince the parties to "settle" a part of the dispute. Indeed, we also see the influence of a tribunal's "long shadow" in the *Gut Dam Arbitration*, which is discussed *infra*.

It also appears that the Justices in the *Arizona* v. *California* dispute forgot the cautionary note that the Court struck in its 1943 decision in *Colorado* v. *Kansas*, which I posit, worked to the detriment of the Parties in this

---

[459] *Sacket v. EPA*, 520 US 154, 155 (2012) (Ginsburg, J. Concurring). ("Not raised by the Sacketts here, the question remains open *for another day* and case."); and *Stop the Beach Renourishment, Inc. v. Florida*, 560 US. 702, 742, 130 S. Ct. 2592, 2618 (2010). (Breyer, J. concurring in part and concurring in the judgment): ("[T]hose Parts the plurality unnecessarily addresses questions of constitutional law that are better *left for another day*.") (Emphasis added.)

[460] The Court declined to adopt Special Master Rifkind's recommendation concerning the boundary issue, explaining "[w]e disagree with the Master's decision to determine the disputed boundaries of the Colorado River Indian Reservation and the Fort Mojave Indian Reservation. We hold that it is unnecessary to resolve those disputes here." *Arizona v. California I*, 373 US 546, 601 (1963).

[461] 320 US 383 (1943).

litigation. There, Justice Owen Roberts, writing for the Court and alluding to the polycentric issues raised by these types of disputes, observed – as noted previously – [462] that the Court must be circumspect in addressing water allocation issues between states, noting that

> [t] he reason for judicial caution in adjudicating the relative rights of states in such cases is that, while we have jurisdiction of such disputes, [footnote omitted] they involve the interests of quasi-sovereigns, present complicated and delicate questions, and, due to the possibility of future change of conditions, necessitate expert administration rather than judicial imposition of a hard and fast rule. *Such controversies may appropriately be composed by negotiation and agreement, pursuant to the compact clause of the Federal constitution.* We say of this case, as the court has said of interstate differences of like nature, that such mutual accommodation and agreement should, if possible, be the medium of settlement, instead of invocation of our adjudicatory power . . . [463]

It is clear to this author that what Justice Owen Roberts was saying, is that the Court would rather not have to deal with these types of disputes because they are more amenable to settlement than to adjudication.[464] Thus, he urges, that if parties negotiate a resolution to a problem on their own, the Court need not be involved.[465] This, of course, is a valid point, which may speak to the issue of the Court's ability to resolve transboundary water problems.

The issue raised by the foregoing, is whether this Court's chief occupation is to adjudicate disputes or to resolve them. If it is the latter it may mean providing a space, under the watchful eye of the Court, for the parties to negotiate a settlement. Justice Roberts' advisory comment also appears to support the theory that States entering into a compact – or treaties in true interstate disputes – may more quickly resolve their differences via

---

[462] *See* text accompanying note 677.   [463] *Ibid.*, 320 US at 391.

[464] Professor Charles Myers, in his criticism of the Court re: the Colorado River, similarly observes that

> [B]asin development plans must necessarily come before Congress, and it is a highly appropriate time when they do so to settle interstate conflicts over water allocation. Without such a settlement development cannot go forward. Not only is the time appropriate but so is the place. *First, a congressional* division is likely to be more expeditious than compact or Supreme Court.

Ibid. at 48. (Emphasis supplied.)

[465] Myers also notes that "[a]s the Lower Basin imbroglio demonstrates, interstate water settlements in the West can involve protracted litigation." *Ibid.* at 27.

mutual accommodation, than by adjudication. Indeed, "[i]n cases where no previous agreements existed, the affected states met in private sessions and negotiated what were, in effect, subcompacts. Moreover, once the states had each been allotted a fixed percentage of the virgin flow, they reached agreements among themselves."[466] Similarly, Kansas and Colorado were able to negotiate a compact within a three-year timeframe. Were Arizona and California to enter into a compact, or some other agreement, regarding how they would apportion the Colorado River's waters, as recommended by Master Rifkind, they might have been able to avoid the prolonged litigation that followed.

Moreover, speedy resolutions of disputes need not always require a courtroom. Whatever method is employed in pacifically resolving a dispute, whether court-mandated mediation, arbitration, or litigation, becomes the most effective. Finally, it is worth bearing in mind that in the universe of conflicts, each dispute is different – different parties, different facts, and different political calculations – and therefore different methods may be required to move the parties to resolve their dispute. Therefore, international courts and tribunals cannot design a "one size fits all" solution.

G *The Aftermath*

The irony of this dispute, is that while California was in the heat of the present litigation, it was swimming through more than 5.2 million acre-feet of water per annum – 800,000 acre-feet above the volume of its allotted 4.4 million acre-feet. Thus, the Court's remedy and judgments appear to have been discounted and not complied with. Indeed, apparently the "Golden State" had failed to abide by its appropriation – and consequently the Court's judgments – since the late 1990s.

Moreover, in 2000, then Secretary of the Interior, Bruce Babbitt, stood before the annual meeting of the Colorado River Water Users Association, "which brings together the men and women who run the Colorado River – the 'water buffaloes' who wring every drop they can out of the river for agriculture and for urban growth,"[467] and announced that the seven Compact states

---

[466] *Ibid.* at 35.
[467] Ed Marston (ed.), Quenching the Big Thirst, in Char Miller, *Rivers of the American West* (2009) 31.

"had signed a peace treaty in the ongoing war over [the river's] water."[468] That document, which Babbitt called the "4.4 Plan,"[469] was spawned as a consequence of the other Compact states "growing larger and thirstier with each passing year."[470] Indeed, the five other compact states fretted that they would never be able to secure the full use of "their . . . apportionments of the Colorado if California's use became institutionalized."[471] Under the "4.4 Plan" California would have to go on a fifteen year water diet, and shrink its water use from the 5.2 million ac-ft. that it was then using, to its allotted amount of 4.4 million ac-ft.[472] The prospect that California would go on a water diet may have been unrealistic a few years post the last judgment, however on April 1, 2015 the state's Governor, Jerry Brown, issued a State of Emergency, in which he found "that conditions of extreme peril to the safety of persons and property continue to exist in California due to water shortage and drought conditions with which local authority is unable to cope . . . "[473] This Order followed one that the governor issued on April 25, 2014,[474] due to an ongoing drought.[475] Moreover, the housing and economic collapse,[476] that hit the other compact states in 2008 and lasted into 2014, did not hit California as hard as it did its neighbors, and, therefore, California's population declined little during the

---

[468] *Ibid.*   [469] *Ibid.* at 32.   [470] *Ibid.*   [471] *Ibid.* at 31.

[472] *Ibid.* at 32. Patrick Tyrell & John Shields, Wyoming State Engineer's Office, *An Update on Colorado Programs and Issues, Presentation to March 25, 2003, Meeting of the Green River Basin Advisory Group*, Purpose of the Plan: "Get California's annual Colorado River water demand back to 4.4 million acre-feet per year (MAY) (CA's basic Apportionment) during normal water supply years." (Mar. 2005), http://waterplan.state.wy.us/BAG/green/brief book/200303Shields1--18.pdf.

[473] *See* Executive Department, State of California, Executive Order B-29–15 (April 1, 2015), https://www.gov.ca.gov/docs/4.1.15_Executive_Order.pdf.

[474] *See e.g.*, Association of California Water Agencies, Save Our Water, Drought 2014: What You Need to Know.

> Governor Brown has declared a statewide drought emergency and is asking all Californians to reduce their water use by 20 percent. California is experiencing a serious drought and the state will be challenged to meet its water needs in the upcoming year.

> Calendar year 2013 was the driest year in recorded history for many areas of California, and current conditions suggest no change is in sight for 2014.

(2014), http://www.saveourh2o.org/content/Drought2014WhatYouNeedtoKnow.

[475] *See e.g.*, Tom Knudson, The Public Eye: As Drought Persists, Frustration Mounts Over California's Well Drilling, *Sacramento Bee*, July 6, 2014, http://www.sacbee.com/2014/07/06/6534974/as-drought-persists-frustration.html.

[476] *See generally*, Susan Heavy, Great Recession Took Deep Toll Across US States, *Reuters*, June 21, 2012, http://in.reuters.com/article/2012/06/21/usa-economy-insecurity-idINL1E8HL3CX20120621.

2008–2012 recession.[477] In contrast, Arizona[478] and Nevada[479] lost a huge percentage of their populations. However, today, the economy in the southwest United States has bounced back, and therefore the two other lower basin-compact states will require their full allocation of water. California, therefore, will not be able to draw any extra water from these states.

Indeed, over-allocation is the central dilemma for the users of the Colorado River. [480]

The seven basin states and Mexico are allotted a total of 16.5 million acre-feet a year. But the allocations were developed based on weather patterns of the early 20th century, which were unusually wet.

Currently, the lower basin shortfall is about 1 million acre-feet annually... The amount is predicated on the upper basin states releasing their agreed-upon amounts of water and varies with the rate of evaporation from Lake Mead [the Hoover Dam's reservoir].

According to a report released by Interior Secretary Ken Salazar in December 2012, the long-term shortfall is about 3.2 million acre-feet annually. An acre-foot is about 326,000 gallons, enough for two single-family households a year.

Lake Mead can hold a maximum of about 29 million acre-feet, according to the US Bureau of Reclamation. Lake Powell, its companion reservoir upstream, holds up to about 24 million acre-feet. Total storage capacity of the Colorado River system is just under 60 million acre-feet.

While that's a lot of capacity, the drought and overuse has over the years drawn down the reservoirs to worrisome levels. Unlike in California, where much smaller storage capacity means that just three or four dry years can

---

477 Southern California Association of Governments, How Much has Southern California Grown Since the Last Census? (2012). City Population 2000 and 2010, Excel Spreadsheet (2012), http://www.scag.ca.gov/census. (Total California Population Apr. 1, 2000, 33, 871, 653; Apr. 1, 2010, 37, 253, 956 Change 10%. But some parts of Southern California grew at a higher rate. E.g., Riverside County 41.7%, San Bernardino County, 19.1%).

478 *See e.g.*, United States Census Bureau (Last Revised: October 6, 2011), http://www.census .go/census2000/states/az.html, and US Census Bureau, Historical Estimates Data: 2000s Main, National Tables (Last Revised: December 8, 2011), http://www.census.gov/popest/data/ historical/2000s/vintage2008/state.html. (According to the US Census, in 2008 Arizona's population in 2000 was 5,130,632; in 2008 it was 6,500,180, and in 2010, it was 6,392,017. In the two-year period 2008–2010, the state experienced a loss in a population of 108,163.)

479 According to the US Census, US, State & County Quick Facts, Nevada (last revised: Thursday, August. 16, 2012) (in 2010 the population was 2,700,551; in 2008, it was 2,600,167; and in 2007 it was 2,718,337).

480 Bradley J. Fikes, 3 States Work to Share the Colorado's Waters, The San Diego Union-Tribune, Nov. 14, 2015, http://www.sandiegouniontribune.com/news/drought/sdut-colorado-mead-water-california-arizona-nevada-2015nov14-story.html.

cause drought, the Colorado River basin's problems have been building for more than a decade. [481]

The foregoing has led to greater cooperation between all of the basin's states, particularly the three lower ones. It is therefore, quite likely that the Court will not be called upon to settle any further differences.

H Polycentricity and Other Challenges for International Courts

Kansas v. Colorado and *Arizona v. California* demonstrate the two major challenges for international courts in adjudicating transboundary water, natural resources, and environmental disputes, generally, and for this Court specifically. The first is the constant task of weighing the competing "community of interests" of state sovereignty. [482] The Court first observed the tension of these competing interests in the transboundary water context in its 1907 *Kansas v. Colorado* judgment. There, in a case of first impression, concerning opposing rights to consumption of the Arkansas River's waters, the Court declared:

> [o]ne cardinal rule, underlying all the relations of the States to each other, is that of *equality of right*. Each State stands on the same level with all the rest. It can impose its own legislation on no one of the others, and is bound to yield its own views to none. Yet, whenever ... the action of one State reaches through the agency of natural laws into the territory of another State, *the question of the extent and the limitations of the rights of the two States becomes a matter of justiciable dispute between them*, and this court is called upon to settle that dispute in such a way as will recognize the equal rights of both and at the same time establish justice between them. [483]

(Emphasis supplied.)

Kansas v. Colorado and *Arizona v. California*, two similar disputes, that were adjudicated by the same court, and for the most part were parallel in time, demonstrate that the law of the Supreme Court's interstate water disputes today, is not at all crystal clear. Undoubtedly, several norms were developed by the Court – particularly, the doctrine of equitable allocation – in these two disputes. However, from an institutional perspective this author believes

---

[481] *Ibid.*

[482] *See e.g.*, Noah Hall, Political Externalities, Federalism, and a Proposal for an Interstate Environmental Impact Assessment Policy, *Harv Envtl L R* (2008) 49, 68; Thomas W. Merrill, Golden Rules for Transboundary Pollution, 46 *Duke L J* (1997) 931, 944–46. (Describing the Supreme Court's principles as elusive in these disputes, and "Given the inherent difficulties in regulation by any single state, transboundary pollution would seem to present a clear case for shifting regulatory authority from local to more centralized levels of governance.").

[483] *State of Kan. v. State of Colo.*, 206 US 46, 97–98 (1907). (Emphasis supplied.)

that the Court honored its mandate providers' goals of declaring what the law is, pursuant to *Marbury* v. *Madison*, 5 U.S. 137 (1803). Another major challenge in the SCOTUS' adjudication of transboundary water disputes,[484] is the fact that these disputes are very fact specific,[485] "and often hinge upon competing arguments over technical and scientific uncertainty."[486] This may result in polycentric problems. Perhaps, for this reason "the Court has made clear its lack of interest and competence in deciding interstate environmental disputes."[487] In contrast, once parties select arbitration, as a mode of pacific dispute settlement, the tribunal is required to adjudicate the dispute, so long as it has *competence materia rationae* to do so. *See e.g.,* the *Bayview Irrigation* v. *Mexico, infra,* and the Permanent Court of Arbitration's *Indus Waters Kishenganga Arbitration (Pakistan/India).*[488]

An example of the Supreme Court's lack of interest in adjudicating transboundary environmental disputes is *Ohio* v. *Wyandotte Chemicals Corp.*[489] There, the state of Ohio filed a motion for leave to file a complaint – invoking the Court's original jurisdiction – against a number of defendant companies. Ohio claimed that the respondent companies caused a public nuisance, due to their dumping of mercury into the State's tributaries, which resulted in the pollution of Lake Erie. Thus, Ohio sought to have the nuisance abated. The Court declined to exercise its jurisdiction over Petitioner's transboundary pollution claims. In so doing, Justice John Harlan, writing for the 8–1 majority (Justice Douglas dissented), stated that "[h]istory reveals that the course of this Court's prior efforts to settle disputes regarding interstate air and water pollution has been anything but smooth."[490]

Harlan also harkened back to *Missouri* v. *Illinois,*[491] observing that there, Justice Oliver Wendell Holmes was "at pains to underscore the great difficulty that the Court faced in attempting to pronounce a suitable general rule of

---

[484] Hall, Political Externalities, *ibid.* at 69.

[485] *See also, Illinois v. City of Milwaukee*, 406 US 91 (1972); *Ohio v. Wyandotte Chems. Corp.*, 401 US 493 (1971).

[486] Hall, Political Externalities, *ibid.* at 69.   [487] *Ibid.*

[488] Final Award, December 20, 2013, *available at* file:///C:/Users/iek32/Downloads/PK-IN %20Final%20Award,%2020%20December%202013.pdf.

[489] 401 US 493 (1971).   [490] *Wyandotte Chem. ibid.* 401 US at 501.

[491] 200 US 496 (1906).

> This was "a suit brought by the State of Missouri to restrain the discharge of the sewage of Chicago through an artificial channel into the Deplanes River, in the State of Illinois. That river empties into the Illinois River, and the latter empties into the Mississippi at a point about forty-three miles above the city of St. Louis. It was alleged in the bill that the result of the threatened discharge would be to send fifteen hundred tons of poisonous filth daily into the Mississippi . . . "

Ibid. at 517.

law to govern such controversies."[492] Moreover, Justice Harlan acknowledged that "the legal challenge of interstate environmental cases is complicated and perhaps eclipsed by the technical and scientific challenges."[493] In this regard he noted that

> [t]he nature of the case Ohio brings here is equally disconcerting. It can fairly be said that what is in dispute is not so much the law as the facts. And the factfinding process we are asked to undertake is, to say the least, formidable... Indeed, Ohio is raising factual questions that are essentially ones of first impression to the scientists. The notion that appellate judges, *even with the assistance of a most competent Special Master, might appropriately undertake at this time to unravel these complexities is, to say the least, unrealistic.* Nor would it suffice to impose on Ohio an unusually high standard of proof. That might serve to mitigate our personal difficulties in seeking a just result that comports with sound judicial administration, but would not lessen the complexity of the task of preparing responsibly to exercise our judgment, or the serious drain on the resources of this Court it would entail.[494]

Clearly, the SCOTUS was "casting-off the yoke of jurisdiction," due to what the Court's majority viewed as a "complicated" or polycentric problem. This rejection is, in my opinion, equivalent to Justice Scalia's refrain in *Massachusetts* v. *EPA*, where he stated "That's why I don't want to have to deal with global warming, to tell you the truth ... "[495] Indeed, Justice Harlan observed that the "Court has found even the simplest sort of interstate pollution case an extremely awkward vehicle to manage."[496] Resolving transboundary water or interstate environmental disputes requires a range of skills, including "factfinding, conciliation, detailed coordination with – and perhaps not infrequent deference to – other adjudicatory bodies, and close supervision of the technical performance of local industries."[497] The want of *ratione materia* jurisdiction was further elaborated upon later in the *Wyandotte* judgment. There Justice Harlan declared the following:

> This Court is, moreover, structured to perform as an appellate tribunal, ill-equipped for the task of factfinding and so forced, in original cases, awkwardly to play the role of factfinder without actually presiding over the introduction of evidence[, which it does routinely in its appellate cases]. Nor is

---

[492] *Wyandotte Chem.* 401 US at 501   [493] Hall, Political Externalities *ibid.* at 69.
[494] *Wyandotte ibid.* at 503–504 (emphasis added).
[495] Transcript of Oral Argument at 22–23, *Massachusetts v. EPA*, 549 US 497 (November 29, 2006) (Emphasis added.)
[496] Wyandotte, *ibid.* at 504.   [497] *Ibid.* at 505.

the problem merely our lack of qualifications for many of these tasks potentially within the purview of our original jurisdiction; it is compounded by the fact that for every case in which we might be called upon to determine the facts and apply unfamiliar legal norms we would unavoidably be reducing the attention we could give to those matters of federal law and national import as to which we are the primary overseers.

Thus, we think it apparent that we must recognize *the need [for] the exercise of a sound discretion in order to protect this Court* from an abuse of the opportunity to resort to its original jurisdiction in the enforcement by States of claims against citizens of other States … *In our opinion, we may properly exercise such discretion, not simply to shield this Court from noisome, vexatious, or unfamiliar tasks, but also, and we believe principally, as a technique for promoting and furthering the assumptions and value choices that underlie the current role of this Court in the federal system.* Protecting this Court *per se* is at best a secondary consideration. *What gives rise to the necessity for recognizing such discretion is pre-eminently the diminished societal concern in our function as a court of original jurisdiction and the enhanced importance of our role as the final federal appellate court.* A broader view of the scope and purposes of our discretion would inadequately take account of the general duty of courts to exercise that jurisdiction they possess.[498]

It is, of course, the justices' duty to protect the Court as an institution that is true to the Framers' – its mandate providers' – principles, role, and value choices. Nevertheless, even if the justices seek to protect the Court, Justice Harlan's statement above, in this author's view, is cramped and ignores the realities of the Court's original jurisdiction framework. For example, for almost a century, special masters have been appointed to undertake "the task of factfinding."[499] Thus, the Court is not *required* to "awkwardly … play the role of factfinder without actually presiding over the introduction of evidence."[500] Indeed, the previous sentence, it is suggested, is a red-herring, since the Court routinely undertakes the practice of not presiding over the introduction of evidence, in its role as the nation's final appellate court.

Moreover, Justice Harlan's declaration "that the diminished societal concern in [the Court's] function as a court of original jurisdiction … "[501] may be highly inflated. If the Court is truly an independent institution, it should not be concerned with society's concern of what it does, so long as it does not stray from its constitutional mandate. Indeed, if we correctly interpret his apprehension, Justice Harlan seems to be suggesting that the Court looks over

---

[498] *Ibid*. at 498–499 (emphasis added).   [499] *Ibid*. at 505.   [500] *Ibid*.   [501] *Ibid*.

its shoulder at societal expectations. Bold courts effect both law and justice regardless of the popularity of their decisions.[502]

Furthermore, as the dissent by Justice William O. Douglas notes "[t]he complaint in this case presents basically *a classic type of case congenial to our original jurisdiction*. It is to abate a public nuisance."[503] Finally, as I have noted previously, judges are political creatures and their politics likely guides or influences some of their opinions. Indeed, the justices were accused as much by the dissent in the Court's 1963 judgment in *Arizona v. California*. There Justice Douglas, who was an ardent Western conservationist, declared: "[t]he present case will, I think, be marked as the baldest attempt by judges in modern times to spin their own philosophy into the fabric of the law . . . "[504]

There is, however, a dichotomy in the Court's interstate jurisprudence that impacts its effectiveness. On the one hand, transboundary water cases and interstate boundary disputes are "readily" granted jurisdiction. *Missouri v. Illinois* is typical of how the Court deems these kinds of disputes. There, the Court held that

> if one State raises a controversy with another, this court must determine whether there is any principle of law and, if any, what, on which the plaintiff can recover. But the fact that this court must decide does not mean, of course, that it takes the place of a legislature. Some principles it must have power to declare. *For instance, when a dispute arises about boundaries, this court must determine the line, and in doing so must be governed by rules explicitly or implicitly recognized.* It must follow and apply those rules, even if legislation of one or both of the States seems to stand in the way.[505]

On the other hand, that is not the situation in transboundary environmental cases, as we saw in *Wyandotte*.[506] Similarly, the Court declined jurisdiction in

---

[502] *See generally, Ryland's v. Fletcher* (1868) LR 3 HL 330; *Brown v. Board of Education*, 347 US 483 (1954); *Griswold v. Connecticut*, 381 US 479 (1965) (Defining privacy); HCJ 5100/94, *The Public Committee Against Torture in Israel v. the Government of Israel*, (Barak, P. J.) (in Hebrew). ("A democracy must sometimes fight with one arm tied behind her back. Even so, a democracy has the upper hand. The rule of law and individual liberties constitute an important aspect of her security stance. At the end of the day, they strengthen her spirit and this strength allows her to overcome her difficulties." *Ibid.* at 845.)

[503] *Ibid.* 401 US at 505–506 (emphasis added).

[504] *Arizona v. California*, 373 US 546, 628 (1963) (Douglas, J. dissenting).

[505] 260 US 519–520. (*Citing Rhode Island v. Massachusetts*, 12 Pet. 657, 737 (1838)) (emphasis added.)

[506] *See e.g.*, Hall, Political Externalities, *ibid.*; Richard Lazarus, Restoring What's Environmental About Environmental Law in the Supreme Court, 47 *UCLA L R* (2000) 73; Richard Lazarus, The Power of Persuasion Before and Within the Supreme Court of the United States, 2012 *Univ Ill L R* (2012) 231.

Missouri v. *Illinois*, ruling that the Petitioner did not offer enough proof to demonstrate that the discharge of raw sewage into the Mississippi River by Illinois, was creating a public nuisance, as it alleged. This dichotomy may arise from the fact that environmental cases require greater awareness and comprehension of complex scientific facts and the polycentric issues that are enmeshed in them than do delimitation disputes.

9

Arbitration of Transboundary Water Disputes

I THE CHAMIZAL DISPUTE

"Conquest gives a title which the courts of the conqueror cannot deny, whatever the private and speculative opinions of individuals may be, respecting the original justice of the claim which has been successfully asserted."[1]

A *Introduction*

The Chamizal dispute between Mexico and the United States was a conflict over a shift in the Rio Grande River's (*Río Bravo del Norte* in Spanish) channel and the movement of a tract of land, which rested upon the principles of accretion and avulsion. Although it did not begin so, the dispute devolved into a conflict over the exact location of the negotiated international boundary. The Chamizal dispute demonstrates how the divisions between states, which we view as international boundaries, are "characterized in law by their inherent rigidity."[2] The boundary between Mexico and the United States, as originally agreed to by the two states, was located in the channel of the Rio Grande River, between the sister cities of El Paso (USA) and Ciudad Juarez (Mexico).

The crux of the dispute was over four treaties negotiated between 1848 and 1884 – beginning with the Treaty of Guadalupe Hidalgo (which ended the hostilities of the Mexican–American War). Each of these designated the boundary between Mexico and the United States, as the center of the river's channel. A shift in the Rio Grande's channel, in 1861, repositioned the 2.4-km (600-acre) Chamizal tract, from the southern bank of the Rio Grande

[1] *United States v. Alcea Band of Tillamooks*, 329 US 40, 60–61 (1946).
[2] John W. Donaldson, Paradox of the Moving Boundary: Legal Heredity of River Accretion and Avulsion, 4 *Water Alternatives* (2011) 155, 155.

River, *i.e.*, the Mexican side, to the northern one, *i.e.*, the American side. The Chamizal tract attached itself to the United States at El Paso, Texas, sandwiched between the Rio Grande as surveyed in 1852, and the present channel of the river.

Some 100 acres of the tract fell within El Paso's business district.[3] The issue: could any of the four treaties contain language that would be of use in interpreting where the boundary was located, once the river's channel moved due to an avulsive episode?[4]

The discord between Mexico and the United States over the Chamizal Tract simmered for over a decade until they entered into a *compromis* on June 24, 1910, and an additional protocol, dated December 5, 1910. That agreement set the stage for a subsequent arbitration that commenced on May 15, and ended on June 24, 1911.[5] The *compromis* required the arbitral commission to award the entire Chamizal tract exclusively to either Mexico or the United States.

However, the arbitrators divided the tract, awarding the lion's share to Mexico. Mexico protested the award, maintaining that the Arbitration Commission's decision was a nullity, *i.e.*, invoking the doctrine of *excès de pouvoir*.[6] Moreover, the American government refused to abide by the award for fifty-three years. Ultimately, the matter was resolved diplomatically.

1 The Rio Grande River and the Physical Setting Which Gave Rise to the Chamizal Dispute

The Rio Grande (Spanish for the big river), as it is known in the United States, or the Rio Bravo del Norte (the North Pass), as it is called in Mexico, has its headwaters 1,885 miles (3,000 km) from the venue of the dispute.

---

[3]   Sheldon B. Liss, The Century of Disagreement: The Chamizal Conflict, 1864–1964 (1965) 1.
[4]   Avulsion is a phenomenon by which a river suddenly jumps or changes the course of its channel and creates a new one. This subject is more fully addressed *infra*.
[5]   United Nations Reports of International Arbitral Awards the Chamizal Case (Mexico, United States) 15 June 1911 Volume XI p. 309 (hereinafter "Award") at 313, *citing* Art. III of the *compromis*. The dates of the arbitration included, May 15, 18, 20, 22, 23, 24, 25, 26, 27, 29, 30. 31, June 2, 10 and 15. US Department of State, International Boundary Commission, United States and Mexico, Chamizal Arbitration, Record of the Daily Proceedings of the International Arbitration Hearings, Herman H. Pechin, Shorthand Reporter. 1911.
[6]   *Excès de pouvoir* is the French term for ultra vires or excess of power. *See generally,* W. Michael Reisman, Nullity and Revision (1971) 246; *see also* W. Michael Reisman, Control Mechanisms in International Dispute Resolution, 2 *US–Mex LJ* (1994) 129, 130–131. The fundamental view of the doctrine is that a tribunal in a *compromis* is granted only the power or subject matter jurisdiction that is expressly conferred upon it within the four corners of the document and no more. Nullity and Revision *ibid.* at 246.

Rising high in Colorado's San Juan Mountains (12,588 feet or 3,387 meters high), at Stony Pass, on the Continental Divide in western Colorado, the river is the second longest in North America. It courses almost due south through central New Mexico to southwest Texas, where it turns southeast and forms the US–Mexican border for the rest of its course. The river flows into the Gulf of Mexico adjacent to Brownsville, Texas, and Matamoros, Mexico.

As part of the ceasefire of the Mexican–American War of 1848, the United Mexican States ("Mexico") and the United States of America ("US") agreed that the lower Rio Grande River would form their southeastern border. This agreement is memorialized in the 1848 Treaty of Peace, Friendship, Limits, and Settlement between the United States and the Mexican Republic (Guadalupe Hidalgo Treaty),[7] and the subsequent Gadsden Treaty of 1853.[8] The Chamizal tract is located between the twin cities of El Paso in the USA, and Ciudad Juarez in Mexico (formerly known as El Paso del Norte). In the simplest terms, the Chamizal is a wedge of land that today is attached to El Paso, Texas.[9] It is composed of two parts: The Island of Cordova and the Chamizal.[10] (See Figure 9.1.)

Although the dispute between the two states centered on a tract of land, the conflict was, in fact, over the movement of the lower Rio Grande's channel.

---

[7] Treaty of Peace, Friendship, Limits, and Settlement Between the United States and the Mexican Republic, Feb. 2, 1848, US–Mex., 9 Stat. 922 [hereinafter Treaty of Guadalupe Hidalgo], at art. V. ("The boundary line between the two Republics shall commence . . . opposite the mouth of the Rio Grande. Otherwise called the Rio Bravo del Norte . . . up the middle of that river, following the deepest channel, where it has more than one, to the point where it strikes the southern boundary of New Mexico . . .")

[8] Gadsden Treaty, Dec. 30, 1853, US–Mex., 10 Stat. 1031. The description of the border established in the Guadalupe–Hidalgo Treaty was modified by Article I of the Gadsden Treaty as follows:

The Mexican Republic agrees to designate the following as her true limits with the United States for the future: retaining the same dividing line . . . as already defined and established, according to the 5th article of the treaty of Guadalupe Hidalgo, the limits between the two republics shall be as follows: Beginning in the Gulf of Mexico, three leagues from land, opposite the mouth of the Rio Grande, as provided in the 5th article of the treaty of Guadalupe Hidalgo; thence, as defined in the said article, up the middle of that river to the point where the parallel of 31° 47' north latitude crosses the same [El Paso, Tex. is located at 31° 48' N latitude, 106° 24' W longitude, while Ciudad Juarez is located at 31° 45' 31" N latitude, 106° 29' 11" W longitude] . . . .

[9] Liss *ibid.* at 1.

[10] The name Chamizal is derived from Chamisa, Spanish for a four-wing salt bush. United States National Park Service, Chamizal National Memorial, *Flood and the Chamizal Issue, The Rio Grande Floods: The Beginning of the Chamizal Dispute* (undated), https://www.nps.gov/cham/learn/historyculture/rio-grand-floods-and-the-chamizal-issue.htm.

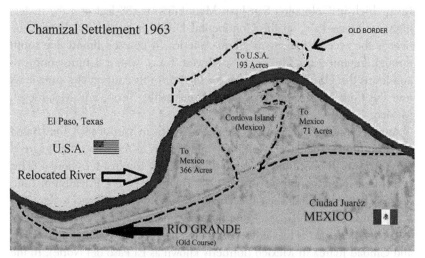

FIGURE 9.1 EL Paso and Ciudad Juarez Separated by the Rio Grande River

Long-standing international law provides that the thalweg[11] or middle, of the main *navigable* channel is to be taken as the true boundary line between two states whose border is a river.[12] It is also established doctrine that when a change occurs in the course of a boundary river, which is caused by a deposit

---

[11]   Thalweg is a German word that means a valley (thal) and way (weg) and translates to mean "the channel continuously used for navigation." L. J. Bouchez, The Fixing of Boundaries in International Boundary Rivers, 12 *Int'l & Comp L Q* (1963) 789, 793. A Thalweg, pursuant to international law, is used to demarcate Boundary Rivers that are navigable. *See generally, Kasikili/Sedudu Island (Bots. v. Namib.)*, 1999 ICJ 1045, 1062 (Dec. 13) ("'Treaties or conventions which define boundaries in water courses nowadays usually refer to the thalweg as the boundary when the watercourse is navigable and to the median line between the two banks when it is not, although it cannot be said that practice has been fully consistent."); *Oklahoma v. Texas*, 258 US 574, 586 (1922) (noting that it is a "settled rule" that "navigability in fact is the test of navigability in law"). Furthermore, the thalweg is not a specific line in the river's channel. Rather it is a broad area. Bouchez, *ibid.* at 793. The term thalweg has also been described as "the middle, or deepest, or most navigable channel..." *Louisiana v. Mississippi*, 202 US 1, 49 (1906), and "the line of the greatest depth or the stream line of the fastest current;" Elihu Lauterpacht, River Boundaries: Legal Aspects of the Shatt-al Arab Frontier, 9 *Int'l & Comp L Q* (1960) 208, 221.

[12]   The United States has also adopted this doctrine. *See e.g., Louisiana v. Mississippi*, 202 US 1, 49 (1906). (No. 11, original). ("The term 'thalweg' is commonly used by writers on international law in definition of water boundaries between states, meaning, the middle, or deepest, or most navigable channel..."); *New Jersey v. Delaware*, 291 US 361, 379 (1934) (No. 13, original). ("International law today divides the river boundaries between states by the middle of the main channel, when there is one, and not by the geographical center, halfway between the banks.")

of alluvium,[13] that is the building up of new land, the boundary changes with the river. However, when change is due to avulsion,[14] the old channel remains the boundary.

Shifts in a river's channel are quite normal.[15] Indeed, like all rivers, the Rio Grande has historically altered its channel.[16] Such shifts frequently cause pieces of land to become detached from the shoreline, forming what in English are termed "cut-offs," or oxbow lakes,[17] and in Spanish are called "bancos del rio," *i.e.*, banks of the river or "bancos." Since these cut-offs have from time to time detached themselves from either the continental United States or from Mexico, both states have asserted title to them. The Chamizal tract likewise, formed as a consequence of the shift in the river.

[13] If riparian land grows by the addition of alluvium, *i.e.*, sediment or soil, until it extends to the mainland, such new made land will become the property of the owner whose property the alluvium attached to.

[14] *See generally, Anderson-Tully Co. v. Walls*, 266 F. Supp. 804, 812 (D. Miss. 1967). (*Citing Mayor, Alderman, etc., of New Orleans v. United States* 35 US 662 (1836).)

> When, however, from any cause, natural or artificial, a boundary river suddenly leaves its old channel and seeks a new bed, this sudden and rapid change is termed an avulsion and the resulting change works no change of boundary, which remains in the middle of the old channel, although no water may be flowing in it, and irrespective of subsequent changes in the new channel.

At common law, a riparian owner automatically took title to dry land added to his property by accretion, but formerly submerged land that has become dry land by avulsion continues to belong to the owner of the bank nearest the avulsion. However, Since Mexico is a civilian or civil law jurisdiction the law is somewhat different. *See e.g.*, Mexican Civil Code Art. 800. *See also*, William Cullen Dennis, International Boundary & Water Commission United States & Mexico, *Chamizal Arbitration: The Countercase of the United States of America, with Appendix and Portfolio Maps* (1911) 562–563 (*citing* Bello, *Derechio Internacional*, at 38, and Pando, *Derechio Internacional*, at 99).

[15] Henning Nolzento, *et al.*, River Channel Position, Regime Shifts Database (Last revised June 21, 2013), http://www.regimeshifts.org/about/item/403-river-channel-position. ("[A] river channel position regime shift occurs when the main channel of the river changes it course to a new river channel. Meandering and braided rivers are especially vulnerable to such shifts. The actual shift of the channel usually follows a large flood event.")

[16] Luna B. Leopold and Thomas Maddock Jr., *The Hydraulic Geometry of Stream Channels and Some Physiographic Implications*, United States Geological Survey (1953). United States Fish & Wildlife Service, Lower Rio Grande Valley National Wildlife Refuge, Texas, *Wetland Management* (last updated, July 9, 2012), https://www.fws.gov/refuge/lower_rio_grande_valley/resource_management/wetlands_management.html. ("For centuries, the Rio Grande regularly flowed over its banks. The river would blanket the Lower Rio Grande Valley and, over centuries, would inevitably alter its own course.")

[17] A cut-off is formed when a river's current rounds a bend of a river cutting that bend off from the river. The abandoned stretch of the river, or bend, forms what is called an oxbow lake. Hal Shelton, *Geology Illustrated* (1966) 144–145.

The *Chamizal Arbitration* provides a number of lessons. The first relates to how states deal with a shift of their transboundary river. Second, it provides lessons in arbitral mechanics, and normative contributions to transboundary water and international law. Third, this dispute demonstrates a lesson in the *ultra vires* behavior by a tribunal and that tribunal's legitimacy on the one hand and a lack of compliance by a state on the other. In addition, when measuring this tribunal's effectiveness, the issue of whether award compliance was a decisive aspect of this adjudication comes to the fore. Of course, award or judgment compliance is only one proxy for effectiveness, and its impact on the overall evaluation of the tribunal's efficacy should not be overstated, since other actions which may yield effective outcomes may be overlooked.

One other key point that should not be neglected, particularly in this dispute, is that the Chamizal *ad hoc* tribunal grew out of a *compromis* negotiated by the two Parties who formed the International Boundary Commission. Indeed, the fact that only one dispute has been litigated in some 125 years of the IBC/IBCW existence, likely points to one of two reasons: (1) the success of the IBC and the model that its mandate providers sought to establish; one that diplomatically resolves disputes over the rivers that flow across the borders of Mexico and the United States; or (2) alternatively, given their experience with this case the Parties decided to pursue diplomatic solutions in all of their future conflicts. I posit that the real answer likely lies somewhere between these two poles.

The *compromis* entered into by Mexico the United States required the commission to adhere to that instrument's terms. However, the tribunal failed to do so. The relevant *proviso* specified that the "commission shall decide solely and exclusively as to whether the international title to the Chamizal tract is in the United States of America or Mexico. The decision of the commission, whether rendered unanimously or by majority vote of the commissioners, *shall be final and conclusive upon both Governments, and without appeal.*"[18]

Given that the arbitrators divided the tract, and awarded the lion's share to Mexico, they disregarded their mandate, even if they thought that their choice was the most equitable one. The United States, therefore, had cause for rejecting the award, albeit, the commission's unique remedy would have benefitted the USA, because it would have retained a portion of the Chamizal tract, rather than lose it all to Mexico. Nevertheless, one scholar has argued that the IBC, under whose auspices the tribunal was formed, and the IBWC, its current reincarnation, have been ineffective when the political spirit of

---

[18] Convention for the Arbitration of the Chamizal Case, June 24, 1910, US–Mex., 36 Stat. 2481, at 2483, art. III (emphasis added).

the two sides was lacking,[19] as was the case in this dispute. He also repeats the point made by Justice Roberts in his 1943 *Kansas v. Colorado* case that when disputes become part of the adjudicatory process they turn out to be very difficult to resolve.[20] Indeed, another author, C. Richard Bath, recommends that states seize every possibility to prevent their disputes from reaching the hands of adjudicatory bodies.[21]

B *The Crux of the Dispute*

Although the dispute became an international one, the Chamizal controversy began as a private title claim made by the Mexican grandson of the original title holder. It was initiated by a November 4, 1895 submission, made by the Mexican Commissioner to the International Boundary Commission (IBC) on behalf of the putative owner of the land, Pedro Ignacio Garcia, a resident of Ciudad Juarez, whose familial title dated to 1827.[22]

That case, denominated as the *El Chamizal, No. 4*, was presented to the IBC in 1896, with the request that the Commission decide to which State the territory belonged.[23] Seeking to establish a factual record of the processes that caused the river to jump its channel's location, in 1861, the Commission examined witnesses and accepted a technical report submitted by its engineers. This evidence appeared to demonstrate that slow and gradual erosion had occurred preceding 1864 and that thereafter "erosion of a perceptible and sometimes violent nature had taken place."[24]

Nevertheless, in an 1896 decision, the two national IBC Commissioners disagreed about how to apply the principles established by a Convention executed by the parties in 1884, to the evidence presented. While the Mexican

---

[19] Peter S. Smedresman, The International Joint Commission (United States–Canada) and the International Boundary and Water Commission (United States–Mexico): Potential for Environmental Control Along the Boundaries, 6 *NYU J Int'l L & Pol* (1973) 499, 502.

[20] *Ibid.*

[21] *Ibid. See also*, C. Richard Bath, Alternative Cooperative Arrangements for Managing Transboundary Air Resources along the Border, 18 *Nat Res J* (1978) 181, 189.

[22] "In 1827, Jose Ponce de Leon received a land grant from the Mexican government. His land was in El Paso del Norte, on the south side of the Rio Grande [River]. Leon's land became known as el Chamizal (the Chamizal tract)..." United States National Park Service, Chamizal National Memorial, *Flood and the Chamizal Issue, The Rio Grande Floods: The Beginning of the Chamizal Dispute* (undated), https://www.nps.gov/cham/learn/historyculture/rio-grand-floods-and-the-chamizal-issue.htm. *See also*, Robert M. Utley *Changing Course* (1996) 90.

[23] Percy Don Williams, Jr., Fifty Years of the Chamizal Controversy – A Note on International Arbitral Appeals, 25 *Tex L R* (1947) 455, 458.

[24] *Ibid.* at 458.

Commissioner maintained that there was no change in the boundary location along the Rio Grande, the United States Commissioner asserted that
the border relocated south when the channel moved.[25] The situation became
so mired in the United States that in his 1889 State of the Union, President
McKinley, observed that the

> Mexican Water Boundary Commission has adjusted all matters submitted
> to it to the satisfaction of both Governments save in three important cases –
> that of the "Chamizal" at El Paso, Tex., where the two commissioners failed
> to agree, and wherein, for this case only, this Government has proposed to
> Mexico the addition of a third member; the proposed elimination of what
> are known as "Bancos," small isolated islands formed by the cutting off of
> bends in the Rio Grande, from the operation of the treaties of 1884 and 1889,
> recommended by the commissioners and approved by this Government,
> but still under consideration by Mexico; and the subject of the "Equitable
> distribution of the waters of the Rio Grande," for which the commissioners
> recommended an international dam and reservoir . . . [26]

1 1910: A *Compromis* is Born

The two states remained far apart until June 24, 1910, when they entered into
the aforementioned *compromis* in an effort to resolve the title issue.[27] That
instrument's preamble expressed the parties' desire to conclude the disputes
that arose between them, concerning the international title to the Chamizal
tract, "upon which the members of the International Boundary Commission
have failed to agree, and having determined to refer these differences to the
said commission, established by the convention of 1889, which for this case

---

[25] *See* Award by the International Boundary Commission, *ibid.* 11 RIAA at 318. At a session of
the boundary commissioners held on September 28, 1894, the Mexican commissioner presented the papers in a case known as "El Chamizal No. 4." These included a complaint made
by Pedro Ignacio Garcia, who alleged, in substance, that he had acquired certain property
formerly lying on the south side of the Rio Grande, known as El Chamizal, which, in consequence of the abrupt and sudden change of current of die Rio Grande, was now on the
north side of die river and within the limits of El Paso, Texas. This claim was examined by
the International Boundary Commissioners, who heard witnesses upon the facts, and who,
after consideration, were unable to come to any agreement, and so reported to their respective
Governments. As a result of this disagreement the convention of June 24, 1910, was signed, and
the decision of the question was submitted to the present commission.

[26] State of the Union Address: William McKinley (December 5, 1898), *available at* Infoplease
.com http://www.infoplease.com/t/hist/state-of-the-union/110.html.

[27] Convention for the Arbitration of the Chamizal Case, June 24, 1910, US–Mex., 36 Stat. 2481;
also at 11 RIAA 309 (June 15, 1911) (*hereinafter* Award).

only shall be enlarged as hereinafter provided, have resolved to conclude a convention for that purpose . . . "[28]

The *compromis'* Article II states that for the Chamizal dispute proceedings, a special panel of the commission would be established, which would include the two existing Mexican and US Commissioners, Fernando Beltram y Puga and Anson Mills, respectively. The commission was to be enlarged with the inclusion of a third commissioner, a Canadian jurist, who would be designated by the Government of Canada. Accordingly, each side would appoint a representative commissioner and the Canadian Jurist would be the arbitral committee's chair. The disputed territory was described as follows in the *compromis*:

> Article I. The Chamizal tract in dispute is located at El Paso, Texas, and Ciudad Juarez, Chihuahua, and is bounded westerly and southerly by the middle of the present channel of the Rio Grande, otherwise called Rio Bravo del Norte, easterly by the middle of the abandoned channel of 1901, and northerly by the middle of the channel of the river as surveyed by Emory and Salazar in 1852.[29]

In executing the *compromis* Mexico and the United States also declared that all previous diplomatic negotiations and offers of settlement regarding the Chamizal case were to be null and void. However, each side did retain the right to submit as evidence, and official correspondence solely for informational purposes.[30] Moreover, the *compromis* provided for detailed procedures, including:

1. The appointment of an agent and counsel to represent each side before the commission, each of whom was entitled to present oral arguments, to examine and cross-examine witnesses, and when the commission decided, to introduce additional documentary evidence;[31]
2. The fee for the Canadian commissioner;[32]

---

[28] Convention and Supplemental Protocol between the United States and Mexico; Award and Dissenting Opinion – Chamizal Tract Arbitration, Jan. 25, 1911, at Proclamation, *in* Papers Relating to the Foreign Relations of the United States (1918) 565–6.

[29] Convention for Arbitration *ibid.* at Art. I. The description refers to

> a map on a scale of 1–5,000 signed by General Anson Mills, commissioner on the part of the United States, and Senor Don F. Javier Osorno, commissioner on the part of Mexico, which accompanies the report of the International Boundary Commission, in Case No. 13, entitled "Alleged Obstruction in the Mexican End of the El Paso Street Railway Bridge and Backwaters Caused by the Great Bend in the River Below" . . .

[30] *Ibid.* at Art. IX.   [31] *Ibid.* at Art. IV.   [32] *Ibid.* at Art. VI.

3. Strict timelines of when documents were to be exchanged between the respective agents, how many copies were to be provided to each side, and when they were to be supplied to the commission;[33]

4. Notice to the parties that the commission would heed the terms of the 1889 boundary Convention, but that it would adopt those rules and regulations that it would "deem convenient in the course of the case."[34]

Finally, the *compromis* provided that the commission's decision was to be final and unappealable.[35]

By appointing the Canadian Eugene LaFluer, a former Professor of International Law at McGill University,[36] as the chairman of this mixed commission, the arbitral tribunal and its "trial"[37] were imbued with an international aura. Indeed, the Arbitration, which began on May 15, 1911, was to "become the single most important factor in the long history of the Chamizal conflict."[38] The Commission was tasked with investigating and considering (1) whether the change in the Rio Grande River's course was gradual or rapid; (2) whether the border as set forth by Guadalupe-Hidalgo and the Gadsden Treaties, among others, was static, or impermanent; and (3) if the 1884 treaty governed.[39]

In its submission Mexico asserted that the boundary was static and never moved, consequently the Chamizal tract remained Mexican territory. Alternatively, the United States argued that an 1861 flood episode swiftly shifted the channel, and, pursuant to the 1884 Treaty, the Chamizal was part of its

---

[33] *Ibid.* at Art. VI. *E.g.*

On or before February 1, 1911, each Government may present to the agent of the other a countercase, with documentary evidence, in answer to the case and documentary evidence of the other party. The countercase shall be delivered in the manner provided in the foregoing paragraph. The commission shall hold its first session in the city of El Paso, State of Texas, where the offices of the International Boundary Commission are situated, on March 1, 1911, and shall proceed to the trial of the case with all convenient speed, sitting either at El Paso, Texas, or Ciudad Juarez, Chihuahua, as convenience may require.

[34] *Ibid.*

[35] *Ibid.* 36 Stat. 2483, at Art. III. ("The commission shall decide solely and exclusively as to whether the international title to the Chamizal tract is in the United States of America or Mexico. The decision of the commission, whether rendered unanimously or by majority vote of the commissioners, *shall be final and conclusive upon both Governments, and without appeal*.") (Emphasis added.) *See also*, Alan C. Lamborn & Stephen P. Mumme, *Statecraft Domestic Politics, and Foreign Policy: The El Chamizal Dispute* (1988) 54–55.

[36] "Eugene Lafleur, one of His Britannic Majesty's counsel, doctor of civil law and former professor of international law at McGill University." Award at 316.

[37] The dispute was over "Title to the Chamizal Tract – Boundary rivers – Effects of natural change in the course of such rivers – Treaty interpretation – Retroactive effects of treaty provisions – Prescription."

[38] Liss *ibid.* at 24.   [39] *Ibid.* at 68–69, 75–77.

territory.[40] The 1884 Treaty included two provisions. Both, concerned the Rio Grande River and its changing course. One of them stated that should the river shift its course gradually, then the transboundary border would move with the river. The other declared that should the Rio Grande's course change swiftly, as it would during a flood, the border would not change.[41]

One odd proviso in the *compromis* provided that

> if the arbitral award provided for by this convention shall be favorable to Mexico, it shall be executed within the term of two years, which cannot be extended, and which shall be counted from the date on which the award is rendered. During that time the status quo will be maintained in the Chamizal on the terms agreed upon by both governments.[42]

If the award were for the United States, however, the implementation would be immediate, because the United States was in de facto control of the territory.[43]

The two antagonists expected the arbitration to "last for several weeks or months."[44] The *compromis* defined the Chamizal tract,

> as being located at El Paso, Texas, and Ciudad Juârez, Chihuahua, and is bounded westerly and southerly by the middle of the present channel of the Rio Grande, otherwise called the Rîo Bravo del Norte, easterly by the middle of the abandoned channel of 1901, and northerly by the middle of the channel of the river as surveyed by Emory and Salazar in 1852 . . . [45]

The arbitrators initially convened in the El Paso Federal Building at 3:00 p.m., on Monday, May 15, 1911.[46] (See Table 9.1). The proceedings were not covered intently. Indeed, the El Paso newspapers did not pay a great deal of attention

---

[40] In 1884, the IBC United States National Park Service, Chamizal National Memorial, Texas, The Arbitration of 1911 (2016), https://www.nps.gov/cham/learn/historyculture/the-arbitration-of-1911.htm.

[41] Convention Between the United States of America and the Mexico States Touching the International Boundary Line Where it Follows the Bed of the Rio Grande and the Rio Colorado, US–Mex., Nov. 12, 1884, 24 Stat. 1011, at Arts. II and III, *available at* http://www.ibwc.gov/Files/TREATY_OF_1884.pdf (hereinafter "Treaty of 1884").

[42] US Statutes at Large, vol. 36, Part 2, 2485, Arbitration Convention-Mexico, Art. IX (June 24, 1910). The original draft provided for the execution of the award within three months.

[43] Kenneth Duane Yielding, The Chamizal Dispute: An Exercise in Arbitration, 1845–1945, Ph.D. Dissertation, Texas Tech University (May 1973) 170.

[44] *Ibid.* at 167.   [45] Statutes at Large, vol. 36, Part 2, *ibid.* at 2482.

[46] The USA appropriated $50,000.00, and the Mexican Congress of the Union (Congresso de la Unión) appropriated $80,000.00 to cover their respective sides' expenses. US, Statutes at Large, vol. 36, Part 1, at 1034; House of Rep., Arbitration of International Title to Chamizal Tract, 61st Cong., 3d Sess., 1910, Doc. 1139, at 1-2.

to the proceedings.[47] Mexico was at the time in the throes of a revolution, and most Mexicans were not optimistic as they were uncertain whether "the territory upon which the city of El Paso is built, stolen from them by the Yankees,"[48] would ever come under their flag again.

In issuing its award on June 10, 1911, the tribunal recommended that the Chamizal tract should be divided between the two parties. As part of their deliberation of the evidence, the arbitrators examined a survey conducted in 1852. Based on that survey they awarded the United States that portion of the Chamizal situated between the Rio Grande's riverbed, during the 1852 survey, and the river's channel during 1864. The remainder was awarded to Mexico. As noted previously, the Government of the United States disavowed the award, as it did not conform to the terms of the *compromis*. This rejection continued until 1963. Although a number of attempts to resolve the matter diplomatically were made during that 52-year period, these failed.

The interests of the United States suffered greatly as a result of its rejection of the award. For example, Liss documents the injuries to the United States' economic and political interests, among others, because of its prolonged failure to comply with the arbitral award.[49] Finally, in 1963, President John F. Kennedy agreed to accept the 1911 arbitration award.[50] He did not live to see the resolution, due to his assassination, on November 22, 1963. Subsequently, President Lyndon Baines Johnson finalized the settlement on January 14, 1964. The settlement terms were those contained in the award and are as follows: Mexico to receive 366 acres (1.48 km²) of the Chamizal tract, as well as 71 acres (0.29 km²) on the adjacent Cordova Island, which lies to the east of the Chamizal. The settlement precluded the parties from paying damages to each other. Nevertheless, the United States did receive recompense for 382 buildings included in the reassignment of the tracts to Mexico. In addition, the USA obtained 193 acres (0.78 km²) from Cordova Island. Furthermore, the two states agreed to re-channel the Rio Grande into a concrete canal so that the river would no longer breach its banks.

---

[47] Yielding *ibid.* at 173-4.   [48] Yielding *ibid.* at 174.

[49] Liss *ibid.* at 68–69, 75–77. Percy Don Williams, Jr., *ibid.* at 25 *Tex. L. R.* 461–462 (1947). (Discussing the Government of the United States problems negotiating with the Government of Mexico issues related to the latter's expropriation of American business' agrarian and petroleum properties.) *See also*, President Kennedy's expression of disappointment in the position of the US Government regarding the Chamizal dispute. Kennedy Says US Was Wrong in Mexico Border Disagreement, NY TIMES, July 6, 1962, at 4. ("President Kennedy indicated [on July 5] that he believed that the United States had been wrong in refusing to accept the decision of a 1911 arbitration commission in a territorial dispute with Mexico.")

[50] The dispute was settled on August 29, 1963, when the United Mexican States and the United States ratified the Convention for the Solution of the Problem of the Chamizal, US–Mex., August 29, 1963, 15 UST 21, which essentially followed the stipulations of the award.

TABLE 9.1 *The Chamizal Arbitration – Time from Compromis to Award*

(1) **June 24, 1910** – *Compromis* executed.	(5) **September 1911** – Award Issued. (2–1 decision placing the international boundary to the 1863 course of the Rio Grande River.) USA Rejects.
(2) **On or before February 1, 1911,** each Government may present to the agent of the other a countercase, with documentary evidence, in answer to the case and documentary evidence of the other party.	(6) **1983** – *Arizona v. California*, 460 US 605. Argued Dec. 8, 1982; Decided Mar. 30, 1983. **= 3 months and 22 days.**
(3) **May 15, 1911** – Arbitration proceedings begin.	(7) **January 14, 1964** – Presidents Lyndon Baines Johnson (USA) and Adolfo López Mateos (U.M.S.) convene at the parties' border to execute the agreement to conclude the dispute.
(4) **August 1911** – Panel convenes in El Paso, Texas.	(8) **September 17, 1964,** the United States Congress introduced the American–Mexican Chamizal Convention Act of 1964, Pub. L. 88–300, Apr. 29, 1964, 78 Stat. 184, enacting 22 USC §§ 277d–17 to 277d–25, finally settling the dispute. In October 1967, Presidents Johnson and Gustavo Díaz Ordaz met at the border to officially proclaim the resolution.

a MEASURING THE TRIBUNAL'S EFFECTIVENESS As noted above, based on these facts and the outcome, the United States had grounds to complain that the tribunal failed to heed the terms of the *compromis*, and consequently failed to promote or encourage **compliance – proxy number 1 – with the governing international norm,** *i.e.*, the Commission was not true to the document governing its existence as an *ad hoc* tribunal. Thus, the commission's actions led to a lack of compliance by the United States. However, the Commission did follow transboundary water law *vis a vis* river courses. Nevertheless, it is unclear whether the award and the tribunal's operation had any impact on the conduct of other States or relevant actors, since the historical and legal literature do not address this issue. Of course, that does not necessarily mean that the award did not, or has not, influenced other actors.

With regards to **proxy number 2, resolution,** we are initially required to evaluate whether this arbitral panel/commission resolved the dispute and the specific problem it was asked to solve. There is no doubt that the tribunal resolved the dispute, although not in accordance with the terms of the *compromis*.

With recourse to **proxy number 3, this dispute's normative impact** and whether the tribunal contributed to the operation of related institutional and normative regimes. I do not believe that the resolution of this dispute provided new remedies nor made any significant normative contributions – although it clarified the law of avulsion. It is also unclear to me whether this arbitration's resolution in 1963 had any impact on international legal norms at that juncture. This dispute also had no polycentric issues that had to be addressed by the Commission. Moreover, since the award has not been cited by other fora, it would suggest that no such contribution was made. Nevertheless, I posit that in adopting certain legal principles, the tribunal's resolution of this dispute, likely had a positive impact on international legal norms; particularly, since the commission's members followed the governing international law regarding certain attributes of river hydrology, *e.g.*, use of the thalweg and the Rio Grande River's position, as compared with the Parties' border.

Long-standing international law provides that the thalweg,[51] or middle of the main navigable channel, is considered to be the true boundary line between two states whose border is a river.[52] Similarly, it is established doctrine that when a change in the course of a boundary river occurs, and is caused by a deposit of alluvium,[53] *i.e.*, that is the building up of new land takes place, the frontier or boundary changes with the concomitant change in the river's channel. However, when a change is due to avulsion,[54] the old

---

[51] Thalweg is a German word that means a valley (thal) and way (weg) and translates to mean "the channel continuously used for navigation." L. J. Bouchez, The Fixing of Boundaries in International Boundary Rivers, 12 *Int'l & Comp L Q* (1963) 789, 793. A Thalweg, pursuant to international law, is used to demarcate Boundary Rivers that are navigable. *See generally, Kasikili/Sedudu Island (Bots. v. Namib.)*, 1999 I.C.J. 1045, 1062 (Dec. 13).

[52] US law has also adopted this doctrine. *See e.g., Louisiana v. Mississippi*, 202 US 1, 49 (1906). (No. 11, original). ("The term *'thalweg'* is commonly used by writers on international law in definition of water boundaries between states, meaning, the middle, or deepest, or most navigable channel...")

[53] If riparian land grows by the addition of alluvium, *i.e.*, sediment or soil, until it extends to the mainland, such new made land will become the property of the owner whose property the alluvium attached to.

[54] *See generally, Anderson-Tully Co. v. Walls*, 266 F. Supp. 804, 812 (D. Miss. 1967). (*Citing Mayor, Alderman, etc., of New Orleans v. United States* 35 US 662 (1836).)

> When, however, from any cause, natural or artificial, a boundary river suddenly leaves its old channel and seeks a new bed, this sudden and rapid change is termed an avulsion and the resulting change works no change of boundary, which remains in the middle of the old channel, although no water may be flowing in it, and irrespective of subsequent changes in the new channel.

channel remains the boundary. Here the commission was true to these two norms, and consequently its support likely furthered this transboundary normative framework, thereby making this part of the award effective.

Concerning the fourth proxy, the tribunal's fairness and legitimation, we can infer that but for the award, the Parties **perceived the tribunal to be a fair, just, and independent forum**, which is **proxy number 4** in Table 7.2. Indeed, both parties were afforded equal due process in presenting their case, including submission of evidence and witnesses. Moreover, there is no suggestion that the commission's proceedings were not fair-minded, impartial, or even-handed. Actually, the contrary is true. During these proceedings the panel was perceived as a fair, just, and independent forum. For example, the *compromis* provided for detailed procedures,[55] and flexibility that is not generally seen in the procedures of international courts, and each party adhered to these rules. Additionally, in appointing an impartial Canadian jurist as the chairman of the arbitral commission the tribunal was imbued at least with the appearance, if not actual, fairness.

With recourse to **regime legitimization**: in dividing the tract in accordance with the evidence, Lafleur, the Canadian Chair, and Puga, the Mexican Commissioner, adopted the view of the United States Supreme Court in *Nebraska v. Iowa*.[56] Noting that in that case, the US Supreme Court observed that up to the year 1877, the shifts in the Missouri River resulted from accretion, and in that year, the river made a new channel for itself. In utilizing this precedent, the tribunal provided legitimacy to the Supreme Court's norm, and to its transboundary water regime. Lastly, as should be clear from the tribunal's history, it was efficient in issuing its award, taking only twenty-seven (27) days – May 15 – June 10 – for the entire adjudication.

II THE GUT DAM ARBITRATION

A Introduction

The Gut Dam controversy grew out of Canada's construction of a dam, the Gut Dam, in the middle of the St. Lawrence River, which caused the flooding of and subsequent damage to 230 private properties in New York State. The dam was erected along the boundary between the Province of Ontario, in Canada and the State of New York, in the United States.

---

[55] Convention for the Arbitration of the Chamizal Case, June 24, 1910, US–Mex., 36 Stat. 2481.
[56] 143 US 359 (1892). Award at 331.

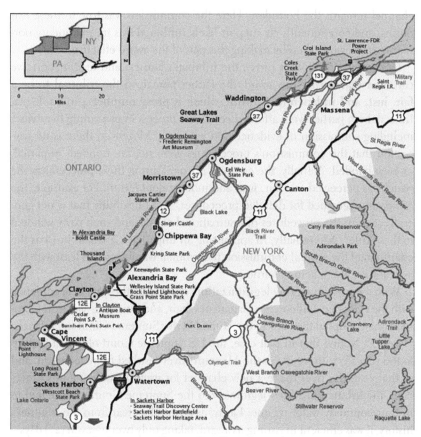

FIGURE 9.2 The St. Lawrence River – Gut Dam Was Adjacent to Ogdensburg, NY

1. The Dispute's Geographic Setting and the Dam's Construction

The St. Lawrence River's drainage basin stretches approximately 2,000 miles (3,219 km). It extends from the westerly portion of Lake Superior, at Duluth, Minnesota, to the Gulf of St. Lawrence, which drains into the Atlantic Ocean. The International Boundary between Canada and the United States cuts across four of the Great Lakes and the St. Lawrence River.[57] (See Figure 9.2.)

The river originates in the northeast portion of Lake Ontario and flows north-easterly into the Gulf of St. Lawrence. Between Belleville, which is situated on Lake Ontario and Montreal in Canada, and Rochester/Oswego New York and Ogdensburg, New York, in the United States. The St. Lawrence was divided into three sections during the period in question. They are as follows:

---

[57] Dr. Lambertus Erades, The Gut Dam Arbitration, 16 *Netherlands Int'l L. Rev.* 161 (1969) (Judge Erades was the Chair of the Lake Ontario Arbitral Tribunal).

(1) The upper section. 62 miles from Lake Ontario to Galops Rapids just below Ogdensburg, NY, in which there is a fall of about two feet; (2) the International Rapids Section, about 54 miles long from Ogdensburg, NY to the mouth of the St. Regis River,[58] forming the upper section the boundary between the United States and Canada; and (3) the lower section, a further distance of 66 miles, which is entirely in Canada.

> A part of the International Rapids Section [which is the section relevant to this dispute] of the St. Lawrence River is called the Galop Rapids Reach which extends from about Ogdensburg, N.Y. to about Cardinal, Ontario. [Cardinal is approximately 13 miles north – northwest of Ogdensburg, as the crow flies, along the St. Lawrence]. Within this reach are the Galop Rapids formed by a rocky ledge extending across the vicinity of [Les] Galop and Adams Islands. [The Gut Dam was located between these two islands in the St. Lawrence]. These islands divide the rapids into three separate channels: the Canadian Galop Rapids, the Gut and the American Galop Rapids.[59]

B *The Construction of the Dam*

In 1874 the Government of Canada's ("GOC") Chief Engineer for Public Works proposed the construction of the dam on the St. Lawrence River between Adams Island on the Canadian side of the river and Galops Island on the United States side.[60] The dam was proposed to improve navigation along the St. Lawrence, as the river flowed easterly into the Atlantic Ocean. It was designed to prevent water from flowing into the Gut Channel, which flowed between the two islands.[61]

The GOC, via the British Ambassador in Washington,[62] requested the United States approval to build the dam. Negotiations over the dam took place during the period 1900–1903. However, these were preceded by several legal events that had a critical effect on these consultations. The first of these was an 1897 decision by the United Sates Supreme Court in *Gibson v.*

---

[58] The St. Regis River is a 138-km (86-mile) long river in Franklin County, in northeastern NY. It flows into the Saint Lawrence River from the St. Regis Mohawk Indian Reservation. US Geological Survey, The National Map Viewer (undated), http://viewer.nationalmap.gov/viewer.

[59] Erades *ibid.* at 162.

[60] *Gut Dam Arbitration*, Reports Prepared by Edward Re. Chairperson, US Foreign Claims Settlement Commission, 4 May 1965, *reproduced in* International Environmental Law Reports, vol. I: Early Decisions (Cairo A. R. Robb ed.) (Cambridge: Cambridge University Press, 1999) 386.

[61] *Ibid.*

[62] Canada was represented by the United Kingdom until it achieved full independence on December 11, 1931, when by Royal Assent of the Statute of Windsor (f/k/a/An Act to Give Effect to Certain Resolutions by Imperial Conference Held in the Years 1926 and 1930) 22 & 23 Geo. 5 c. 4.

United States.[63] There the Court held that "[a]ll navigable waters are under
the control of the United States for the purpose of regulating and improving
navigation, and although the title to the shore and submerged soil [maybe
titled to others], it is always subject to the servitude in respect of navigation
created in favor of the federal government by the Constitution."[64] The Court
also cited its long-held view that only the Congress can authorize the building
of obstructions in the navigable waters of the United States[65]

The second event was the 1899 amendment to the Rivers and Harbors Act of
1894.[66] Section 9 of the Act states in relevant part that "[i]t shall not be lawful
to construct or commence the construction of any bridge, causeway, dam, or
dike over or in any port, roadstead, haven, harbor, canal, navigable river, or
other navigable water of the United States until the consent of Congress to the
building of such structures shall have been obtained . . . "[67] Similarly, Section
10 of the Act states "[t]hat the creation of any obstruction not affirmatively
authorized by Congress, to the navigable capacity of any of the waters of the
United States is hereby prohibited . . . "[68] Examples of the types of prohibited
constructions include "any bridge, dam, dike or causeway over or in navigable
waterways of the United States that are interstate in nature."[69]

But for these two laws the Government of the United States ("GOUS")
would not be able to authorize the dam's construction. Thus, when on
November 2, 1900, Lord Minto, the Governor General of Canada, approved
a communication with the GOUS, seeking its consent that "a dam should

---

[63] 166 US 269 (1897).   [64] *Ibid.* at 271–2.
[65] *Ibid.* at 272.

> In *South Carolina v. Georgia*, [93 US 4 (1876)] a proposed improvement of the Savan-
> nah River consisted of the practical closing of one channel around an island and the
> throwing of water into other channels, to the substantial improvement of the harbor of
> Savannah. This Court held that, in view of the general rule, although structures deemed
> by Congress to be in aid of navigation might in fact be in obstruction of certain meth-
> ods of navigation of the particular stream, their construction was nevertheless within the
> federal power.

[66] 30 Stat. 1151 (1899). Codified at 33 USC § 401 *et seq.*   [67] 33 USC § 401.
[68] 33 USC § 403. ((Act of Mar. 3, 1899, ch. 425, §10, 30 Stat. 1151; amended July 26, 1947, ch. 343,
title II, §205(a), 61 Stat. 501.)
[69] *Ibid.* Stating in the relevant section that

> The creation of any obstruction not affirmatively authorized by Congress, to the naviga-
> ble capacity of any of the waters of the United States is prohibited . . . and it shall not be
> lawful to excavate or fill, or in any manner to alter or modify the course, location, condi-
> tion, or capacity of, any port, roadstead, haven, harbor, canal, lake, harbor or refuge, or
> inclosure within the limits of any breakwater, or of the channel of any navigable water
> of the United States, unless the work has been recommended by the Chief of Engineers
> and authorized by the Secretary of the Army prior to beginning the same.

be constructed from Adams' Island to Les Galops Islands, the former being Canadian, the latter American territory, the International Boundary laying midway between the two ... the work of constructing this dam and its maintenance shall be defrayed by the Dominion,"[70] the executive branch of GOUS could act upon the request.

In a response dated November 12, 1900, Secretary of State John Hay communicated the following to the British Ambassador in Washington: "The matter has been referred to the Secretary of War [who at that time was Elihu Root] for examination with a view to bringing it to the consideration of the Congress under the provisions of the River and Harbour Act, approved March 3, 1899."[71] Initially, not much seems to have occurred with the GOC's request.[72] Therefore, in 1902, the British Ambassador sent a reminder to Secretary Hay and the matter began to move through the Department of War's Army Corps of Engineers.

These engineers had questions regarding the potential damage to US property owners.[73] Indeed, when on June 18, 1902, the Congress enacted Public Law 164,[74] which authorized the construction of the Gut Dam; it inserted qualifications into the Act. One of the relevant ones, was whether:

---

[70] Erades, The Gut Dam Arbitration, *ibid.* at 164.　　　[71] *Ibid.*　　　[72] *Ibid.*

[73] *Ibid.* Indeed, two reports that were generated by the Corps of Engineers, which described the engineers' concerns, were not turned over to the GOC. Judge Erades in his article appears to suggest that these reports would have aided in an earlier resolution of the case. *Ibid.*

[74] Chap. 1123.-An Act Allowing the construction of a dam across the Saint Lawrence River.

Preamble. Whereas it is represented that the government of the Dominion of Canada, with a view of improving the navigation of the channel excavated through the rapids at the head of Les Galops Island, in the Saint Lawrence River, proposes to construct a dam from Adams Island, in Canadian territory, to Les Galops Island, in United States territory; and

Whereas the consent of the United States to the construction of that part of the work which will be upon United States territory is desired:

Therefore,

Be it enacted by the Senate and House of Representatives of the United Saint Lawrence States of America in Congress assembled, That consent is hereby given for the construction of the portion of the aforesaid dam which crosses or abuts upon the territory of the United States: Provided, That the proposed dam and the plans of construction and operation level of Lake Ontario, thereof shall be such as will not, in the judgment of the Secretary of War, materially affect the water level of lake Ontario or the Saint Lawrence River or cause any other injury to the interests of the United or any citizen thereof: And provided further, That the work of construction on United States territory shall not be commenced until plans and details of the work shall have been submitted to and approved .by the Secretary of War.

Approved, June 18, 1902. Pub. L. 57–164 (Ch. 1123, Sess. 1). 132 Stat. 392 (1902).

(1) the type of the proposed dam and the plan for construction and operation
thereof shall be such as will not in the judgment of the Secretary of War (a)
materially affect the water level of Lake Ontario or the St. Lawrence River or
(b) cause any other injury to the interests of the United States or any citizen
thereof;[75]

From the date that Congress passed the Act through August 18, 1903, the
United States Army Corps of Engineers undertook an intensive investigation
of the region where the dam was to be built. The Corps' principal concern
was "the effects of Gut Dam at extreme high levels,"[76] *i.e.*, water levels above
the base level of "ordinary water" of 244.49 feet above the tidal level. Following
a series of back and forth correspondence the GOC formally agreed, by correspondence to the Secretary of War, to the insertion of a provision wherein
it would indemnify US landowners from any damage to an increase or rise in
both Lake Ontario's and the St. Lawrence River's water level. That provision
stated in part

1. That if, after said dam has been constructed, it is found that it materi-
    ally affects the water levels of Lake Ontario or the St. Lawrence River
    or causes any injury to the interests of the United States, the Govern-
    ment of Canada shall make such changes therein, and provide such
    additional regulation works in connection therewith as the Secretary of
    War may order.
2. That if the construction and operation of said dam shall cause dam-
    age or detriment to the property owners of Les Galpos Island or to the
    property of any other citizens of the United States, the Government of
    Canada shall pay such amount of compensation as may be agreed upon
    between the said Government and the Parties damaged, or as may be
    awarded the said Parties in the proper court of the United States before
    which claims for damage may be brought.[77]

Finally, on August 18, 1903, Secretary of War Root executed the document,
and provided the GOC with the authorization, from the GOUS, for the construction of the Gut Dam. The dam's construction began on September 10,
1903, and was completed on November 11, 1903. However, the dam was too
low to have any of the sought-after results. Consequently, in 1904 Canada once
again requested the consent of the United States to build up the dam. That
approval was provided, again, with the inclusion of the same two conditions,
noted above.

[75] 32 Stat. 392 (1902).   [76] Erades, The Gut Dam Arbitration, *ibid.* at 166.   [77] *Ibid.*

Canada raised the height of the dam, and all went well from 1904–1951 – but for a few minor changes that increased the rate of water flow, which swelled the water level of the St. Lawrence River and Lake Ontario. One of the changes was the diversion of water from the St. Lawrence to the Great Lakes in order to increase the generation of hydropower. The United States, once again agreed to this change and Canada, in turn and as part of the bargain, made available electric power to the U.S. In turn, Canada reduced its rate of water withdrawal from the Great Lakes system via the Chicago Diversion into the Chicago Sanitary and Ship Canal.[78] There were also a series of other diversions, both in Canada and the United States; the latter, from Lake Michigan via the Chicago Diversion,[79] and the former, via a number of rivers in Canada.[80] These diversions caused the level of Lake Ontario, the lowest of the five Great Lakes, to rise above its mean datum or level of 248.8 feet (75.8 meters).

During the 1951–52 winter, storms buffeted the St. Lawrence and all five of the Great Lakes. As a result, the water level of the lakes and the river, which were already high, reached unparalleled levels. This combination caused widespread flooding on both shores of the St. Lawrence River and the Great Lakes. 230 property owners on New York's Galops Island and nearby properties in the Town of Lisbon sustained extensive damage.

Similarly, in 1952 the Great Lakes Division of the Army Corps of Engineers reported that:

> It...found that severe damage by wave action and flooding has occurred to property along the shores of the Great Lakes during the past year. These damages were sustained principally during storms and local temporary rises in the water surface at the time. Field surveys showed a total estimated damage of 61 million dollars of which total [sic] 50 million dollars resulted from wave action and 11 million from flooding. [The causes of the high-water levels during 1951 and 1952 were abnormal storms and abnormal precipitation].[81]

[78] The Chicago Diversion diverts water from Lake Michigan to the Mississippi River watershed at Chicago. It is the most long-standing and biggest out-of-basin transfer from the Great Lakes. *See generally Wisconsin v. Illinois*, 281 US 179 (1930).

[79] This diversion led to a suit filed in the United States Supreme Court in 1922, by the State of Wisconsin against the State of Illinois. *See, Wisconsin v. Illinois*, 278 US 367 (1929).

[80] These included the Long Lake Project, which diverted water from Hudson Bay into Lake Superior, and a second diversion, this one from Lake Ogoki River to Lake Nipigon in Ontario, Nipigon River, then drains into Nipigon Bay which finally drains into Lake Superior.

[81] Erades, The Gut Dam Arbitration, *ibid.* at 182.

That report also found that Lake Ontario's water level had increased to 249.29 feet during June 1952, the Lake's highest level to date, as compared to its lowest level of 242.68 feet, during the month of November in 1934.[82] Outraged at the flooding, the New York residents complained to the two governments. This prompted the US and Canadian governments to request that the International Joint Commission ("IJC") study the fluctuations in the river and the Great Lakes and, to determine whether the dam and/or other factors contributed to the flooding. The IJC's jurisdiction is provided by The Boundary Waters Treaty[83] whose Article VIII requires the IJC to approve any artificial movement of water across the border between the two states. Similarly, Article IX requires the IJC to conduct investigations and author reports regarding differences between the two states. These reports however are not binding.

Consequently, on June 25, 1952, the two governments invoked Article IX, and filed a Reference with the IJC.[84] In order to carry out the terms of the Reference, the IJC created the International Lake Ontario Board of Engineers ("ILOBE"), in April of 1953.[85] The ILOBE was composed of one expert from each country. These two specialists were tasked with harnessing the necessary agencies on each side of the border in order to investigate the scientific and engineering issues associated with or raised by the Reference. The ILOBE and the IJC reported that the Gut Dam, did raise the water level of Lake Ontario, however, the height was less than that contended by the Les Galops landowners. Moreover, the experts suggested that this was one of several factors, natural and artificial that caused the property owners' damages.

Based on these results, in 1959, the United States Ambassador submitted a letter to the relevant authorities of the Canadian government, that the claimants would settle their claims for $875,000. Previously, in November of 1952 the Canadian Ambassador to the United States dispatched a note to Dean Acheson, the then United States Secretary of State, acknowledging, that the GOC recognized, that as per ¶ 2 of the 1903 conditions, in principle it had an obligation to pay for the damage to the property of the 230 landowners,

---

[82] *Ibid.* at 179.
[83] Recall the Boundary Waters Treaty was executed by the two governments in 1909.
[84] Erades *ibid.* at 182.
[85] The International Lake Ontario Board of Engineers, Water Levels of Lake Ontario, Final Report to the International Joint Commission (Under the Reference of 25 June 1952) (Dec. 1958), *available at* http://www.ijc.org/files/publications/K89.pdf. ("The duties of the Board will be to undertake through appropriate agencies in Canada and the United States, the necessary investigation and studies and to advise the Commission on all technical engineering matters which it must consider in making a report or reports to the two Governments under the Reference of 25 June 1952.") *Ibid.* at 2.

provided, however, that the landowners could demonstrate that the harm they suffered resulted from the Gut Dam.

Apparently not satisfied with the IJC's progress, in October 1952, the property owners commenced a series of suits in the United States Federal District for the Northern District of New York (the trial court), against the Dominion of Canada.[86] These actions were consolidated and in 1956 that federal district court issued its judgment, dismissing the action for lack of personal jurisdiction ineffective service,[87] which was made on Canada's Counsel in New York. The Second Circuit Court of Appeals affirmed that decision.[88]

C Preliminary Steps at Resolution

One of the institutional aspects of the IJC which, added to its effectiveness of this dispute, is its flexibility. For example, during the diplomatic phase of this controversy – and post the work of the ILOBE – the United States Congress established and authorized the Foreign Claims Settlement Commission of the United States, in order to resolve the claims of the New York landowners (and US citizens) against Canada. One of the Commission's mandates was to determine the validity of all claims presented by the landowners, and the amount of each claim. The property owners were given until October 15, 1963 to submit their claims. Notices of the filing date were provided with "appropriate publicity."[89] During the Congressional discussion over the establishment of the Commission, estimates were provided to the legislators that suggested that up to 1,000 landowners may have incurred injury to their properties, and that the harm would likely total millions of dollars. Nevertheless, the Commission only received 542 claims, which claimed damages of $8,473,043.

However, documentation of damage attached to the claims was insubstantial. There were probably two reasons for the poor documentation. First, the claims at this point were some 13–14 years old, memories faded, and paperwork

---

[86] *Oster v. Dominion of Canada* (class action); *Clay et al. v. Dominion of Canada; Clay v. Dominion of Canada; Dollinger v. Her Majesty Elizabeth, Queen of Canada and Canada* (among others), 144 F.Supp. 746 (NDNY1956).

[87] "It is apparent from the whole record that the sufficiency of such service was disputed at the time." *Ibid.* at 748. Moreover, the Counsel had limited powers "and his power is limited by the terms thereof to the protection of the interests of Canadian citizens within his consular district. He is in no sense a managing agent." *Ibid.* Current Fed. R. Civ. Pro 12(b)(4) "ineffective process" would govern the issue.

[88] *Aff'd per curium* (without opinion), sub nom. *Clay et al. v. Dominion of Canada*, 238 F.2d 400 (2nd Cir. 1956), *cert den.* 353 US 936 (1957).

[89] *The Gut Dam Arbitration ibid.* at 396.

was thrown out. Second, since the legislation giving rise to the Commission did not provide any assurance that the property owners would be compensated for their damages, they were likely reluctant to invest too much time and resources into what was probably seen as a futile process. The Commission worked for three years with little success. Thus, on March 25, 1965, both Parties agreed to establish the Lake Ontario Claims Tribunal.[90] At the same time, as per the terms of its establishment, the United States was required to disband the unilateral Commission.[91]

Once the Parties recognized that the Claims Settlement Commission was moribund, the IJC's institutional regime allowed both Canada and the United States to agree to refer the dispute to the IJC, without having to negotiate a treaty or other instrument, so that a tribunal could be seated. Since every dispute or arbitration is required to adjudicate the issues before it, the newly appointed Lake Ontario Claims Tribunal was tasked by the Parties' *compromis* with (1) assessing the amount of damages that Canada would have to pay to the 230 property owners; (2) who would sit on the arbitral panel; and (3) establishing the procedural aspects of the adjudication.

1 The Parties' *Compromis* Proceedings

The two governments ultimately settled their dispute. Nevertheless, initially, it must be stressed that since the parties agreed to the *compromis*, neither had any grounds to suggest that the procedural aspects of the tribunal were unfair. An example of the terms of the Agreement, which demonstrates the *compromis'* procedural fairness, is presented in Article II, which addressed the Tribunal's jurisdiction. It provided the following:

1.   The Tribunal shall have jurisdiction to hear and decide in a final fashion each claim presented to it in accordance with the terms of this Agreement. Each decision of the Tribunal shall be based on its determination of any one or more of the following questions on the basis of the legal principles set forth in this Article: [e.g.,] Was the construction

---

[90] The United States agreement to establish the Tribunal was based on the Congressional enactment of Public Law 87–587 approved August 15, 1962 (76 Stat. 387). The Act gave the Foreign Claims Settlement Commission of the United States "the unique assignment of conducting a program to determine the validity and amounts of claims of citizens of the United States for damages caused during 1951 and 1952 by the Government of Canada's construction and maintenance of the Gut Dam in the Saint Lawrence River." Foreign Claims Settlement Commission of the United States, Department of Justice, 2010 Annual Report 29 (2010), *available at* www.justice.gov/fcsc/annrep10.pdf.

[91] *See* United Sates Pub. L. 87–587.

and maintenance of Gut Dam the proximate cause of damage to the property that is the subject of such claims?

The *compromis'* Art. I, para. 4 set forth the qualifications of the members of the Tribunal. That provision states that "Each member of the Tribunal shall be a judge or a lawyer competent to hold high judicial office in his national State. No member prior to his appointment shall have been associated directly or indirectly with any matter related to this Agreement."

The Tribunal was composed of the chair, a Dutch national, Dr. Lambertus Erades, a Canadian National Member, Judge Wilfred D. Roach, and the United States National Member, Professor Alwyn V. Freeman, all familiar with international law. Prior to the Tribunal's initial meeting the two Governments exchanged drafts of suggested procedural rules that would be submitted to the Tribunal. Following these exchanges the parties met and resolved, that the joint draft, should be submitted to the panel at its first meeting, to assist the panel members in establishing the procedural rules for the arbitration.

Two procedural items remained unresolved. First, how were documents to be admitted into evidence? The GOUS's designate advised, via correspondence, to the Canadian Government's designate, that all statements made by each claimant were governed by 18 USC § 1001, which provides for criminal sanctions for false statements.[92] Additionally, the letter provided information regarding the qualifications and authority of notaries' public in New York State, so that there would be no questions with regards to notarized claim documents. These provisions and authorities were accepted by the GOC's designee. Second, was the procedural issue of how to admit oral testimony. Here, the Governments agreed that the Tribunal would require the guidance of experts and that expert testimony from engineers and others would be essential.

One sticking point was whether the GOUS would call individual claimants and other fact witnesses to testify before the Tribunal. The GOUS was opposed to calling the fact witnesses for several reasons, including the amount of time that direct and cross-examination of these witnesses would require and,

---

[92] 18 USC § 1001 states in pertinent part:

   (a) Except as otherwise provided in this section, whoever, in any matter within the jurisdiction of the executive, legislative, or judicial branch of the Government of the United States, knowingly and willfully –
     (1) falsifies, conceals, or covers up by any trick, scheme, or device a material fact;
     (2) makes any materially false, fictitious, or fraudulent statement or representation; or
     (3) makes or uses any false writing or document knowing the same to contain any materially false, fictitious, or fraudulent statement or entry; shall be fined under this title, imprisoned not more than 5 years . . .

the fact that calling these witnesses might cause tensions that could affect relations between the two states. Another concern by the USA was that issues related to the parties' earlier failures, would be raised by the fact-witnesses during the proceedings. The GOC also understood that if it were to be viewed as a "defendant" without first establishing the facts of individual claims, it would be placed in an untenable light, and could cause friction with the GOUS. Thus, the two Governments agreed to a rule that was thereafter incorporated as Rule XI of the Rules of Procedure, wherein the Canadian Agent would provide the US Agent with written fact interrogatories to be served upon the respective claimants.

Pursuant to this element, the GOC would be able to gather the factual information that it required. Additionally, the Tribunal sought to reserve the right to call expert witnesses to either testify or to submit written reports, and to have either party question these witnesses pursuant to procedures, which would be developed later by the Tribunal. Finally, testimony of fact witnesses was not to be taken, except in extraordinary circumstances, as established by the Tribunal. The foregoing was incorporated into Article XII of the Rules of Procedure. Accordingly, the rules for the arbitration were put into place.

Subsequently, the Canadian Agent submitted 150 sets of interrogatories that were addressed to the claimants and others. The two Agents discussed these, and any objections by the GOUS's Agent were remedied. Accordingly, the GOC received responses to the individual interrogatories, which were incorporated into its Memorials as well as the supplemental Memorials for the claims. The interrogatory process worked so well that no oral testimony was required. Indeed, the interrogatory process is viewed as a "significant aid in unearthing facts which may be of significance."[93]

One other element remained for the GOUS to address. As is well known, under the doctrine of diplomatic protection, all international claims require that the petitioning state provide proof that each claimant is a national of that state.[94] Here the United States had to establish before the Tribunal that

---

[93] Report of Carl Goodman, US Agent, Lake Ontario Claims Tribunal, 22 November 1968, 8 ILM 118, *reproduced* in Cairo, International Environmental Law Reports: Early Decisions *ibid.* at 418.

[94] See e.g., *In the Matter of: The Loewen Group, Inc. and Raymond L. Loewen, Claimants/Investors, v. The United States of America, Respondent/Party.* ICSID Case No. ARB(AF)/98/3, Reply of the United States of America to the Counter-Memorial of the Loewen Group, Inc. on Matters of Jurisdiction and Competence (Apr. 26, 2002), available at http://www.state.gov/documents/organization/9947.pdf, at 10. ("[C]ustomary international law requires that a claimant maintain a nationality other than that of the respondent State from the date of injury (the dies a quo) through the date of the award (the dies ad quem)." Robert

every claimant was a United States national. Moreover, the GOUS's Agent, Carl Goodman, offered confirmation of ownership and the damage incurred due to the high-water condition caused by the Gut Dam. Nevertheless, these issues were not addressed by the Tribunal, as it decided that its first task was to determine liability. Mr. Goodman, in a report that he issued subsequent to the proceedings, theorized that this decision was based on the Tribunal's determination that liability and the percentage of damage attributable to dam, was a question common to each of the claims.[95]

The arbitration was conducted in the two States' capitals, Ottawa and Washington, DC, and the Tribunal's respective headquarters. Both sides presented extensive oral arguments. The rules of procedure granted the GOUS, as the claimant state, wide latitude in its presentation to the Tribunal. Nevertheless, the parties agreed at the hearings that as a matter of fairness and justice, they would continue their various arguments until they and the Tribunal felt that there was no more point to an argument.

Most treaties and other international instruments are incorporated into one bilateral document. The Gut Dam agreement was not. Consequently, the GOC's Agent argued that

[t]he agreement giving rise to the issue before this Tribunal is an unusual agreement in the sense that unlike most of the international agreements which have been reviewed by tribunals and international courts, it is not evidenced by one document which was negotiated, revised from its drafts, and finally signed and by the representatives of our respective nations. It consists . . . in a series of documents and acts, and it is to that series of documents and acts in the context of the times that we must seek to determine what the agreement was and what it means.[96]

The Tribunal held three separate proceedings. The first took place on January 15, 1968. During that hearing the panel members addressed two issues: (1) whether Canada was liable for the Gut Dam's damages? and (2) whether that obligation was limited not only to persons but also as to time? Canada contended that it was only liable to a small class of property owners: The owner of Galops Island, in New York State. It also asserted that its liability extended

Beckman and Dagmar Butte, *Introduction to International Law* (undated), https://www.ilsa .org/jessup/intlawintro.pdf. ("Under the principle of nationality of claims, if a national of State A is injured by State B through internationally unlawful conduct, State A may make a claim against State B on behalf of its injured national. This is known as the doctrine of diplomatic protection.")

95 *The Gut Dam Arbitration ibid.* at 414.
96 Report of Carl Goodman, *reproduced* in Cairo, *ibid.* at 418.

only to 1908. Alternatively, the GOUS asserted that pursuant to the 1902 Congressional Act and the 1903 agreement, Canada was liable for all damage, and therefore it was bound to compensate any US citizen whose property was injured from the date of construction through 1952.

The 1902 Act stated

(1) that the type of the proposed dam and the plan for construction and operation thereof shall be such as will not in the judgment of the Secretary of War (a) *materially affect the water level of Lake Ontario or the St. Lawrence River or* (b) *cause any other injury to the interests of the United States or any citizen thereof* . . . [97]

Similarly, Secretary of War, Elihu Root's August 18, 1903, letter authorizing the GOC to construct the Gut Dam contained the following provision:

2. That if the construction and operation of said dam shall cause damage or detriment to the property owners of Les Galops Island or to the property of any other citizens of the United States, the Government of Canada shall pay such amount of compensation as may be agreed upon between the said Government and the Parties damaged, or as may be awarded the said Parties in the proper court of the United States before which claims for damage may be brought.

Recall that Canada argued that it was only liable for damages to the owner of Los Galops Island. However, given the plain language of ¶ 2, above, which references "*the property of any other citizens of the United States,*" the Tribunal was faced with a broader picture of damages. Accordingly, the Tribunal's award in this phase found for the United States, holding that Canada was liable for damages, and noting that "[t]he Government of Canada admitted liability, and if the 1952 damage were attributable to the dam . . . The obligation extended not only to owners of Les Galops Island *but to any citizen* of the United States."[98]

The next hearing took place on February 18, 1968. At this sitting the Tribunal was required to address the second issue: whether Canada's argument that there was a limitation of time on its obligation to compensate the New York landowners for the injury caused the Gut Dam, or in the alternative to adopt the United States' position that there was no time limitation? Observing that in correspondence between the two Governments, Canadian officials stated that they recognize in principle the GOC's obligation to pay compensation to US citizens that are attributable to the construction of the Gut Dam;

[97] 32 Stat. 392 (1902), *ibid.*   [98] Report of Carl Goodman, *reproduced* in Cairo, *ibid.* at 418.

the panel members pointed to two pieces of correspondence: One was dated November 10, 1952,[99] while the second was dated May 13, 1953.[100]

Thus, the Tribunal held that

> In official diplomatic representation the Canadian Government clearly rec-ognized its obligation to pay compensation as far as the 1951–1952 claims are concerned... It is clear to the Tribunal that the only issues which remain for its consideration are the questions of whether Gut Dam caused the damage for which claims have been filed and the quantum of such damages.[101]

In a later informal session, the panel recommended that the two Govern-ments attempt to reach a compromise settlement. This "nudge" caused the two governments to negotiate a settlement of a lump sum of $350,000, which was presented to the Tribunal. Consequently, on September 27, 1968, the Tri-bunal approved the agreement, noting that

> the Government of the United States on its part will not further prosecute the claims before the Tribunal and will recognize this payment as being in full and final satisfaction of all claims before the Tribunal and will recognize this payment as being in full and final satisfaction of all claims of United States nationals for damage allegedly cause by Gut Dam.[102]

All that remained was the distribution of the proceeds to the claimants.

D Analysis of the Dispute

There is a good deal to analyze about the Gut Dam Arbitration, although the parties settled their dispute, particularly with regard to the tribunal's attributes, its effectiveness, and state behavior. These include the following: (1) the fact that the parties negotiated their own procedural rules, which they submitted to

---

99 The November 10, 1952 letter from the Canadian Embassy in Washington to the US Secretary of State advised:

> I am directed to inform you that the Government of Canada recognizes in principle its obligation to pay compensation for damages... provided that they are attributable to the construction of the Gut Dam...

Report of Carl Goodman, *reproduced* in Cairo, *ibid.* at 421.

100 Similarly, in the 1953 correspondence "Canadian Minister Pierce informed the United States Government of terms of a press release to appear the following day," wherein the GOC stated that it was liable to US citizens. *Ibid.* at 421.

101 *Ibid.* at 422.

102 *Ibid.* at 423. The final settlement was confirmed on November 18, 1968, UTS, vol. 19, Part 6 (1968) at 7862.

the Tribunal. This element contrasts with other international courts and other tribunals, for example, NAFTA investor–state disputes,[103] the International Tribunal for the Law of the Sea,[104] among others, who have set rules of procedure; (2) how one government, in this case, the United States, agreed to accept a token $350,000 payment in settlement of damages to its harmed citizens, when its ambassador originally offered to settle these injuries for $850,000 and the Claims Commission's presentation of 542 claims, which it asserted damages of $8,473,043; (3) the tacit understanding, by both parties but especially Canada, from its experience in the *Trail Smelter Case*, that the principle of *sic utere tuo ut alienum non laedas*, or, the principle of customary international law which mandates that a state sovereign is bound to eschew transboundary injury to its adjacent sovereign; and (4) how a prudent tribunal's narrowing of issues, here, Canada's liability, "avoided entanglement in the international law of torts. [And] elegantly circumnavigated difficult questions such as the standard of liability for transnational damage."[105]

The procedural and adaptive flexibility[106] afforded the GOC and GOUS in the Gut Dam Arbitration, and the discretion to bargain over these rules under the shadow of good faith and fair dealing, led to the two states' ability to alter the procedures should they be improperly vague or overreaching.[107] These aspects were hallmarks of this adjudication. Indeed, discretion in selecting rules of procedure lies within a movement occasionally termed "delocalization," by which arbitration has turned out to be less reliant on

---

[103] International Centre for Settlement of Investments Disputes, Rules of Procedure Proceedings (Arbitration Rules), Part F (2016), *available at* https://icsid.worldbank.org/ICSID/StaticFiles/basicdoc/partF.htm; United Nations Commission on International Trade Law Rules on Transparency in Treaty-based Investor–State Arbitration and Arbitration Rules (as revised in 2010, with new article 1, paragraph 4, as adopted in 2013), *available at* http://www.uncitral.org/pdf/english/texts/arbitration/arb-rules-2013/UNCITRAL-Arbitration-Rules-2013-e.pdf.
See also, International Chamber of Commerce, International Court of Arbitration, Arbitration Rules/Mediation Rules which simply state at Art. 25 that the arbitrator may establish the facts by 'all appropriate means' (2012), http://www.iccwbo.org/Products-and-Services/Arbitration-and-ADR/Arbitration/Rules-of-arbitration/Download-ICC-Rules-of-Arbitration/ICC-Rules-of-Arbitration-in-several-languages.

[104] International Tribunal for the Law of the Sea, Rules of the Tribunal (Mar. 17, 2009), at Part III, Arts. 43 *et seq.*, *available at* https://www.itlos.org/fileadmin/itlos/documents/basic_texts/Itlos_8_E_17_03_09.pdf.

[105] Rudolf Bernhardt, *Encyclopedia of Public International Law: Decisions of International Courts and Tribunals and International Arbitrations* (1981) 128.

[106] On the procedural and adaptive flexibility in arbitrations, *see* Walter Mattli, Private Justice in a Global Economy: From Litigation to Arbitration, 55 *Int'l Organizations* 619 (2001).

[107] Examples include, the awarding of interest; procedural rulings that disallow a claimant the absolute last word in arguments; and interim determinations on the extent of the arbitrator's authority that overlap merits phases of the arbitration.

the characteristics of the arbitral seat or its rules.[108] This "trend remains of great practical significance, given that most established arbitration rules provide few precise canons for the conduct of proceedings in matters such as evidentiary standards, presentation of testimony and briefing schedules."[109]

Moreover, as was plainly evident in this dispute, where parties agree to arbitrate their case, via a *compromis*, the arbitral process provides a forum within which the two states can resolve their "international dispute." This fact is true of these types of arbitrations, as contrasted with the national courts of one of the Parties,[110] international courts, or other types of arbitrations, where issues of jurisdiction may preclude adjudication. Finally, although, the two litigants concurred that they would abide by the award, if they were to go back on their word, international arbitration awards are simpler to enforce than are national court judgments.[111]

Similarly, the significance of prompt resolution of this and, as will be seen *infra*, other international arbitrations is reflected in the arbitral rules of the foremost arbitral bodies.[112] Nevertheless, the Gut Dam arbitrators provided the two parties with sufficient time to make their case, which is as it should be. Arbitrators should also not unfairly regulate parties' opportunity to litigate their dispute only for the sake of hasty determination.[113]

In the normal course of arbitrations before international *ad hoc* Tribunals fact witnesses are generally a critical element of the trial. That was not the

---

[108] William W. Park, Two Faces of Progress: Fairness and Flexibility in Arbitral Procedure Two Faces of Progress: Fairness and Flexibility in Arbitral Procedure, 23 *Arbitration International* 499, 500 (2007).

[109] *Ibid.*

[110] See *e.g. Oster v. Dominion of Canada*, 144 F. Supp. 746, *ibid.* ("the problem involved in each of the above actions is one of jurisdiction.")

[111] United Nations Convention on the Recognition and Enforcement of Foreign Arbitral Awards – a/ka/a the "New York Convention" – gives effect to arbitral awards in both Canada and the United States, as well as over 118 other countries which have ratified the treaty. 330 UNTS 38, 21 UST 2517, TIAS No. 6997 (1958).

[112] International Arbitration Rules of the International Centre for Dispute Resolution of the American Arbitration Association ("ICDR"), Article 16.2 states, "[t]he tribunal, exercising its discretion, shall conduct the proceedings with a view to expediting the resolution of the dispute." *See also*, London Court of International Arbitration ("LCIA"), Rule Article 14.1 directs arbitrators "to adopt procedures suitable to the circumstances of the arbitration, avoiding unnecessary delay or expense, so as to provide a fair and efficient means for the final resolution of the parties' dispute."

[113] ICDR *ibid.* at Article 16.1 states that: "[s]ubject to these rules, the tribunal may conduct the arbitration in whatever manner it considers appropriate, *provided that the parties are treated with equality and that each party has the right to be heard and is given a fair opportunity to present its case.*" (Emphasis added). Article 15.2 of the ICC Rules provides that "the Arbitral Tribunal shall act fairly and impartially and ensure that each party has a reasonable opportunity to present its case."

case in the *Gut Dam* dispute. Recall that the parties' *compromis* detailed the fact that witnesses would only be called to testify in extraordinary circumstances, which were to be determined by the Tribunal, another element of the flexibility of this arbitration – although parties in an international court could stipulate to certain facts, so that witnesses need not be called. Additionally, the GOC and the GOUS decided to utilize a panel of three arbitrators, rather than select the less costly and more convenient single arbitrator process. Although the majority of transboundary water disputes have selected three arbitrator panels,[114] a single arbitrator is able to decide a dispute quicker and at less cost than three arbitrators.[115] Greater effort is required to coordinate the schedule of three panel members than for one.[116] In addition, clearly, a single arbitrator is generally able to respond faster than three in most pre-hearing issues.[117] However, the choice of multiple panel members likely reflects the parties' belief that there is a lesser chance for error in the proceedings.

Furthermore, by focusing solely on Canada's liability – as detailed in the correspondence between the parties – the Tribunal avoided potential entanglement in the law of torts, particularly strict liability, as a consequence of the harm caused by Canada's construction of the Gut Dam.[118] Indeed, by utilizing its "long shadow" to encourage the two parties to settle their dispute, the Tribunal sought to disentangle itself from having to address issues dealing with "causation" or remedies, including consequential damages. This is the second instance where an international court or tribunal utilized its long shadow as an influence over the two litigants in order to resolve their dispute without a trial – the previous case was the *Kansas v. Colorado* dispute following the Court's 1943 adjudication. There, too, the "court's long shadow" was the catalyst for the parties to initiate negotiations, which led to the formation of their 1949 compact.

---

[114] *Lake Lanoux Arbitration*. However, in the *Indus Waters Kishenganga Arbitration* (Pakistan v. India), the parties selected seven arbitrators. *See* https://www.pcacases.com/web/sendAttach/48.

[115] John Fellas, A Fair and Efficient International Arbitration Process, 59 *Dispute Res. J* (2004) 78.

[116] *Ibid.*   [117] *Ibid.*

[118] See e.g., Alezah Trigueros, The Human Right to Water: Will Its Fulfillment Contribute to Environmental Degradation? 19 *Indiana J of Global Legal Stud* (2012) 599, 609 ("[t]he tribunal simply interpreted and applied the provisions of the agreement, it never made any broader holding on State liability for extraterritorial environmental damage, and therefore the imposition of strict liability in the Gut Dam case is inextricably linked with Canada's consent to be held strictly liable."); *Cf.* Günther Handl, State Liability for Accidental Transnational Environmental Damage by Private Persons, 74 *Am J Int'l L.* (1980) 525, 538 (dismissing the claim that "[a]n even clearer illustration of the application of strict liability in the context of environmental injury is the Gut Dam arbitration ... " and that the Tribunal was "clearly adopting a standard of strict liability.")

Scholars who study the effectiveness of international courts and tribunals do not generally address the notion of a tribunal's "long shadow." For example, Posner & Yoo only looked at compliance and usage rates, while positing that independent tribunals are more "effective" than dependent tribunals. Similarly, Helfer & Slaughter did not address a court or tribunal's long shadow in their factors for measuring effectiveness.

Furthermore, an external "shadow" cannot be discounted. That aspect here was the possibility of more private litigation, by other claimants in the courts of the United States or Canada against the latter. Although such suits might be dismissed on the grounds of sovereign immunity, assuming service was not a problem, it would both be a nuisance and a financial burden for Canada. Thus, this possibility may have also affected Canada's thinking regarding the settlement of this dispute. One more possibility for both parties was that the arbitral panel would make an award that neither party would be satisfied with.

1 Measuring the Tribunal's Effectiveness

Employing the proxies for effectiveness, the tribunal demonstrated that as an institutional construct it was effective in several ways. First, from an institutional perspective, the Tribunal's promotion of the resolution of this dispute is a critical goal. Second, there is no question that these Parties complied with their agreement. Thus, I posit that in encouraging the settlement, the Tribunal promoted **compliance – proxy 1**, with a critical governing norm: honoring agreements. Furthermore, I posit that the panel implicitly strengthened the doctrine of *sic utere*.

As for the four other proxies listed in Table 7.2, clearly even where litigants settle a dispute, the proceedings and the results can demonstrate effectiveness. **Proxy-2, Resolution & Satisfaction**: the dispute was resolved, and given that the parties settled the dispute "full and final settlement of all claims for damage allegedly caused to the United States national by Gut Dam,"[119] one believes that they were satisfied, otherwise they would have continued the litigation. As for **Proxy-3, Normative Impact**: the settlement precluded the development or enhancement of new norms. However, with regards to this proxy I could not find any evidence that the results of this dispute had any impact on the conduct of other States. Nor could one find any evidence that the present adjudication had any effect on the improved compliance by other relevant actors. The tribunal, however, did contribute to the operation of the

---

[119] *Canada–United States Settlement of Gut Dam Claims*, Report of the Agent of the United States Before the Lake Ontario Claims Tribunal, 8 ILM 118, 140 (1969).

TABLE 9.2 *The Gut Dam Arbitration – Time from Compromis to Award*

(1) 1968 – *Compromis* executed.	(3) **February 12, 1968**, the tribunal decided the second question: whether that obligation was limited not only to persons but also to time?.
(2) **January 15, 1968** – The arbitrators empanel. They address the disputes one of the two central issues: whether Canada was liable for the Gut Dam's damages?	(4) **February 12, 1968** – Panel finds found that the Canadian Government clearly recognized its obligation to pay compensation so far as the 1951–1952 claims are concerned. However, it did not issue. Rather, it recommended a compromise settlement.

International Joint Commission, although not to other adjudicative bodies. **Proxy-4, Fairness and Legitimation:** the panel demonstrated a high degree of fairness and it did provide legitimacy to the IJC, the institution that created it; and **Proxy-5, Efficiency:** there is no question that this panel was both efficient and effective in managing the proceedings. Of course, this dispute is only one point on the graph. More work is required to assess whether settlements can be utilized to measure tribunal and court effectiveness.

From an institutional perspective, there is also the issue of how the IJC is perceived by its many stakeholders – including the property owners, and whether its actions are considered appropriate or desirable within the legal regime that its mandate providers (the two states' federal legislatures) established for it. For our purposes, which include an assessment of the specific role of the adjudicative body on the one hand, and its ability to enforce its awards and norms on the other: The latter is a facet of the tribunal's and the IJC's sphere of authority, "which may well in turn vest [it with] norm-creating power."[120] One was unable to find any information regarding how stakeholders other than the two IJC state-parties perceived the tribunal's outcome. Again, the two governments seemed pleased to get the matter resolved. However, as noted above, the United States Government ultimately seems to have done an injustice to its citizens, by agreeing to such a small sum: ($1,522.00/claimant).[121]

Finally, I, once again, wish to discuss the view that there is a critical difference between what Posner & Yoo term dependent and independent

---

[120] Hans Kelsen, *General Theory of Law and State* (1945) 113.
[121] $350,000/230 = $1522.00.

tribunals.[122] As noted previously, I am unable to accept this distinction. Indeed, as will become clear from the following discussion, the logic of this thesis is peculiar. These authors also argue that the independence of a tribunal affects its willingness to create new law or methods of dispute resolution. Such a conclusion would, however, in my view, be incorrect. I posit that the Parties in the *Gut Dam Dispute* – or possibly Canada more than the United States – were influenced by the Tribunal's "long shadow."

Posner & Yoo's views – at least, in light of the arbitrations that are discussed in this work, as well as in investment arbitrations, and those adjudicated by the Permanent Court of Arbitration – seem to belie what actually occurs in most State-to-State arbitrations. For example, they posit that

> [a]rbitration limits the involvement of the third party: an arbitral panel is set up to resolve only one dispute or class of disputes, and it follows an *ad hoc* set of procedural and substantive laws that remain within the control of the parties. Arbitration's main weakness is that the disputing states, whose interests and passions are engaged, need not consent to a panel's jurisdiction; nor need they comply with its judgment, though they frequently do.[123]

But here is the rub. First these authors state that disputing states "need not consent to a panel's jurisdiction; nor need they comply with its judgment..." Nevertheless, they concede that States generally do consent to an arbitral panel's jurisdiction. What is not stated is that in most, if not all cases, including in the *Gut Dam Arbitration*, States choose this mode of adjudication. (*See also* the *Indus Waters Kishenganga Arbitration* (Pakistan v. India), and the *Lac Lanoux Arbitration*.) Of course, the Parties in the present dispute could have litigated their case before the ICJ or the PCA. Obviously, they chose not to, possibly because they had greater control in this forum.

Posner & Yoo's thesis appears to be flawed on one other ground. That is, in many international court adjudications the litigants also limit the court's involvement. The clearest example of that fact is the ICJ's *Gulf of Maine Case*.[124] There, Canada and the United States established the rules for the

---

[122] Posner & Yoo *ibid.* at 72. These authors take the position that dependent tribunals are more effective than independent ones. They define "dependent" tribunals as those where arbitrators or judges are party appointed. Independent tribunals are characterized as those peopled by fixed-term judges, *e.g.*, the ICJ or the ITLOS, as opposed to tribunals where the adjudicators are *ad hoc* arbitrators. Moreover, they also assert that dependent adjudicators are more successful than those who populate independent tribunals. Similarly, these authors reason that the success of dependent tribunals is grounded in the fact that if these arbitrators/judges fail to please the State-party that engaged them, they won't be employed again.

[123] Posner & Yoo *ibid.* at 9.

[124] *Delimitation of Maritime Boundary in Gulf of Maine Area* (Can/US), 1984 ICJ 246,

litigation, chose the members of the Chamber, utilized the Chamber process for the very first time, and laid down the geographic line that would divide their delimitation. Similarly, it can be argued that the use of *ad hoc* judges in international courts also limits the court, since in many cases *ad hoc* judges vote in favor of the party that hired or seated them.[125]

III BAYVIEW IRRIGATION DISTRICT V. UNITED MEXICAN STATES

A *Introduction*

The present case arose out of a claim by the Texas-based Bayview Irrigation District *et al.* ("Claimants," "Texans," or "Bayview")[126] against the United States of Mexico ("Mexico" or "Respondent"), under Chapter 11 of the North American Free Trade Agreement ("NAFTA").[127] The Claimants alleged that Mexico appropriated or "took" their water rights, thereby violating NAFTA's Chapter 11, investment sections, specifically articles 1102, 1105, and 1110. Although the water was located in Mexico, and under what appeared to be Mexico's sovereign territory, the Texans claimed rights to that water.

Bayview also asserted that they possessed the "fully adjudicated exclusive legal right to withdraw 1.2 million acre-feet (1.5 billion cubic meters) of water annually from the lower Rio Grande River,"[128] on the Mexican side of the Rio Bravo/Rio Grande River.[129] These rights were claimed under the Treaty

---

[125] *See e.g.*, Dapo Akande, Trivia: Cases Where Judge Votes Against National State or Appointing Party, *EJIL Talk* (Sept. 20, 2012), http://www.ejiltalk.org/category/international-tribunals/ad-hoc-judges.

> In international tribunals it is often the case that a judge will vote in favour of a State that appoints that particular judge or that a judge will vote in favour of their State of nationality where that State is involved in a case before the tribunal. Sometimes, the suggestion is made that these facts show that judges have some sort of bias in favour of their national State or in favour of the State or party that appointed them.

[126] The claim was submitted by 46 parties, composed of seventeen Texas irrigation districts, sixteen individuals, two trusts, two limited partnership, two estates, four corporations and three general partnerships...," located in Cameron County, the southeatern most county in Texas. *Bayview Irrigation District et al. (Claimants) v. United Mexican States (Respondent)*, ICSID Case No. ARB(AF)/05/1 (June 19, 2007), Award at ¶ 1.

[127] Dec. 17, 1992, Can.–Mex.–U.S., 32 ILM 296 and 32 ILM 605 (1993).

[128] Notice of Intent to Submit a Claim to Arbitration Under Section B, Chapter 11 of the North American Free Trade Agreement (2004), at 1, [hereinafter NOI], http://naftaclaims.com/Disputes/Mexico/Texas/TexasNoticeOfIntent.pdf.

[129] The River is called the Rio Bravo in Mexico and the Rio Grande in the United States. *See generally*, Mary E. Kelly, Water Management in the Binational Texas/Mexico Rio Grande Rio Bravo Basin, in Human Population and Freshwater Resources: US Cases and International Perspectives, *Yale Schl Forest & Envtl Stud Bul* (Karin M. Krchnak ed., 2002) 107, 116.

between the United States of America and Mexico Relating to the Utilization of the Waters of the Colorado and Tijuana Rivers and of the Rio Grande, signed on February 3, 1944 ("1944 Treaty").[130] That is, the Claimants sought private rights to the transfer of water under the treaty. The central issue in the case was whether the Texans possessed an absolute right to withdraw the 1.2 million acre-feet of water each year from the lower Rio Grande River in Mexico. Another issue that concerned the International Centre for Settlement of Investment Disputes ("ICSID") arbitral tribunal was whether it had jurisdiction over the case. A subsidiary issue, which also informed the jurisdictional question, was whether the Claimants were investors, as defined by NAFTA's Chapter 11. Ultimately, the Panel unanimously adjudged that the Claimants were not investors, or had an investment in Mexico, as defined by NAFTA, and therefore that the Tribunal had no jurisdiction to hear the matter.

A Geographic Setting

The Rio Grande's geographic setting, as well as the history of the 1944 Treaty, were discussed in the Chamizal Arbitration case, *ibid.*, and will therefore not be repeated here. However, where additional aspects of the geographic setting and the 1944 Treaty bear on this dispute, they will be supplemented. Figure 9.3 depicts the River and Cameron County, Texas, where Bayview is situated, northeast of San Benito. The river flows through the city of Brownsville and empties into the Gulf of Mexico, south of Port Isabel.

B The Texans' Allegations

As indicated above, Bayview claimed that they possessed "fully adjudicated rights to withdraw 1.2 million acre-feet of water annually from the lower Rio Grande River."[131] They also made nine other assertions in support their claims,[132] but only five of them will be addressed here. They are:

(1) In diverting the water that allegedly belonged to them, the Texans claimed that Mexico thereby nationalized or appropriated Bayview's investment, without compensation and due process in violation of NAFTA's Article 1110.[133]

---

[130] 59 Stat, 1219, USTS 994 (effective November 8, 1945) (*hereinafter* "1944 Treaty"), http://www.ibwc.state.gov/Files/1944Treaty.pdf.

[131] NOI, *ibid.* at ¶ 1. Paul Stanton Kibel & Jonathan R. Schutz, Rio Grande Designs: Texans' NAFTA Water Claim Against Mexico, 25 *Berkeley J Int'l L* 228, 251 (2007).

[132] *See generally*, Kibel & Schutz, *ibid.* at 250–252.

[133] NOI, *ibid.* at ¶ 4; Kibel & Schutz, *ibid.* at 250–252. Article 1110: Expropriation and Compensation, provides in pertinent part:

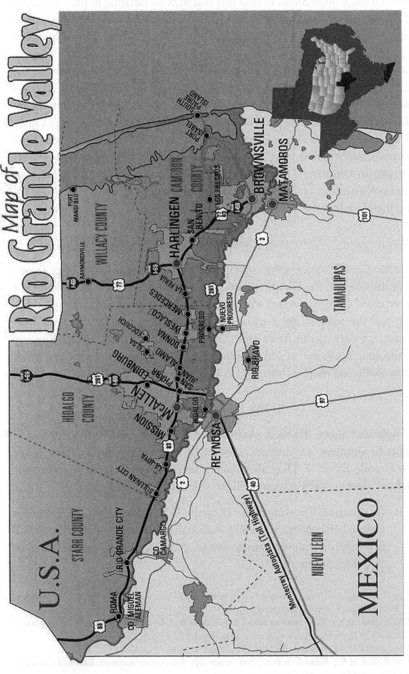

FIGURE 9.3 Bayview Irrigation District – lies to the northeast of Brownsville, approximately where the words Cameron County are. The Rio Grande meanders through the county and is generally followed by highway 281.

(2) For the period 1992–2000, Mexico captured and diverted, the Texans' "investment [of] (approximately 1,013,056 [acre-feet] of irrigation water) located in Mexico and owned by Claimants."[134]

(3) In diverting Claimants' water for use by Mexican farmers, Respondent improved its agricultural production and injured Bayview's agricultural production.[135]

(4) Claimants asserted that in so doing Mexico dealt less favorably with their investments as opposed to those of its own investors' and therefore breached NAFTA's Article 1102.[136]

(5) The thrust of the Claimants' Chapter 11 allegations was that they were the authorized or legal owners of 1.2 million acre-feet of irrigation water that Mexico unlawfully diverted from the Rio Grande River, "the expropriation and diversion of which has severely damaged the ability of the Texans and the farmers they represent to produce crops."[137] Bayview therefore claimed that they possessed an "integrated investment" under the definition of Article 1139(g) of NAFTA[138] that allegedly included:

> rights to water located in Mexico; facilities to store and distribute this water for irrigation and domestic consumption; irrigated fields and farms; that Claimants invested millions of dollars in an integrated water delivery system, including pumps, aqueducts, canals, other facilities for the storage and conveyance of their water to the land on which it is used . . . Each Claimant's Investment is entirely predicated on this right to receive water located in Mexican tributaries.[139]

Finally, the Texans alleged that they suffered damages totaling "nearly $1 billion [due to losses] . . . in decreased business activity and that 30,000 jobs ha[d] been precluded."[140]

---

1. No Party may directly or indirectly nationalize or expropriate an investment of an investor of another Party in its territory or take a measure tantamount to nationalization or expropriation of such an investment ("expropriation"), except:
   (a) for a public purpose;
   (b) on a non-discriminatory basis;
   (c) in accordance with due process of law . . . ; and
   (d) on payment of compensation . . .

[134] NOI, *ibid.* at ¶ 7. (Emphasis added.)   [135] *Ibid.* Notice of Arbitration, *ibid.* at ¶ 32–33.
[136] *Ibid.*   [137] Kibel & Schutz, *ibid.* at 251–252; NOI, *ibid.* at ¶ 7.
[138] Kibel & Schutz, *ibid.* at 252; Notice of Arbitration, *ibid.* at ¶ 27.   [139] *Ibid.*
[140] Kibel & Schutz, *ibid.* at 251–252; NOI *ibid.* at ¶ 7.

C Pre-Arbitration History and Procedural Aspects

On August 27, 2004, the Texans submitted to the ICSID their notice of intent to seek arbitration under Chapter 11. Subsequently, on January 19, 2005, Bayview submitted their application, to ICSID, requesting an arbitration proceeding under the Additional Facility Arbitration Rules ("the Request").[141] As is required in most arbitrations involving nationals of a State who sue another State, see e.g., the Gut Dam Arbitration, the "Request for Arbitration" declared that each of the individual Claimants, at the time of filing, is or was a resident of Texas and a national of the United States of America ("USA"), and not a national of Mexico, and that each of the juridical persons, e.g., corporations, was organized and existed under the law of Texas.[142] Thereafter, on January 27, 2005, the Centre confirmed its receipt of the Application.

On July 1, 2005, the Secretary-General of the Centre approved access to the Additional Facility.[143] As arbitrators, the Claimants appointed an American national, Edwin Meese, III, former Attorney General in the Reagan Administration, and the Respondent appointed a Mexican national, Professor Ignacio Gómez-Palacio.[144] Both parties then, agreed to the appointment of Professor Vaughan Lowe, a British national, as president of the Arbitral Tribunal. Subsequently, on December 15, 2005, the arbitral panel was regarded as constituted and the proceedings to have been commenced.[145]

---

[141] The request was received by the International Centre for Settlement of Investment Disputes ("ICSID") Secretary on January 19, 2005. *Bayview Irrigation District ibid.* at ¶ 1.

> The Claimants' Counter-Memorial on Jurisdiction refers in ¶ 1 to 'the 42 investor Claimants'. The Tribunal regards the detailed list of Claimants in the Request for Arbitration, as amended by the letter of 20 May 2005 referred to in ¶ 4), below, as the definitive list of Claimants in the absence of any other formal notice of amendment to that list.

[142] A list describing the nature of each Claimant, its address and place of incorporation, was attached to the Request.

[143] Both parties were notified of the registration of the Request per Article 4, Access to the Additional Facility in Respect of Conciliation and Arbitration Proceedings Subject to Secretary-General's Approval. Additionally, and as required by Article 5(e) of the Additional Facility Arbitration Rules, the Secretary-General invited the Parties to constitute an Arbitral Tribunal in accordance with Chapter III of those rules. Schedule B Conciliation (Additional Facility) Rules Chapter I, Art. 5, "Notice of Registration, provide. The notice of registration of a request shall: (e) invite the parties to proceed, as soon as possible, to constitute a Conciliation Commission in accordance with Chapter III of these Rules."

[144] *Bayview Irrigation District et al. ibid.* at ¶ 6.

[145] *Ibid.* "Pursuant to Rule 25 of ICSID's Administrative and Financial Regulations, the parties were notified that Ms. Gabriela Alvarez Avila, ICSID Senior Counsel, would act as Secretary of the Arbitral Tribunal."

D *The Tribunal's First Sitting*

The Tribunal held its First Session on February 14, 2006 in Washington DC ("the First Session").[146] During that sitting, the Parties agreed that the arbitration would proceed in accordance with ICSID's Additional Facility Rules, which were then in force[147] and as modified by NAFTA's Chapter 11, Section B. Also, at that session, the Tribunal determined, following consultations with the Parties, that "the question of jurisdiction would be considered as a preliminary issue."[148] Concomitantly, the Tribunal requested that Mexico file its Memorial on Jurisdiction by April 19, 2006 and that the Texans would thereafter file their Counter-Memorial by June 23, 2006.[149] The Tribunal also decided that the Respondent would file its Reply Memorial no later than July 26, 2006, and that the Claimants would file their Rejoinder by August 28, 2006.[150] The hearing to determine the Tribunal's jurisdiction was scheduled for three days, November 14, 15 and 16, 2006, in Washington D.C., while further hearing dates would be determined, at a later date.[151] Finally, the Tribunal also advised the disputants that pursuant to Article 1128, the two other NAFTA Parties would be invited to submit their comments by September 18, 2006.[152]

Subsequently, on August 31, 2005, employing Article 1128, the Tribunal requested the NAFTA parties to submit any submission that they felt was appropriate in the proceedings, no later than September 18, 2006.[153] The Government of Canada advised the Tribunal on September 15, 2006, that it would not file any submissions on Jurisdiction before the due date, but that it reserved the right to comment during the hearings.[154] There is no indication in the Judgment that the Government of the United States responded by the due date.

On September 26, 2006, the Centre acknowledged receipt of a letter from Kathleen Harnett White, Chairwoman of the Texas Commission on Environmental Quality, dated September 20, 2006, which was conveyed to both the Tribunal and the Parties.[155] The letter involved the scope of the 1944 Water Treaty, as well as, "the negotiations over Mexico's water debt. It stated that the claims of water districts and individual water users were not within the scope of the negotiations and settlement concerning the water debt between the United States and Mexico."[156]

---

[146] *Ibid.* at ¶8.   [147] These Rules were in force since January 1, 2003. *Ibid.* at ¶ 9.
[148] *Ibid.* at ¶ 10.   [149] *Ibid.*   [150] *Ibid.*   [151] *Ibid.*
[152] *Ibid.* Article 1128 provides the following: "'Participation by a Party' On written notice to the disputing parties, a Party may make submissions to a Tribunal on a question of interpretation of this Agreement."
[153] *Bayview Irrigation District et al. ibid.* at ¶ 12.   [154] *Ibid.*
[155] *Ibid.* at ¶ 13.   [156] *Ibid.*

Then, on October 31, 2006, The Tribunal asked the Parties to address the following three issues at the hearing:

(1) two points pertaining to the issue of the law applicable under NAFTA Article 1131. These included (a) "What is the role, if any, of national law?" Specifically, "(i) Did Texas law and (ii) Mexican law have any bearing on the proceedings?" and (b) What is the role, if any, of the principles of private international law?

(2) with regards to the use of the term "investment" in NAFTA's article 1139 in the case *sub judice*, the litigants were requested to answer, whether that term had any significance to the term "property" under NAFTA? and

(3) What was the aim in this case of the NAFTA term "in the territory of the Party"?[157]

E *The Tribunal's Second Sitting: The Hearing on Jurisdiction*

On November 14–15, 2006, the Tribunal held its second hearing on Jurisdiction,[158] and addressed the Parties' contentions.[159] The Parties were also advised that the Panel would invite the NAFTA Parties to file written submissions, by November 27, 2006, on the following questions: "a) . . . the standing of the Irrigation Districts as Claimants under NAFTA, and b) . . . the concept of territoriality in relation to Articles 1102 and 1105 of NAFTA." In addition, on November 16, 2006 the Tribunal requested the Parties to present it with the following, no later than December 11, 2006: a) any comments on the questions that were to be addressed by the NAFTA Parties, *i.e.*, Canada and the United States; and b) any supplementary comments or observations that the litigants sought to address in addition to what they had previously included in their submissions, regarding the case of the *City of San Marcos* v. *Texas Commission on Environmental Quality*,[160] alluded to in the Texans' submissions; and c) any comments on the concept of water as a "good in commerce", in both Texas and Mexico, as addressed during the Tribunal's jurisdictional hearing.[161]

Moreover, the Tribunal also invited the Parties to provide a concise explanation regarding the following three questions: "(a) what, if any, action the State of Texas could take in the event of noncompliance with conditions attached

---

[157] *Ibid.* at ¶ 14.   [158] *Ibid.* at ¶ 15.

[159] *Ibid.* "Transcripts of that hearing were made in English and Spanish and were distributed to the Tribunal and the Parties at the end of each day of the hearing." *Ibid.* at ¶ 15.

[160] 128 SW 3d 264 (Tex. App. 2004).   [161] *Bayview Irrigation District et al. ibid.* at ¶ 19.

to the exercise of water rights of the kind held by the Claimants?[162] (b) is it likely under Texas' water law for an owner of a water right to bring a claim against an Irrigation District for its breach of whatever the legal responsibilities that the Irrigation Districts may have pursuant to the relevant Texas legislation?"[163] and "c) the availability of copies of resolutions of the board of directors of the water districts authorizing the initiation of these arbitral proceedings."[164] In response to the Tribunal's request the United States filed their submissions on November 27, 2006.[165] Finally, on December 15, 2006 the State of Texas made a submission in support of the Claimants, and via correspondence dated December 18, 2006, the Commissioner of the Texas Department of Agriculture also submitted a letter in support of the Texans' position.

F *The Parties' Arguments*

1 The challenge to jurisdiction and admissibility

a. **Mexico's Memorial on Jurisdiction asserted the following three objections to the Tribunal's jurisdiction and admissibility:**
   i) the Texan's claim fell outside NAFTA "in light of NAFTA's object and purpose and of the nature of the treaty";[166]
   ii) the Texan's assertion was untimely and therefore inadmissible;
   iii) there were defects in the individual claims, with respect to the proof of each claimant's eligibility.[167]

Each of the foregoing assertions is elaborated upon below.

(a) THE FIRST ALLEGATION: As to the first assertion, that the claim falls outside the scope of NAFTA, Mexico argued that the Tribunal's jurisdiction is limited by the limitations of the consent of the parties, and that such consent must adhere to NAFTA's article 1122, which is limited to "arbitration in accordance with the procedures set out in this Agreement."[168] It also asserted that a NAFTA claim must relate to an investment within the scope of Chapter 11, and within the scope of Respondent's consent to arbitration.[169] Moreover, Mexico argued that NAFTA is founded upon a "territorial principle of jurisdiction."[170] It pointed to numerous NAFTA articles, in particular to article 1101, in buttressing its point. The pertinent section reads as follows:

---

[162] *Ibid.* at ¶ 20.   [163] *Ibid.*   [164] *Ibid.*   [165] *Ibid.* at ¶ 21.
[166] *Ibid.* at ¶ 24.   [167] *Ibid.*   [168] *Ibid.* at ¶ 25.   [169] *Ibid.*   [170] *Ibid.* at ¶ 26.

(i) Article 1101. Scope and Coverage.

1. This Chapter applies to measures adopted or maintained by a Party relating to: -
(a) investors of another Party;
(b) investments of investors of another Party *in the territory of the Party* . . . .[171]

In support of its position Mexico cited the *Methanex* case Award,[172] which held that " . . . the phrase 'relating to' in Article 1101(1) of NAFTA which, signifies something more than the mere effect of a measure on an investor or an investment and . . . requires a legally significant connection between them . . . "[173] Mexico similarly stressed that in its view Chapter 11 applies to "protect *investors of one NAFTA State Party* or their investments *in the territory of another NAFTA State Party*. [Respondent also stressed that the Texans maintained that each one of them] is 'an Investor and owner of an integrated Investment' which includes 'rights to water located in Mexico.'"[174]

Respondent likewise pointed to the definition of the term "investment" in Article 1139, which in pertinent part reads as follows:

"**investment** means: . . .

(g) real estate or other property, tangible or intangible, acquired in the expectation or used for the purpose of economic benefit or other business purposes;

investment of an investor of a Party means an investment owned or controlled directly or indirectly by an investor of such Party;

---

[171] *Ibid.* (emphasis added).
[172] *See Methanex Corp. v. United States*, First Partial Award on Jurisdiction and Admissibility (NAFTA Ch. 11 Arb. Trib., Aug. 7, 2002), http://www.state.gov/documents/organization/12613.pdf.
[173] *Ibid.* at ¶ 27. One set of commentators has observed that

> the expansive notion of 'investment' that underl[ay] the Texans' NAFTA water claim is at odds with the ruling made by the Chapter 11 arbitration panel in *Methanex Corporation v. United States of America*. Kibel & Schutz, *ibid.* at 260.

> The Chapter 11 claim in *Methanex* was brought by a manufacturer of methanol, one of the main ingredients in methyl tertiary-butyl ether ("MTBE"). [Footnote omitted . . .] In a decision issued on August 7, 2002, the *Methanex* panel dismissed claims for compensation for damages on the grounds that Methanex Corporation did not constitute an "investor" under Chapter 11 because its investments in the production of methanol were insufficiently linked with California's ban on MTBE.

> *Ibid.*
[174] *Ibid.* at ¶ 28 (emphasis added).

investor of a Party means a Party or state enterprise thereof, or a national or an enterprise of such Party, that seeks to make, is making or has made an investment."[175]

Mexico also urged that, based on the foregoing definition, the Texans do not and cannot have any property rights in the waters of the Rio Bravo/Rio Grande or its tributaries, which are located wholly within Mexico's territory, even if they have an ownership right in the River's waters when it flows across the border into the territory of the United States.[176] Moreover, Mexico argued that the Texans' claims were based on the contention that Mexico breached the bilateral 1944 Treaty.[177] Pointing to assertions that the Texans made in their Request for Arbitration, where Bayview referred to violations of the 1944 Treaty by Mexico, the Respondent concluded that "the only basis the Claimants could have for any expectation of receiving any volume of water from the Mexican tributaries of Rio Bravo is the Bilateral Treaty of 1944, and it is precisely the alleged non-compliance with that international agreement on which the claimants assert a purported breach of the NAFTA."[178]

Furthermore, Mexico asserted that pursuant to the 1944 Treaty each State may at its discretion distribute its assigned Rio Grande/Rio Bravo River water rights, as it sees fit under its municipal laws. Additionally, it also argued that both it and the Government of the United States ("GOUS") agree that the 1944 Treaty did not create any private rights of action for individuals in either State. Indeed, the GOUS articulated that position in an earlier case lodged in a United States federal court, where it intervened.[179] Mexico also argued that the circumstances concerning its water shortfall did not represent a breach of the 1944 Treaty, and that the GOUS did not assert any breach occurred.[180]

Similarly, relative to the 1944 Treaty Mexico quoted the United States' Reply Memorial in the *Methanex* case, where the GOUS declared that "[n]umerous treaties, many of which have either no mechanism for resolving disputes between States or highly specialized mechanisms, are in effect among the NAFTA Parties. The limited consent to arbitration granted in Chapter 11

---

[175] *Ibid.* at ¶ 29. (Emphasis in the original.)

[176] *Ibid.* (*Citing Mexico's* Memorial on Jurisdiction, ¶¶ 88–89.)

[177] *Ibid.* at ¶ 30 (*citing Mexico's* Memorial on Jurisdiction, ¶¶ 102–104).

[178] *Ibid.* (*citing Mexico's* Memorial on Jurisdiction, ¶ 105).

[179] *Ibid.* at ¶ 31 (*citing Mexico's* Memorial on Jurisdiction, ¶¶ 111, and Memorandum in Support of United States' Motion to Dismiss Counts 1–4 & 7–8, *Consejo de Desarrollo Economico de Mexicali, AC v. United States*, 20 (D. Nev. September 19, 2005) (NO. CV-S-05–08700-KJD-GWF), 438 F.Supp.2d 1207, 1221 (D. Nev. 2006), *rev'd on other grounds*, 482 F.3d 1157 (9th Cir.2007)).

[180] *Ibid.* at ¶ 32.

cannot reasonably be extended to the international law obligations embodied in those treaties."[181] Mexico also argued that in the case *sub judice*, the same logic applies with regards to the claimed breaches of NAFTA founded on the asserted breaches of the 1944 Water Treaty.[182]

(b) THE SECOND ALLEGATION: THE CLAIMS ARE UNTIMELY Here, Mexico asserted that the Request for Arbitration was submitted on January 20, 2005 and the "acts or omissions of Mexico that occurred before the entry into force of the NAFTA on 1 January 1994 are beyond the Tribunal's jurisdiction *ratione temporis*."[183] It cited NAFTA's Article 1116(2), which states that "2. An investor may not make a claim if more than three years have elapsed from the date on which the investor first acquired, or should have first acquired, knowledge of the alleged breach and knowledge that the investor has incurred loss or damage."[184]

(c) THE CLAIMANTS DID NOT ABIDE BY NAFTA'S MANDATORY PROCE-DURAL REQUIREMENTS: Initially, Mexico asserted that the Tribunal lacked jurisdiction over the dispute because the Texans did not comply with various sections of NAFTA's Chapter 11. Additionally, Mexico asserted that Bayview failed to observe ICSID's Arbitration Rules, requiring documentation that identifies that each claimant is a US national, investor,[185] and that the Irrigation District's claimants were not authorized by their members to submit this claim.[186] Moreover, Mexico claimed that the Texans' counsel had not provided proof that they were properly authorized by the Claimants who were juridical persons to represent them.[187]

2 Bayview's Counter-Memorial on Jurisdiction

The Texans' Counter-Memorial on Jurisdiction initially alleged that "[b]eginning in 1992, Mexico set about a course of purposeful and systematic capture, seizure, and diversion of the water belonging to Claimants, while it was located in Mexican territory, for use by farmers located in Mexico."[188] Furthermore, Bayview averred that they have owned the water at issue since

---

[181] *Ibid.* at ¶ 33. (*Citing* "Reply Memorial of Respondent United States of America on Jurisdiction, Admissibility and the Proposed Amendment (12 April 2001), pp. 32–33.")

[182] *Ibid.* (*Citing Mexico's* Memorial on Jurisdiction, ¶ 114.)

[183] *Ibid.* at ¶ 34 (*citing Mexico's* Memorial on Jurisdiction, ¶ 90).   [184] *Ibid.* at ¶ 35.

[185] *Ibid.* at ¶ 37.   [186] *Ibid.* at ¶ 38.   [187] *Ibid.* at ¶ 39.

[188] *Ibid.* at ¶ 40. (The Texans submitted their Counter-Memorial on Jurisdiction dated June 23, 2006.)

1969, when they were granted the right of ownership by a Texas state court.[189] Claimants Counter-Memorial on Jurisdiction then went on to address Mexico's objections to jurisdiction and admissibility.

(a) THE CLAIM DOES NOT FALL OUTSIDE THE SCOPE OF NAFTA: The Claimants asserted that their petition related to a Mexican action concerning investors of another Party, the USA, and to an investment located within the territory of Mexico. That action constituted the impoundment by Mexico of the Texans' water "while that water was in transit to the Claimants' fields in Texas, and its diversion by the Respondent for use by Mexican farmers in Mexico."[190] Pointing to disparities in the wording of Articles 1102 (National Treatment), 1105 (Minimum Standard of Treatment), and 1110 (Expropriation and Compensation), the Texans urged that Articles 1102[191] and 1105,[192] in contrast to Article 1110, apply to all actions taken by Mexico relative to investors of another Party or to their investments, regardless of whether those investments were located within Mexico.[193] They also asserted that neither Article 1102 nor Article 1105 contain any requirements pertaining to the location of the investor or the investment.

Furthermore, the Texans argued that under the 1944 Treaty Mexico had relinquished ownership of the Claimants' irrigation water, and that this water was an investment located in Mexico and within the scope of

---

[189] *Ibid.* at ¶ 41. (Claimants cited the decree in *State v. Hidalgo County Water Control & Improvement Dist. No. 18*, 443 S.W. 2d 728 (Tex. Civ. App. 1969).)

[190] *Ibid.* at ¶ 43.

[191] *Ibid.* **Article 1102: National Treatment** provides in pertinent part

    1. Each Party shall accord to investors of another Party treatment no less favorable than that it accords, in like circumstances, to its own investors with respect to the establishment, acquisition, expansion, management, conduct, operation, and sale or other disposition of investments.

    2. Each Party shall accord to investments of investors of another Party treatment no less favorable than that it accords, in like circumstances, to investments of its own investors with respect to the establishment, acquisition, expansion, management, conduct, operation, and sale or other disposition of investments.

[192] *Ibid.* **Article 1105: Minimum Standard of Treatment** provides in pertinent part

    1. Each Party shall accord to investments of investors of another Party treatment in accordance with international law, including fair and equitable treatment and full protection and security.

    2. Without prejudice to paragraph 1 . . . each Party shall accord to investors of another Party, and to investments of investors of another Party, non-discriminatory treatment with respect to measures it adopts or maintains relating to losses suffered by investments in its territory owing to armed conflict or civil strife.

[193] *Ibid.* at ¶ 44. (*Citing* Counter-Memorial on Jurisdiction, ¶ 49.)

Article 1101(1)(b).[194] They also asserted that the water rights were "transferred from Mexico to the United States in 1944, and from the United States to Claimants under the national law of the United States."[195] The Texans more-over claimed that the Joint Communiqué was an interpretation of NAFTA that was binding on the Tribunal pursuant to Article 1131(2).[196] They additionally asserted that water turns into a commercial good or product when an investment of human activity translates it into a tradable commodity, and that Bayview's water, "which flows within... Mexican tributaries before reaching the Rio Grande, where it is stored in... reservoirs, sold on the Water Market, and delivered through a complex of irrigation works, is clearly a good or product in commerce."[197]

Likewise, Bayview quoted from a 1906 Mexico–United States Convention on the Equitable Distribution of the Waters of the Rio Grande, which they declared is equally applicable to the 1944 Treaty.[198] Indeed, in their view, "[f]ollowing the conclusion of the [1944] Treaty, each nation owned the water resources allotted to it, and relinquished ownership of the water allotted to the other nation."[199] The 1944 Treaty, the Texans claimed, consisted of an actual fixing of water rights in the Rio Grande and its tributaries, "much like the fixing of the territorial boundary between the two nations".[200]

---

[194] *Ibid.* at ¶ 45.

> Article 1101: Scope and Coverage, provides in pertinent part
>
> 1. This Chapter applies to measures adopted or maintained by a Party relating to...
>   (b) investments of investors of another Party in the territory of the Party...

[195] *Ibid.* (*Citing* Counter-Memorial on Jurisdiction, ¶ 57.)
[196] *Ibid.*

> Article 1131: Governing Law, states
>
> 1. A Tribunal established under this Section shall decide the issues in dispute in accordance with this Agreement and applicable rules of international law.
> 2. An interpretation by the Commission of a provision of this Agreement shall be binding on a Tribunal established under this Section.

[197] *Ibid.*
[198] *Ibid.* at ¶ 47. That statement includes the following passage:

> "The 1906 Water Convention equitably distributes the surface waters of the Rio Grande above Fort Quitman. Other than the waters to which it is entitled under the 1906 Water Convention, Mexico has waived all claims to the waters of the Rio Grande for any purpose.... Rights to utilize the water resources within the boundaries of each nation are controlled by their respective domestic laws."

> (*Citing* Counter-Memorial on Jurisdiction, ¶ 67.)

[199] *Ibid.*   [200] *Ibid.* at ¶ 48. (*Citing* Counter-Memorial on Jurisdiction, ¶ 74.)

In addition, Bayview asserted that Texas' municipal law controls in the case: Citing the fact that the Texas Court of Appeal "took judicial custody of the American waters of the Rio Grande"[201] in the 1969 *Hidalgo* case and "made substantial quantities of water available to Texas residents (including Claimants), even though the 1944 Treaty itself did not apportion these rights."[202] Furthermore, the Texans claimed that Mexico cannot lawfully seize property which either a United States or Canadian investor owns in "Mexico simply on the ground that Mexico did not create [a property] right[] over the property in question." Finally, Claimants argued that they were seeking private rights for breaches of NAFTA, rather than a ruling on the rights and obligations of Mexico and the United States under the 1944 Treaty.[203]

(B) THE CLAIMS ARE NOT UNTIMELY: The Texans also asserted that Article 4(B)(c) of the 1944 Water Treaty declares that the United States' share of the flow "shall not be less, as an average amount in cycles of five consecutive years, than 350,000 acre-feet [432 million cubic meters] annually."[204] Accordingly, Bayview took the position that, strictly speaking, the United States' minimum allotment was a right to 1,750,000 acre-feet (2.2 billion cubic meters) (as a minimum) every five years, rather than a right to compel 350,000 acre-feet each year from Mexico.[205] Therefore, the Claimants averred that there was no violation of their water rights until after September 30, 2002, since Mexico was obligated to deliver water on October 1, 2002, and only subsequent to that date would Respondent become delinquent.[206] Consequently, October 1, 2002, fell within NAFTA's three-year period of limitation.[207]

(C) THE CLAIMANTS HAVE COMPLIED WITH MANDATORY PROCEDURAL REQUIREMENTS: The Texans contended that they had presented sufficient evidence regarding the nationality of each of the Claimants. These proofs included birth certificates and passports.[208] Finally, both Parties filed a Reply and Counter-Reply, in which each of them enlarged its arguments.

---

[201] *Ibid.* at ¶ 49. (*Citing* Counter-Memorial on Jurisdiction, ¶ 76.) This contention is only partially correct. It will be further addressed below.
[202] *Ibid.* (*Citing* Counter-Memorial on Jurisdiction, ¶ 77.)
[203] *Ibid.* at ¶ 51. (*Citing* Counter-Memorial on Jurisdiction, ¶ 83.)   [204] *Ibid.* at ¶ 52.
[205] *Ibid.* (*Citing* Counter-Memorial on Jurisdiction, ¶ 29.)
[206] *Ibid.* at ¶ 53. (*Citing* Counter-Memorial on Jurisdiction, ¶ 34.)
[207] *Ibid.* (Article 1116(2) states the period of limitations.)
[208] *Ibid.* at ¶ 54. (*Citing* Counter-Memorial on Jurisdiction, ¶ 36.)

3 The United States Submission

On November 27, 2006, the GOUS tendered its submission under Article 1128. It addressed the issue of the extent of safeguards provided to investors and investments by Articles 1102 and 1105, stating that

> all of the protections afforded by the NAFTA's investment chapter extend only to investments that are made by an investor of a NAFTA Party in the territory of another NAFTA Party, or to investors of a NAFTA Party that seek to make, are making, or have made an investment in the territory of another NAFTA Party.[209]

In support of this view the GOUS pointed to the function of Article 1101 as the "gateway" to Chapter 11's dispute resolution provisions. The United States took the position that the statement in Article 1101(1)(b), that Chapter 11 pertains to actions espoused by a Party, which relates to "investments of investors of another Party in the territory of the Party"[210] that has implemented those measures. Accordingly, the GOUS view was that this characterized the scope of the safeguarding of investments in Article 1105. It also asserted that Article 1102's scope in protecting "investors" is not explicitly limited to the protection of investors with regards to the investments "in the territory of the State adopting the measures of which complaint is made."[211] Accordingly, the USA suggested that it is obvious that Article 1102 is limited and that any other theory would be absurd.[212] It would, for instance, result in circumstances where there was a requirement to provide "national treatment to an investor even though there was no obligation to accord national treatment to the investment itself."[213]

Finally, the Tribunal also received letters from the following: The Attorney General, the First Assistant Attorney General, and the Solicitor General of Texas, who argued that Bayview's claim fell within the purview of territoriality under Chapter 11 and therefore does not conflict with the "interpretative position" submitted by the GOUS in 2006.[214]

4 The Tribunal's Analysis

Initially, the Tribunal established that it had the jurisdiction under NAFTA to adjudicate the claim. It then found that pursuant to NAFTA Arts. 1101–1114, it had the jurisdiction to hear a claim by an investor from a NAFTA party.

---

[209] *Ibid.* at ¶ 71.   [210] *Ibid.*
[211] *Ibid.* at ¶ 54. (*Citing* Counter-Memorial on Jurisdiction, ¶ 36.)
[212] *Ibid.* (*Citing* United States Submission, at ¶ 8.)
[213] *Ibid.* (*Citing* United States Submission, at ¶ 10.)   [214] *Ibid.* at ¶ 72.

The Tribunal also noted that it had to determine whether the claimants were investors pursuant to Art. 1101. The Panel's members noted that Art. 1101[215] provides that the reach of a tribunal's jurisdiction to hear Chapter 11 claims is apparent from the article's title, because it defines the 'scope and coverage' of the entirety of Chapter 11. Moreover, the Tribunal's members observed that the question before the Tribunal was therefore whether, in the terms of Art. 1101, the claim involved "measures adopted or maintained by a Party relating to:

(a) investors of another Party;
(b) investments of investors of another Party in the territory of the Party."[216]

Consequently, the Tribunal decided that it would assume *arguendo* that the claims against Mexico concerned "measures adopted or maintained" by it.

Moreover, since the claims related to asserted violations of NAFTA's Arts. 1102, 1105, and 1110,[217] the first issue the Tribunal had to address was whether the claims concerned "(a) investors of another Party; and/or (b) investments of investors of another Party in the territory of the Party." The Tribunal, therefore, looked to Article 1139, the definitions section of Chapter 11, to determine whether the term "investor" was defined. It found that the term "investor of a Party means a Party or its state enterprise, or a national or an enterprise of a Party that pursues an investment opportunity, is making or has made an investment."[218] The Tribunal therefore determined that the Bayview claimants included "persons who have invested in farms and irrigation facilities within the State of Texas. There is also no doubt that the Claimants include persons who own[ed] or control[ed] directly or indirectly those farms and facilities in Texas."[219] Nevertheless, the issue was whether these farms, located in Texas, constituted "not simply as an 'investment' in general terms but as an 'investment' which entitles the owner to initiate under the NAFTA the specific claims against Mexico in this case."[220]

The Panel observed that the Parties were split on the issue of whether, as Mexico argued, an "investment" must be one that the Claimants were seeking to make, were making, or had made *"in Mexico,"*[221] or whether, as the Texans asserted, the undeniable fact that they had made an investment in Texas was adequate.[222] The Tribunal noted that it was clear that a prominent characteristic "w[ould] be that the investment [wa]s primarily regulated by the law of a State other than the State of the investor's nationality, and that this law

---

[215] *Ibid.* The text of Art. 1101, is located at note 171 and 194 *ibid.*   [216] *Ibid.* ¶¶ 85–86.
[217] *Ibid.* ¶ 87. (*Citing* Request for Arbitration, at ¶ 59.)   [218] *Ibid.* ¶ 91.
[219] *Ibid.*   [220] *Ibid.*   [221] *Ibid.* at ¶ 93.   [222] *Ibid.*

is created and applied by that State which is not the State of the investor's nationality."[223] Indeed, the Panel cited the submission of the GOUS, which stated the following:

> The aim of international investment agreements is the protection of *foreign* investments, and the investors who make them. This is as true with respect to the investment provisions of free trade agreements (FTAs) as it is for agreements devoted exclusively to investment protection, such as bilateral investment treaties (BITs). NAFTA Chapter 11 is no different in this regard. One of the objectives of the NAFTA, expressly set forth in Article 1102(1)(c) is to "increase substantially investment *opportunities* in the territories of the Parties" which refers to, and can only sensibly be considered as referring to, opportunities for *foreign* investment in the territory of each Party made by investors of another Party . . . [224]

Consequently, based on the foregoing the Panel ruled that to be an "investor" within the definition and scope of Art. 1101, an enterprise is required to make an investment in another NAFTA State, and not in its own. Indeed, it found that an investment must have a "legally significant connection" with the NAFTA Party creating and applying the measure complained of by the investor.[225] That relationship, the arbitrators adjudged, did not exist between Bayview and Mexico because the Texans were not "foreign investors" in Mexico. Rather, they were domestic investors in Texas.

Furthermore, the Tribunal deemed that there was no "investment" in Mexico. Since Bayview did not "make or has made an investment *in the territory of another NAFTA Party*."[226] The Panel found that pursuant to Art. 1101(1)(b), Chapter 11 applies solely to "investments of investors of another Party in the territory of the Party."[227] Accordingly, the arbitrators ruled that the Texans did not make an investment in Mexico. They also observed that their interpretation was supported by the construction publicly espoused by the three NAFTA Parties, prior to these proceedings. The Panel furthermore, rejected the Texans claim, that they in fact had an investment in Mexico, in the *form of rights* to water situated in Mexico, which were unjustly or illegally confiscated by Mexico, because it conflicted with Mexican law.

Indeed, the Tribunal observed that water law in Mexico allows for an award by the (GOM) of "legal rights to extract water from rivers in Mexico for defined periods, in defined amounts, and for defined purposes. Similarly, the law of Texas provides for the grant by the State of Texas of legal rights to extract water from rivers in Texas for defined periods, in defined amounts,

[223] *Ibid.* at ¶ 98.   [224] *Ibid.* at ¶ 100.   [225] *Ibid.* at ¶ 101.   [226] *Ibid.* at ¶ 105.   [227] *Ibid.*

and for defined purposes."[228] The foregoing, the arbitrators found brought them "to the crucial question of, whether the Claimants had an investment 'in the territory of [Mexico]'."[229] In their view it was patently obvious that Bayview did not. In fact, the Texans' investments were strictly within Texas, particularly, "in the form of the infrastructure for the distribution of the water that they extract from the Rio Bravo/Rio Grande. They have investments in the form of the water rights granted to them by the State of Texas. They [we]re certainly 'investors'";[230] however, these investments were solely situated in Texas, and therefore the Texans were not "investors in Mexico or vis-à-vis Mexico."

Finally, the Panel noted that water in a river, such as the Rio Grande/Rio Bravo, is not owned, as when one owns the water in a bottle of mineral water. Consequently, if a person takes the bottle without consent, that act constitutes a theft of property. However, a holder of *a right* granted by the State of Texas is granted an entitlement "to take a certain amount of water from the Rio Bravo/Rio Grande he does not 'own', does not 'possess property rights in', a particular volume of water as it descends through Mexican streams and rivers towards the Rio Bravo/Rio Grande and finds its way into the right-holders irrigation pipes."[231] The Tribunal's award consequently held that the Texans did not own any of the water within Mexico; nor did they hold any *water rights* in Mexico or, for that matter any rights enforceable against the Government of the United Mexican States. Their water rights were created in Texas, granted to them by the State of Texas, and could only be exercised within that state.

5 Lack of Jurisdiction and an Assessment Proxies

Consequently, the Tribunal dismissed the case for lack of jurisdiction. It reasoned that:

> it is quite plain that NAFTA Chapter Eleven was not intended to provide substantive protections or rights of action to investors whose investments are wholly confined to their own national States, in circumstances where those investments may be affected by measures taken by another NAFTA State Party. The NAFTA should not be interpreted to bring about this unintended result.[232]

---

[228] *Ibid.* at ¶¶ 112.   [229] *Ibid.*   [230] *Ibid.*   [231] *Ibid.* at ¶ 116.
[232] *Bayview Irrigation District et al. (Claimants) v. United Mexican States (Respondent)*, ICSID Case No. ARB (AF)/05/1 (June 19, 2007), Award at ¶ 103.

Moreover, in rejecting Bayview's expansive definition of "investment," the panel relied upon several NAFTA Chapter 11 precedents. For example, in construing the award in *US v. Methanex*,[233] the panel's principal precedent, the tribunal declared that in order to be an "investor" within the meaning of NAFTA Art. 1101 (a), an enterprise must make an investment in another NAFTA State, and not in its own . . . [I]t is necessary that the measures of which complaint is made should affect an investment that has a 'legally significant connection' with the State creating and applying those measures.[234]

In assessing the five proxies listed in Table 7.2, what can one learn from the Tribunal's award? First, with regards to **Proxy 1, Compliance: with governing international norms**: the *Bayview* award expanded the definition of "investor" and demarcated NAFTA's *rationae materia* jurisdiction. Indeed, in employing precedents, the award likely enlarged the normative reach/framework of both investment law and more pertinent here, transboundary water law in the NAFTA context – by finding that this dispute over water was not within NAFTA's purview. This broadened interpretation of the "investor" may have an impact on other international investment legal norms, *e.g.*, those of bilateral investment treaties or, World Trade Organization disputes, as well as aid other tribunals in future classifications of the term.

The crux of the panel's ruling, in this case of first impression, was that since the water that Bayview sought was physically situated in Mexico, there could be no investment by an American claimant, since no investment was made in Mexico. The Bayview panel also construed the 1944 Treaty between the United States of America and Mexico,[235] and rejected Bayview's argument that they had private rights in Mexican river water. This reading of treaty law reinforces the view of international law by adjudicative bodies and scholars.[236] Moreover, the Panel found no evidence in the Treaty to support the Bayview's claim that "Mexico alienated or relinquished title [to any Rio Grande/Rio Bravo River water] just as States sometimes relinquish land territory in treaties."[237]

---

[233] *Methanex Corp. v. United States*, First Partial Award on Jurisdiction and Admissibility, 44. ILM 1343 (2005).
[234] *Bayview Irrigation, ibid.* at ¶ 101. (*Citing Methanex ibid.* at ¶ 147.)
[235] Treaty Relating to the Utilization of Waters of the Colorado and Tijuana Rivers and of the Rio Grande, US–Mex., Feb. 3, 1944, 59 Stat. 1219.
[236] Sital Kalantry, The Intent-to-Benefit: Individually Enforceable Rights under International Treaties, 44 *Stanford J Int'l L* (2008) 63, 65. ("International tribunals, however, are not typically receptive to claims brought by individual litigants for treaty violations.") Restatement (Third) of Foreign Relations Law § 906 (1987) ("International tribunals and other fora are generally not open to claims by private persons.").
[237] *Bayview Irrigation, ibid.* at ¶ 119.

TABLE 9.3 *Bayview Irrigation v. Mexico – Time from Filing to Award*

(1) **August 27, 2004** – Bayview submits Notice of Intent to Arbitrate, pursuant to Chapter 11.	(7) **February 14, 2006** – Tribunal requests Mexico, to file its Memorial on Jurisdiction by April 19, 2006 and that Bayview file its Counter-Memorial by June 23, 2006.
(2) **January 19, 2005** – Bayview submits application to ICSID, requesting an arbitration proceeding under the Additional Facility Arbitration Rules.	(8) **November 14–16, 2006** – Tribunal hears arguments on Jurisdiction.
(3) **January 27, 2005** – ICSID confirms receipt of the Application.	(9) **August 31, 2005** – Tribunal requests NAFTA parties to submit submissions appropriate to the proceedings, no later than September 18, 2006.
(4) **July 1, 2005** – ICSID's Secretary-General approves access to the Additional Facility.	(10) **October 31, 2006** – Tribunal asks the Parties to address three key issues.
(5) **December 15, 2005** – The arbitral panel was regarded as constituted and the proceedings to have been commenced.	(11) **November 14–15, 2006** – Tribunal holds its second sitting: addresses Jurisdiction
(6) **February 14, 2006** – Tribunal holds its first Sitting. Parties agree to proceed in accord with ICSID's Additional Facility Rules.	(12) **June 19, 2007** – The Tribunal issues its award.

With recourse to **proxy 2, Resolution** there is no question that the panel resolved this dispute. Furthermore, with regards to **proxy no. 3, Normative Impact**, it is unclear whether there was any impact on the conduct of other States, although other investors may have been dissuaded from filing similar claims. As to whether the NAFTA tribunal was **fair and legitimate, proxy no. 4**, there is no question that based on the transcript and the award, the panel was fair and just to both sides, and the panel's members acted in an impartial and independent fashion. Additionally, this award likely added to the legitimization of the ICSID and NAFTA regimes, as well as to its norms, since the panel employed NAFTA precedents in its analysis and the arbitrators found that there are no private rights of action under the 1944 Treaty.

Finally, with respect to **proxy no. 5, efficiency**, this litigation took **2.4 years** from filing to the issuance of the award. (See Table 9.3). The award does not evince any wasting of time by the panel's members. Thus, the process appears to have been both fair and efficient.

One issue that remains is the voting patterns of party-appointed arbitrators. In this regard, Posner & Yoo contend that party-appointed arbitrators will side with those who appoint them if they want more work. That thesis must be contested as to this dispute. The evidence here demonstrates that Bayview's appointed party arbitrator, Edwin C. Meese, III, voted with the other two arbitrators to dismiss the case for lack of jurisdiction. Similarly, given Posner & Yoo's assertion that dependent tribunals, *i.e.*, *ad hoc* adjudicative bodies, are more effective then are independent ones, the record from this award provides no evidence that these authors' theory is valid. Indeed, their hypothesis does not appear to be convincing for any of the three arbitrations analyzed here.

These voting patterns of the arbitrators, however, are supported by Daphna Kapeliuk's empirical data.[238] Her study finds that arbitral bodies are likely more independent than courts. Indeed, Kapeliuk[239] demonstrates that in the arbitral context repeat presiding arbitrators are much less reluctant to issue extreme awards than are party-appointed arbitrators.[240] Additionally, her research reveals that when an arbitrator's decisions are examined individually, they do not always show a pattern of awards that is balanced across time.[241] She also demonstrates that an arbitrator's motivation to preserve his/her reputation, as an experienced or an impartial adjudicator, often leads the arbitrator to make an award that is uninfluenced by the asserted need to satisfy the parties that engaged him/her.[242]

Finally, as noted previously, Andreas Follesdal coined the term "social legitimacy,"[243] which he defined as a measure of the public's support for the judiciary, and whether the judiciary is worthy of the public's support, *i.e.*, "does the judiciary command general public belief that it has the *rightful authority* to secure general *compliance*?"[244] Moreover, he asked two critical questions:

---

[238] See Daphna Kapeliuk, The Repeat Appointment Factor: Exploring Decision Patterns of Elite Investment Arbitrators, 96 *Cornell L R* (2010) 47.
[239] *Ibid.* at 60–62.   [240] *Ibid.*   [241] *Ibid.*
[242] *Ibid.* at 87–88.

> The arbitrators' decision records, examined individually, do not always display a tendency towards a balanced decision pattern. For example, when appointed by the claimant, [a given] arbitrator [identified as arbitrator] number 2 awarded the claimant a partial monetary award in the first three awards (27.3%, 53.6%, and 29.9%). In the fourth award, the same arbitrator dismissed all claims when acting as a respondent-appointed arbitrator. While this sequence of awards might suggest bias in favor of the appointing party, this arbitrator dismissed all claims in the fifth award when serving as a claimant-appointed arbitrator. Thus, if the first three awards insinuate favoritism towards the claimant, then the fourth award balances out such perceived favoritism.

[243] Andreas Follesdal, The Legitimacy Deficits of the Human Rights Judiciary: Elements and Implications of a Normative Theory, 14 *Theoretical Inquiries L* (2013) 339, 345.
[244] *Ibid.*

(1) whether a given court or tribunal has the legal authority or jurisdiction that it claims over a specific issue(s); and (2) are a court's or tribunal's judgments or awards in keeping with the proper principles of the law?[245] These two factors are employed herein to assess the legitimacy of the adjudicative bodies assessed here.

The Supreme Court of the United States has in the main enjoyed social legitimacy[246] as an institution and for its judgments within the public. Nevertheless, some recent decisions may have whittled away some of that legitimacy away, *e.g.*, on issues regarding campaign spending and gay marriage. Although the Court's decisions have certainly had a 100% rate of compliance in transboundary water disputes, over half of the American population disapproves of the Supreme Court as an institution.[247]

Moreover, for the most part, the public is either unaware of or, *dis*interested in transboundary water disputes. Even in cases where it may affect their well-being.[248] Since transboundary water disputes involve decades-long state rights in interstate rivers and lakes that affects the rights of millions of people, *see e.g.*, *Arizona* v. *California*, the fact that the Court does not engage the public, specifically during the litigation before the master, is disquieting and clouds its legitimacy. The fact that state-litigants can repeatedly call on the Court to resolve their interstate water disputes,[249] *i.e.*, the states can ask for decrees to be altered on a whim, I believe, also detracts from the Court's legitimacy.

The International Joint Commission, where the public is aware of it, benefits from social legitimacy; however, given that it has only arbitrated two disputes – the *Trail Smelter* and the *Gut Dam Arbitration*, the last one concluded in 1968 – it is unclear whether today the wider public or even the

---

[245] *Ibid.*

[246] On social legitimacy and the law, *see generally*, Leisy Abrego, Legitimacy, Social Identity, and the Mobilization of Law: The Effects of Assembly Bill 540 on Undocumented Students in California, 33 *Law & Social Inquiry* (2008) 709.

[247] Gallup, Supreme Court (2016), http://www.gallup.com/poll/4732/supreme-court.aspx. (From to 2001 to 20016 the rate of disapproval increased from 25% to 52%.)

[248] Seth Motel, What Kinds of Supreme Court Cases Interest Americans? Not Campaign Finance, Pew Research Center, Fact Tank (Apr. 10, 2014), http://www.pewresearch.org/fact-tank/2014/04/10/what-kinds-of-supreme-court-cases-interest-americans-not-campaign-finance. ("In part, the lack of attention might be related to the fact that there were other big stories dominating the news...."); Jay Famiglietti, Can We End the Global Water Crisis? *National Geographic*, June 10, 2013, http://voices.nationalgeographic.com/2013/06/10/can-we-end-the-global-water-crisis. ("And a crisis of understanding: does the public and do our elected officials truly understand what's happening with water, nationally and globally? If they did, I contend that we could make some real progress towards managing this crisis.")

[249] James G. Mandik, The Modification of Decrees in the Original Jurisdiction of the Supreme Court, 125 *Yale L J* (2016) 1880.

legal community believes that the Commission has the rightful authority to secure general compliance. Albeit, the two awards it issued were fully complied with.

With regards to the IBC/IBWC, the *Chamizal Arbitration*, the Commission's sole adjudicated dispute, the wider American public, at the time of the award, did not ascribe either social legitimacy to the Commission nor any lawful authority to secure general compliance with its award.[250] On the other hand, the Mexican public had the opposite perspective. Finally, with recourse to ICSID, its *ad hoc* tribunals, including those that adjudicate NAFTA disputes, do produce both social legitimacy and compliance legitimacy within the legal community. Indeed, social science research suggests that institutional demands, such as those placed on ICSID, as a consequence of the different arbitral schemes[251] that parties are able to select, lead to contrasting effects in the arbitral process.[252] Consequently, use of different arbitral rules may produce changes in how these standards are applied.[253] They may also lead to a uniformity of performance.[254] Nevertheless, few people outside the population of international lawyers generally, and investor–state or trade lawyers, in particular, are aware of either ICSID or NAFTA's Chapter 11 disputes.

---

[250] Kenneth Duane Yielding, The Chamizal Dispute: An Exercise in Arbitration, 1845–1945, Ph.D. Dissertation, Texas Tech University (May 1973) 212.

> American writers have generally reacted with hostility toward the award. In fact, several "old timers" in El Paso declared immediately that the river of 1864 was near its present course, apparently in an effort to justify the United States' claim to the entire tract. [Footnote omitted] One El Paso attorney termed the award a "judicial abortion," a view shared by the President in his message to Congress of December 7, 1911. Taft declared that "our arbitration of the Chamizal boundary question with Mexico was unfortunately abortive."

[251] *See e.g.*, ICSID Article 1120: Submission of a Claim to Arbitration.

[252] Mark C. Suchman, Managing Legitimacy: Strategic and Institutional Approaches," 20 *Acad Manag J* (1995), 571.

[253] Paul J. DiMaggio & Walter W. Powell, The Iron Cage Revisited: Institutional Isomorphism and Collective Rationality in Organizational Fields, 48 *Am Soc R* (1983) 147.

[254] *Ibid.*

10

Conclusion

In law, we must beware of petrifying the rules of yesterday and thereby halting progress in the name of process. If one consolidates the past and calls it law he may find himself outlawing the future.

Judge Manfred Lachs[1]

A INTRODUCTION

At the outset of this volume I addressed two issues, international court and tribunal effectiveness in the adjudication of transboundary water issues. Initially, I will focus on what can be learned from the transboundary water issues. The three US Supreme Court disputes were focused on rivers flowing through arid lands or deserts. The contests over the water of each of these rivers, the Arkansas, the Laramie and the Colorado, was for a divertible amount for irrigation. It did not include any uses other than for irrigation. Not for fish! Not for potable water! Not for nature!

Today, in an era of climate change, long-term droughts and lack of potable water, the sharing or allocation of transboundary water for multiple uses is still moribund, because we live in an era where world leaders have failed to utilize that which they should have learned in kindergarten: "share everything" and "play fair." Sustainability requires new approaches, both legal and extra-legal, that policy-makers and lawyers may wish to take, once they realize that people are beneficiaries of the earth's water, but not the sole beneficiaries. Nature too has an entitlement for water. Indeed, humankind "cannot have an effect on nature, cannot adopt any of her forces, if [it] does not know the natural laws . . ."[2]

---

[1] Judge Manfred Lachs, President of the International Court of Justice, Commemorative Speech at the United Nations General Assembly (Oct. 12, 1973).

[2] Science Quotes by Baron Friedrich Wilhelm Heinrich Alexander von Humboldt, Today in Science History (2010), available at https://todayinsci.com/H/Humboldt_Friedrich/HumboldtFriedrich-Quotations.htm.

In this regard, the doctrine of equitable apportionment, as established in *Kansas* v. *Colorado's* 1907 decision, may need to be employed for uses other than irrigation. The doctrine is now part of customary international law, and has been incorporated into numerous international instruments. Modern international law, nevertheless, provides that the Parties to a water convention should take all appropriate actions to *preserve water and cooperate in taking sustainable actions to protect transboundary waters*. For example, the 1992 Helsinki Convention,[3] in force in the member states of the Economic Commission for Europe ("ECE") provides the following:

> The Parties shall, in particular, take all appropriate measures:
> (a) To prevent, control and reduce pollution of waters causing or likely to cause transboundary impact;
> (b) *To ensure that transboundary waters are used with the aim of ecologically sound and rational water management, conservation of water resources and environmental protection;*
> (c) To ensure that transboundary waters are *used in a reasonable and equitable way*, taking into particular account their transboundary character, in the case of activities which cause of activities which cause or are likely to cause transboundary impacts;
> (d) To ensure conservation and, where necessary, *restoration of ecosystems.*[4]

As for *ad hoc* arbitrations, they too may need to consider what priorities, if any, nature and potable water should be given, in disputes that come before them.

Next, is the issue of effectiveness of international courts and tribunals in adjudicating transboundary water disputes. As part of that introduction I selected five proxies for measuring the effectiveness of these adjudicative bodies. They are: (1) **Compliance**; (2) **Resolution and Satisfaction**; (3) **Normative Impact**; (4) **Fairness and Legitimation**; and (5) **Efficiency**.

Nevertheless, these five proxies do not and cannot purport to be exclusive. Rather, they are *one set* of tools for measuring judicial and arbitral efficacy. Their non-inimitability is one of the conundrums that confront researchers in this subfield of international law, because there is no unique suite or concrete empirical methodology or set of criteria for measuring effectiveness.

I also introduced four courts and tribunals that have adjudicated transboundary water disputes in North American, that were analyzed. These

---

3 Convention on Protection and Use of Transboundary Watercourses and Lakes (Helsinki, March 17, 1992), 3 ILM 1312 (entered into force October 6, 1996).
4 *Ibid*. (Emphasis added.)

adjudicative bodies are extremely diverse and have had to adjudicate a wide-ranging suite of disputes. In measuring their effectiveness, I found that arbitral tribunals were much more efficient than courts and they also had no problems dealing with polycentric issues. Although two of the SCOTUS disputes spanned decades, their individual adjudications were quite efficient. Moreover, these disputes also demonstrated the strain between finality of the dispute when the Court delivered its original decrees and insuring that changed circumstances or unexpected events would be addressed in the future.

This work has made the following findings and contributions:

(1) This is the very first study of its kind in any geographic venue/location.

(2) Transboundary water disputes are resolved by courts' and tribunals' use of equity, or equitable remedies. My research finds that this is the first study of its kind that definitively demonstrates this fact.

(3) In one respect, *ad hoc* international tribunals are more effective than international courts in adjudicating transboundary because they are more adept at addressing polycentric issues.

(4) The results yielded in this study demonstrate that within the universe of disputes *ad hoc* tribunals are much more efficient – that is, *overall* they adjudicate disputes quicker – than do courts.

(5) I have also compared the length of time from the execution of the *compromis* until the issuance of the arbitral awards for the three arbitrations analyzed herein: the *Chamizal Dispute*; the *Gut Dam Arbitration*; and the *Bayview Irrigation District Case*, with the *Bering Sea Arbitration (Fur Seals)*, the *Trail Smelter Case*, The *San Juan River Case* and the *Lac Lanoux Arbitration*, and found that the average time for resolution of these disputes is between 1.9 years and 2.2 years, while most court cases, particularly those of the United States Supreme Court, take much longer – for the *Kansas v. Colorado* and *Arizona v. California* SCOTUS disputes analyzed here it took 86 years and 102 years, respectively, to resolve. Thus, I argue that arbitral tribunals are more effective, in resolving these types of case. (See Table 10.1, below.)

(6) The use of precedents and the development of norms is one characteristic that runs through the cases that were analyzed, particularly to fill lacunae. The use of precedents, which I term "cross-pollination," leads to greater coherence in international law, and helps the development of new norms; regardless of whether an adjudicative body employs its own case law or imports it from another jurisdiction. Thus, if we think about the use of precedents as pieces of a puzzle that fit together to provide a fully integrated archetype, we can comprehend and envisage the building of a system of international law.

TABLE 10.1 *Courts and Tribunals Efficiency in Natural Resource Disputes*

Case Name	Time to Resolution
Bering Sea Arbitration (Fur Seals)	*compromis* signed Feb. 29, 1892; Award signed and published on Aug. 15, 1893 **= 1 year ± 6 months (1.5)**
Trail Smelter Case	special agreement executed Apr. 15, 1935; Award on damages, Apr. 16, 1938; **= 3 years** -March 11, 1941 on remaining issues. **4 years 11 months (4.9 years)**
The San Juan River Case	*compromis* executed on Dec. 24, 1886, by Costa Rica and Nicaragua. Award rendered, Mar. 22, 1888, by President Grover Cleveland. **= 1 year 3 months (1.25)**
Affaire du Lac Lanoux	*compromis* executed Nov. 19, 1956; Award Nov. 16, 1957 **= 362 days (1 year)**
Chamizal Dispute	**1 year 9 days**
Gut Dam Arbitration	**1 year 351 days (2 years)**
Bayview	**2.4 years**
Kansas v. Colorado	**104 years (overall)**
Wyoming v. Colorado	**35 years (overall)**
Arizona v. California	**86 years (overall)**

This volume also contributes to an increasing body of literature on the nature of international dispute resolution and the significance of transboundary networks in shaping and enforcing international law.[5] Spearheaded by Harold Hongju Koh and other scholars, these "transboundary legal process theorists" postulate that, in contrast to the realist camp, international law is not a mere construct that is contingent upon state consent.[6] Rather, it is, more often than not, a product of a vibrant interplay buttressed by municipal

[5] See Harold Hongju Koh, The 1994 Roscoe Pound Lecture: Transnational Legal Process, 75 Neb L R 181, 182:

> Throughout my career, I have sought to understand this puzzling void in international legal scholarship. To many domestic legal scholars, the reason seems self-evident: they consider the very term "International Legal Scholarship" to be a complex oxymoron, – like the Holy Roman Empire (which was neither Holy, Roman, nor an Empire) or the New York Giants (which are neither New, from New York, or Giants) – may be distinguished from the more familiar simple oxymoron, such as "jumbo shrimp" or "working vacation." Other complex oxymorons of which I have been reliably informed include the Uniform Code of Military Justice, the Chicago School of Law, and the Union of Soviet Socialist Republics.

[6] Ibid. at 183–86 (addressing transnational legal process as the "theory and practice of how public and private actors . . . interact in a variety of public and private, domestic and international fora to make, interpret, enforce, and ultimately, internalize rules of transnational law").

legal experience and international interests, which are advanced by numerous transboundary constituencies that import, introduce, "and adapt ideas across boundaries."[7] New legal rules are informed by established practice and conducting experiments in both the domestic and international realms. They also form and contour novel legal rules in a reciprocally flowing fashion.

Indeed, it is "networks of state and non-state actors [that] drive this phenomenon."[8] An example of this occurrence is cited by Peter Haas, who "has described epistemic communities of scientific and policy experts that worked to address problems such as the transboundary pollution of the Mediterranean Sea,[9] and threats to the ozone layer."[10] Haas posits that these epistemic communities behave like "channels through which new ideas circulate from societies to governments as well as from country to country."[11] Finally, in her book, *A New World Order*, Anne-Marie Slaughter details how these "[n]etworks of government officials – police investigators, financial regulators, even judges and legislators – increasingly exchange information and coordinate activity to . . . address common problems on a global scale."[12]

In addition, this volume also contributes to the field of dispute resolution by offering case studies of transboundary water disputes and legal issues that transit state borders. For the most part, the cases assessed herein are from an era pre-dating modern international environmental law. Nevertheless, these international courts and tribunals set the stage for the modern era by establishing new norms. Finally, although one might expect that the new tribunals,

---

7 Eric Dannenmaier, Environmental Law and the Loss of Paradise, Book review, Oliver A. Houck, Taking Back Eden: Eight Environmental Cases that Changed the World, 49 *Colum. J Transnat. L* (2010) 463, 488. *See also,* Koh *ibid.*

8 *Ibid.* at 488.

9 *Ibid.* (*Citing* Peter M. Haas, Do Regimes Matter? Epistemic Communities and Mediterranean Pollution Control, 43 *Int'l Org* (1989) 377, 384–87. John Ruggie is one of the first to employ the term "epistemic communities." He utilized the concept to describe communities that evolve about shared policy ideas. *See* John Gerard Ruggie, International Responses to Technology: Concepts and Trends, 29 *Int'l Org* (1975) 557, 569–70. (Ruggie analogized what Michele Foucault referred to as "*epistemes,* 'through which the political relationships acted out on the international stage' are visualized.")

10 Dannenmaier, *ibid.* (*citing* Peter M. Haas, Banning Chlorofluorocarbons: Epistemic Community Efforts to Protect Stratospheric Ozone, 46 *Int'l Org* (1992) 187, 189–96).

11 Peter M. Haas, Introduction: Epistemic Communities and International Policy Coordination, 46 *Int'l Org* (1992) 1, 27; *see also* Emanuel Adler & Peter M. Haas, Conclusion: Epistemic Communities, World Order, and the Creation of a Reflective Research Program, 46 *Int'l Org* (1992) 67, 370–71 (these authors explain the instrumental value of epistemic communities "when they promote more international coordination and a greater affinity between the values and practices of states and the policies advanced through international regimes and institutions"). Dannenmaier, *ibid.* at 489.

12 Anne-Marie Slaughter, *A New World Order* (2004) 1.

where non-state parties can litigate disputes, would behave differently than previously established tribunals – those where only states can litigate – that in fact is not the case. Other than access, the tribunals, such as NAFTA's Chapter 11 investor–state arbitrations, function in the same manner and with similar rules, as their state–state counterparts.

B THE IMPACT OF COURT AND TRIBUNAL EFFECTIVENESS

Future studies should consider the impact that remedies imposed upon a losing party may have on future litigation, *i.e.*, if the remedy is too harsh, a respondent may not comply with the remedy that the court or tribunal fashioned. Indeed, the results in two disputes analyzed herein, exemplify several remedies: compensation in the *Gut Dam* Arbitration and restoration to the *status quo ante* in *Arizona v. California*.

In closing, a more significant aspect of the evolution of international law, in the field of transboundary water law, is how its geographic scope has expanded over the years? This enlargement was made possible by the adoption of two local/municipal legal doctrines by foreign adjudicative bodies. These doctrines are (1) the principle of equitable allocation – established in 1907 by the United States Supreme Court – and adopted by most, if not all international courts and tribunals,[13] as well as legal publicists; and (2) the principle of *sic utere*, developed by the *Trail Smelter* Tribunal, and tacitly accepted by the *Gut Dam* tribunal.

---

[13] *See e.g., Indus Waters Kishenganga Arbitration* (Pak. v. India) (Final Award of Dec. 20, 2013), *supra* note 129. One of the questions before the Court was "[w]hether under the Treaty, India may deplete or bring the reservoir level of a run-of river Plant below Dead Storage Level (DSL) in any circumstances except in the case of an unforeseen emergency?" (Award at 1). The response to this question at page 3 of the Award was, In relation to the Second Dispute, (1) Except in the case of an unforeseen emergency, the Treaty does not permit reduction below Dead Storage Level of the water level in the reservoirs of Run-of-River Plants on the Western Rivers... (3) *Accordingly, India may not employ drawdown flushing at the reservoir of the Kishenganga Hydro-Electric Plant to an extent that would entail depletion of the reservoir below Dead Storage Level.* (Emphasis added.)

Index